DIFFERENTIATED SERVICES FOR THE INTERNET

Kalevi Kilkki

MACMILLAN
TECHNICAL
PUBLISHING
U·S·A

Differentiated Services for the Internet

Kalevi Kilkki

Published by:
Macmillan Technical Pulishing
201 West 103red Street
Indianapolis, IN 46290 USA

International Standard Book Number: 1-57870-132-5

Library of Congress Catalog Card Number: 99-62122

2002   01   00   99   4   3   2   1

Interpretation of the printing code: The rightmost double-digit number is the year of the book's printing; the rightmost single-digit, the number of the book's printing. For example, the printing code 99-1 shows that the first printing of the book occurred in 1999.

Composed in Galliard and MCPdigital by Macmillan Computer Publishing

Printed in the United States of America

Trademark Acknowledgments

All terms mentioned in this book that are known to be trademarks or service marks have been appropriately capitalized. Macmillan Technical Publishing cannot attest to the accuracy of this information. Use of a term in this book should not be regarded as affecting the validity of any trademark or service mark.

Warning and Disclaimer

This book is designed to provide information about **Internet technologies**. Every effort has been made to make this book as complete and as accurate as possible, but no warranty or fitness is implied.

The information is provided on an as-is basis. The authors and Macmillan Technical Publishing shall have neither liability nor responsibility to any person or entity with respect to any loss or damages arising from the information contained in this book or from the use of the discs or programs that may accompany it.

Feedback Information

At Macmillan Technical Publishing, our goal is to create in-depth technical books of the highest quality and value. Each book is crafted with care and precision, undergoing rigorous development that involves the unique expertise of members from the professional technical community.

Readers' feedback is a natural continuation of this process. If you have any comments regarding how we could improve the quality of this book, or otherwise alter it to better suit your needs, you can contact us at network-tech@mcp.com. Please make sure to include the book title and ISBN in your message.

We greatly appreciate your assistance.

PUBLISHER
David Dwyer

EXECUTIVE EDITOR
Linda Ratts Engelman

MANAGING EDITOR
Patrick Kanouse

ACQUISITIONS EDITOR
Karen Wachs

DEVELOPMENT EDITOR
Thomas Cirtin

PROJECT EDITOR
Theresa Wehrle

COPY EDITOR
Keith Cline

INDEXER
Larry Sweazy

AQUISITIONS COORDINATOR
Jennifer Garrett

MANUFACTURING COORDINATOR
Brook Farling

BOOK DESIGNER
Ann Jones

COVER DESIGNER
Karen Ruggles

PRODUCTION TEAM SUPERVISOR
Tricia Flodder

PRODUCTION
Lisa England

PROOFREADER
Elise Walter

Dedication

To: Eija, Olli, and Juho

Acknowledgments

First, I would like to thank my management at Nokia Research Center, in particular Raj Bansal and Antti Ylä-Jääski, for allowing me to work on the book with minimal attention to other tasks. I would like to express my appreciation to several colleagues at Nokia, among them Jussi Ruutu, Ove Strandberg, Ravikanth Rayadurgam, Jarno Rajahalme, Pasi Väänänen, and Matti Alkula. I have consumed their time with numerous intricate questions during the past months.

I also am indebted to the technical reviewers, Shivkumar Kalyanaraman and Jon Crowcroft, for their critical comments and beneficial suggestions. I am grateful to all the experts at Macmillan Technical Publishing for editorial assistance and for keeping the project on track although the schedule and the target appeared unattainable from time to time.

Finally, I heartily thank my family for their support and patience during this project.

About the Author

Kalevi Kilkki is a principal scientist at Nokia Research Center in Burlington, Massachusetts. He holds a master of science and doctor of technology in electrical engineering from Helsinki University of Technology, Finland. His comprehensive background includes research projects related to telephone networks at Helsinki University of Technology, to ATM networks at Telecom Finland (now Sonera), and to IP networks at Nokia Research Center. The ATM research work has been carried out in connection with several European research projects, such as COST242 and Eurescom P105, while the framework for IP research has been the Differentiated Services Working Group in IETF.

During the last three years, Kalevi's main effort has been to develop feasible traffic handling mechanisms required for service differentiation in the Internet. He has given numerous presentations at international conferences about diverse topics, from the application of genetic algorithms in connection admission control to pricing models for the Internet. Dr. Kilkki also has continuously delivered lectures about traffic theory and telecommunication systems at the Helsinki University of Technology and has instructed various master's theses. Finally, one of his main hobbies, philosophy, gives a specific flavor to the treatment of these intricate topics.

About the Technical Reviewers

These reviewers contributed their considerable practical, hands-on expertise to the entire development process for *Differentiated Services for the Internet*. As the book was being written, these folks reviewed all the material for technical content, organization, and flow. Their feedback was critical to ensuring that *Differentiated Services for the Internet* fits our reader's need for the highest quality technical information.

Shivkumar Kalyanaraman is an assistant professor for the department of electrical, computer, and systems engineering at Rensselaer Polytechnic Institute in Troy, New York. He received a B.Tech degree from the Indian Institute of Technology, Madras, India, in July 1993, followed by master of science and doctoral degrees in computer and information sciences at Ohio State University in 1994 and 1997, respectively. His research interests include traffic management, multicast, Internet pricing, multimedia networking, and performance analysis of distributed systems.

Shivkumar is a co-inventor in two patents (the ERICA and OSU schemes for ATM traffic management) and has co-authored several papers, IETF drafts, and ATM forum contributions. He is a member of IEEE-CS and ACM. His World Wide Web site is located at `http://www.ecse.rpi.edu/Homepages/shivkuma`.

Jon Crowcroft is a professor of networked systems in the department of computer science, University College London, where he is responsible for a number of European and U.S. funded research projects in multimedia communications. He has been working in these areas for over 18 years. Jon graduated with a degree in physics from Trinity College, Cambridge University, in 1979. He gained his master of science in computing in 1981 and his doctoral degree in 1993.

Jon is a member of the ACM and the British Computer Society. He is a Fellow of the IEE and a senior member of the IEEE. He also is a member of the IAB and general chair for the ACM SIGCOMM. He is also on the editorial team for the ACM/IEEE Transactions on Networks. With Mark Handley, Jon is the co-author of *WWW: Beneath the Surf* (UCL Press). He also wrote *Open Distributed Systems* (UCL Press/Artech House).

Overview

Contents

Figures

INTRODUCTION

The status of the Internet has changed fundamentally during the past few years, particularly after the emergence of convenient Web browsers. Although this statement seems to be self-evident—one would even say that it is a cliché—it is an elusive statement as well. What has really happened? Internet traffic has exploded in such a way that it now surpasses the amount of telephony traffic in many parts of communication networks. Many extraordinary applications have found their place on the Internet. (Perhaps you bought this book from a virtual bookstore on the World Wide Web.) Email addresses are nowadays nearly as important as street addresses or telephone numbers.

However illustrative and valid this kind of assessment is, it does not provide proper guidance for the next steps in the evolution of the Internet. Thorough preparation requires a good understanding of the fundamental issues and a solid knowledge of the available tools for reaching this goal. This book strives to meet these requirements in a systematic manner.

Differentiated Services is one of the key concepts that can lead toward a more robust, more versatile, and more efficient Internet infrastructure. But this is a vast project that requires good planning:

1. Develop a robust technical basis that consists of the traffic-handling mechanisms—including queuing and scheduling systems implemented in network nodes.

2. Design a feasible network based on the nodes.

3. Devise the services provided to customers.

These tasks are complicated and need a solid understanding of traffic processes and network performance issues. This book addresses all these technical levels of Differentiated Services, and gives a lot of practical examples of how to optimally apply different mechanisms and methods.

The project is not finished when the technical issues are well resolved. Marketing the service to customers and keeping them satisfied enough that they are willing to pay for it is as important as the technical realization. The history of telecommunications has shown that *this part of the project could be the main obstacle to success.* Therefore, this book focuses a lot of attention on evaluating the actual needs and expectations of ordinary users.

Who Will Benefit from This Book?

This book is intended both for readers who have knowledge of networking concepts and protocols and for readers who are more interested in the service aspects than the underlying technology. This book does not require a thorough understanding of communications technology or mathematical modeling, although both are used to explain the characteristics of different services.

This book is aimed at the following audience:

- Business and marketing managers at Internet service providers developing new Differentiated Services

- Engineers developing routers and other type of nodes for packet networks

- Operators responsible for the planning, operation, and management of the Internet and other packet networks

- Researchers, scientists, and students at universities and research institutes developing traffic-management systems for communication networks

Key Features of This Book

This book contains the following features that make it a practical guide for developing and implementing Differentiated Services:

- Concrete examples are highlighted throughout the book to demonstrate implementation and to anchor the abstract concepts in reality.

- Figures throughout the book illustrate technical issues and procedures. For easy access to the technical data, a table of all the figures appears at the beginning of this book.

- Tables convey crucial technical information at a glance.

- Numerous notes and sidebars are sprinkled throughout the text to provide information about tangential issues related to the principal topics.

- The glossary defines terms related to Internet traffic management. It is a handy reference to use when reading this book or working to implement Differentiated Services.

Organization of the Book

To expedite the learning process required in mastering Differentiated Services concepts and technologies, this book follows a three-part sequence of related topics—beginning with explanations of essential concepts and quickly moving to technical information and descriptions of solid implementation practices. The book's organization is described in detail in the following sections.

Part I: Background for Differentiated Services

Chapter 1, "The Target of Differentiated Services," defines the viewpoint of the book by introducing the primary building blocks of packet networks and the fundamental characteristics required by a feasible network service.

Chapter 2, "Traffic Management Before Differentiated Services," reviews the traffic-management principles applied in earlier networks. Concepts such as best-effort service in the current Internet, guaranteed services designed for the future Internet, and variable bit rate (VBR) service of ATM networks are explained and evaluated. Finally, this chapter discusses the target of Differentiated Services in relation to the advantages and disadvantages of the former approaches.

Chapter 3, "Differentiated Services Working Group," is reserved for the approach taken by the Differentiated Service Working Group of the Internet Engineering Task Force (IETF). Because of both the historical background and the status of IETF, the scope of the Working Group is carefully defined: IETF specifies only certain functions inside the network, but the design of the network services is left to service providers. In consequence, although the IETF specifications offer good basis for the implementation of Differentiated Services, they do not address all the necessary aspects.

Part II: Building a Network Domain Based on Differentiated Services

The ideas introduced in Chapter 4, "General Framework for Differentiated Services," fill the deficiency of IETF specifications. The framework provides a consistent view of the key aspects of Differentiated Services on traffic handling and network service levels.

In the future Internet with diversified services, the most prevalent expectation of customers could be high quality comparable to telephone service, or the affordability of the current Internet, or something else. These service and pricing issues are discussed in Chapter 5, "Differentiation of Customer Service."

Chapter 6, "Traffic Handling and Network Management," introduces the technical core of telecommunications networks: the mechanisms available to realize the desired services. You must understand numerous concepts before it is possible to build a reasonable service. These concepts include such things as packet marking, traffic shaping, weighted fair queuing (WFQ), random early detection (RED), and bandwidth broker.

The first six chapters provide a good foundation for Chapter 7, "Per-Hop Behavior Groups," which evaluates the various approaches proposed within the wide scope of Differentiated Services.

Part III: Building Global Networks Based on Differentiated Services

Interworking is the main area of difficulty that can delay the realization of practical Differentiated Services. Chapter 8, "Interworking Issues," covers issues such as interoperability between a pure best-effort Internet and a Differentiated Services network; mappings between Differentiated Services and Integrated Services; and the implementation of Differentiated Services in ATM-based networks.

To get a realistic feel for what Differentiated Services can accomplish, Chapter 9, "Implementing Differentiated Services," provides several concrete examples in which different acute problems of the Internet are solved. There will be a lot of new things that are difficult to foresee, but I hope this book makes it possible to understand and, in the best case, anticipate the evolution of Internet services.

PART I

Background for Differentiated Services

The Target of Differentiated Services

Service differentiation is an old topic in many business areas. Nevertheless, if you search for references to Differentiated Services or service differentiation dated 1996 or earlier, you probably won't find much about the Internet and its services. During the past year, however, Differentiated Services of the Internet has become a popular concept. But why do we need a novel concept within the specific field of the Internet? As Ludwig Wittgenstein (1889–1951) said, "He who controls vocabulary controls thought." In the best case, a new concept with a new vocabulary provides a useful framework for the development of new ideas and the analysis of old ones.

This chapter explains the main motivation behind the Differentiated Services effort: how the Internet has changed and how this change has altered the requirements for Internet services and traffic management. I introduce the fundamental building blocks needed to realize reasonable customer service, and the desirable characteristics at all levels of implementation. These characteristics, or attributes, are then used as a thread throughout the whole book. This chapter elucidates the philosophical basis of the book.

> **Note**
>
> Although it could be useful to give an exact definition of Internet service, that is a somewhat risky approach because the Internet service model is still evolving and is prone to significant changes. Chapter 4, "General Framework for Differentiated Services," further illustrates the various aspects of the service models. Which one of them will be prevalent in the future is still an open issue—and the development of Differentiated Services may have a crucial role in that service evolution.

1.1 *The Core of Differentiated Services*

Imagine yourself as a mechanism inside the Internet, something like an intelligent sorter in a post office. You are working at a service provider that transmits packets between end users. The service provider in this case has different end-to-end services using different "postage." More expensive services may require quicker treatment inside the "post office" as well as different transmission tools, such as a "courier" rather than a "mailman." The network needed to accomplish this task consists of a number of packet-handling centers and paths between them.

When you, working in one of those centers, receive a packet with certain information in its tag (or *header* in Internet terminology), you will decide how to treat the packet. You can choose from only a limited number of different actions:

- You can deliver the packet immediately, before all other packets, because you consider it very urgent.

- You have a number of boxes in which you can put the packet waiting for delivery.

- You can totally discard the packet because you think that you cannot deliver all incoming packets anyway.

How has the Internet changed from the viewpoint of this mechanism? What changes are coming in the near future?

Previously, your task would have been relatively easy. Basically you would have needed to look at the address on the packet and then, based on a routing table, you would have forwarded the packet in the right direction. From time to time, some packets marked as *urgent* would have arrived, and you would have had to deliver them as soon as possible. If the box (or queue) seemed to overflow, you would have had to discard some incoming packets to lighten your load. You could have expected that if you had to discard some packets, the senders would have been informed about the situation and, consequently, they would have sent packets more slowly. Finally, if there had steadily been too many packets for your capacity, you would have had to be retired and a new handler with a tenfold capacity would have been substituted for you.

In this case, most of the packets deserved equal treatment, independent of the sender or receiver; there was not much need for calculating how many packets someone had sent during the past hour or what kind of packets were waiting for delivery.

And everything worked fine with this simple scheme. Why? Mainly because the Internet population was relatively coherent in the sense that the communication between Internet users made it possible to build the Internet based on the principle of reciprocity.

Reciprocity means that anyone is allowed to send a large amount of important packets because other users could expect the following:

- They could do the same when necessary.

- No one wasted network resources by sending useless packets.

- Most users decreased their sending rate when capacity limits were exceeded.

The Internet community, with both network engineers and users, was coherent enough for this kind of system 10 years ago. Things have changed during the past few years, however, and you cannot—whether in your actual role as a network device or not—expect that all packets are equal anymore. In the same Internet, fundamentally different packets are delivered: Some packets are vital to someone's business; some packets become obsolete within fractions of a second; a lot of packets are sent just for curiosity; and some packets contain information that could be considered totally valueless by some other users.

Now you, as a network device, must decide how every individual packet will be treated. The core of the problem is that the current Internet environment is heavily fragmented. No single cooperative group sends packets; instead, a large number of groups and even separate end users—all with potentially different desires, different requirements, and a different willingness to pay for different properties—are sending packets. To treat all the packets fairly seems to be almost an impossible task, even if you have all the necessary information and enough time to make reasoned decisions.

This is the very area of problems that Differentiated Services aims to resolve, this "fragmentation" problem. This book seeks to clarify exactly what Differentiated Services is and how you can maximize its utility. The main goal of this book is to present a consistent view of the development of the Internet toward Differentiated Services, using a limited number of key concepts. The introductory concepts discussed here relate to the components that either are crucial for building the appropriate Differentiated Services or have a significant effect on the whole system of Differentiated Services.

1.1.1 *Basic Entities of Differentiated Services*

Differentiated Services consists of an array of technical issues, but that's not all. Differentiated Services must also be understood as having an inherent business and even psychological aspect. To provide a common reference point for this discussion, it is important to first identify the basic entities of Differentiated Services. Three of these basic entities were introduced in the preceding example of a packet-handling center and are explained in this section:

- The service provider

- The end user

- The mechanism that treats packets in different ways

After briefly discussing these basic entities, this section introduces three other important entities of Differentiated Services: applications, networks, and vendors.

The Service Provider

The term *service provider* is often used to refer to two different things: the actual service provider responsible for customer relations (the broad sense of the term, and the way in which it is used here), and the network operator responsible for operation and management of the network. Although not used in the first simplified illustration of Differentiated Services, this distinction is necessary when assessing several issues, such as business models or interworking. (See Chapter 8, "Interworking Issues," for more information.)

In an extreme case, a service provider can be just a brand name (much like Coca-Cola or Nokia). All the technical devices required to implement the marketed service are collected in the same way that many branded articles are produced and marketed all over the world—that is, without having much more in common than the name. Subcontractors make the actual product (or service), even though the end users might think that they are doing business directly with the holder of the brand name.

At the other extreme, a service provider may be responsible for all parts of the service—from network construction to customer care. In addition, the relationship between end users and the service provider can vary significantly: The service provider might work within the same corporation as all the end users, or the service provider might sell small pieces of service(s) to a large number of individual users. An enterprise that brokers bandwidth and services between users and multiple providers is another alternative. Yet a more complex situation is when several brokers negotiate with each other. As this discussion hopefully makes clear, the term *service provider* applies to many different business models (both impossible and unnecessary to elucidate exhaustively here).

End User

An *end user* is you or any other person who is using the Internet for any purpose. The key point is that the end user is a human being, even though the chain from the real bit transfer to final end user can be long. If the network is used to convey data automatically from a meteorological station to a host computer, for example, some human need is still prompting that bit transfer request. It is fair to suppose, therefore, that end users have a variety of emotions that influence the use of the service.

If you think that you are getting poor service, for example, you can change your service provider (regardless of what is actually causing you to think that the service is poor). From the service provider's point of view, your reasoning might actually be irrelevant, flawed, irrational, and/or based on limited information. The applications running on your own computer might be incorrectly configured, for example, or you might have heard that your provider is somehow unreliable. The important thing to remember is that customers do not always make their selections based on technical facts.

Mechanism

The third basic entity, the mechanism used to illustrate the principles of the network, is an integral part of Differentiated Services. Technically speaking, it can be called a *mechanism*. A mechanism can be understood here to be any piece of equipment or software that does a particular job inside the network nodes. A typical example is a device that categorizes packets into two classes of importance based on some rules defined in the service-level agreement.

Applications, Networks, and Vendors

End users use *applications* to satisfy some demand that can vary from serious to entertaining. The demand can be to find product information, to converse with a colleague abroad, or to spend some time surfing the Net. At this point of the discussion, the particular use or aim of the application is not important; it is important, however, to notice that the underlying need is rarely just to transfer some bits through the network.

The term *application* should also be understood broadly: It covers typical user applications as well as all protocols not controllable by the service provider, such as TCP/IP protocols running in customers' computers. In contrast, the *network* as a basic entity is something totally managed by the service provider and used to transmit information from one end user to another.

Finally, *vendors* supply network components (both hardware and software) to service providers, network operators, and end users. Without these components, Differentiated Services would be an empty idea.

Note

This introductory picture should be refined. One principal circumstance not yet addressed is that several service providers that are connected to each other may provide the same services (more or less). Moreover, a Differentiated Services network does not form an insulated region; instead, a lot of other network technologies are used in parallel with it—and all these networks raise interworking concerns. The success of Differentiated Services depends crucially on how effectively these concerns are addressed. This is a substantial topic and is covered more fully in Chapter 8, "Interworking Issues."

1.1.2 The Relationships Among the Basic Entities

Something crucial is still missing, however: Although the preceding section drew a skeletal outline of the basic entities, it is important to flesh out that skeleton by defining the relationships among the basic entities. To accomplish anything useful on the Internet, an awareness and understanding of these relationships is necessary.

The relationship between end user and service provider can be called *customer service*. Customer service includes all the issues that have a significant effect on customer satisfaction. The issues encompass both technical details, such as packet-loss ratio, and non-technical details, such as the friendliness of help desk staff. The formal part of customer service can be called the *service-level agreement*. The service-level agreement may relate to a specific need of transmission, such as connection to a video server, or it may specify some general issue, such as the appropriate response time for customer technical support. In addition to the formal service-level agreement, customer expectations play an important role when customers are assessing the quality of a product (in this case a service), even though these expectations are not recorded in any document.

Another fundamental relationship between user applications and the network can be called *network service*. There are a lot of network services that vary in characteristics, such as packet-loss ratio, delay variation, and available bit rate. In other words, network service defines what an application is supposed to do on a technical level, in such a way that the quality level is usually straightforward to measure.

The relationship between the network, which often covers all possible technical issues, and the mechanism, which is apparently part of the network technology, tends to be artificial. If you think of the network as a unit that has a general purpose, however, you can use the term *traffic handling* to refer to this relationship; this term illustrates the low level of service provided by mechanisms.

The relationship between the service provider and the network and mechanisms can be called *operation and management (OAM)*. OAM covers such issues as building reasonable services based on available mechanisms, making traffic measurements for network-planning purposes, and solving fault situations. In many cases, OAM is the main single cost factor—in particular, if any of the OAM functions require manual operations (and usually they do).

Finally, the vendors provide applications and network components. Although vendors are definitely crucial to applications, services, and networks, they do not usually have any specific role in the actual service. Therefore, it is unnecessary to define any particular relationship between vendors and other basic entities. It is necessary from time to time, however, to remember that there are extra players, called vendors, in the field and that these extra players have their own specific interests.

1.2 The Four Attributes of Differentiated Services

The many special ingredients of Differentiated Services have yet to be described *per se* here. To that end, it is important to regard the *differentiated spirit* as the principal target of the whole effort and to consider the four attributes discussed in this section as secondary targets.

End-user needs should be the paramount focus of any Differentiated Services approach. Unfortunately, most end users have no idea what their future needs will be, particularly with regard to Differentiated Services. This discussion, therefore, reviews the following four universal attributes of Differentiated Services:

- Fairness

- Robustness

- Versatility

- Cost efficiency

These attributes often intertwine, and a Differentiated Services approach might also apply other attributes to a job at hand. These four specifically listed attributes relate to this discussion, however, because they can be applied both at the customer-service level and at technical levels; in addition, together they can cover all the key aspects discussed earlier (provided the terms are used generally).

1.2.1 Fairness

The concept of fairness relates directly to the essence of human viewpoint. For business managers and administrators, it is of great importance to thoroughly comprehend what customers want and what they think or "feel" about the service. It is not enough to look at money and technology only. The other three attributes focus on the hard values, such as earnings, efficiency, and reliability. *Cost efficiency* emphasizes the need to assess technologies from a realistic business viewpoint, for example, and *robustness* calls for reliability.

One of the several meanings of *fair* is concisely expressed as "reasonable according to most people's ideas of justice" (taken from *Longman Language Activator*, Longman Group UK Limited, 1993). This definition emphasizes the emotional aspect of the term. Note also that *fair* does not necessarily mean equal treatment; fair just means that the treatment is acceptable to *most* people. In addition to the psychological aspects, technical aspects of fairness must be considered when appraising the properties of mechanisms and network services. These aspects of fairness are secondary, however, in the sense that fairness is finally assessed in a person's mind and is not very well represented by any mathematical formula.

Fairness is the key attribute of the relationship between the end user and the service provider. Whatever the service provider is selling to customers, it must be regarded—first and foremost—as fair by customers. In fact, the fairness of the service from the customer viewpoint is the first issue to be addressed when this discussion turns to other networking technologies in Chapter 2, "Traffic Management Before Differentiated Services," and Differentiated Services proposals in Chapter 7, "Per-Hop Behavior Groups."

Fairness Versus Quality of Service

You may be curious about why the popular term *quality of service (QoS)* has not been introduced into this discussion. The reason is that the QoS concept is often used in a limited sense, in which it means support for service with certain predefined characteristics that can be directly measured. In the case of communication services, however, typical measures of service are maximum delay and loss ratio. With regard to these measures, a premature or excessive use of technical parameters can lead to somewhat misleading conclusions. In particular, it should be noted that technical parameters cannot cover all the substantial aspects of customer service—most users are hardly willing to consider technical details, and even fewer users will make measurements to verify the actual quality of service.

To express it simply, most customers just assume that the market somehow establishes the right price level (whatever the word *right* means). An average customer just decides whether the price offered is low enough to justify buying the product. Nevertheless, the customer wants to be sure that the market is fair—that is, that everyone pays the same price for the same product. This is the essence of fairness.

Because the essential characteristics of customer service can be more precisely discussed using the word *fairness* rather than *quality*, *fairness* is used as the key term. In this book, the term *quality of service* is used only when it is possible to accurately define the required characteristics and to verify whether the service actually meets these requirements.

Groups and Fairness

Before diverting this discussion to technical matters, it is important to understand another very important concept: the *group*. A group is a set of entities located close together or classed together. The basis of classification is often a certain quality that each individual entity has in common with the other entities so classed. Why is *group* such an important term? Because it is impossible to evaluate fairness without having a good understanding of the group to which an end user or a packet belongs.

A group must be coherent to be meaningful. (*Coherent* here refers to something that has unity of ideas and/or interests.) Within a coherent group, each member is somehow responsible for the behavior of all other members, or, at least, this is considered fair from an outsider's view. The other side of the same issue is that each member of the group expects to benefit from the group membership.

An example that relates to Differentiated Services might help to explain the use of the word *group* in this discussion. A similar contract between several end users and one service provider makes a basis for an inherent group. The source of cohesion is the contract between the user and the service provider. The user joins a group with certain rights and responsibilities, partly described in a service-level agreement and partly based on common sense. Each user expects certain predictable behavior from all users within the group, and will be content with the service. In a best-effort service, for example, a user buys access to a network. That access has a certain physical bit rate. The user won't (or at least shouldn't) expect to obtain any definite bit rate from the network; instead, the user should expect a fair share of bandwidth and be content with that service.

Some service-level agreements, or contracts, might differ slightly from one user to the next. These relatively minor differences do not necessarily justify the formation of several groups. If that were to happen, the management of the total system would quickly become too troublesome. On the other hand, it is difficult for end users to assess the fairness and other key properties of a service if contracts vary too much—that is, there are a large number of small differences from contract to contract. One reasonable solution to this problem is for the service provider to offer only a couple of service levels. (The airline industry is using this approach to market and manage their services.)

Fairness and Service Provision

At all times, potential for group to overlap exists, possibly with a certain hierarchy. Unfortunately, it is not always clear which grouping is relevant in each case. To further illustrate this complex issue, consider the following example, "Limiting the Load Level to Avoid an Overload."

> **Note**
>
> This book uses a fictitious company and service to provide concrete examples of various aspects of implementing Differentiated Services: Fairprofit, an Internet service provider, and Quicksure, a service supplied by Fairprofit and other ISPs that provides reliable service for real-time applications.

Limiting the Load Level to Avoid an Overload

Several Internet service providers, Fairprofit among them, share a backbone network for transmitting traffic between customers of different service providers. All providers have the same service structure, including Quicksure. Now the combined load of Quicksure from Fairprofit customers significantly exceeds its normal traffic level, even though every individual user complies with his or her service-level agreement. In consequence, the backbone operator is compelled to somehow limit the load level because of the imminent overload situation. The operator can apply several different approaches to manage the situation:

- Limit the traffic of the customers belonging to both Fairprofit and Quicksure groups.
- Limit the traffic of all Fairprofit customers independently of the service group.
- Limit the traffic of all Quicksure users independently of the service provider.
- Limit the traffic of all customers belonging to either Fairprofit or Quicksure.
- Limit the traffic of all customers.

Further, these approaches can be combined in different manners—for instance, by more tightly limiting all traffic from Fairprofit and less tightly from traffic belonging to the Quicksure service (independently of the service provider). Now the fundamental question is, which one of the possible approaches is most fair?

The right answer apparently depends on the situation—in particular, how tight the groups are and what contracts have been made between different parties. A service provider with individual customers makes for a relatively loosely coupled group; users within a corporation, on the other hand, are tightly coupled. The importance of Quicksure service may depend on such a non-technical issue as how the service has been marketed, because marketing creates expectations, and expectations have an effect on what is considered fair.

Considerations About Fairness in Reality While not going too deep into the details of service provision, in reality the situation is even more complicated. Several more alternatives emerge if the services form a hierarchy. If Quicksure is high in the service hierarchy, for example, an overload situation of Quicksure service could have different effects on any of the lower-level services. This intricate issue is addressed further in the section titled "Sharing Network Resources Fairly Among All Users" in Chapter 9, "Implementing Differentiated Services."

Another question that might arise is, what is the cohesion among a service group (for instance, among IP telephony users)? A tentative answer is that correlation in behavior may justify the grouping. This is, at least, a reasonable answer from the service provider's point of view because the grouping based on similar behavior may facilitate the network dimensioning and management and by that means improve the cost efficiency of the network. It is not clear, however, whether this is sufficient cohesion to justify any grouping that has considerable effect on the capacity allocation.

The most desirable treatment of a packet depends on the grouping of packets. One more viewpoint can be condensed into the issue of how much an individual packet is responsible for the past traffic process. When a packet arrives at a network node and requires a treatment, for example, the network defines a group of packets for controlling purposes. The group consists of the last packet with some other earlier packets; that is, the treatment of the packet depends on the arrivals of some previous packets. The earlier packets may belong to a flow of packets generated by an application, to an individual user, or to a larger user group.

The most reasonable and fair approach may considerably differ from case to case. As a consequence, the underlying mechanisms and other building blocks must be able to support different arrangements. That is, network service should be versatile in the sense that it supports purposeful grouping of packets and flows and logical treatment of packets inside the network.

1.2.2   Technical Issues: Versatility and Robustness

Now it is relevant to discuss the most important aspects of technical issues. The next issue to be assessed is the relationship between applications and the network—that is, *network service*. As expressed earlier, the thorough changes in the Internet might be summed up in one word: *fragmentation*—not on the technical level of packet handling, but on the level of applications, users, and business models. If and when the service provider attempts to fulfill all the differing needs, network services must be as *versatile* as possible.

Versatility is, to some extent, an important service attribute for end users as well. Still, it is not clear whether end users want to work with very versatile services and applications, because versatility may bring about complexity and opacity. Hence, versatility is an essential characteristic of the network service to the degree that is necessary for the service provider to offer reasonable service packages for different customers, but it should not be exaggerated by adding insignificant features to customer service packages.

The Internet has relied so far on the benevolence of most end users; that is, the Internet community has been quite a coherent group. Unfortunately, the increased fragmentation of the Internet community brings about an increased threat of undesirable behavior of some end users because of inexperience, greediness, or malevolence. In consequence, it is extremely important to design *robust* network services. Without robustness, it is impossible for the service provider to offer fair and credible customer services. End users must be able to trust that some malevolent or greedy users cannot significantly deteriorate the service of other users.

Three attributes of Differentiated Services have been discussed thus far: fairness, versatility, and robustness. There are, certainly, several other desirable properties, such as reliability, consistency, and simplicity. Although all these could be of primary importance in some cases, they are not used as basic attributes in this book (mainly because they serve some other, more fundamental targets). If the target is making a profitable business, for instance, simplicity usually means less-expensive management and high reliability means more desirable customer service. This business aspect can be taken into account by an additional attribute, namely, *cost efficiency*.

1.2.3   Cost Efficiency

Efficiency is a common term in the field of communication technology. It usually refers to the relationship between beneficial outcome and the resources spent to realize the desired outcome, such as the average load-to-link capacity ratio. After defining the efficiency by a mathematical formula, it is often thought that the optimal solution is one that just maximizes the efficiency. Although this approach may work well in some cases, it tends to be too limited for practical purposes because it is not reasonable to separate one technical issue from a meaningful framework. As a simple example, just maximizing the number of delivered packets is not a rational target if the cost of the maximization is totally ignored.

Therefore, to emphasize this aspect, the adjunct *cost* is added to the term of efficiency. Cost efficiency refers to the balance of effectively meeting other targets (fairness, versatility, and robustness) at the lowest price; it does not refer to some purely technical issue, such as the number of transmitted packets.

Now it is possible to draw a picture depicting the main entities of Differentiated Services, the main relationships among the entities, and the main targets of the whole project. Figure 1.1 shows the relationships inside the Internet system: customer service between the service provider and the customer, the network service between the network and the application, operation and management between the service provider and the network, and traffic handling between the mechanism and the network.

The main purpose of Figure 1.1 is to illustrate the general structure of Differentiated Services rather than to make any exact statements about the implementation:

- The bold arrows depict the concrete information flow going through the network: Applications send packets into the network, and networks use mechanisms to handle packets in an appropriate manner.

- The standard arrows illustrate the other relationships between entities; for instance, end users use an application through a user interface, and service providers manage the network by using proper tools.

- Double lines illustrate a high-level set of functions, such as services and management. Many of them are somewhat equivocal: It is not clear what issues should be included in customer service or network management. The position of this book, and Figure 1.1 in particular, is that customer service is a broad concept that covers all issues important for customer satisfaction, including the usefulness of applications.

- Broken arrows are used for those interrelations important for real implementations, but of lesser interest in this book.

Figure 1.1   Main entities of the Internet and the relationships among them.

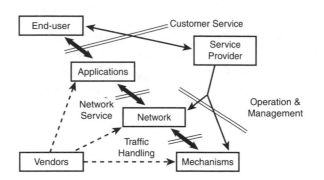

Summary

The technical core of Differentiated Services is the mechanisms used to treat packets in different ways inside network nodes. It is not practical or sufficient, however, to limit this study to the technical level because it does not make it possible to obtain a sufficiently broad view of the primary issues. Therefore, this chapter introduced six other basic entities:

- Service provider

- End user

- Mechanism

- Application

- Network

- Vendor

This basic entity list was introduced mainly to organize the presentation, and it needs further refinement before it is possible to evaluate several complicated issues related to Differentiated Services.

The relationships among these basic entities and the target(s) of their efforts result in Differentiated Services. A target is fixed by four attributes (used extensively in the following chapters):

- Fairness

- Versatility

- Robustness

- Cost efficiency

Throughout this book, the fulfillment of these attributes when using various approaches that have different mechanisms, network services, and customer services is evaluated.

If you look at this introductory chapter, you might notice that it does not have any tight relationship to the Internet Protocol (IP) or the Internet itself. All the basic concepts and ideas can be applied to almost any networking technology based on packets or similar independent information units. It is possible on the one hand, therefore, to apply most of the primary ideas of Differentiated Services to many other networks, such as ATM and Frame Relay; on the other hand, it is possible to exploit the experiences obtained in other networks.

CHAPTER 2

Traffic Management Before Differentiated Services

Because engineering, so far, is a human activity, the evolution of traffic management is similar to that of any other human effort. Thomas Kuhn (1922–1996) presented one of the most popular theories describing this process of theory development in the early 1960s. His central statement is that science does not progress in an orderly fashion from lesser to greater truth, but rather remains fixated on a particular explanation (Kuhn 1996). Only with great difficulty can this explanation, or paradigm, be replaced by a new one.

Engineering, an application of science, is quite similar to science in this respect: There is always a prevalent notion about how a certain engineering problem should be solved and such notions are difficult to change, requiring a lot of time and effort. The additional factor affecting engineering is the rapid evolution of environment; paradigm changes are necessary purely because of altered problems. Differentiated Services may in fact turn out to be a new paradigm. To design a new one, however, the old paradigms—including their strengths and their weaknesses—must be understood.

2.1 Fundamental Concepts, Models, and Technologies

This chapter outlines the basic vocabulary and concepts of telecommunication networks and services, and shows which are the most appropriate. In the best case, vocabulary provides a useful framework for developing new ideas and analyzing old ones. In the worst case, inappropriate concepts may limit our thoughts; for instance, mathematical concepts may lead to an idea that everything essential can be expressed in mathematical formulae.

The viewpoint in this chapter is mainly that of an Internet service provider with a goal related more to the service business than to technical excellence. Hence, the following pages introduce the basic concepts and some basic issues related to the Internet services provision; the purpose is to prepare your thoughts for the thorough examination of the Differentiated Services approach in the rest of this book.

2.1.1 Customer Service

First, you have to decide what kind of service you are selling and to whom. For this discussion, three main customer groups are identified: residential, business, and academic. These groups differ considerably in certain aspects. In the academic environment, for instance, usage control has traditionally been relatively loose. As a consequence, quality control has been slight, also. Typical business customers are much more concerned about quality and performance because even a short service outage can cause significant losses.

In addition, it is important to notice that there are three network types:

- The public Internet
- A private network
- A virtual private network (VPN)

Private networks are physically separate from any public network. A *VPN* may use the same network resources as public services and other VPNs as well. Because the topic of this book is Differentiated Services for the Internet, the main concern is with public services; the secondary issue is VPNs, because they share the same resources and can, therefore, be thought to be a part of the public network. In contrast, although the same principles of Differentiated Services can be applied in private networks, the special issues of private networks are not extensively discussed in this book.

Business and academic users, although with diverse needs and expectations, have some predictable characteristics; residential customers, on the other hand, as a group of Internet users, comprise a mostly unexplored field of business. It is unclear what quality most users really need, or how much they are willing to pay for better quality. You may personally assess whether you would rather have a predictable price of service (a flat-rate charge) than have a predictable quality of service (guaranteed service with time-dependent pricing). Based on practical business experience so far, Internet service providers have found that most residential customers prefer the first option.

It is not, however, obvious that this inference is valid with regard to new services, such as video or audio multicasting. Could it be possible to combine quality differentiation with flat-rate pricing? It seems that if you can realize that kind of service, you may have a significant business advantage. Section 5.1.3, "Pricing as a Tool for Controlling Traffic," in Chapter 5, "Differentiation of Customer Service," shows how you can use Differentiated Services to achieve this.

A *service-level agreement (SLA)* is the formal part of the relationship between a service provider and a customer. If you look at the Web pages of an ISP, you usually find general assurances for residential Internet service related to the following issues:

- Throughput—that is, the bit rate available at the access point of the network

- Network availability, with compensation in case of unavailability and reporting of unavailability within a specific time

- Time to install new services and to respond and repair faults

- Round-trip transmission delay within the operator's domain, and possibly to some other destinations as well

In addition to these assurances, there could be more complex guarantees relating to more specific technological issues. A potential problem, however, is that ISPs' SLAs are often convoluted, and "[I]f you are not an educated buyer, you may not understand what you are really getting," as stated in *PC Weeks* online article (Neil 1998). This is just one question that this book seeks to address thoroughly.

2.1.2 *Network with Services*

If you have successfully acquired a sufficient customer base for your business and have made appropriate service-level agreements, you need a network to satisfy the customer needs and meet your obligations under the SLAs. This section addresses some of the attendant technical issues of network services.

A packet network consists of nodes that are practically computers with some special hardware and links between them. A node that handles packets is usually called a router. Depending on the capabilities of the node, however, it may instead be called a bridge or a switch.

> **Note**
>
> The term *node* is used as a general term, covering bridges, routers, and switches, and the capabilities of a node are defined as exactly needed in each case. This book focuses primarily on networks with point-to-point links—that is, each link connects only two nodes.

Although the concepts are overlapping and there is not any single criterion to distinguish them, it is fair to say that a bridge has much less knowledge about network topology than a router or a switch. The key property of switching is that a switch makes the forwarding decision (for a packet or some other information unit) based on a label rather than the full destination address. The main advantage of this arrangement is that it allows better exploitation of hardware, which means it can accelerate forwarding functions (Davie, Doolan, and Rekhter 1998).

A large network can usually be divided functionally into two sections: the access network and the backbone (or core) network (see Figure 2.1). The main tasks of the access network are to physically connect your customers to the network and to provide appropriate tools, such as pricing capabilities, to manage the relationship between operator and customer. For these reasons, the total capacity of a boundary node connecting access and core networks, measured in bit rate, is usually much smaller than that of an interior node. On the other hand, however, a boundary node has more "sophisticated" tools that enable it to control and measure individual flows. Interior nodes, for their part, govern large bundles of aggregate traffic. Therefore, an interior node's main task is to efficiently transmit high-speed traffic.

Figure 2.1   The main building blocks are boundary nodes (A), interior nodes (B), and customer equipment (C).

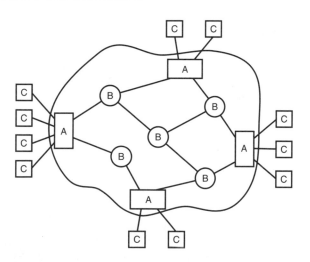

2.1.3 *Network Operation and Management*

The quality of network service depends basically on two issues: the sufficiency of network resources and the capability of a traffic-handling mechanism to efficiently utilize the available resources. If there are not enough resources, even advanced traffic-handling mechanisms cannot solve all problems. From an operator viewpoint, therefore, it is extremely important to manage the resources appropriately. The following section, "Traffic Handling," briefly introduces the principles of resource allocation, or network dimensioning, in circuit-switched and packet-switched networks.

The goal of network dimensioning is to make certain that the network has enough capacity to keep customers satisfied with the service. In a circuit-switched network, such as a telephone network, the main effect of insufficient capacity is that some of the call requests must be discarded. The standard measure of this quality parameter is call-blocking probability. Call blocking can be either directly measured or estimated by using a mathematical modeling.

Direct measurement—that is, counting the number of calls rejected because of insufficient capacity and the number of successful calls—is a useful tool to estimate the quality level of a real network. This approach is obviously not suitable for determining the required capacity of a future network. (How can you measure an imaginary network?) For such cases, you need an indirect approach.

The indirect approach is based on the measurement of traffic load and on certain assumptions about the statistical characteristics of traffic process. First, a base calculation must be determined. To do so (for this discussion), make the following assumptions:

- Every call reserves one channel.

- The average call arrival rate is λ (calls/s).

- The arrival process is Poisson—that is, the inter-arrival time between call attempts is exponential.

- The average call holding time is h (s).

- A link has together S channels.

Under these conditions, the call-blocking probability can be calculated by using the Erlang loss formula. (See Chapter 5, "Differentiation of Customer Service," for further information.) Although the underlying assumptions of the Erlang formula are seldom exactly valid, it can be used to illustrate certain important phenomenon of any service with capacity reservations.

If the call-blocking probability is fixed—say, to 0.1%—the allowed load level (A/S) depends largely on the number of channels (S). The main message is that, if you divide the link into fixed parts in a way that each part has its own traffic that can use only that part of the link capacity, the allowed link utilization may decrease dramatically, as shown in the examples in Table 2.1.

Table 2.1 Link Utilization for a 0.1% Call-Blocking Standard

Link Parts	Number of Channels	Theoretical Load Level
1	500	448 calls (90%)
10	50	325 calls (65%)
100	5	76 calls (15%)

Further, it should be noted that you must be able to divide the load evenly among the 100 parts to get even the figures in Table 2.1. From an efficiency point of view, therefore, it is always questionable to divide the available capacity into a large number of fixed parts.

A similar phenomenon is noticeable in packet networks as well, although the effect is not as prominent because the buffering of packets softens some problems—but only provided that the link capacity can be divided proportionally to the load level of each part. If the load of one of the parts exceeds the capacity of that part, the corresponding buffer eventually overflows even though the other buffers are empty. In this case, also, a fixed division of link capacity (without the possibility to use the other part of the link capacity) may lead to a significant waste of resources.

This kind of division approach could be reasonable, but only if there are clear reasons behind it (for instance, because different user groups must be tightly separated for security reasons). The same dilemma arises with regard to some standardization efforts by the Internet Engineering Task Force (IETF), such as Multiprotocol Label Switching (MPLS) and Resource Reservation Protocol (RSVP).

2.1.4 Traffic Handling

When you have successfully finished the network dimensioning phase, you have enough network resources to handle the traffic demand. The next step is to ascertain that you have appropriate traffic-handling mechanisms in your network because, in reality, the performance of traffic handling determines the quality of packet flows.

The first, and fundamental, requirement is that your network must be able to transmit the packet to the required destination. This fundamental task of a packet network is actually done by two processes: routing and forwarding. *Routing* is a mechanism implemented in the network nodes to collect, maintain, and distribute information about paths to different destinations in the network. In other words, routing does not directly concern packets, but it enables an efficient packet *forwarding* mechanism that is in charge of conveying packets to the right destination. These two processes together make sure that packets reach the right destination, provided that there are enough resources for the transmission.

Another aspect of traffic handling is the treatment of the packets inside the network nodes. Traffic handling can be done on different levels of aggregation. The lowest level in a packet network is one arriving packet as an independent entity without any information about any other earlier packets in the network. In this case, traffic handling must rely on the information available in the packet.

From a traffic-handling viewpoint, the main fields in an Internet Protocol version 4 (IPv4) packet header are the source address, destination address, type of service (ToS), and protocol. The node may treat the packets differently based on these fields; for instance, a node may immediately drop all packets coming from a certain source address, or may give fast delivery for all packets that use a certain protocol. Although routers may, in principle, apply quite complex rules, the implementation and management of the system may become impossible when millions of packets are arriving every second. Further, any system without any knowledge about past traffic is inherently limited because it does not take into account the amount of resources used by different flows in the past.

Therefore, it is often desirable to classify packets into groups, follow the traffic process of the group, and make the required decision based on the information collected in this way. Basically, there are two different approaches to accomplish the task:

• Make the measurements at every node for every individual group.

• Make the measurements only at certain points in the network (usually at the edge of the network), and convey the needed information somehow through the network.

Both approaches have their advantages and disadvantages. If the number of groups is very large, the measurement system in interior nodes could limit the system performance (and note that the same measurement must be done at every node). Further, in many control schemes, it is not enough just to measure the traffic; some information related to the groups is also required—for instance, how much each customer is paying for his service. Because this kind of information is usually available at the boundary node, one reasonable approach is to make the necessary measurement only once in the boundary node and then transfer the relevant information to other nodes. Now there are two options:

• The information can be placed in every IP packet.

• The information can be transferred by using special control packets.

The first option is often more realistic in packet networks (although the second option is possible as well). In particular, if the information content can be expressed by a couple of bits, and it is changing frequently, the transmission of additional packets with large IP headers is not an efficient solution. Therefore, it is desirable to reserve some bits in the packet header to transmit relevant information in every packet. Actually there is one octet, ToS, reserved for this purpose in an IPv4 packet, although it is not yet widely used. The basic philosophy of Differentiated Services is to utilize the ToS octet in a way that enables service differentiation throughout the network without keeping track of all flows at every node.

2.1.5 Traffic Models for the Internet

The network dimensioning of a packet network is traditionally based on delay characteristics. This dimensioning problem can be divided into the capacity allocation problem of each individual link in the network. Because packet networks inherently rely on statistical multiplexing, at least one queue is needed for each outgoing link. (The actual queuing systems are discussed further in Chapter 5, "Differentiation of Customer Service.")

In the simplest queue model using the *first in, first out (FIFO)* discipline, Poisson arrival process, and exponential service-time distribution, there is a simple formula, as shown in Formula 2.1, that connects the average load (ρ) and average waiting time in the queue (D), and average service time (h).

Formula 2.1

$$D = h\rho/(1-\rho)$$

You can apply this formula to a case where packets arrive at a buffer and are sent to a link with a certain speed. The service time of a packet is determined by the packet size and link speed. If the average packet size is 500 bytes, link rate is 100Mbps, and the average load is 0.5 (that is, 50Mbps), for example, the average waiting time of a packet according to Formula 2.1 is only 0.04 milliseconds. Even if the average load is as high as 0.99, the average, theoretical, queuing delay is less than 4 milliseconds.

This simple calculation may indicate that delay is not any problem in high-speed networks. Unfortunately, this is not a right conclusion because of several reasons. First, even if all other assumptions were valid but the average load increases by 1% from 0.99 to 1, the theoretical delay grows to infinity. Therefore, information about average load only is not sufficient for making practical conclusions.

Second, extensive studies have shown that the Poisson assumption is not valid for modeling Internet traffic, as noticed in the studies made at Bellcore in the early 1990s (Leland *et al.* 1993, 183–193). In particular, the aggregate arrival process of packets is not Poisson, but it contains a long-term correlation process that essentially changes the characteristics of traffic process. It is said that the traffic process is *self-similar*. Self-similarity in this context means that there are similar traffic variations on every time scale from milliseconds to weeks. Because of this fundamental nature, it is almost impossible to calculate any exact delay or packet-loss ratio for typical Internet traffic.

Moreover, even with the right formula, it is difficult to measure the required traffic parameters; one characteristic of self-similar traffic is that extremely long measurement periods are needed to acquire accurate results. Even if you did have both the formula and the parameters, a relatively small change in some of the parameters could result in a remarkable effect on the delay or loss figures. Therefore, this kind of approach may give some understanding about the system, but probably not any definite numbers for resource-management purposes.

> **Note**
>
> One additional warning is also valid: On the Internet, there is no such thing as traffic process independent of the network resources. This is evident if you consider the nature of TCP, which adjusts the bit rate of each connection based on the load situation in the network. (See section 2.3.2, "Basic Best-Effort Service Based on TCP," later in this chapter.) Consequently, analytical formulae are seldom useful. Instead, cumbersome simulations are usually needed to investigate Internet performance issues.

Simplistic models can be misleading. It is much easier to implement a network with three nodes and three links; you could have complete information about everything going on in this small network. If you have only three nodes, for instance, you can easily configure permanent connections between each pair of nodes and even reserve capacity for several different classes. On the contrary, if you have 1,000 boundary nodes and five service classes, this simple scenario is totally impractical.

If you want to establish a permanent connection with a specific bit rate between each boundary node pair for every service class, you need to manage 2,497,500 connections. Either you have a superb automatic management system or you have to forget the whole idea. Besides, as stated earlier, division of the link capacity into distinct parts is an inefficient way to utilize your resources. Therefore, you need a sensible, somewhat flexible, approach with some level of control over the traffic.

2.1.6 Technological Progress

The progress of optical transmission systems has been amazing during the past few years. The most advanced systems with *wavelength division multiplexing (WDM)* can provide bit rates as high as 100Gbps. To understand the real capacity of those systems, suppose that you have one transatlantic link with a capacity of 100Gbps in both directions. How many minutes of telephone calls can every inhabitant in the United States make during a day?

A straightforward calculation leads to this theoretical result: Each of the approximately 268,000,000 inhabitants could speak about 8.4 minutes every day if 64kbps coding is used. This is a considerable length, even though it is not realistic to suppose that the whole link capacity can be exploited by phone calls. On the other hand, if you are not using the standard PCM coding, but a more efficient coding scheme, you can lengthen the duration of 7.5 minutes up to even an hour!

Such a huge capacity means that the network nodes must be extremely capable. If the same link is used to transmit IP packets with an average size of 500 bytes, for instance, the nodes must be able to handle an average of 25 million packets coming from one link. That is certainly a hard task, although not impossible, even when taking into account the rapid development of information-processing technology. Therefore, although the transmission capacity may seem to be limitless, some bottlenecks will continue to occur in the foreseeable future (either inside network nodes or at access networks).

A consideration of the growth of network capacity, bottlenecks, and Internet traffic models leads to the conclusion that traffic engineering is needed even in networks with huge capacity. There are too many uncertainties to allow a feasible solution without any traffic control.

2.2   Traditional Telecommunication Approaches

The telephone network has a long tradition. Some significant changes in technology have occurred: first the emergence of automatic exchanges, and then digital transmission, and finally digital exchanges. All these developments have been important inside the network, and they have had certain effects on customer service as well. The operational principle has remained the same, however, in such a way that telephone networks have been able to smoothly evolve from one technological phase to another. What is the continuity of telephone networks? One apparent answer is the target—that is, to provide a medium for transmitting voice over long distances.

Telephone networks are now used for other purposes as well. These other uses are possible because the applications, such as fax and data connections, have adapted to the characteristics of the telephone networks. Certain limits do apply, however, with regard to this approach—for instance, a voice channel is too slow for many advanced applications. These issues are analyzed in Section 2.2.1, "Circuit-Switched Networks."

The main solution for these telephone network problems is Asynchronous Transfer Mode (ATM). Because of the telephone background, some of the basic principles of telephone networks can be found in ATM as well; in particular, a connection should be established before any user traffic can be transmitted through the network. The main objective of Section 2.2.2, "ATM Networks," is to provide an outline of the main strengths and weaknesses of the ATM approach.

2.2.1   Circuit-Switched Networks

In circuit-switched networks, a dedicated channel (or circuit) is established for the duration of a transmission. Telephone networks, the most universal circuit-switched networks, initially applied an utmost mode of circuit switching in which the network provided an unbroken, undivided electrical circuit for a specified frequency region between two telephones.

The technical evolution, including thorough digitalization of communication networks, has obscured this clear situation of electrical circuits: Very seldom anymore is there any fixed circuits between end terminals; instead, there is usually a certain type of transmission channel. Therefore, a circuit-switched network can be recognized by the following list of determinants:

- The network reserves certain fixed capacity for the information transmission for every channel.

- The network service provides a small additional delay to the fixed delay determined by speed of light, and a minimal end-to-end delay variation.

- The distinguishing of different channels during the transmission is based on the location of the information in the frame structure rather than the information inside the transmission channel.

Although the previous characteristics are typical for circuit-switched networks, you can find several deviations from the basic form of circuit switching in current networks. First, it is possible even in analog telephone networks to detect idle periods in a telephone conversation and to use these periods for transmitting some other information. As a consequence, although it appears for the user that he has a continuous connection to the other end, the connection could be of an on/off nature.

In digital networks, the possibilities are even more versatile. If all information is presented in digital form, for example, a basic circuit-switched network can manipulate information inside the network. Digital telephone exchanges, for instance, store all (or almost all) information for a short duration before it is transmitted forward. This is an unavoidable action, because it is possible that two different incoming channels that have exactly the same arrival time but a different incoming link will be multiplexed to the same outgoing link. Either of the channels has to be delayed.

Despite the development of circuit-switched technology, it is still evident that circuit-switching systems are primarily ideal for communication systems that require data to be transmitted in real-time during a relatively long period of time. Because they provide a tool for transmitting information from one place to another, however, they could, in principle, be used as a basis for any communication network. What does this actually mean if you have 1,000,000 end users who require transmission service for Internet traffic?

In a circuit-switched network, you typically can establish only connections with a predefined bit rate. Because the digital telephony network is based either on a bit rate of 56kbps or 64kbps, for instance, it is difficult to support a connection with an arbitrary bit rate because only certain multiples of the basic bit rate are usually supported. If, and when, your end users have various and continuously changing bit-rate needs (from some kilobits per second to several megabits per second), you could have big troubles with your customer and network services. Your customers will have to use certain predefined bit rates even though they might need something else most of the time.

You may be able to acquire an exceptional circuit-switching system capable of transmitting a very large number of different bit rates. For example:

n*1kbps where n = 1,2,3,..., 1,000,000

Does this kind of network solve your problem? Unfortunately, although it does solve a part of the problem, significant difficulties still exist. First, the network will always either establish a new connection or modify an old one when the required bit rate of a connection changes—and there will be a huge number of changes every second in your network. Consequently, your network must have a very advanced signaling system to transmit all information related to bit-rate changes—and a signaling system may require a considerable amount of transmission capacity.

The second problem is that each customer or application must be able to predict what bit rate the application needs within the next second, minute, or hour. This is definitely possible in the case of certain established applications, such as telephony calls in current networks. However, many Internet applications are not based on any fixed bit rate.

If your network did have an excellent signaling system and all applications were able to predict their bit rate, you would still encounter fundamental problems. If the bit rate changes, say, once a second, the network probably cannot update the capacity reservations in a way that no resources are wasted.

Finally, if you were able to solve all the previously discussed problems, you would have to dimension your network in such a way that your customers would remain satisfied. This is the same task you need to do if you are responsible for telephony service. You must go through the following phases for all links in the network:

Phase 1	Predict the offered traffic during busy hours for all the network links.
Phase 2	Specify quality of service target—for example, the allowed probability that a connection attempt is rejected because of insufficient link capacity.
Phase 3	Determine, based on the traffic prediction, the capacity required to satisfy QoS.

Phase 4	Find out what is the cheapest product that has at least the capacity calculated at Phase 3.
Phase 5	Order the required product (or update the current product).
Phase 6	Make the installation or update.

A lot of problems can arise during all these phases. You cannot assume that your Internet traffic prediction is accurate: An increased traffic demand might be either 100% or 200% per year, resulting in a relatively high probability that you will either overestimate or underestimate the actual demand.

In telephony networks, Phase 3 is usually done with the aid of the Erlang loss formula, which gives the call-blocking probability as a function of offered traffic and the number of channels. Because your customers will have variable connection requests, Phase 3 is much more complicated than in the case of telephony networks. You need a more advanced tool; although several methods are available, they require some effort to be applied (Roberts, Mocci, and Virtamo 1996).

If you want to build your own network based on real products, you must cope with quite rough expansion steps. The available increments in a backbone network based on optical transmission systems, for example, are 155Mbps, 622Mbps, and 2.488Gbps. As an inescapable result, even if you are a skillful network planner, you are using your network resources inefficiently. As a target, a long-term average load of 20% is more ambitious than easy. Therefore, a traditional circuit-switched network does not seem to be a cost-efficient approach to transmitting Internet traffic; and because there is only one guaranteed service class (although with several bit rate levels), it is not versatile.

The most significant advantage of this approach is robustness: Customers can use exactly the bit rate they have requested (and paid for), but not a bit more than that. Further, there are no lost packets or bits inside the network, provided that your network is working properly. For the same reasons, the customer service can be considered fair.

Note

Some intricate issues make the assessment of fairness more complicated than what could be expected, however: The call-blocking probability may depend on the bit rate requested by the customer, on the time and date of the request, and on the number of links on the connection path. Although the question whether the result is fair is surely interesting, this discussion skips it because it seems that a pure circuit-switching network cannot provide a proper solution to the purpose of transmitting Internet traffic.

Although the preceding considerations seem to lead to an impractical result, such considerations serve one purpose: Identifying several key problems that most likely are solvable by any networking technology specifically designed for the transmission of Internet traffic. The problems can be summarized as follows:

- Many flows are of very short duration.

- Connection establishment tends to require complicated actions inside the network.

- Quality and capacity requirements of new applications vary within extremely wide bounds.

- Traffic characteristics of flows (or connections) are difficult to predict.

- The use of a resource-reservation principle tends to leave the majority of network capacity unused.

The third item in the preceding list relates to the fundamental attribute of versatility. The other items relate mainly to cost efficiency. With circuit-switching systems, no significant problems seem to be related to fairness or robustness. As discussed later, these attributes are the main concerns of some packet-switching systems.

You might be wondering why this discussion has so far focused on the evaluation of circuit-switched networks. The answer is that, if you want to improve the quality of service of a packet network by separate connections with fixed bit rate and quality, you will most likely encounter the same problems evident with circuit-switching technologies.

2.2.2 ATM Networks

Asynchronous Transfer Mode (ATM) has been regarded as a promising solution to some of the problems described in Chapter 1, "The Target of Differentiated Services,"—such problems as the lack of versatility in circuit-switched networks, for example. A wide standardization effort within the International Telecommunications Union (ITU) and ATM Forum has led to an extensive set of standards that specifies all the issues needed to build a workable ATM network.

Taking into account these facts, it is quite surprising that there are so few real demonstrations of customer service based on end-to-end ATM connections. (Although ATM has definitely been widely used as a backbone technology, that type of use exploits only a relatively small part of the whole set of ATM standards.) Chapter 3, "Differentiated Services Working Group," sheds light on this issue.

The target of the original project that led to the ATM technology was real-time cable TV using a high-speed digital transport (Coudreuse 1997). Therefore, the main challenges were high-speed switching (note that the project took place almost 20 years ago) and delay control. It soon became apparent, however, that a network with those characteristics could be useful for almost any imaginable purpose. So flexibility, or *versatility* in the terminology of this book, was given priority at an early stage of ATM development.

In the case of ATM, flexibility is achieved by an intrinsic property: All types of information are presented in the same form using equal-sized packets, called *cells*. The size of an ATM cell is 53 bytes (424 bits), of which 5 bytes are used for the header and 48 for user information. The size of the cell was a result of significant debate between two camps: those who wanted to keep the relative overhead of the cell header small by a large cell, and those who wanted to keep the packetization delay short by a small cell. Unfortunately, the final compromise of 48 bytes cannot meet either of these targets very well, as the following examples illustrate.

The packetization delay for an 8kbps audio stream can be calculated as shown in Formula 2.2.

Formula 2.2

```
Delay = 48*8 bit / 8000 bit/s = 48 ms
```

This is the time needed to fill the information field of an ATM cell if a bit rate of 8kbps is used. Although 48 milliseconds is not a very long delay as such, it is a significant part of the allowed delay of a high-quality telephone call. According to Multimedia Communications Forum, delay shall be less than 160 milliseconds with echo controller, and a low delay limit of only 22 milliseconds is applicable when supporting connections to conventional telephones without supplementary echo control.

Because of the small size, the minimum overhead of an ATM cell is relatively large—that is, $5/53 = 9.4\%$. The real overhead when ATM is used to transmit IP packets is larger because IP packets should be adjusted into the cells with an extra protocol layer, the *ATM Adaptation Layer (AAL)*, that requires an additional byte in the ATM cell. In addition, because an IP packet is rarely a multiple of 47 bytes, one ATM cell per IP packet is partly unused. As a result, a typical overhead of ATM layers when used for transmitting IP packets is approximately 20%.

ATM can delicately solve one problem circuit-switched networks face: lack of versatility. Any user or application can transmit any bit rate whatsoever, limited only by the physical bit rate of the links, and the ATM network can aggregate any combination of different bit rates into one link, even without knowing what the real bit rate of each connection is. In that sense, ATM is surely versatile. The other side of this advantageous property is that every ATM node must have advanced tools to control traffic if and when it attempts to guarantee specific quality of service.

Virtual Connections

The key instruments of traffic handling in ATM networks are virtual circuits (VCs) and virtual paths (VPs). Because the quality control is based on connections, ATM is fundamentally a connection-oriented technology even when used to transmit IP packets. On the other hand, because ATM utilizes packet-based technology (rather than circuit switching) to transfer information, every packet (or cell) includes information about the destination address. Because the cell size is relatively small, it is not reasonable to convey the whole address in every cell; instead, a local identifier specifies the connection to which the cell belongs. Because of this locality, the required size of the identifier field is of moderate length—in ATM, 24 bits (assuming that the first 4 bits of the ATM header are not used for this purpose).

These 24 bits makes it possible to distinguish 16,777,216 connections on every link—that is, a large number. The downside of largeness, agreeable as such, is that it generates other strict requirements if really applied as a whole. Suppose, for example, that the average lifetime of a connection is three minutes. The node should be able to handle, in theory, 93,206 connection requests every second on every link. Although this could be realized technically, it would certainly bring about a serious operational and management burden unless the connection handling is truly straightforward.

To solve this dilemma, ATM uses the two levels of identifiers mentioned earlier: *virtual circuit (VC)* and *virtual path (VP)* identifiers. The basic idea of this arrangement is that a VP forms a relatively permanent pathway for cells between two ATM nodes, possibly far away from each other; and VCs can then be established and terminated without making any actions in the intermediate nodes. Figure 2.2 illustrates this system.

Node B2 in Figure 2.2 is a so-called VP cross-connect node that looks and takes into account only the VP identifiers, but leaves all VC identifiers unchanged. The other backbone node, B1, can support both VCs and VPs. The result is that virtual circuits can be established and modified inside a permanent VP from A1 to A4 through B1 and B2, without any actions in nodes B1 and B2.

Although VPs are generally useful, they have some negative effects as well. One of the key problems of VPs is that, because a VP usually needs a fixed bandwidth reservation, an excessive use of VPs tends to severely deteriorate the efficiency of statistical multiplexing. Note that if the bandwidth reserved for the VP is always changed when a new connection is established, you lose the fundamental advantage of VPs (because all intermediate nodes should be informed of all changes).

Figure 2.2 Virtual circuits and virtual paths in an ATM network.

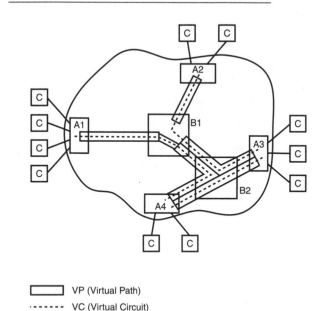

VP (Virtual Path)
- - - - - - VC (Virtual Circuit)

To provide versatility in quality characteristics, a third set of building blocks for ATM traffic management is needed: the service categories. ATM Forum has so far defined six services with the following admission criteria and efficiency of statistical multiplexing:

- *Constant Bit Rate (CBR)*: Admission control is based on the peak rate of the connection, usually without statistical multiplexing.

- *Real-Time Variable Bit Rate (rt-VBR)*: Admission control is based on several parameters that make it possible to apply more efficient statistical multiplexing.

- *Non-Real-Time Variable Bit Rate (nrt-VBR)*: Admission control is similar to rt-VBR, but statistical multiplexing could be more efficient because of better possibility for buffering ATM cells.

- *Available Bit Rate (ABR)*: Connection-level admission control is based on a minimum bit rate; in addition, a cell-level admission control is based on load level inside the network. It provides high statistical multiplexing—at least in theory.

- *Unspecified Bit Rate (UBR)*: With no or minimal admission control, UBR provides very efficient statistical multiplexing.

- *Guaranteed Frame Rate (GFR)*: Admission control is based on a minimum bit rate available for a connection; GFR provides efficient statistical multiplexing. (The standardization is unfinished.)

Constant Bit Rate (CBR)

The CBR service category is intended for real-time connections that need tight synchronization between the traffic source and destination. Further, it is supposed that the source sends traffic with a constant bit rate or, actually, with a constant cell rate (because the source is sending cells, not individual bits). It is unrealistic, however, to require that a source send cells with exactly the same inter-arrival time (because the ATM network itself may generate jitter to any originally regular flow). Therefore, CBR service allows a small variation in cell rate, but not any persistent excess of cell rate.

Because network-management systems must rely on the assumption that CBR connections are really using a constant bit rate, or at least that the bit rate is below a specified limit, there must be tools for restricting offered traffic of every CBR connection. To guarantee robust service, therefore, two traffic control functions are used: *Usage Parameter Control (UPC)* and *Connection Admission Control (CAC)*.

Excessive cells are rejected by the UPC mechanism situated at the ingress ATM node. (A similar function at network-to-network interfaces is called *Network Parameter Control [NPC]*.) CAC mechanism decides whether a new connection request can be accepted into the network without compromising quality of service of existing connections. The technical aspects of these control functions are discussed in Chapter 5, "Differentiation of Customer Service."

In addition to end-to-end virtual connections, CBR service is regularly used in the case of VPs because statistical multiplexing between VPs that are used to transmit VBR VCs inside them is extremely difficult to manage. Therefore, even though the traffic inside a typical VP is anything but constant, VPs are usually supplied with constant resources.

Variable Bit Rate (VBR)

The next two categories, rt-VBR and nrt-VBR, are aimed at improving the statistical multiplexing of CBR service. As the name indicates, the basic difference between CBR and VBR is that VBR allows more fluctuations in traffic process than CBR service does. A VBR connection is characterized by three parameters: Peak Cell Rate (PCR), Sustained Cell Rate (SCR), and Maximum Burst Size (MBS). Based on these parameters and on information about network resources, ATM nodes calculate the required bandwidth for a set of connections. This task has turned out to be very difficult to carry out in real-time; in particular, it should be noted that the required parameter for any flow may depend essentially on both other connections and the available link rate.

The nrt-VBR service is applicable for those VBR connections that have no inherent need for time synchronization between source and destination. The rt-VBR service category was principally designed for transmitting compressed video traffic. There are two principles of video coding. With constant bit-rate coding, the output of video coder is constant-bit-rate and the quality of the picture is variable. In particular, scene changes generating high peaks of information to be transmitted are difficult to support with CBR coding without temporarily deteriorating picture quality. You can avoid this problem by variable bit-rate coding that makes possible a constant quality.

Available Bit Rate (ABR)

The ABR service category tries to combine definite quality guarantees with flexible use of network resources. This target is ambitious: How can a network give any guarantees if it at the same time allows users to send traffic with arbitrary bit rates? Actually it cannot; it must regulate the bit rates used by customers quite tightly.

The principal assumption behind ABR is that the applications using the service do not have any strict bit-rate requirements, but that they can benefit from increased bit rate. In addition, it supposes that packet losses are so harmful, either for users or for the network, that they should be avoided even at the expense of complicated control mechanisms. The control mechanism is designed to offer a fair share of network resources for each ABR connection, basically by dividing the available bandwidth at each bottleneck link according to a definite rule. Information about available bandwidth is then transmitted through the network by specific cells, called Resource Management (RM) cells.

ABR service is suited only for those systems and applications that can quickly adjust their bit rate. (Otherwise, a lot of cells might be lost at the ingress node before the cells enter the ABR network service.)

It is fair to say that ABR service is *versatile* in the sense that it provides various and variable bit rates; *robust*, because it tightly controls traffic sent by the user; and *fair*, because the available capacity is divided equitably. The major concern regarding ABR is whether it can be cost efficient because of its inherent complexity.

Unspecified Bit Rate (UBR)

The UBR service category differs fundamentally from the other ATM service categories in the sense that UBR sources neither specify nor receive any bit rate, delay, or loss guarantee. UBR service can be used by applications that can adjust their bit rate in case of lost or delayed cells.

The lack of guarantees and of strict control mechanisms bring about fairness problems; in fact, fairness issues are either left for upper-layer protocols, such as TCP/IP, or the network operator supposes that most of the time there are no critical fairness problems (for instance, because of low network utilization). The fairness problems related to UBR are basically the same as those with the best-effort service model in IP networks (see Section 2.3.2, "Basic Best-Effort Service Based on TCP"). In particular, greedy users capable of modifying protocols may get much more bandwidth than users relying on standard protocols.

Guaranteed Frame Rate (GFR)

The most recent development to ATM services is GFR. According to Report Q7/13 of the ITU documents, the main motivation behind GFR is that some applications may not be best suited for any of the ATM-transfer capabilities described earlier. Such applications are too bursty for CBR, have traffic characteristics that are not suitable for VBR, and cannot use explicit feedback as in ABR.

The main advantage of GFR over UBR is that it provides a minimum guaranteed frame rate for every connection. Furthermore, new signaling messages are needed for establishing the reservations. Although the standardization is still unfinished as of this writing, and it is not totally clear what the actual meaning of guarantee is with regard to GFR, it is likely that there will be strict rules for controlling GFR connections. Yet, the rules may be looser than those of other ATM services. Because of the inherent vagueness of the applications of this service, however, the design of an optimal and mathematically accurate control method might be a very laborious process. In general, it seems that a combination of applications with unpredictable traffic patterns, loosely defined control mechanisms, and guaranteed services is difficult, if not impossible, to realize.

A short summary of the basic engineering philosophy of ATM is as follows:

- For most of a network, the basic unit for traffic engineering is a connection—that is, a continuous flow of cells.

- ATM provides two levels of aggregation (VC and VP) that may facilitate traffic management.

- An ATM network offers guaranteed services for most of the connections.

- The rest of the capacity is divided among UBR, GFR, and ABR service categories, suitable for adaptive applications.

- An ATM network favors statistical multiplexing to improve network utilization even at the expense of complicated control architecture.

2.2.3 Evaluation of Connection-Oriented Approaches

It can be argued that if the philosophical basis of ATM is the right one, the overall result cannot be much better than what ATM technology offers independently of the amount of effort put in to develop the service architecture. It is impossible, however, to be certain that the starting point is totally relevant with regard to the Internet. Hence, it's important to consider the requisite attributes—fairness, versatility, robustness, and cost efficiency—when assessing this issue. Although this evaluation concerns mainly ATM networks, most of the issues are common to any connection-oriented technology.

Versatility

Several arguments can be made for the superior versatility of ATM technology:

- Five different service categories can meet, in principle, almost any imaginable service need. More specifically, the rt-VBR service (and CBR as a special case of it) can provide superb real-time characteristics, and ABR and UBR are designed for adaptive data applications.

- The network can distinguish each individual connection and give everyone a network service with user- or application-specific characteristics, including appropriate bit rate. Therefore, the bit-rate granularity problem of circuit-switching systems can be solved exquisitely by ATM.

- The advanced traffic-control functions make it possible for the operator to adjust and optimize the use of network resources in a flexible manner. Thus, the use of virtual paths enables the network operator to handle a lot of connections inside the network without detailed information about individual connections.

Further, it is possible, at least in theory, to provide various levels of cell-loss ratios within the VBR service categories. There is even a bit in every cell reserved for dividing cells of each connection into two cell-loss categories: Cell Loss Priority (CLP). It might also be possible to provide two different virtual paths within one link in a way that the cell-loss ratio is different. In practice, this kind of system is cumbersome to implement and manage. (This is discussed further in Chapter 5, "Differentiation of Customer Service.")

Although it can be argued that ATM operators or service providers will rarely actually use all these service categories and traffic-control features, the overall conclusion is that there are not many problems related to versatility. Besides, it seems that the standardization organizations are able to develop new standards if any deficiency is identified.

Robustness

Robustness is the other area to which ATM standardization has paid a lot of attention. If this discussion ignores, for a while, the UBR service category, all the other ATM services are designed in a way that definitely restricts the possibility of misuse of the network. The traffic contract between a user and a network specifies in detail, on the one hand, what the user is allowed to send into the network, and, on the other hand, what performance the network promises to offer for compliant connections. There is not much more room for misuse than in circuit-switching networks.

Of course, the principle of statistical multiplexing results in some level of uncertainty. It is theoretically possible, for example, that a large number of users exploiting VBR service will synchronize their transmission in such a way that the momentary load exceeds the network capacity even though every individual user is complying with the traffic contract. In general, any traffic-control mechanism relying on statistical properties of traffic behavior can be challenged by an intentional attack from malicious users. It is possible to limit this kind of threat with well-defined customer services and by appropriate network dimensioning.

Another possible, and perhaps more serious, concern relates to the inherent complexity of ATM traffic engineering. It is apparent that the more parameters to be specified, the more possibilities for errors. Errors can be made either by users when defining their requirements or by network operators when specifying the characteristics of networks services. Consider, for example, what you would think if you put an extra zero in the required bit-rate box (say, 500kbps rather than 50kbps) and then received a bill 10 times more expensive than what you expected? Correspondingly, a reverse error made by a network operator may wreak havoc on the performance of a whole service category. If there are dozens of parameters, as ATM service categories in total have, it is very likely that something will go wrong (because of the complex architecture and the large number of parameters).

Finally, it is important to say something about the robustness of UBR service category. UBR is, in this respect, contrary to other ATM services: Complex service architecture does not induce any problems, but the lack of strict traffic control might. If all other service categories can be insulated from the effects of excessive UBR traffic—and ATM traffic management surely provides tools for doing that—the problems can be kept on an appropriate level. Further, the users of UBR service will comprehend that the cheapness of the service is directly related to the lack of any strict service guarantees.

Fairness

Fairness is an elusive term. Because this is the first time that this discussion is attempting to thoroughly assess the fairness of a service model, it is important to first consider this central issue more generally. It is possible to clarify some issues by limiting the viewpoint to a specific case. You have bought a service from a service provider for transmitting information through the network, for example. The structure of the service could be of any form, simple or complex. One thing is certain, however: You must pay for the service. For the sake of simplicity, assume that you get a monthly bill that consists of either a constant flat rate or a very complicated composite of separate fees. Other customers get similar bills, or perhaps dissimilar bills because of a different service model, every month. The most essential issues to consider when assessing the fairness are as follows:

- Total amount of payment

- The service you and other customers have obtained

- Clarity and predictability of both the service and the bill

Note

The viewpoint of this book is that the structure of the bill is of minor significance. This book assumes that the customer doesn't much care whether the monthly invoice consists of several itemized charges or of one flat rate (only that the content should be, in any case, understandable).

Another issue to consider is the relative services obtained by different customers compared to the service obtained by one customer and the costs related to realize that service. One would argue that the charge of a service could be unfair even though all customers get the same service with the same price. This is definitely possible—for example, the price of some telephony services seems to significantly exceed the real costs of the service.

Nevertheless, these are new services with tough competition. It seems fair to suppose that the competition keeps the average price level of Internet services reasonable. In this case, it is important to ask the hard question: What is a fair price structure when service diversity is as wide as it is predicted to be in the future Internet?

What would be the result if you were to take as a starting point the monthly bill rather than the technical characteristics of service categories? You might get a monthly bill with an extremely detailed description of what you have used, something like the one depicted in Figure 2.3.

Note

It is not important to this example to understand all the terms appearing in the monthly statement in Figure 2.3. You can just suppose that an ordinary customer is not willing to read the handbook, and that it is too long to include here. There could be 100 items every month if the Internet service is used for Web browsing, telephone calls, file transfer, and various other applications. As a result, the total bill is hard to compress into fewer than 10 pages, and a customer needs to spend quite a lot of time to check the bill carefully.

Figure 2.3   Part of a fictitious ATM service bill.

Item	date time	destination	service or deviation	parameters	ref. (manual)	tariff $	charge $
21	10/23/98 9:56:27– 10:37:45 (2478 c)	XXZ.XYZ. YXY.XZY	rt–VBR	PCR=200kbit/s SCR=120kbit/s MBS=200byte CLR(clp0)<10e^{-7} maxCTD=50ms	p.24		
				EffBand=172kbit/s	p.45	2.00/Gbit	0.85
			excess	SCR=+18kbit/s	p.48	5.00/Gbit	0.22
			excess	maxCTD=+15ms	p.49	–5%	–0.05
						total	1.02
21	10/23/98 19:05:23– 20:22:05 (4602 s)	XXY.XYZ. XYY.YXZ	UBR	Mbits up = 4.7 Mbits down = 96.7 linkrate = 2Mbit/s	p.26	1.00/Gbit 0.50/Gbit 0.01/Gbit	0.00 0.05 0.09
						total	0.14
Total amount of payment							32.45

What about fairness? Is there any problem? The service and the tariffs are designed carefully in a manner that could be considered as fair as possible. Every traffic and quality parameter has been taken into account; the price levels of different service categories have been pondered sincerely; and the hard competition takes care of the overall level of tariffs.

Although every detail seems to be fair, something in the whole system is inappropriate. Can you understand the bill in Figure 2.3 without looking at some ATM textbook? If not, don't be worried. A great majority of ordinary customers lose track in the first row of the bill and move immediately to the only figure that they certainly understand: the total amount to be paid.

Although the bill might be exhaustive, consisting of fair details, most customers cannot assess the service they get from their service providers or compare the price performance of different service providers. For these reasons, a scheme in which an ATM service provider offers all service categories to all users is not in reality a very likely approach.

Moreover, because one service provider can seldom offer connections to all required places, many important issues—such as the availability of service classes, pricing, and quality of service—depend on the approaches applied by other service providers and network operators. The reality of multiple providers makes the fairness assessment by an ordinary customer even more difficult.

What could be a solution to this disagreeable situation? There are, of course, various pricing approaches with different properties, as discussed in Section 5.1.3, "Pricing as a Tool for Controlling Traffic," in Chapter 5, "Differentiation of Customer Service." One feasible approach is to simplify the service construction as much as possible. The most concise, but still somehow feasible, structure is a combination of CBR and UBR (or GFR) services.

You can use UBR service whenever the network performance is high enough for your purposes; otherwise, you must use CBR service that is basically able to meet all imaginable quality requirements. In the simplest model, the price of the UBR service is based purely on your access rate into the network and CBR services are charged in the same way as ordinary telephone calls, except that the price depends on the required bit rate. Note that the basic philosophy of the GFR service model is quite similar to this combination of CBR and UBR services.

Can this simple scheme be fairer than the complex scheme with all ATM service categories? Let's try to look at this fundamental question more thoroughly by supposing three groups of customers:

- Customers using CBR service

- Customers using UBR service with moderate demand of information transfer

- Customers using UBR service with high and continuous demand for transferring information

Although customers can change the group whenever they want, for this discussion suppose that customer groups are permanent during a month. Three main questions relate to fairness: Does this service structure enable relatively fair pricing for CBR customers, for the CBR-group and the UBR-groups, and for the two UBR-groups?

The first issue raises questions as to whether the tariff should depend on the destination address or on the date and time of the connection and whether the CBR tariff should be a linear function of the bit rate. Because the CBR service is similar to that of telephone service, many service providers with telephony background will answer *yes* to the first two questions. There is no evidently right or fair scheme, however, when looking at the technical costs of two CBR connections, a local connection, and a connection to a destination on the other side of the globe. The situation is too complicated and changeable to provide means for accurate evaluation. Markets, customer behavior, and regulatory issues will determine the situation in real networks.

There is no apparent answer to the linearity question either. A simple calculation shows that a linear tariff either limits the usefulness of CBR service for high-quality video transfer or offers free telephone calls:

- A three-minute telephone call with a bit rate of 20kbps generates 3.6Mb of traffic.

- A movie coded by 2Mbps and lasting 100 minutes generates 12Gb of traffic.

Consequently, a movie may generate 3,333 times more bits than a telephone call, which means that if the telephone call costs $0.003, transmitting the video will cost $10 when using the same linear tariff. Neither of these are reasonable: The cost of billing a telephone call is probably more than 0.3 cents, and $10 for transmitting a video through the network is a prohibitive price for most users. Therefore, although linear pricing could meet basic fairness criteria if judging by the technical realization of the service, it is not necessarily a reasonable solution in practice. (This issue is discussed further in the section titled "Price of Bandwidth" in Chapter 5, "Differentiation of Customer Service.")

The next topic is fairness of CBR pricing compared to UBR pricing. The same basic problem is encountered as in the case of different CBR calls: Customer willingness to pay depends much more on the usefulness or entertainment of the end application than on the number of bits transmitted through the network.

A tariff of $0.05/minute for a 64kbps connection means $13/Gb. If you assume that your UBR usage is moderate (say, on average 5MB per day), the same tariff means $15/month. Because the price per bit for UBR service will be lower than that of CBR service due to lower quality, the result could be quite appropriate in this case—for instance, $5/month for UBR services is a quite reasonable tariff.

But again, a linear-pricing model may bring about problems because customer willingness to pay is probably not a linear function of transmitted bits. How to avoid this problem? One possible approach is to ignore totally the transmitted bits and apply a pure flat rate. This approach may certainly solve some problems, but may also generate some new problems when assessing the fairness between the two UBR customer groups with light and heavy usage. This primary question of Internet services is addressed later in Section 2.3, "The Best-Effort Approach."

Cost Efficiency

It seems that a very versatile service provision, even though somehow desirable, is difficult to design and manage in a truly fair manner from an ordinary user's viewpoint. If you conclude that service structure should be as simple as possible, something like a combination of CBR and UBR categories, you have to ask whether ATM is the most efficient way to realize these services.

UBR service seems to be needed mainly for IP packet transmission. As mentioned earlier, the ATM overhead when transmitting IP packets is approximately 20%. In some cases, an overhead of this level is acceptable; sometimes, however, it is not acceptable. Another, probably more serious, source of extra costs is the management of an extra layer: ATM has its own signaling and routing and management systems. Therefore, if you consider only IP over UBR service, it is somewhat difficult to identify any compelling reason to use ATM between IP and the physical layers.

This picture changes significantly when you consider needs other than IP traffic—in particular, real-time applications such as voice and video. The cell-based switching and transmission and strict quality control of every connection are powerful tools to satisfy the most demanding requirements. The question now is whether this is enough to justify the large contraptions of ATM. If ATM, or any similar technology is used, you must first of all be certain that the quality-control scheme applied in ATM is exactly what you need.

Real Quality of ATM Services

ATM traffic management and quality assurance are based on three cornerstones: virtual connections, capacity reservations, and quality guarantees. The terms and concepts of this system—connections, reservations, and quality—are easily misleading. (For example, reservation models and calculations are often based on certain assumptions that are not necessarily valid in reality.)

If you try to guarantee a definite cell-loss ratio, the actual result in practice could be like that shown in Figure 2.4. The figure illustrates a situation in which a service operator offers three service classes: low, high, and guaranteed. They are treated using two basic principles:

- All packets are delivered if possible.

- During congestion, packets belonging to higher service classes are delivered whenever possible (ahead of lower classes).

It is probable that most of the time (90% in the figure) there is enough capacity to transmit all packets. Consequently, if you consider a short period, the probability that there is no packet loss even on the lowest service level is 90%. Then during some high peaks of traffic load (or traffic variation), some packets belonging to the intermediate class should be discarded; all guaranteed service packets, on the other hand, can still be successfully transmitted. The highest class will suffer packet losses only if something exceptional happens—for instance, a cable break. Even so, the loss ratio is likely very high. Note that the unavailability value of 0.001% means only 5 minutes per year.

Figure 2.4   The difference in real service quality of three service classes.

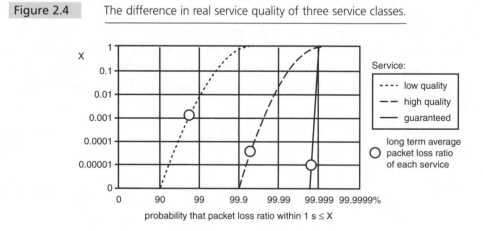

probability that packet loss ratio within 1 s ≤ X

Exceptional cases may occur, for instance, due to operational errors that are more likely when the system is complicated, as ATM is. If you want to provide several QoS classes, there will be a real difference between classes perhaps only 0.01% of the time. This is always a likely result when a network relies on reservations and preventive traffic engineering.

The difference in quality does not mean so much difference in cell-loss ratio, but rather differences in reliability or availability of the service. For most applications, the service is either available or not; seldom is the quality only moderate. For most end users, the real reason for the unavailability of service is usually of no importance. Most end users will want to know when the service will be available again, not the "fascinating" reason(s) for temporary unavailability—excessive load in the network, cable break, management error, and so on.

2.3   The Best-Effort Approach

There are actually two traffic management philosophies: In the first one, traffic management is needed only during congestion; in the other one, the main task of traffic management is to avoid congestion whenever possible. With ATM, the engineers had something permanent in mind, such as long video connections with relatively stable bit rate demand that are totally independent of what is occurring in the network. Congestion avoidance is a reasonable approach in that case.

On the contrary, in IP or Internet, the fundamental idea has been almost the opposite: Most of the traffic is anything but stable, and there are inherent relations between network capacity, load situation, and traffic demand. Therefore, the starting point of IP has been that if there is no congestion, no traffic-control actions are needed. It is important now to clarify the main reasons that have led to this traffic-control paradigm in IP networks.

2.3.1 Service Model

The foundation of Internet technology has been the assumption that packet switching is much more suitable than circuit switching for computer networks. The Internet has shown that this assumption is valid. However, the technological differences between packet and circuit switching do not totally explain the remarkable differences in the history of the Internet and telecommunication networks.

Part of the difference stems from the amount of time that each has taken to develop. There has been much time for building bureaucratic standardization and development processes since the invention of telephony in 1876. In contrast, the development of the Internet during the first 20 years was a much less bureaucratic, and a much more flexible, process.

The Development of the Internet

The Internet started as a research project connecting four computers in 1969. The experimental network, called ARPAnet, was funded by Advanced Research Projects Agency (ARPA), now called Defense Advanced Research Projects Agency (DARPA), an agency of the U.S. Department of Defense. Since then, a lot has occurred:

- The number of computers has grown steadily, by approximately 75% per year.

- The Request for Comments (RFC) series was established in 1969.

- The first email system was introduced in 1972.

- Wide deployment of TCP/IP began January 1, 1983.

- First IETF meeting took place in January 1986 with 21 attendees.

- Tim Berners-Lee at CERN (*Conseil European pour la Recherche Nucleaire*, translated as European Laboratory for Particle Physics Research) invented the World Wide Web in 1990, which added graphics capability to the Internet and positioned the network to become a vehicle of commerce.

- The Internet Society was founded in 1991.

- The number of computers connected to the Internet exceeded 1 million in 1992.

- During the past few years, TCP/IP has become the dominating networking protocol.

- The number of attendees to the forty-second IETF meeting, in August 1998, was 2,106.

continues

A few key principles have guided the evolution of the Internet:

- Open architecture means that the network architecture does not dictate the use of any network technology, but rather the provider may select it freely.

- The simplicity and robustness of the system has been promoted by specifying that the network nodes do not keep any information about the individual flows of packets passing through.

- The Internet has not been designed for just one application, but as a general infrastructure.

These principles distinguish the Internet from most other networking standards.

For further information about the history of the Internet, see `http://www.isoc.org/internet/history/`.

In traditional telecommunication networks and services, the specification and implementation phases are clearly and separately defined. With regard to the Internet, however, specification work and implementation proceed parallel. This is explicitly stated in RFC 2026: "An Internet Standard is a specification that is stable and well-understood, is technically competent, has multiple, independent, and interoperable implementations with substantial operational experience, enjoys significant public support, and is recognizably useful in some or all parts of the Internet."

Therefore, an Internet document may reach a standard status only after there are independent implementations. In addition, it should be noted that the standardization body, the Internet Engineering Task Force (IETF), is a loosely self-organized group of people who make technical and other contributions rather than a hierarchical organization with official representatives from different organization. Basically, the same people who are the most intensive users of the Internet are participating in the standardization effort (and may as well be involved with the operation of the network). Although this situation has changed somewhat as the user population has expanded, it is safe to say that Internet engineers are still developing standards for themselves.

It is, therefore, somewhat artificial to speak about customer service in the case of former IP networks. The engineering philosophy was based on the model of a homogeneous community that had common interest to design a workable network rather than on a model of service providers and customers.

The fairness of the Internet service, or more generally the fairness of the whole Internet, has relied on the assumption that there is in essence one user group consisting of all

Internet users. In that case, the fairest situation is when everyone is allowed to use the network for any sensible purpose, and only when there is not enough capacity for all demand, would there be a need for controlling or limiting the traffic sent to the network.

Even during congestion, it is supposed that all or at least most users behave agreeably. Agreeable behavior could be that users stop transferring enormous files if they notice any performance problems in the network, or even better, if everyone sends only truly necessary information through the network. The situation was earlier eased by the fact that transferring information through the network was a much more complex operation than nowadays; back then, only persons with some level of experience in the field of data transmission sent much data through the network. It is evident that this kind of approach has serious limitations when the population contain tens of millions of users and the use of the network becomes a simple task for anyone (even those without any knowledge about data networks and protocols).

The next step has been to specify protocols that automatically adjust the sent traffic to the network. If everyone is using a similar protocol and does not evade the adjustment control by using other more greedy protocols, the system could partly solve the problem of different user behaviors, because most users are neither able nor willing to modify any traffic-control protocols.

Within these limits, any user who has been connected to the network has been allowed to utilize any available network resources independent of the actual purpose of the application or information. The network then provides a service that is called *best effort* because the network tries to transmit as many packets as possible and as soon as possible but does not give any guarantees. As a result, the realization of best-effort service consists of three main parts:

- The network transmitting packets

- The TCP protocol controlling the bit rate

- The application capable of working in changing conditions

2.3.2 *Basic Best-Effort Service Based on TCP*

Jon Postel wrote the Transmission Control Protocol specification, RFC 793, in 1981. It is worth noticing what was said about the objective: "This document focuses its attention primarily on military computer communication requirements, especially robustness in the presence of communication unreliability and availability in the presence of congestion, but many of these problems are found in the civilian and government sector as well."

Because of this background, TCP provides an effective tool to recover from data that is damaged, lost, duplicated, or delivered out of order. This is achieved by assigning a sequence number to all data transmitted in the network, and requiring a positive acknowledgment (ACK) from the receiving TCP. If the ACK is not received within a timeout interval, the data is retransmitted. As a result, if all TCP implementations function properly and the Internet does not become completely partitioned, TCP is able to recover from transmission errors.

Moreover, TCP provides a means for the receiver to control the amount of data sent by the sender. This property is achieved by returning a "window" indicating a range of acceptable sequence numbers. The window indicates an allowed number of octets that the sender may transmit before receiving further permission.

These characteristics are specified in the original TCP document. The basic TCP scheme does not, however, provide reasonable tools for efficiently avoiding or alleviating congestion situations inside the network. In a worst-case scenario, a combination of retransmissions and a rapidly growing load in congested links may lead to a so-called congestion collapse.

The situation may start when a new file transfer begins to fill a buffer assigned to an already loaded link. When this buffer fills up, the round-trip time for all connections rises quickly. In that case, TCP connections suppose that packets are lost, and retransmit them. Finally, several copies of the same packet may exist at the same time in the network. Consequently, the throughput of the network is permanently reduced to a small fraction of normal. This problem was addressed by RFC 896 in 1984 and various proposals to solve it, such as RFC 2001, have been presented thereafter.

2.3.3 Improvements to the Basic TCP Behavior

The fundamental problem of the old TCP implementations based on RFC 793 is that the sender may start a connection by sending lots of data up to the window size advertised by the receiver. Although this simple scheme may work in small networks with large capacity, it may be harmful in large networks with several routers and possibly low or highly loaded links.

Slow-start is a solution to this problem. In essence slow-start means that after connection establishment, the sender is allowed to send only one packet before getting acknowledgement from receiver (supposing that the sender is using the packet size announced by the receiver). When the sender receives a whole window of ACKs, the sender can double the amount of data it can put in the network, until a packet is discarded and the sender notices that the maximum available capacity in the network is reached.

Congestion can be alleviated by going into a slow-start when the sender notices a congestion situation in the network. Several different schemes are used to increase packet rate after congestion. This discussion does not address them further, but it should be noted that they all induce a sawtooth pattern in which the window size (and also the bit rate) goes regularly up and down, as illustrated in Figure 2.5.

All connections also encounter intermittent packet losses when the total load exceeds link capacity and the buffers get full. Note that there is a delay between packet loss and window size reduction because of the round-trip delay. Both the sawtooth and packet losses are intrinsic characteristics of TCP and usually are insignificant to most end applications.

Figure 2.5   Sawtooth pattern of a TCP connection.

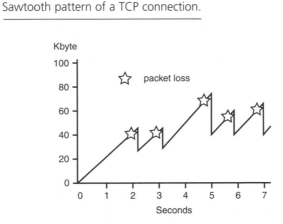

An elementary part of the congestion problem is that the network nodes have applied a pure first in, first out (FIFO) principle in the buffers—packets are discarded only when the buffer is totally full. If most network nodes are built with FIFO buffers, TCP flow-control algorithms are about the best that can be done (Keshav 1998, 421). Although a FIFO principle may seem to be the most efficient and fair in general, in certain situations it is both inefficient and unfair.

A FIFO buffer yields a similar packet-loss ratio to every connection at certain point in time. When measured during a short period when the buffer is full, the packet-loss ratio could be very high, and consequently, almost all senders get notice of congestion at the same time. If they are also reacting at the same time, the total traffic will drop dramatically. Then for a certain period of time, the congested link will be underutilized because every connection begins to increase its packet rate from a low value.

One possible solution to this problem is that some randomly selected packets are discarded even before the buffer becomes full. In that way, some senders are informed about the imminent congestion in the network. Because the senders are not synchronized, it could be possible to keep the bottleneck link utilized most of the time. The selection of discarded packets can be totally random, or some more complicated procedure can be applied. These mechanisms are discussed thoroughly in section 5.3, "Traffic Handling Functions in Interior Nodes," in Chapter 5, "Differentiation of Customer Service."

Although it seems possible to develop TCP protocol and buffering algorithms in a way that maximizes the network utilization, there remain some serious difficulties with fairness. If and when well-behaved TCP connections must live with other connections with different behavior, the final result could be that TCP connections are continuously in the slow-start phase, and aggressive connections without any adjusting mechanism seize most of the capacity.

Is there any means to alleviate this situation? Yes, if you are ready to distinguish individual flows somehow inside the network. During a congestion situation, you should discard packets from those connections that have exploited most of the resources and leave other connections alone. There is not any obvious way to select the discarded packets, however, particularly if you want to share the network resources based on individual traffic contracts rather than on even shares. Actually, this is one of the fundamental questions of the Differentiated Services approach.

2.3.4   Evaluation of the Best-Effort Approach

The best-effort approach has been a successful service model for the flourishing Internet. Why should we change one of the cornerstones of such a successful technology? One plausible opinion is that we actually should not do that, but we only have to increase the network capacity as quickly as possible without changing the best-effort service model. The reasoning behind any new, likely more complicated model has to be strong and clear; a mere vague idea that best effort is not satisfactory for the future is not enough.

Chapter 1, "The Target of Differentiated Services," introduced "attributes" exactly for this purpose—that is, to facilitate the analyzing of different approaches. The attributes—cost efficiency, versatility, robustness, and fairness—are used in the next four sections to look at the best-effort approach from different viewpoints. Cost efficiency gives emphasis to the economical aspects; versatility stresses the various needs of future applications; robustness and fairness shed light on the issues related to the intrinsic weakness of a service model based on the TCP protocol.

Cost Efficiency

One potential efficiency problem of the best-effort service model using TCP as a control method is that at the bottleneck node, some packets are always lost because the algorithm detects overload situations using discarded packets. You would argue that a lost packet always means wasted resources. In a sense, you are right: Some resources are used to transmit the packet to the bottleneck node. Despite this fact, it is fair to infer that in a simple situation with only one bottleneck, no significant resources are wasted.

In any modern telecommunication system, the actual costs are practically independent of the traffic load if the infrastructure and amount of customers are fixed (personnel, electricity, and so on) and costs are constant. What is the real nature of costs in telecommunication networks then? Definitely they depend somehow on the traffic, and lost packets are considered part of the traffic load. Traffic load can be related to costs is two ways.

First, the network dimensioning is based on the offered traffic load, and perhaps on the packet-loss ratio as well. If the load exceeds a certain limit, you update the network by acquiring more capacity—and that definitely entails costs. Because you are aware of the nature of the TCP mechanism, however, you should not be too hurried to buy new capacity if a moderate amount of packets are lost. A "normal" packet-loss ratio is acceptable and does not imply a need to expand the network. Only if the packet-loss ratio exceeds a certain higher threshold is it an indication of insufficient capacity. Therefore, there is not necessarily any direct relation between wasted packets and costs.

Second, a potentially more important issue is that a packet lost in the bottleneck node has used link and buffer capacity somewhere else in the network and, therefore, may give rise to an unnecessary packet discarding in those points. But that happens only if there is another bottleneck in the route of the packet, and at the same time there is a suitable packet to be transmitted through the network. Although this kind of situation may induce additional costs, it seems that under normal traffic conditions the total effect is negligible. This issue is discussed further in Chapter 7, "Per-Hop Behavior Groups," and Chapter 8, "Interworking Issues," because it is common to most of the Differentiated Services schemes.

It is fair to conclude that best-effort service based on TCP control makes possible highly efficient networks. In addition, the network costs seems to be low because no signaling is required, and a relatively simple buffering system gives satisfactory results; even a pure FIFO is workable. But this assessment is valid only with adaptive applications that can utilize the intrinsic characteristics of the service.

A lot of applications cannot do that, however; if you want to satisfy the needs of those applications, you must keep the overall load level in the network so low that packet losses are rare and delay variations small. In that case, best-effort service is not technically efficient because of low utilization; it can be more cost efficient than a complicated system, however, because of low implementation and management costs.

Versatility

The lack of versatility is one of the key questions related to best-effort service—and one of the fundamental questions of the whole effort of Differentiated Services. Versatility can be divided into several aspects: bit rates, delays, packet-loss ratios, and network environment.

As to the bit rate, best effort can be applied with any bit rate, low or high, constant or variable; there are no definite limits for granularity. The problems are related to the other aspects. It could be possible to devise a real-time best-effort service applying a similar mechanism to TCP. Unfortunately, some fundamental problems arise with this approach. A workable best-effort implementation requires that buffers be big enough to handle the bursty TCP connections; with very small buffers, the system does not work efficiently. However, if a large buffer is really used, it also means long delay unless the bit rate is very high.

Therefore, the basic best-effort service cannot properly support truly real-time connections except if the load level is so low that buffers are continuously almost empty. In practice, real-time service requires additional tools to be feasible, such as its own buffers and proper buffer management inside the nodes. Because TCP counts on packet losses to adjust bit rate, it cannot offer loss-free service or different levels of loss ratios. This kind of service is beyond the scope of the basic best-effort model, but surely belongs to the field of Differentiated Services.

It is also reasonable to ask whether TCP is suitable in all network environments. In most cases, it is; this fact is comprehensible if you remember the basic target of TCP including potentially unreliable networks. Nonetheless, one area of networks causes problems to TCP connections: wireless networks. In most current transmission systems, the bit error rate is very small. Therefore, the main reason for lost packets is congestion, just as the TCP mechanism assumes. On the contrary, in wireless networks bit error rate could be occasionally high and cause packet losses because every packet with bit errors is discarded. Consequently, TCP supposes there is severe congestion and moves into slow-start phase. Chapter 8, "Interworking Issues," addresses this issue.

Robustness

One severe problem of TCP-based traffic management is that the TCP protocol is usually running in customer equipment and, therefore, not within the direct control of the network operator or service provider. As a result, the boundaries between network service and applications are considerably blurred, which makes it difficult to provide a consistent network service.

The current situation is that a main part of the traffic on the Internet utilizes only a couple of different TCP implementations, and that a large majority of users are using them without any modifications. Unfortunately, this situation leaves the field open for rogue users who try to maximize the bandwidth they attain from the network—and in a worst-case scenario, intentionally interfere with the normal network operation. Therefore, although best-effort service works well in many conditions, the whole service structure is susceptible to rogue users and new applications with different requirements.

Fairness

When you want to offer higher-quality connections for some customers, you need tools to at least limit the effect of different TCP implementations on the best-effort service class, and if possible, to also limit the effect of mischievous users within that class.

Internet users can be divided into two primary groups to assess fairness: ordinary users with no or minor knowledge about Internet technology, and skillful users with considerable ability to tune their computer systems. The latter can still be divided into two subgroups: friendly and harmful. Friendly users, even though they possess harmful potential, are chiefly interested in just getting somewhat more capacity than ordinary users from time to time, but without a desire to damage the network. Harmful users, who are unfortunately not unknown on the Internet, may instead try to abuse networks resources (sometimes even regardless of how much real benefit they actually get themselves).

As for the best-effort service, the group of unskillful users is usually not problematic; and similarly, most users belonging to the friendly expert group are not a threat as such. If every user is behaving appropriately, the best-effort service is a feasible approach within its intrinsic limits. The main threat seems to be that a programmer devises an innovative product that does not need much expertise to use but that significantly improves the bandwidth the user is getting compared to other users. This kind of product could become so popular that most experts, friendly or not, will exploit it.

In the worst case, this may decline the service of ordinary users and, therefore, impede overall customer service. Unfortunately, this seems to be possible because of weak or nonexistent control mechanisms at the user-network interface. If this happens on a large scale, it does not only deteriorate overall fairness but also deteriorates the service of all users. One of the areas in which this may happen is multicasting applications sending real-time audioand video streams.

2.4 Integrated Services Model

The history of *Integrated Services* can be traced to the Birds of Feather (BOF) session, "The Real-Time Packet Forwarding and Admission Control BOF," in November 1993. The first sentences of the BOF minutes stated: "The demand for multimedia communication and the success of IETF audio/videocasts will soon create an urgent requirement for resource reservation and control in the Internet. From an architectural viewpoint, this represents a new Internet service model." (For more information, visit the Integrated Services mailing list archive at `ftp://ftp.isi.edu/int-serv/int-serv.mail`.)

This statement defines the main area of concern: real-time audio and video multicasting services. It was recognized that these services could not be properly supported by the basic best-effort mechanisms. From the very start, some fundamental questions were discussed:

- Why do we need a new service model?

- What should the fundamental nature of the service model be, explicit or implicit?

- Is admission control necessary?

As to the last issue, the primary philosophy of the Working Group was that occasional blocking of a connection request is a more economical approach than vast over-provisioning. That is the whole point to resource reservations and the guaranteed service model adopted by the Integrated Services Working Group.

It was observed that behavioral characterization of functionality is a very difficult intellectual problem, and that it was important that the community not get bogged down in this exercise. It seems, unfortunately, that this very intellectual problem is still unresolved. In the Differentiated Services effort, the behavioral characterization of functionality is one of the fundamental issues, and yet real experience is required in the same way it was required during the first phase of Integrated Services five years ago.

The Integrated Services Working Group focused on defining a minimal set of global requirements that would transform the Internet into a robust, integrated-service communication infrastructure, including the following issues:

- Defining the services to be provided

- Defining the interfaces between application and network service, routers, and subnetworks

- Developing router validation requirements

In January 1994, Bob Braden expressed a concern about poor activity in the Integrated Services mailing list; this was a somewhat premature concern, because four years later the mailing list archive consisted of more than one million words. In addition, a part of the effort, namely the Resource Reservation Protocol (RSVP), has been discussed on a separate mailing list. The following sections outline the results of these activities.

2.4.1 *Customer Service*

One interesting theme of discussion when the Working Group started was the importance of convincing the public at large that IP is suitable for Integrated Services. Although making major technological developments is difficult, it can be much more difficult to change public opinion. When the public has experienced a moderate level of Internet service with regard to quality and reliability for several years, you may encounter severe difficulties when attempting to ensure people that some Internet services can be both reliable and of a good quality.

If you want to offer high-quality telephony service over the Internet, for example, you will certainly meet a lot of doubts about the reliability of the service. Your customer is not likely to assess technical details; instead, he or she will compare the current telephony service with the current Internet service in general—and, right now, customers perceive a big difference. Although you may deem this unjust from an operator's viewpoint, you must face reality (and reality does not consist of technical facts only, but also of opinions).

So what is the right reference point for high-quality Internet service? The service that all Internet users are familiar with is ordinary telephony service. The current situation, in most developed countries, is that you practically always get a telephone connection with the same quality. The quality, albeit definitely sufficient for most purposes, is not actually very high; this is evident if you listen to classical music on the telephone. The strongest feature of digital telephone service is predictability: You can obtain the same service independent of time, date, location, or distance.

Note
The characteristics of mobile services are somewhat different, with some reliability and quality problems. The success of mobile services strongly indicates that users can cope with a lower level of quality, provided that the service can offer something unique. In this case, the uniqueness is mobility. Therefore, each ISP must find and define the uniqueness of its service offering.

Customer service—composed of both high- and moderate-quality parts—must, consequently, be credible in its good characteristics. One possibility is to build the highest-quality service on a mathematically provable basis. If you select this option, you clearly are aiming to compete with the current services with their own field. It will be very hard to surpass the delay or loss characteristics of circuit-switching networks or CBR service in ATM networks even with mathematical proofs.

Do the basic attributes—fairness, robustness, versatility, and cost efficiency—offer any clue about what could be the competitive strength of Integrated Services as a *customer service*?

Perhaps *fairness* could be the issue. Telephone operators now have several years of experience with customer expectations and competitive markets. So, there is probably not much opportunity to gain a marketing edge in this area. Because the Integrated Services must rely on the same infrastructure as the current Internet, it is not likely that *robustness* can be the main marketing point of integrated services on the Internet.

As to *versatility*, it may indeed offer real possibilities. Although the telephone network is very reliable, it is also inflexibly in the sense that totally new service features, if feasible at all, require complicated and cumbersome standardization processes. The problem of the ATM network is the lack of much real end-to-end ATM services. What is the meaning of versatility if it does not reflect on customer services? On the contrary, the Internet and the applications used through it are famous for rapid and innovative development.

The other potential advantage of the integrated-service model is *cost efficiency*. This advantage, however, remains unclear (because of the difficulties of identifying and assessing all the associated costs) until there are widespread implementations. The technical foundation of Integrated Services is likely to be at least as cost efficient as any other corresponding technology; whether it can offer cost savings related to the major cost sources, such as network operation, management, customer care and billing, is not so sure.

2.4.2   Implementation of Integrated Services

RFC 2215 defines the set of general control and characterization parameters used in the Integrated Services framework. Each parameter has a common definition across all QoS control services. For instance, NON_IS_HOP provides information about the presence of network nodes that do not support QoS control, and AVAILABLE_PATH_BANDWIDTH provides information about the available bandwidth along the path.

From the traffic management viewpoint, the key parameter is TOKEN_BUCKET_TSPEC (or the shorter TSpec) that describes traffic parameters using a token-bucket mechanism. (For more details, see the section titled "Measuring Principles" in Chapter 5, "Differentiation of Customer Service.") Data senders use this parameter to describe the traffic they expect to generate; the purpose is exactly the same as that of traffic parameters in ATM networks. TSpec uses the parameters shown in Table 2.2.

Table 2.2   Tspec Parameters

Parameter	Description
b	Token bucket with a bucket depth
r	Bucket rate
p	Peak rate
m	Minimum policed unit
M	Maximum datagram size

There are two IP-specific parameters: resource allocation and policing. All IP datagrams less than size m are treated as being of size m, and maximum packet size defines the biggest packet that can conform to the traffic specification.

Guaranteed Service

One of the first Internet drafts already stated that a guaranteed service shall provide firm, mathematically provable guarantees that the end-to-end delay experienced by packets in a flow will not exceed a set limit. This basic philosophy has been realized by RFC 2212, "Specification of Guaranteed Quality of Service."

A *guaranteed* QoS flow is specified by two sets of parameters: traffic parameters (TSpec) and service-level parameters (RSpec). The reservation specification, RSpec, consists of a data rate (R) and a slack term (S). In addition, two error terms, C and D, which describe the accuracy of the implementation compared to a perfect one, characterize the implementation of guaranteed service. Users can compute the maximum delay for a packet transmitted through the path by combining the parameters from the various service elements in a path. This discussion does not, however, go into the details of this calculation because it is quite complicated.

As a result, if the QoS control defined in RFC 2212 is deployed widely enough in the network, guaranteed service gives applications considerable control over their delay. Delay has two parts: a fixed delay and a queuing delay. The *fixed delay* is a property of the chosen path, which is determined not by guaranteed service but by the setup mechanism. Only *queuing delay* is determined by guaranteed service. In other words, an application can usually accurately estimate, *a priori*, what queuing delay guaranteed service will likely promise. If the delay is larger than expected, the application can modify traffics token bucket and data rate to achieve a lower delay.

Controlled-Load Service

The key pronouncement of the controlled-load service specification, as stated in RFC 2211, is the following: "Controlled-load service provides the client data flow with a quality of service closely approximating the QoS that same flow would receive from an unloaded network element, but uses capacity (admission) control to assure that this service is received even when the network element is overloaded."

What does this actually mean, and what is the motivation for this somewhat peculiar definition of a service? As already discussed, best-effort service may offer high quality provided that the network is slightly loaded. It is impossible to give any exact generally applicable numbers, but probably a 5% load is low enough even if the traffic variations are high. (A higher load is acceptable if variations are moderate.) Therefore, if you can give a higher priority for certain flows and limit the traffic and traffic variations of those flows, you might be able to offer a high, albeit not perfect, service with a relatively simple mechanism. Basically three components are needed:

- A prioritization mechanism to separate controlled-load flows from pure best-effort flows

- A mechanism to allocate appropriate resources inside the network to the flows (see `http://www.eecs.umich.edu/~wuchang/ered`)

- Traffic control to limit traffic and traffic variations

Users requesting controlled-load service give an estimation of the data traffic they will generate: the `TSpec`. The service provider ensures that a very high percentage of transmitted packets are delivered successfully and that the delay does not greatly exceed the minimum delay experienced. The controlled-load service does not make use of specific target values for control parameters—such as delay or loss—so the service philosophy is better than best effort, but without any hard guarantees.

If the traffic of a flow exceeds the limits specified by `TSpec`, the flow obtains a similar service, but not necessarily exactly the same, as best-effort flows with the possibility of long delays and dropped packets. So the transition from *best-effort* to *controlled-load service* is a relatively easy operation for users. Moreover, because the specification is quite spacious, the network implementation may either rely on low utilization, traffic measurements to predict traffic behavior or on strict traffic control and accurate calculations.

Resource Reservation Protocol (RSVP)

The Integrated Services architecture enables users to request a higher quality than that of the best-effort service. In addition to the service specifications including the requirements for network element behavior, there has to be a mechanism to communicate the requirements to the network nodes along the transmission path. The Resource Reservation Protocol (RSVP) is designed for that purpose.

Basically, RSVP is doing the same task that is accomplished in connection-oriented networks by signaling. Several significant differences stem from the different starting points (the Internet is connectionless while traditional signaling is used in connection-oriented networks) and the different primary uses of the reservations (multicast applications, in the case of RSVP, but most connections in traditional networks are point-to-point). When compared to signaling in connection-oriented networks, such as ATM, the most prominent characteristics of RSVP are as follows:

- In RSVP, the receiver rather than the sender generates reservations.

- RSVP requires that the reservation be refreshed about once every 30 seconds; a permanent reservation, on the other hand, is explicitly finished.

- An RSVP receiver may modify the requested QoS at any time; usually the QoS is permanent for the life of the connection.

- In RSVP, the establishment of the route is an independent process; traditionally, however, the reservation and routing are concurrent.

- RSVP allows heterogeneity in trafficparameters, a characteristic not usually provided in any traditional networks.

Although all these characteristics could be reasonable and useful, they may complicate the cooperation with other networking technologies, such as ATM. For more information about RSVP, see the corresponding RFCs: 2205, 2210, and 2380.

2.4.3   *Evaluation of the Integrated Services Model*

Although the overall characteristics of Integrated Services are similar to those of corresponding ATM services, it is important to briefly assess the main attributes of the Integrated Services model.

Versatility

There seem to be no major problems, although there is a kind of gap between guaranteed services and best-effort services. In general, a technical standardization body like IETF is not necessarily the best organization to define services because its viewpoint could be too limited. Service providers and customers should have a more integral role in the service specification. Nevertheless, the Internet is such aversatile and flexible technology and environment that the possible gaps can likely be filled (one of the tasks left to Differentiated Services).

Fairness

One of the main problems with the Integrated Services model is that it seems to be difficult to build a reasonable—that is understandable and consistent—customer service. This is a complicated task with both technological and marketing challenges. The additional concern with the Internet is that a large part of the public does not deem the Internet reliable and, as a result, may have serious doubts about high-quality service offered as part of service selection.

Robustness

Because of the inherent mathematical basis, if the service is properly implemented and managed, significant problems are not probable. If the operators and service providers do not possess enough experience in this field, however, they may have big problems with reliability, quality of service, and network performance.

Cost Efficiency

Cost efficiency seems to be the main concern of the integrated-service model. The original intent was to solve primarily a rather limited problem of audio and video multicasting services. As time went on and the Internet changed, however, the objective apparently became more extensive. It is not, however, reasonable to assume that the relatively complex and heavy Integrated Services system with all the parameters and per-flow reservations can be used with most of the millions of flows traversing the Internet continuously. In short, the Integrated Services model has scalability problems.

2.5   Targets for Differentiated Services

The assessment of the other technologies—ATM, best effort, and integrated service—offers a good basis for considering the targets of Differentiated Services. It is important that Differentiated Services can provide a consistent and efficient model on different levels of realization: customer service, network services, operation and management, and traffic handling. Before entering into these special areas, however, it is important to define the general meaning of Differentiated Services:

> Differentiated Services refer to a simple service structure that provides quality differentiation mainly by the means of packet marking.

This definition consists of three parts:

- Differentiated Services is a target model rather than a specification that contains detailed information about the required implementation. (This target is evaluated in the following sections.)

- From the service perspective, Differentiated Services provides a moderate level of quality differentiation without strict guarantees.

- The distinctive technical characteristic is that the quality of service is not attained by reserving capacity for each individual flow or connection, but by marking packets at the network boundaries.

2.5.1   Customer Service

The primary goal of customer service is for most (preferably all) customers to consider it fair. Traditionally, this issue was left out of the standardization of networking technologies.

It is too easy to just remark that service providers are allowed to adopt any existing or new pricing scheme or customer-care system. Unfortunately, the freedom is often superficial, because the underlying service model dictates to a large extent the structure of customer service.

The guaranteed service model, for instance, requires that you understand the essence of the service in a way that you can select the proper service level, request it, and assess whether the service you obtained satisfies the service contract. In addition, if the provision of guaranteed service is based on per-connection pricing, you have to be able to understand the bill. If you want to avoid all these tight requirements, you had better not to apply guaranteed service as your main service paradigm.

It could be better to take a different approach. Users naturally have expectations about the service. You should not to create too high expectations; those might be too expensive and difficult to realize. Instead, you should control customer expectations in a "soft" manner and keep customers so satisfied that they are willing to pay more than the basic flat rate. This requires a predictable pricing and understandable service structure.

2.5.2 Network Services

The fundamental attribute of network service is that it must be robust. This means that the service provider or network operator must control the function of the actual service. This is the main problem with the current best-effort service based on TCP: even though it works surprisingly well most of the time, it is vulnerable to attacks by malicious users.

ATM and IETF's Integrated Services model provides examples of inherently robust service models. The robustness is achieved through the use of advanced control mechanisms, including a lot of traffic parameters, resource allocation and reservation tools, and tight control over the traffic sent by the user. The drawback to this kind of system is that it is prone to errors because of the overall complexity and large number of parameters needed to manage it.

Differentiated Services should be able to combine inherent robustness achieved by traffic control and simple service structure without excessive parameters. Although this apparently is a big challenge, it is target that must remembered all the time when designing the Differentiated Services architecture.

2.5.3 Operation and Management

Operation and management of a network can be costly. Therefore, cost efficiency is a major concern. The rapid progress of information technology makes it possible to develop complicated systems that can work under very hard, real-time requirements. The productivity of human labor, on the other hand, has improved only slowly. Therefore, one of the main targets should be to minimize the human actions needed to manage Internet traffic.

One apparently labor-intensive task is to solve fault situations. As the possible reasons for one fault type increase, the difficulty of fixing the fault also increases. If one connection encounters excessive packet-loss ratio, for instance, there are numerous explanations:

- One of the traffic parameters of that connection is incorrectly set.

- One of the quality parameters of that connection is incorrectly set.

- The service class is inappropriate.

- The application sends more packets than the user supposes.

- The operator has not reserved enough capacity for an aggregate stream.

- The operator has installed some of the service classes incorrectly; then, there are several operators, and so on.

The possibilities are almost limitless.

The overall structure of Differentiated Services should be so clear that the management burden remains limited. Therefore, a consistent, robust set of automatic functions is highly recommendable.

2.5.4 Traffic Handling

The previous aspects emphasize the need for simplicity. If you have no tools to build the service differentiation, however, you end up either with the current best-effort model or with a simple connection-oriented model. What is needed, therefore, is one consistent set of traffic-handling mechanisms that allows different treatment of packets.

This versatile set of mechanisms has to be sufficient to support a variety of network services. Consistency makes it possible to build an effective system with inexpensive network management and customer care. Finally, overall efficiency means that you can provide services that are not too expensive, but that still give reasonable profit for service providers and network operators.

Summary

As a summary of this relatively long assessment of other networking technologies, consider the following list of questions for Differentiated Services:

1. How can you sell a service package to ordinary customers without any technical background?

2. What kind of billing system do you need to support your service model and to make it fair?

3. Do you understand all interactions between the building blocks of services, and do they allow efficient troubleshooting?

4. How efficient is the model when used in a large network with millions of users?

5. Is the service model robust enough to limit the effects of intentional misuse of network resources?

6. Does the service model provide a realistic evolution path from the current best-effort network?

If a service model can acceptably answer all these questions, it has a good chance of being successful.

CHAPTER 3

Differentiated Services Working Group

This chapter provides an overview of the evolution of Differentiated Services. A short history is provided to illustrate the main ideas that formed the basis for the Differentiated Services Working Group.

Most of this chapter discusses the principle achievements of the first year of the working group. The first two documents reached the RFC status in December 1998: RFC 2474, "Definition of the Differentiated Services Field (DS Field) in the IPv4 and IPv6 Headers," and RFC 2475, "An Architecture for Differentiated Services." Those documents describe the theoretical foundation of a Differentiated Services network. The third document reviewed in this chapter is "A Framework for Differentiated Services" (Bernet *et al.* 1998), which supplements the view of the two RFCs by giving more practical guidance for the application Differentiated Services.

3.1 A Short History of Differentiated Services

This brief historical overview is based primarily on the mailing list discussion of the Integrated Services working group. The mailing list archive offers useful documentation of the Differentiated Services effort before the establishment of the Differentiated Service Working Group and the corresponding mailing list in February 1998. (These mailing lists are available at http://www.ietf.org/html.charters/diffserv-charter.html and http://www-nrg.ee.lbl.gov/diff-serv-arch/, respectively.) It can even be safely claimed that that the Differentiated Services activity is a direct extension of the effort made by the Integrated Services and RSVP Working Groups, because the goal of all these efforts is basically the same: the provision of service differentiation in IP networks.

It should be stressed, however, that this introduction provides only one view of the complex development process of Differentiated Services. The End-to-End research group discussed some of the same issues several years before the establishment of Differentiated

Services, for instance (The Internet Research Task Force). This overview tries to disclose the chief motivation behind the effort to develop Differentiated Services by picking some occurrences during the evolutionary process that finally led to the establishment of the Differentiated Services Working Group.

The first mention of differentiation took place in a mailing in November 1995; Mark Garrett mentioned a claim that ATM was the first network technology to have meaningfully differentiated QoS (in contrast to X.25 and ISDN). Note that although the verity of this statement is arguable, the main point here is that until then there was no mention at all of differentiation on the mailing list. The prevalent view seemed to be that real QoS required hard guarantees, and without them there was no QoS at all. (Not everyone held this view, however.)

After that, the general discussion about service differentiation seems to have been buried in the standardization effort of Integrated Services and RSVP. The concerns about the scalability of RSVP gradually increased, however. Consequently, preliminary arguments that something simpler was needed to obtain better scalability began to be bantered about.

The first culmination point was the "Future Directions for Differential Services" BOF session arranged at the IETF meeting in April 1997. The final remarks concluded that the taxonomy of Differentiated Services could include three options (Mankin 1998):

- Service with extremely high predictability

- Two services, one cheap and one expensive; interoperability issues integral

- A lot of finely differentiated services (although apparently this was not a popular idea at the meeting)

A couple of weeks after the meeting, the real discussion started about the basis for a new Differentiated Services model. Figure 3.1 depicts the nature of the discussion. The figure shows the days in which there were messages in the Integrated Services mailing list related to two topics: the need of drop precedence levels (the terms *drop preference* and *drop priority* have also been used) and delay classes (or *delay categories*).

The main reason for presenting Figure 3.1 is to illustrate the emergence of these fundamental issues. Better delay characteristics are required in the future Internet because of real-time applications, and Differentiated Services must provide those characteristics. The concept of drop precedence seems to be more controversial. Drop precedence basically provides a tool with which you can inform the network about the relative importance of packets. It is still somewhat unclear, however, how drop precedence bits should be actually applied. Differentiated Services attempts to give one answer to this issue.

Figure 3.1 Discussion activity on the Integrated Services mailing list.

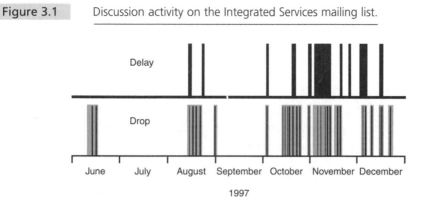

The following three general observations can be made:

- This *traffic* process is very similar to that of any Internet traffic process, with intermittent bursts of activity and relatively long idle periods.

- Traffic streams can be highly correlated. In the case of Figure 3.1, a possible reason for correlation is that both threads of discussion have basically the same objective to specify the fundamental architecture of Differentiated Services. Some of the aspects of both issues could be discussed separately, but several aspects of the issues do indeed overlap.

- The third observation relates to the general behavior of mailing list discussions. The same threads of discussions emerge repeatedly at arbitrary points of time, which makes following the discussion somewhat difficult.

Moreover, by calculating the number of mailings within one day and the length of the mailings, a *self-similar* process results. This correlation between discussions and Internet traffic is not so far-fetched as it might seem at first sight: Internet traffic reflects complex human processes, largely in the same way as does a discussion in a mailing list. The lesson of this brief exercise is that controlling Internet traffic could be as difficult as controlling the discussion in the mailing lists.

The seven months from June to December were crucial for the emergence of Differentiated Services. In August, IETF had a meeting in which the subject of service differentiation was discussed in the Integrated Services Working Group session (Wroclawski 1997). Several presentations related to different service models were made. The presentations and ensuing discussion revealed the basic arguments as well as the basic factions. The following principle factions were obvious:

- The scalability of RSVP is the problem to be solved.

- Highly reliable IP service is the key target.

- The main tool is several drop priority levels.

- Low-dclay service is also important.

- The core network mechanism should allow the implementation of any imaginable service.

This list may appear somewhat disordered: The list includes some target services, tools to meet the targets, and more general objectives. This list illustrates the reality of the mailing list—with diverse objectives and viewpoints. A systematic and coherent list would be "spin" because the reality has been unsystematic.

A lively discussion emerged after the IETF meeting in August, as shown in Figure 3.1. The most controversial issue among the many topics was whether Differentiated Services should be based on drop preferences. This particular controversy crystallized into two opinions expressed in the mailing list [Int-Serv]:

> ...I really like the idea of using the IP precedence bit field, allowing eight (0–7) levels of distinction, so that something similar to WRED can provide for differentiated drop in the core.

> —Paul Ferguson, 17 August 1997

> Support for drop preference creates an undesirable incentive for applications to send packets that will not reach their destinations (knowing that the routers will discard the "less important" or "out of profile" packets at a point of congestion).

> —Steve Deering, 15 October 1997

This division was detectable also in the five Internet drafts that were submitted in November 1997.

Despite the diversity of the proposals, the activity clearly indicated that there was significant support for Differentiated Services in the Internet community, although the service structure was still an open issue. (Another important thing to note is that every IETF session related to Differentiated Services has been very crowded.) After the public discussions at the IETF meeting in December (Wroclawski 1997), a smaller group took over the reins of the Differentiated Services effort, mainly to attain a compromise that would satisfy the various needs of the different parties. The IESG approved the working group on 26 February 1998.

3.2 The Position of the Differentiated Services Working Group

The goal of Differentiated Services is clearly explained in the description of the working group that was published on March 1, 1998 (available at `http://www.ietf.org/html.charters/diffserv-charter.html`). It emphasizes the need for simple, but versatile methods of providing service differentiation. The essence of the approach is that *a small set of building blocks is defined and services are built from those blocks.* Two building blocks are explicitly mentioned: DS byte and Per-Hop Behavior (PHB). Further, interoperability is required to enable the provision of reasonable end-to-end services.

The original description identifies the need for two documents: a standard track document and an informational document. The standard track document defines the general use of the DS byte. In addition, it standardizes a number of *codepoints* that are applied to Per-Hop Behaviors that are commonly used in the current Internet. (See the section "Terminology" later in this chapter for definitions of key terms.) The objective of the informational framework document is to define architecture and common language for Differentiated Services.

An additional goal of the working group was to experiment with different Per-Hop Behaviors. After successful experiments, these Per-Hop Behaviors could be specified in experimental RFCs, or they could become standardized. Although the main building blocks were clearly DS byte and PHBs, one goal of the working group was to investigate other components required to build services, such as traffic shapers and packet markers. Moreover, as a general requirement for any IETF standard, security issues had to be analyzed. Finally, the working description declared two issues to be beyond of scope of the working group: mechanisms for the identification of individual traffic flows within the network, and signaling mechanisms to support the marking of packets.

The description defined a tight timetable for the working group. It gave 10 months to prepare documents for the basic DS standard, framework, boundary mechanisms, and traffic conditioners. Although the working group was not able to totally comply with the timetable, it made good progress in 1998.

3.3 Basic Working Group Documents

The Differentiated Services Working Group prepared three main documents during 1998: RFC 2474, "Definition of the Differentiated Services Field (DS Field) in the IPv4 and IPv6 Headers," RFC 2475, "An Architecture for Differentiated Services," and an Internet draft, "A Framework for Differentiated Services" (Bernet *et al.* 1998). There is a clear difference between the status of the first two and the last of these documents.

Internet Drafts Versus Request for Comments

Internet drafts are working documents, and therefore do not have any official status at all—in fact, they can be removed or replaced at any time by a more recent version of the same document. Consequently, a mere Internet draft is not a published document, which makes it questionable to use them as references.

Unfortunately, some significant documents are not available in any other form than Internet drafts, and therefore are used in this book as a reference—or rather as a pointer to a text (but this is avoided when possible).

Request for Comments (RFCs) are much more stable. There are two special subseries within the RFCs (Bradner 1996):

- *Standard track*: These RFCs may reach an Internet standard status after there is enough evidence that the standard is appropriate for practical use.

- *Nonstandard track*: These RFCs are either experimental or informational. They are supposed to provide useful information about the application of an Internet standard, but do not contain any strict requirements for implementation.

The DS Field document (RFC 2474) is a standard track document; as a result, it is the most important document made by the Differentiated Services working group (Baker *et al.* 1998). However, it provides only limited guidance as to how to apply the building blocks defined in the document. Therefore, the architecture document, RFC 2475, is also essential even though it is not a standard track RFC. It is fair to say that RFC 2475 reflects the opinion of a large group within the Differentiated Services Working Group. The viewpoints of this book and the architecture document are mostly congruent, although there are a couple of differences. (See the section "Provisioning and Configuration" later in this chapter for some of the differences in viewpoint.)

The framework document did not reach a RFC status by the end of 1998 (Bernet *et al.* 1998). A revised version will be submitted to the RFC editor as a Proposed Standard for the Internet Community probably in 1999. Nevertheless, the document was prepared by some of the key authors in this field, and it is also a kind of working group draft, which means that it has a certain level of acceptance among the working group. This book and the framework document disagree on a couple of fundamental issues. Those differences are explained in Chapter 4, "General Framework for Differentiated Services."

3.3.1 *Introduction to Differentiated Services Model*

The abstract of the RFC 2474 clearly states one of the most important characteristics of the Differentiated Services model: There is a definite distinction between boundary functions and interior functions, or boundary nodes and interior nodes. Boundary nodes are responsible of the setting of DS bits in the packet, and of the conditioning of packets; interior nodes, on the other hand, forward packets in different ways based on the value of the DS field.

Service providers can build different network services from the main building blocks: setting of bits, conditioning of packets, and forwarding of packets. Without any common rules, however, there is no consistent service. The rules define how bits are set and how packets are conditioned at the boundaries and forwarded inside the network. The actual substance of the service is the system, consisting of the rules and of the proper design of the building blocks. Moreover, the importance of operation, management, and planning of the system cannot be overemphasized. Figure 3.2 shows these elements of service provision.

Figure 3.2   Construction of Differentiated Services.

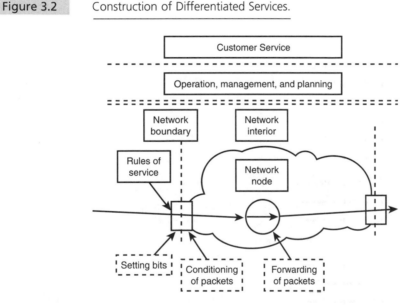

Because the service construction as such is beyond the scope of IETF, IETF documents do not usually give detailed examples of how to apply the specification for business purposes. This book attempts to satisfy the evident need for examples.

The following example, "Real-Time Service Versus Best-Effort Service," illustrates a realistic scenario in which the fictional ISP Fairprofit can improve the network service with a quite simple system that is in accordance with RFC 2474. It should be stressed, however, that the example is only for illustration purposes, and any of the details mentioned here can be realized in different ways. (Note that Fairprofit was used in the section titled "Fairness and Service Provision" in Chapter 1, "The Target of Differentiated Services," to assess the fairness issues related to overloads.)

Real-Time Service Versus Best-Effort Service

The service provider Fairprofit wants to offer two types of service: real-time service for interactive applications and best-effort service for data applications. First of all, Fairprofit must define the basic rules to be applied:

- Customers are allowed to send IP packets into the network, basically with any bit rate, limited only by the physical access rate.

- At the network boundary, packets are marked as real-time packets based on the information in the IP header; that is, the marking divides the traffic into real-time and data substreams.

- If the data traffic sent by the customer exceeds a certain limit, packets are marked as lower importance, but are sent into the network.

- Every user is allowed to send real-time traffic at a certain bit rate, and all excessive packets are discarded at the network boundary.

The system for setting bits requires that the boundary node make a proper decision about what packets should be marked as real-time packets. Traffic conditioning means that the boundary node measures the bit rate of both real-time and data traffic streams, and then according to the result can either re-mark a data packet with lower importance or discard a real-time packet.

The forwarding system inside the network then treats the packet according to the marking. There are three groups of packets: real-time, data with normal importance, and data with low importance. Real-time packets have their own queue that is served before the queue for data packets, to achieve delay differentiation. During overload situations—that is, when the occupancy level of the data queue (or real-time queue) is very high—data packets with low importance are discarded.

The main task of the operation and management system is to keep the real-time traffic low enough to guarantee that real-time queue is not filled, and that there is enough bandwidth for data traffic. In addition, the traffic level of data packets with normal importance should be low enough to keep the packet-loss ratio for those packets very low.

Finally, even though this service model does not necessarily require any changes made by the customers, the Fairprofit Corporation has to be able to explain why the service model is better than the current best-effort model, and how the customer can use the new service offering in the best manner. Their brochure could include such statements as better suitability for interactive applications and relatively high assurance that certain minimum bandwidth is always available for data services. The professionals of Fairprofit can then expect that customers will be ready to pay for these service characteristics.

3.3.2 *The Differentiated Services Field in IPv4 and IPv6 Headers*

The title of RFC 2474, "Definition of the Differentiated Services Field (DS Field) in the IPv4 and IPv6 Headers," indicates that the main issue of the document is to specify the contents and meaning of the DS field. In addition, it provides useful information about the terminology and basic structure of Differentiated Services.

Terminology

RFC 2474 defines the basic terminology of Differentiated Services. Although it is impractical to explain all the terms in different words, some additional explanations of the key terms can be useful:

- Per-Hop Behavior

- Customer service

- Network service

- PHB class

- Codepoint

- Mechanism

The term *Per-Hop Behavior (PHB)* is both difficult to comprehend and important for understanding the whole idea of Differentiated Services. Technically speaking, PHB denotes a combination of forwarding, classification, scheduling, and drop behaviors at each hop. However, PHB is not only a technical concept; instead, the main purpose of PHB is to make a comprehensible connection between packet-level implementations and service models. PHB is, in a way, an intermediary term.

Based on the wording of RFC 2474, it is possible to derive the following guidelines for designing a Per-Hop Behavior. (Note that this is only an interpretation of the formal standard from the viewpoint of this book.)

- PHB is primarily a description of desired behavior on a relatively high abstraction level; in particular, a PHB must have a comprehensible motivation.

- PHB should allow the construction of predictable services.

- The desired behavior should be externally observable—for instance, the description of behavior should not use any internal terms, such as queue.

- The desired behavior should be local—that is, it should concern behavior within one node rather than the whole network.

- The description of behavior is related to an aggregate that consists of all packets belonging to the same PHB in a certain point of the network.

- The packets belonging to a PHB should experience the same treatment independent of other information in the packet and independent of the traffic process of individual flow inside the aggregate.

- The PHB description should not suppose any particular conditioning function at the network boundary.

Consequently, the first two items together specify the general target of PHBs: They should provide meaningful basis for understanding the behavior of the Differentiated Services system. The other items limit the terms that can be used to describe the desired behavior. Figure 3.3 shows a simplified model for PHB specification that concerns the treatment of an aggregate stream inside a black box—that is, an interior node in a Differentiated Services network.

As to the last, somewhat arguable item, there are two opposite needs:

- To keep each PHB as multipurpose as possible

- To make it possible to design predictable end-to-end services

The view adapted in this book is that the last instruction item should always be applied when there is not a compelling reason to bind a certain PHB to a specific traffic-conditioning function. Note that the architecture document (RFC 2475) declares explicitly that Differentiated Services architecture should *decouple* traffic conditioning and service provisioning functions from forwarding behaviors.

The main reasoning behind this decoupling, or separation, of traffic conditioning and forwarding behaviors is flexibility. After the core network system is specified and the applications of core network functions have been established, the service evolution can continue by inventing new traffic-conditioning functions for boundary nodes.

Figure 3.3   Per-Hop Behavior (PHB).

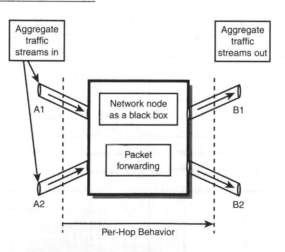

Even though not directly stated in RFC 2474, one permissible approach is to divide the whole network capacity into several parts in a static manner, in a way that each part is operated separately as an independent network although all packets use the same transmission resources. In that case, the PHB description concerns one individual part of the network resources rather than the whole network.

Chapter 1 introduced two service concepts: customer service and network service. The definition of service in RFC 2474 can refer to either of them. *Customer service* is a description of the overall treatment of a customer's traffic (including with other aspects such as pricing); *network service* refers mainly to a subset of a customer's traffic.

Now it's time to introduce one supplementary term not used in RFC 2474—a *class*, or more accurately, a *PHB class*. This term has been used in some important PHB specifications (Baker *et al.* 1998). A PHB class is a collection of PHBs intended to be applicable for transmitting packets of one application. Technically this means that the service provider is allowed to re-mark packets within a PHB class, but not from one class to another class. The main requirement for a PHB class is that packets should not be reordered inside the network. A PHB class with proper traffic-conditioning functions at the network boundary is the nearest equivalent for the network services in connection-oriented networks, such as ATM networks.

Codepoints are the handles used to inform inside nodes about the PHB of the packet. The fundamental requirement is that the codepoint of the packet unambiguously define the PHB. On the contrary, several different codepoints can map to the same PHB, which means that an aggregate can consists of packets with different codepoints. In that case, the treatment should be the same within one PHB regardless of the actual codepoint used in the packet.

According to RFC 2474, a *mechanism* is the implementation of one or more Per-Hop Behaviors according to a particular algorithm. A mechanism can be used for implementing several PHBs, and several mechanisms are usually needed to implement a PHB. Figure 3.4 depicts the total picture of this Differentiated Services structure. (See Chapter 1 for a description of the main structure of Differentiated Services.) The following example, "Implementing Real-Time Service and Data Service," illustrates using PHBs to effect services.

Figure 3.4   The main building blocks of Differentiated Services.

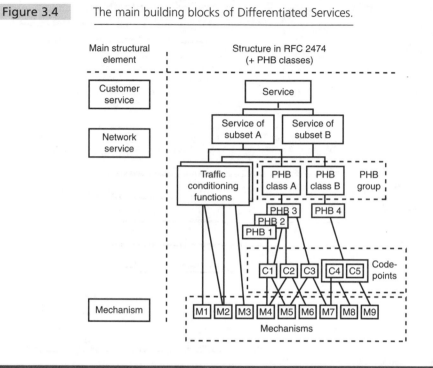

Implementing Real-Time Service and Data Service

The fictional service provider Fairprofit can implement the services introduced in the preceding example, "Real-Time Service Versus Best-Effort Service," by means of one PHB group consisting of two PHB classes: one for real-time service and another one for data service. The real-time service consists of one PHB (11); whereas the data PHB class consists of two PHBs (21 and 22) with different importance. Figure 3.5 shows this PHB structure.

We may ask whether the two classes should belong to a PHB group. This issue is not totally clear; for management purposes, however, it is certainly useful to define the relationship between the two classes and, effectively, to make a PHB group.

Hence, as to the PHB description, it could be enough to say that real-time aggregate is served with shorter delay than the data aggregate and that packets marked with PHB21 encounter smaller discarding probability than PHB22 packets. The actual performance of end-to-end service depends then crucially on traffic-conditioning functions at the network boundaries. In general, it is not feasible to define exact performance values for PHB because PHB as such does not cover traffic-conditioning functions at network boundaries.

Figure 3.5   Per-Hop Behavior group with two PHB classes.

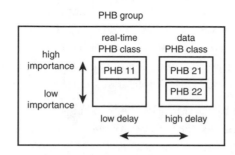

DS Field Definition

The PHB information is transmitted in the Differentiated Services field (DS field) that consists of an octet IP header. Section 3 in RFC 2474 defines the structure of this field, shown in Figure 3.6. This new definition replaces the older definitions of the IPv4 TOS octet and the IPv6 Traffic Class octet. The DS field is divided into two parts: the first six bits (DSCP field) are used as a codepoint to select the PHB, and the two last bits (CU bits) are reserved for future use.

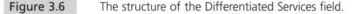

Figure 3.6   The structure of the Differentiated Services field.

A DS-compliant node uses all the six bits of the DSCP field, but not any other bits to select the PHB. Further, RFC 2474 requires that the implementation of codepoint mapping should be very flexible: The field should be treated as an index without any internal structure, and the operator should be able to map any codepoint to any PHB.

Historical Codepoint Definitions

If a packet with an unrecognized codepoint is received, it should be forwarded according to the default behavior. Therefore, the default PHB must be available in every DS node. This default behavior corresponds to the best-effort service provided in current networks—that is, the network tries to deliver as many packets as possible and as soon as possible. The other part of the service (although not formally a part of the PHB) is the traffic conditioning functions. Although according to the conventional best-effort paradigm there is no particular traffic conditioning at the network boundary, in a Differentiated Services network some conditioning is possible, but not mandatory, for default PHB traffic.

The main issue related to the default PHB is the relationship between it and other PHBs used in the network. In general, the operator may apply any kind of policy in this respect. It is recommended that the service policy ensure that default PHB always gets reasonable amount of resources, however, regardless of the other PHBs. This allows a smooth coexistence of both Differentiated Services–aware and non-aware traffic streams in the same network. Because of this backward compatibility issue, the codepoint 000000 must map to the default PHB (or to another PHB with similar characteristics).

In addition to the default behavior, RFC 2474 defines a PHB group called *class selector PHB* with defined codepoints. The reason for this standardization is that the IP Precedence field defined in RFC 791 has been used in some real networks. The specification of this PHB group is described further in RFC 2474 and also in Chapter 7, "Per-Hop Behavior Groups," in section 7.2, "Class Selector PHB Group," of this book.

Per-Hop Behavior Standardization Guidelines

RFC 2474 provides some guidelines for those who write PHB specifications. First, according to the common rule applicable to any IETF specification, implementation, deployment, and proven usefulness are prerequisites for any PHB to be standardized. Because no mechanisms are standardized, vendors can use any appropriate mechanisms that together satisfy the definition of a PHB, PHB class, or PHB group.

It is assumed that certain common Per-Hop Behaviors will evolve in such a way that an established set of services will emerge. Although this is a likely scenario, it is premature to predict how the PHB field will evolve and which one of the PHB proposals will be commonly used and which will vanish.

Although the DSCP field is in principle unstructured, three different pools are introduced in Chapter 6 of RFC 2474, mainly for codepoint-management purposes. The first pool with codepoints xxxxx0 is for standard action, the second pool with codepoints xxxx11 is for experimental and local use, and the third pool with codepoints xxxx10 is initially for experimental use, but may be later used for standard PHBs.

3.3.3 Architecture for Differentiated Services

RFC 2475, "An Architecture for Differentiated Services," defines the architecture for implementing scalable service differentiation on the basis of the DS field specification (Black *et al.* 1998). Because the architecture itself is not a matter of standardization, this architecture document is an informational RFC. This document both further clarifies some issues addressed in the standard track RFC 2474 and, of course, discusses architectural issues.

Terms and Targets

The introduction section of RFC 2475 further illuminates the terminology of Differentiated Services. It states that service characteristics may be specified in terms of *throughput, delay, jitter, loss,* or *relative priority* of access to network resources. This list is actually a central tool for the development of PHBs: The differentiation made possible by a PHB should concern some of the essential service characteristics.

The introduction section also provides a quite comprehensive and useful list of terms. The basic architecture of Differentiated Services is described by a list of requirements. The main points of the list are as follows:

- *Versatility:* A wide variety of end-to-end services should be possible to realize; network services should be independent of applications, and they should be directly applicable with current applications and with current network services.

- *Simplicity:* The overall system or parts of it should not depend on signaling for individual flows; only a small set of forwarding behaviors should be necessary.

- *Cost efficiency:* Information about individual flows or customers should not be used in core nodes, but only states of aggregate streams should be used in core nodes.

As you can see, part of the terminology presented in Chapter 1 is also used here. A similar list of terminology also appears in Chapter 4.

Comparison with Other Approaches

The introduction section of RFC 2475 also provides a concise overview of other approaches for service differentiation. Although the basic arguments are similar to those in Chapter 2, "Traffic Management Before Differentiated Services," it is worthwhile to make an overview to explain the target of the Differentiated Services Working Group (which might differ slightly from that of this book).

The categories applied in the comparison are relative priority marking, service marking, label switching, Integrated Services/RSVP, and static per-hop classification. In the priority-marking approach, the application or some other entity selects a relative priority for each packet, and the network nodes use it to decide which kind of forwarding behavior should be applied to the packet. Differentiated Services can be considered a refinement of this model.

The difference between priority marking and service marking is subtle. In the service-marking approach, the required end-to-end service is more definitely expressed—for instance, "minimize delay" or "maximize reliability." This information is not only used to select the forwarding behavior, but also the route; the Differentiated Services field, on the other hand, is not particularly intended for route selection. Because the Differentiated Services approach leaves as much space as possible for further evolution, it is considered that the possible services are not built-in parts of the Differentiated Services structure. (You may deem this self-contradictory; Differentiated Services really does not consider services, but only building blocks for services.)

The label-switching (or virtual-circuit) model includes Frame Relay, ATM, and MPLS. In this model, the granularity of resource allocation can vary from individual flows to large aggregate streams. The cost of the fine granularity is the complex management and configuration needed to establish and maintain all the information related to the large number of flows. The main difference of Integrated Services/RSVP model compared to label switching is that it relies on traditional packet forwarding as the underlying technology. The additional element of RSVP is that it allows sources and receivers to inform network nodes about the needs of applications and make reservation through the network.

The main problem of the RSVP model is scalability in high-speed core routers. Therefore, it is supposed that by using Differentiated Services in the core network, the scalability problems of RSVP can be avoided; in the access network, however, RSVP can be used to make definite reservations. Furthermore, different combinations of technologies and service models are needed in practical implementations. If ATM is used as the underlying technology for Differentiated Services, for example, the end-to-end service could be a compromise between the ATM service model and Differentiated Services model.

Architecture Model

The basic elements of the architecture model are explained thoroughly in the second chapter of RFC 2475, "Architecture for Differentiated Service." The key elements for building Differentiated Services are DS boundary nodes, DS interior nodes, ingress nodes, and egress nodes, as shown in Figure 3.7. These elements are virtual in the sense that one physical node may contain all characteristics of all node types. It can be said that each type of node is a collection of characteristics:

- *Boundary node*: A collection of functions needed to interconnect a DS domain to another DS domain or to a non-DS–capable domain

- *Interior node*: A collection of functions needed if a node is connected only to other DS-capable nodes

- *Ingress node*: A collection of functions needed to handle incoming traffic streams to a DS domain

- *Egress node*: A collection of functions needed to handle outgoing traffic streams from a DS domain

In particular, a real boundary node can (and typically does) contain all these functions: The same node can be a boundary node for some traffic stream and an interior node for some other streams. Moreover, any interior node can have part of the functions of boundary nodes—for instance, the interior node may have a limited capacity of traffic conditioning.

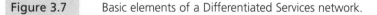

Figure 3.7   Basic elements of a Differentiated Services network.

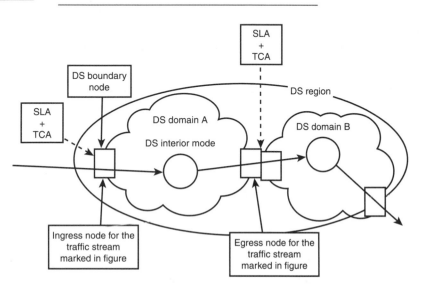

Further, it should be noted that there are two levels of agreements:

- *Service-level agreement (SLA)*: A contract between a customer and a service provider that specifies the forwarding service

- *Traffic-conditioning agreement (TCA)*: Defines the rules used to realize the service, such as metering, marking, and discarding

The same SLA and TCA concepts are also applicable between two network domains. SLA seems to be rather a customer service and/or network service concept; TCA, on the other hand, should be defined by terms that belong to the traffic-handling level (compare to Figure 1.1 in Chapter 1).

A DS domain is a part of a network in which nodes are DS compliant and in which a set of PHB groups are applied based on the same service-provisioning policy. At interfaces where PHB structure and/or the service policy is otherwise significantly changed, a boundary node is needed to make appropriate mappings between PHBs. A contiguous set of DS domains forms a DS region. Differentiated Services can be provided over a DS region, although significant differences in service structure and PHBs make it difficult to design and provide useful end-to-end services.

Traffic Classification and Conditioning

Figure 3.8 presents the logical structure of traffic classification and conditioning functions. This structure is based on the assumption that classification is made according to the information in the packet header (such as source address and destination addresses and DS field) and the incoming interface (RFC 2474). This model seems to exclude the possibility that traffic metering has any effect on the classification. This is a feasible approach if you suppose that the classification means the selection of a PHB class rather than an individual PHB. In such a case, marking is something done within the class, but does not cross the boundaries of PHB classes.

Figure 3.8   Packet classifier and traffic conditioning according to the architecture document.

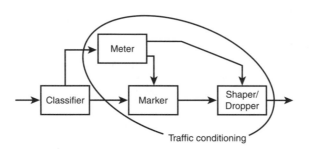

A traffic profile is one way to present the traffic-conditioning rules. In the simplest model, each packet is either *in-profile* or *out-of-profile* based on the metering result at the arrival time of the packet. In-profile packets obtain better traffic-conditioning and forwarding treatment than out-of-profile packets. This model is further evaluated in this book in section 7.4, "Assured Forwarding PHB Group," of Chapter 7.

According to the architecture document, the *meter element* measures each traffic stream. (*Stream* seems to correspond here to the concept of a PHB class, although the term is not used in this document.) Meter then informs the marker, shaper, and dropper mechanisms about the state of the stream:

- *Marker*: This sets an appropriate codepoint to the DS field of the packet. Actually this means that the marker is allowed to change the original value of the DS field. To avoid re-ordering within the network, the marker should comply with certain rules when re-marking packets.

- *Shapers*: These can be used to smooth the traffic process of particular aggregate streams.

- *Dropper mechanisms*: Based on the content of SLA and TCA, some packets can be discarded at the traffic-conditioning element.

Traffic conditioners are usually located in DS boundary nodes. The basic assumption is that all complicated classification and conditioning procedures are made near the source, while inside the network only some straightforward actions are necessary. Consequently, the most advisable approach could be that shaping is done in the private network, marking is done in boundary nodes, and dropping in interior nodes.

PHB as a Tool for Resource Allocation

According to RFC 2475, Per-Hop Behavior is the means by which a node allocates resources to aggregate streams; the given example is that a PHB gets x% of the capacity of a link. This definition satisfies the technical requirements of PHB specification (see the list in the beginning of this chapter); it is more difficult to comprehend how this PHB definition allows constructing predictable services, however. The core of the problem is that a larger capacity for an aggregate stream than for another one does not automatically produce better service because the final result depends crucially on the traffic load of each aggregate stream.

Further, the document states that PHB groups shall effectively partition the link and node resources between aggregates. However, it is not clear how this requirement can be deduced from the general requirements for PHB specification presented in the standard track document (RFC 2474) or from the desired service characteristics presented earlier in the architecture document (throughput, delay, jitter, loss, or relative priority; RFC 2475). Even though the aggregate bandwidth and throughput are similar terms, you can expect that end users are interested in the throughput of their own flow rather than the bandwidth of an aggregate stream.

Although the overall assessment depends on the interpretation of the word *effectively*, the idea that PHB essentially means resource allocation seems to be somewhat restricting and does not necessarily cover all Differentiated Services systems. Chapter 7, in section 7.4, "Assured Forwarding PHB Group," examines this issue in more detail.

Per-Hop Behavior Guidelines

The architecture document, RFC 2475, gives 15 additional instructions for PHB designers. According to the first item, a PHB must include recommendation about the DS codepoint. Furthermore, PHB specification should include the following:

- An overview of the general purpose of the PHB group

- Specification of interactions between individual PHBs within a PHB group

- Provisioning restrictions if necessary (for example, whether the proper function of the PHB depends on the traffic-conditioning actions)

- A statement as to whether the PHB group is considered for general or local use

- A statement about the circumstances under which a packet can be re-marked within the PHB group from one PHB to another PHB

In addition, a PHB specification should discuss various issues such as interactions with previously defined PHBs, tunneling, conformance requirements, security, impacts on higher-layer protocols and link-layer mechanisms. A PHB specification that fulfils all the mentioned recommendations would certainly be very useful and comprehensible (unfortunately this not the case with all proposals).

Interoperability Issues

A non-DS–compliant node is a node that does not appropriately interpret the PHBs used within the DS domain. A specific case of a non-DS–compliant node is a so called legacy node that uses the first three precedence bits defined in RFC 791. Chapter 4 of RFC 2475 briefly considers interoperability issues, mainly in two specific cases. In the first case, a non-DS–compliant node is situated within a DS domain. One possibility to solve the apparent problems of this situation is to keep the overall load level so low that quality characteristics (delay and loss) are good enough for all aggregates. If that is not possible, one solution could be that the DS domain uses only class selector codepoints defined in RFC 2474.

An even more difficult case is when Differentiated Services traffic is sent to a non-DS–capable domain. The main alternatives in this case seems to be that all packets are marked with default PHB, or packets are mapped into class selector codepoints. The latter approach may provide a limited version of Differentiated Services, although the overall result is difficult to predict.

Multicast Streams

RFC 2475 briefly discusses two issues related to multicast streams. First, an incoming multicast packet can consume much more network resources than an incoming unicast packet. Note that multicast packets usually consume fewer resources than unicast packets given the number of recipients. In addition, the amount of resources needed inside the network is difficult to predict at the ingress node. This may cause fairness problems between unicast and multicast streams. One approach to alleviate this problem involves the understanding that multicast packets use different codepoints and different PHBs than unicast packets.

The second issue relates to a situation in which a multicast packet coming through an ingress node may be transmitted to several different network domains. This makes if difficult to select a DS codepoint that conforms to all the service agreements of the different domains.

Security and Tunneling issues

The main security issues considered both in RFC 2474 and RFC 2475 are the so-called denial-of-service attacks and the interactions with security protocols. Because certain PHBs and the corresponding codepoints provide better service compared to majority of traffic, some users may try to modify codepoints in their packets to try to obtain better service. In the worst case, this kind of behavior can yield to a denial-of-service attack, in which the modified packets exhaust the resources available for other traffic streams.

Moreover, because interior nodes are allowed to rely purely on the codepoint's value set by the boundary nodes, it is of great importance to design boundary nodes in such a way that every packet gets an appropriate codepoint value and properly traffic-conditioning actions are applied to all traffic streams marked with any preferential PHB.

3.3.4 A Framework for Differentiated Services

The framework document, RFC 2475, addresses basically the same issues as this book. In general, it provides a lot of helpful ideas, concepts, and recommendations for building networks and services based on the Differentiated Services approach: The document is one step toward real service differentiation in the Internet. Because practically all the issues considered in RFC 2475 are discussed in Part II, "Building a Network Domain Based on Differentiated Services," it is not worthwhile to review the whole document. Nevertheless, certain issues may need clarification, particularly in cases where the viewpoint of this book differs from that of the framework document.

Service Models

According to the framework document, the service provider forms the service by combining PHBs, traffic conditioners, provisioning strategies, and billing mechanisms (Bernet *et al.* 1998). Without doubt, this is a reasonable statement. Two additional qualifiers presented in the framework document are as follows:

- DS services are for unidirectional traffic.

- DS services are for traffic aggregates.

On certain levels of the system, these seem to be reasonable and valid statements.

Remember, however, that because customers are surely interested in traffic in both directions (most applications need a transmission channel in both directions), both directions must be somehow taken into account on the customer service level. Another issue is the technical implementation that can be based on unidirectional transmission channels. Moreover, it is somewhat questionable to equate the treatment of aggregate and service, because service depends crucially on the traffic-conditioning actions at boundary nodes, and these actions can be customer specific or even flow specific.

The fundamental difference between the Differentiated Services of this book and the framework document is the *basic model of service*. Part of the framework is generally applicable with various situations and with various service models. A good example of this is the taxonomy of services that discerns three basic categories: qualitative, quantitative, and relative. The examples presented in the framework document are illustrative. The service definitions related to packet-loss ratio could be as follows:

- *Qualitative service*: Low loss ratio.

- *Quantitative service*: Less than 5% packet-loss ratio.

- *Relative service*: Packet-loss ratio on service level A is smaller than that on service level B.

This practical classification will be used in the Chapter 4 of this book as well. Nonetheless, part of the framework document seems to be based on the assumption that service differentiation definitely means different levels of quantitative service (Bernet *et al.* 1998). Section 4.2 of the framework document states that TCA is an important subset of the SLA, for example, and it specifies detailed service parameters for each service level. Examples of service parameters are *throughput*, *drop probability*, and *latency*. Moreover, there are several references to traffic profile with conforming and nonconforming traffic; without quantitative parameters, the meaning of conformance is a somewhat unclear concept. Obviously, the assumption is that customer service is always based on a strict control regardless of the nature of the network service.

The reasoning seems to be that the customer requires certain service that is defined by a detailed TCA including traffic parameters, such as bit rate. The service provider offers a service with a certain price that likely depends on bit rate and quality requirements of the connection. Based on the TCA, the service provider measures the traffic sent by the customer at the boundary node and marks each packet either in-profile or out-of-profile. This is a very similar model to that of VBR service in an ATM network when CLP bit is applied. The main difference between ATM/VBR service and this service model is the implementation of traffic-control functions inside the network.

Without doubt, this is one possible approach, but not the only one. If the service provider wants to adopt a significantly different service model, some of the ideas presented in the document are difficult to apply. It should be noted, however, that the framework document clearly states that static SLAs are the norm at the present time. Therefore, changes in TCA can occur on the order of days or weeks rather than seconds or minutes. The framework document seems, in a way, to hover between the traditional connection-oriented service model and a new Differentiated Services model that is still to be defined. (This book endeavors to fill this gap.)

Despite this minor criticism, the framework document offers many useful instructions that provide additional tools for effective service differentiation. The fourth section, for instance, discusses problems related to the requirement of controlling received traffic and to the provision of dynamic SLAs.

Further, section 5 introduces three possible service models: better than best-effort service, leased-line emulation service, and quantitative assured media playback service. Better than best-effort gives higher priority than the normal best-effort service. By that means, the content provider can transmit packets with a higher rate than other content providers can. Leased-line service can be used by corporations to transmit, for instance, IP telephony calls between network sites of a corporation. Media playback service provides similar character-istics as the leased-line service, but with lower level of assurances. All these services can be implemented by using the EF and AF PHB groups. (See sections 7.3, "Expedited Forwarding PHB," and 7.4, "Assured Forwarding PHB Group," in Chapter 7.)

Provisioning and Configuration

Provisioning and configuration issues are discussed thoroughly in Chapter 4. It could be, however, helpful to illustrate the main points in the framework document, as well as the main differences between the view of the framework document and this book.

The boundary provisioning is the easy part of the issue, in particular in the direction from the boundary node to the core network. The much harder question is the interior provi-sioning—that is, the dimensioning (to use the term applied in Chapter 4 of this book) of link or service class capacity inside the network. As appropriately noticed in the framework document, a good understanding and control of traffic is necessary for efficient provision (Bernet *et al.* 1998). The statement is that although traffic volumes cannot be anticipated with 100% accuracy, the internal provision is still a tractable problem. Although this state-ment could be partly true, the whole issue is so complicated that it could be overoptimistic to rely on the predictability of the traffic process unless both the route and the traffic sent by the customer are strictly controlled.

One approach to alleviate the provisioning problems is to make certain that quantitative and qualitative services are isolated by using different PHBs. In general, quantitative ser-vices should have higher priority than qualitative services, although this definitely depends on the level of quantitative assurance. In this respect, relative services can be considered as a system consisting of several qualitative services. Moreover, it is supposed that only a small fraction of traffic uses the quantitative services.

In section 6.2 of the framework document, it is said that dynamic provision techniques are desirable because traffic volumes are likely to change dynamically, even if TCA is static (Bernet *et al.* 1998). Dynamic provision means in this connection either that capacity requests are signaled through the network, or that the nodes adjust resources based on measurement results. Dynamic provision is in principle an apprehensible idea, and in some cases certainly necessary. It should be noted, however, that signaling mechanisms do not belong to the main tools used by the Differentiated Services Working Group.

Viewpoint of This Book

It is not clear whether the dynamic provision truly is the best approach to optimize the use of network resources. Figure 3.9 illustrates the basic dilemma of dynamic provision. There are two traffic streams sharing a link with a fixed-capacity reservation for both; the streams can represent two service classes with different quality requirements. The starting point could be that a fixed capacity is reserved for both traffic classes. (Case A in Figure 3.9 shows this.) This is probably not a very efficient approach if traffic streams are highly variable.

One possible way to improve the situation is to dynamically adjust the capacity of service classes based on the momentary traffic load of the streams. (Case B in Figure 3.9 shows this.) Some issues limit the usefulness of dynamic provision, however. First, there is usually an ultimate limit for the total reservation because link capacity seldom can be adjusted dynamically. Therefore, an increase of reservation for stream 1 must be taken from somewhere, either from another reservation or from a free pool. Second, reservations as such consume some resources, and moreover they can never follow every change in traffic demand.

A third alternative could be the key to better use of network resources. It is based on solving a conflicting situation when it really occurs rather than on proactive reservations. (Case C in Figure 3.9 shows this.) As long as there is enough capacity for all traffic streams, no special action is needed: The system merely transmits packets forward. Only when there are momentary overloads is a decision system activated in a way that makes possible an efficient use of the network and fair service for all traffic streams.

In this model, no explicit capacity reservation is used to avoid conflict situations, and no explicit mechanism is used to warn senders about possible overloads. This is a fundamental idea of Differentiated Services presented in this book—but note that there still are differing opinions about the basic principles of Differentiated Services.

Figure 3.9 Three approaches to sharing link resources.

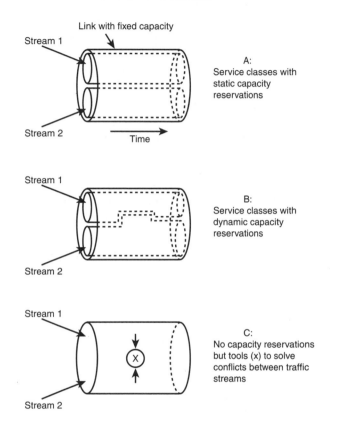

Summary

The evolution of Differentiated Services has been eventful and fast. Although part of the frenetic activity could be classified as hype rather than progress, the establishment of a dedicated working group has systematized the effort (thanks to the co-chairs of the working group, Brian Carpenter and Kathleen Nichols).

This chapter provided an historical overview that illustrated the many various goals for Differentiated Services. This variety has had a significant effect on the development process so far, and it is likely that the diversity of proposals will be even greater in the future. Whether all proposals truly comply with the principles of Differentiated Services is a matter of continuous debate.

The most concrete results of the first year are two RFCs that specify the structure of the DS field in IP packets and the basic architecture for Differentiated Services. This chapter provided an overview on these documents, as well as an overview of a framework document that contains instructions about the application of Differentiated Services models in real networks.

The most important concept of Differentiated Services is Per-Hop Behavior (PHB). Although PHB is primarily a technical term, PHB should not specify mechanisms. Moreover, PHB is also used to depict the purpose of the whole system; it should not be a service specification, however. It will take a lot of expertise and effort to define the PHB proposal in an appropriate manner.

The final part of the chapter illustrated the main differences between the working group documents and the later chapters in this book. The main reason for developing Differentiated Services, from the perspective of this book, is not merely to provide scalable implementation of the integrated services model. In technical terms, this book resolutely promotes an approach based on flexible sharing of network resources rather than capacity reservations. This starting point makes it necessary to reconsider the whole service model of the Internet, which is the topic of Chapter 4.

PART II

Building a Network Domain Based on Differentiated Services

CHAPTER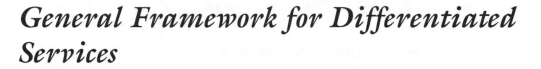

General Framework for Differentiated Services

This book tries to give as consistent a view as possible on the Differentiated Services effort—its targets, available methods, and the most promising service models. One way to meet this objective is to build a framework based on an evaluation of various aspects. The framework built in this chapter attempts to have the same meaning for Differentiated Services as grammar has for a language: "Essence is expressed by grammar," Ludwig Wittgenstein once remarked (Wittgenstein 1973).

Although the introduction section of this chapter is quite extensive, it is important to remember that all considerations are inevitably based on simplified models of complex reality, and some aspects are inevitably ignored. The real challenge of this whole effort is to acknowledge the many relevant issues that could be considered, while realizing that there is no hope of a grand unified theory that can explain everything. Even taking into account this inescapable limitation, however, the ensuing evaluation may provide useful tools for understanding and building Differentiated Services.

This chapter first attempts to clarify the philosophical standpoint of this book by analyzing the complexity of the matter and the most fundamental concepts of service differentiation. Then the chapter briefly reviews the basic limitations of the documents made within the Differentiated Services Working Group. Based on this evaluation, a target is set for a more general framework.

A closer examination is made of three issues: the efficiency of statistical multiplexing, the need for high predictability of quality, and a tool that can be used to compare service models from guaranteed services to relative service. Finally, a concise, but general framework with three primary dimensions is introduced.

4.1 Basis for the Framework

This section defines the position of the Differentiated Services framework introduced in this chapter. Together, three parts make up this framework:

- The outer limit defined by the fundamental concepts

- The inner limit defined by the scope of the Differentiated Services Working Group

- The general target for the framework

Two fundamental terms, *differentiation* and *service*, together define the extreme limits for this effort. All the issues presented in this book and the framework will be related to service differentiation. It is so vast an area, however, that it cannot be exhaustively covered.

The scope of the Differentiated Services Working Group defines the minimum region for the framework. Nevertheless, that region is quite limited because of some fundamental restrictions of a standardization organization. Particularly, service and business models are largely excluded from the specifications made by the Working Group.

The reasonable area for the framework is situated somewhere between the outer and inner limits. The primary purpose of the framework is to facilitate the designing and implementation of Differentiated Services. Because the ultimate goal is to provide service for customers, however, service and business aspects should be essential parts of the framework.

It also is useful to remember the large number of issues discussed in Chapter 1, "The Target of Differentiated Services." A pivotal requirement for the framework is that it should be applicable to various cases in a consistent manner.

4.1.1 Basic Terminology

It is important to first consider the meaning of the primary term of the whole book: *differentiation*. One definition for differentiation can be found in the glossary of *The Origin of Species* (Darwin [1859] 1972): "the separation or discrimination of parts or organs that in simpler forms of life are more or less united." This definition is surprisingly usable in the context of the Internet, where differentiation may mean that the current, simpler form of service is separated or discriminated into several forms. The Oxford Dictionary, which offers a more recent definition of differentiate, says it is "to constitute the state of being distinguishable in nature, form, or quality." These three attributes provide a good starting point also for considering service differentiation.

The meaning of *service* may seem evident. However, one general remark is useful: Service is not necessarily something that is truly sold, nor is any specific mechanism necessary to limit the use of the service. Indeed, one characteristic of the original Internet service used by the academic community was that it was available free of charge for the end users. Users were, however, supposed to carry out research that benefited the community. It is useful to remember this background because it has significantly affected the way the Internet is still working.

When the word *differentiate* is added, some changes in the service model are inevitable. First, there seems to be a strong incentive to attach different prices to different services (where price could also be something other than money). Therefore, the innocent-looking word *differentiate* may yield fundamental changes in Internet service.

4.1.2 Limitations of the Differentiated Services Working Group

The Differentiated Services Working Group made noteworthy progress during the first year after its establishment, in particular taking into account the complexity of the questions and the different views about the target of the effort. However, the results do not cover all relevant issues in the form they are presented. You can find these results in RFC 2474, "Definition of the Differentiated Services Field (DS Field) in the IPv4 and IPv6 Headers" (Baker *et al.* 1998), RFC 2475, "An Architecture for Differentiated Services" (Black *et al.* 1998), and some Internet drafts. There seem to be three primary reasons why the results aren't all inclusive:

- Some issues cannot be addressed formally in an IETF working group (business models).

- Issues are left open mainly because it is better to obtain more experience before making any final decisions (service models).

- There is a lack of common understanding about some fundamental issues, such as the real need for per-flow guarantees.

Customer service paradigms and pricing models are often kept out of the standardization process, because an official document that gives too much guidance relating to these business aspects is seen as potentially limiting competition in the area. Fortunately, because this book is definitely not a standard, it is possible here to address to some extent the delicate area of business models for the Internet. It should be stressed, however, that all suggestions and recommendations presented in this book are based purely on this author's best understanding of the issue, and they are not aimed to limit the application of any kind of Internet business model. Nevertheless, without any business considerations, the usefulness of this book might be seriously deteriorated.

It is hard to decide exactly when the time is right for making a standard. In the beginning, there is not enough understanding about the target and the best mechanisms to meet the target. Then, all of a sudden, it might be too late to devise a standard because someone has already brought a successful product to market without any standardization. One approach for solving this dilemma is to first make a quite loose standard that defines the frame for products or services without specifying the details of implementations. Later, when more experience is gained, it is possible to refine the standard. Many IETF working groups employ this basic approach (including the Differentiated Services Working Group).

The Differentiated Services Working Group, as explained in Chapter 3, "Differentiated Services Working Group," deliberately leaves many technical issues for further study or to be decided by service providers and network operators. The Working Group's reasoning is that this approach encourages the development of a wide variety of Differentiated Services without limiting the scope of acceptable models. Although this is certainly a reasonable approach, and this book also emphasizes the need for experiments and trials to evaluate different models, there seems to a need to give more comprehensive guidance for implementation even before thorough practical experience (even trials should be based on some understanding).

Finally, even though there seems to be relatively wide consensus that something like Differentiated Services could be very useful for the future Internet, there is still much controversy about how it should be done and what is the right basis for development. The main effect of the growing consensus seems to be that new experts are ceaselessly coming to the field of Differentiated Services. Every new person has his or her own opinion about how things should be done—although this is quite natural, it yields an acute problem of making any progress difficult because the discussion circles the same topics time after time.

4.1.3   Target of the Framework

In short, the target of the framework presented in this chapter is to provide better order in the wild field of Differentiated Services. The ordering is not accomplished by punishing for wrong acts or opinions, but rather by harmonization of comprehension. Harmonization can, however, be seen as a double-edged sword: In addition to the benefits of harmonized systems, there could be the danger of limiting the variability of ideas. To avoid this pitfall, the framework should be, in addition to mandatory consistence, as versatile as possible.

The task at hand can be divided into three phases: to lay the foundation, to erect the skeleton of the building, and to add all other necessary elements.

First, a solid grounding is needed. Because of the lack of common understanding of some fundamental issues, a lot of effort is made in this chapter to build a solid and legitimate basis. This phase focuses on issues such as the efficiency of statistical multiplexing and the usefulness of network service for different applications.

Second, a comprehensible and consistent structure is required. For this, it is important to identify all the integral building blocks and the main relationships among them. As for

Differentiated Services, this means that the purpose of the six bits in the DS field must be clearly defined. Moreover, it is not enough to define the meaning of a single bit combination, or codepoint, but it is of great importance to define the structure of relationships among codepoints. Finally, the outcome is practicable in the sense that it is applicable to solving various practical problems. Based on the foundation and skeleton, it must be possible to construct Differentiated Services (and that should be more useful than a grand monument similar to some former network services).

Recall the attributes introduced in the first chapter of this book: cost efficiency, robustness, versatility, and fairness.

As discussed in Chapter 2, "Traffic Management Before Differentiated Services," neither a pure best-effort model nor a pure guaranteed-service model can provide an efficient solution in a multiple-service environment. In fact, a combination of high-quality requirement of some flows and a highly variable traffic process of some other flows tends to result in low utilization, if there is only one service class. If a large number of service classes are used, the management overhead tends to increase and impair cost efficiency. But how should these considerations be reflected in the framework of Differentiated Services? A clear and consistent structure and avoidance of any useless mechanisms seem to be the key means to reach this target. The same conclusion is largely valid with robustness: A logical and solid structure is the tool that enables the building of a robust system.

Because the main purpose of the framework is technical—that is, the design and implementation of Differentiated Services—it is reasonable to emphasize technical aspects. Because the ultimate goal is to provide service for customers, however, consideration should also be given to marketing and customer care. In the best case, the framework could be useful for both marketing and supporting the service. That is possible, however, only if the framework is really clear, almost self-evident. One should check, from time to time, whether it's possible to convince ordinary customers of the fairness of certain characteristics of the service structure. Or more concretely, the service providers should be able to explain to their customers why they should pay more for one service than for another service.

If IP and the Internet dominate the future of communications, as it now seems, all imaginable, and even not yet invented, services have to be supported by IP. The view presented in this book supports the idea that this versatility requirement should be met by one all-encompassing service model rather than by a collection of separate services—and the most promising versatile service model is Differentiated Services.

4.2 Tools for Evaluating Service Models

This chapter elaborates some fundamental issues of service provision and service differentiation. The general target is to offer as wide a perspective as possible in the sense that substantially different service models can be evaluated with the same concepts and within the same framework. To reach this target, questions such as these should be answered:

What does better service mean?

Which fairness aspects are relevant in case of several layers of aggregation?

A primary concept for accomplishing this task is "availability of quality." The following pages introduce the concept and give some numeric examples to illustrate its applicability. Moreover, another aspect of fairness is assessed—that aspect related to multiple levels of differentiation (between parts of the application, between users, and so on) as presented at the beginning of this chapter.

4.2.1 Availability of Quality

One of the integral issues related to service differentiation is the actual meaning of "better service." Better service seems to be used as a synonym for higher quality and, surely, they have a close relationship with each other. There is an apparent danger of making the wrong conclusions, however, if these terms are taken as exact synonyms. The term *higher quality* may readily lead our thinking to an analysis of a situation in which a connection through the network is already available, and only the quality of the connection is assessed. This kind of viewpoint could be feasible if there were significant pricing only when the service is really used by the customer. On the contrary, in case of flat-rate pricing without a direct relationship between actual use and price, this kind of approach may lead to a peculiar conclusion: Quality can be improved just by arbitrarily rejecting service totally to some customers. Therefore, better service is the broader target than high quality.

Instead of merely using the term *quality*, this book applies a concept of the *availability of quality*. In practice, this term is used in such a way that quality is defined in some traditional terms, such as packet-loss ratio, available bandwidth, and maximum delay; then the availability of that given quality is calculated or measured. Thus availability of quality is the probability that the network service can meet a given quality requirement.

The basic idea is very simple: Service is available for an application only if certain quality criteria are fulfilled; otherwise, the service is unavailable. For a data application requiring an attainable bit rate of at least 50kbps over 10 seconds, availability could be high, say 99.9%, even though the service is only best effort. The availability of the same best-effort service is much lower, perhaps 50%, for an IP telephony application that requires a delay variation of less than 50 milliseconds. Consider the following numeric example.

This simple example evaluates the availability of quality on one link used by a number of customers. Based on long experience, the operator knows that the average load is 10Mbps, whereas the network operator does not know beforehand what is the actual momentary bit rate (say, within 10 seconds). Based on the same experience, the uncertainty of the traffic prediction can be described by a variance of $(1\text{Mbps})^2$. In other words, even though the operator knows that the average load is 10Mbps, there are unpredictable variations with variance of $(1\text{Mbps})^2$.

To make some progress, it is necessary to suppose something about the bit-rate distribution. Supposing that the average bit rate measured over 10 seconds is normally distributed, it is relatively easy to calculate the momentary packet-loss ratio for a given link capacity by assuming that all packets within the capacity are transmitted and all excessive packets have to be discarded. Note that this simplified model ignores the effects of short timescale variations and buffering.

Figure 4.1 shows the result in case of three link capacities: 12, 13, and 14Mbps. The vertical axis illustrates the quality criterion, in this case, the packet-loss ratio (P_{loss}); the horizontal axis is the availability of the quality. With a capacity of 12Mbps, for instance, a packet-loss criterion of 1% yields availability of 98.3%.

Figure 4.1	Availability of quality for a packet-loss ratio.

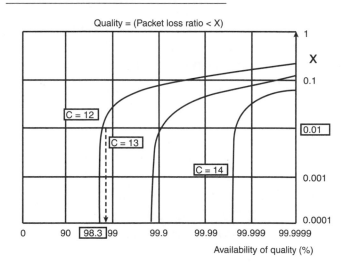

One conclusion seems to be evident: In this case, it is almost irrelevant whether the quality criterion is $P_{loss} = 10^{-4}$, 10^{-6}, or even 0, because almost always P_{loss} is either 0 or more than 10^{-4}. The quality of service should, therefore, be specified as the availability of certain quality criteria rather that as the average packet-loss ratio. Table 4.1 provides some numeric values that further illustrate the situation. In particular, note the tiny differences between the figures on the first three rows.

Table 4.1   Availability of Quality for Different Packet Loss Ratios

Quality Criterion	Capacity Mbps		
	C=12	C=13	C=14
$P_{loss} = 0$	97.720	99.864	99.9968
$P_{loss} <10^{-6}$	97.720	99.864	99.9968
$P_{loss} <10^{-4}$	97.726	99.865	99.9968
$P_{loss} <10^{-2}$	98.300	99.913	99.9983

It should again be stressed that a simple illustrative model cannot cover all relevant aspects. In reality, the dynamics of the packet losses could be very complicated—the human perception of quality can be complicated also. Figure 4.2 illustrates this phenomenon by showing the availability of quality for one fictitious video stream with a length of 1 hour, an average bit rate of 100kbps, and an average packet size of 500 bytes. Supposing that two packets were lost in all, the average packet-loss ratio measured over the total duration is $1.1*10^{-5}$.

If the packet-loss ratio is measured over a period of a second, and the packets are lost during the same second, the packet-loss ratio is either 0 (during 3,599 periods), or 8% (one period). Therefore, the availability of quality is 3599/3600 = 99.97% for any packet-loss criterion less than 8%. If the average packet-loss ratio is measured over a period of 100 seconds, the result differs remarkably: Availability is only 35/36 (97.2%) for any value of packet-loss ratio less than $8*10^{-4}$, and 100% for any packet-loss ratio greater than $8*10^{-4}$.

Figure 4.2   Availability of quality with a theoretical curve and two practical examples.

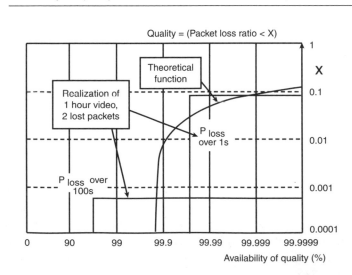

Without further information on the dynamics of traffic variations and on the effects of packet loss to the perceivable quality of the applications, it is impossible to say which one of the alternative results is most relevant. Nevertheless, the concept of availability of quality, as described in the following sidebar, can be used to illustrate characteristics of services better than what is possible with average quality parameters.

Criterion for Quality Availability

It is possible to make the evaluation more concrete by assuming that the customers of the fictional service provider, Fairprofit, are using one link for real-time applications that require a packet-loss ratio of 10^{-6}. What is the required link capacity if the average bit rate and bit-rate variations are the same as in the case with M = 10Mbps and V = (1Mbps)^2 illustrated in Figure 4.2?

The service provider cannot answer this question without specifying the availability criterion. For instance, availability of 99.99% means approximately 1 second of unavailability in every 3 hours. If the service provider believes that this is good enough for customers, a reservation of 13.7Mbps/s is sufficient. What is gained by changing the packet-loss criterion from 10^{-6} to a very high 10^{-2} while keeping the availability criterion the same? According to the present model, 13.6Mbps is needed, and that is only 100kbps less than originally required.

If the service provider looked at the average packet-loss ratio only, the result would be totally different. A theoretical (long-term average) packet-loss ratio of 10^{-6} is achieved by a capacity of 13.8Mbps, whereas a packet-loss ratio of 1% is achieved by a capacity of 10.8Mbps. That is not necessarily the best method for network dimensioning, however, because the situation is most probably that the packet-loss ratio is either 0 or very high for a short period.

4.2.2   Levels of Aggregation

One of the fundamental obstacles in the application of the Differentiated Services model is that the mechanisms inside the network are related to individual packets or aggregate streams, but the desired behavior is usually best specifiable in terms of flows—that is, a sequence of packets transmitted by one application. In addition, there are other important levels of aggregation: the customer, possibly using several applications at the same time; and the organization, which may pay for the service used by the end users.

The desired effects of all these levels should be mapped into a couple of PHB, and that seems to be almost an impossible mission. One way to make the entire system work is to identify the requirements of different entities, and then compare them in terms of desired characteristics and fairness:

- In a pure application model, applications need enough resources for sufficient quality (but waste of resources is undesirable).

- In a customer model, each customer should get a fair amount of resources relative to the price.

- In an organization model, organizations should get the right amount of total resources relative to the total price and support of optimal use of resources within the resource pool.

If you had to support only one of these basic cases, the task of service differentiation could be relatively easy. The reality is that in some parts of the network all these requirements must be satisfied simultaneously. It might be helpful, however, to start by looking briefly at each individual case.

The perspective of one application is somehow very attractive—what else could be the target of a network than to meet the requirements of each application? A natural approach is to list the requirements of all known applications and then design a network that can satisfy all imaginable quality requirements of all applications. This approach seems to lead to a system with one flow versus $n-1$ flows, where n is the number of all active flows in the network. A good service means that one flow is somehow protected from the effects of other flows in a way that high enough quality is available for every individual flow. If an application needs more bandwidth or better quality than another application, it is fair that it gets better service, isn't it? Yet, it is somewhat difficult to assess the real fairness because an application as such is unemotional and does not usually make any significant decisions.

Another possible perspective is that the network provides a quite rudimentary service structure without any tight connection between any service model and any application. The customer is allowed to use any network service in any way (for instance, a real-time network service for data transfer or vice versa). In this customer model, the fairness criterion is whether an individual customer gets a fair amount of bandwidth and quality relative to the price she is paying. This fairness criterion seems to be almost opposed to that of the application model.

Which one of the criteria is more important in cases where there is an actual conflict? Apparently, the answer depends on the service model provided by the service provider. Supposing that all customers behave agreeably and do not waste resources, the application model may yield a better overall result. In case of egoistic customers, however, the application model is more vulnerable than the customer model.

In the third case, with a number of end users within an organization that pays for the service, it is possible to apply both the application model and the customer model. The total capacity should be divided among organizations based on the prices (customer model), while the capacity of one organization divided based on requirements of applications. The model shown in Figure 4.3 summarizes this introduction to fairness issues. The fairness aspects in the figure are as follows:

F1: Between two applications used by the same end user

F2: Between two applications used by different end users within the same organization

F3: Between two applications used by different end users belonging to different organizations

F4: Between two end users within the same organization

F5: Between two end users belonging to different organizations

F6: Between two organizations

Figure 4.3   Fairness aspects on different levels of aggregates.

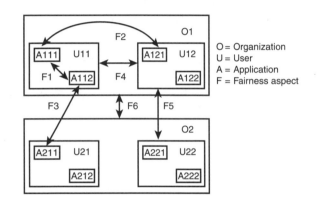

Based on this model, it is possible to define three service models according to the significance of the different fairness aspects:

Application model: F1=F2=F3>0, F4=F5=F6=0,

End-user model: F4=F5>0, F1=F2=F3=F6=0,

Organizational model: F1=F2>0, F6>0, F3=F4=F5=0

Fx > 0 means that the fairness aspect is essential for the service model, Fx = Fy means that the two relationships are managed equally, and Fx = 0 means that the aspect is ignored in the service model. In addition, there are different variations of these basic models—for instance, if end users have different rights for using the networks resources in the organizational model, then F4 > 0.

4.3 *Customer Service*

The first chapter of this book emphasized the fairness aspect of customer service. Although it is definitely a significant aspect, it may not cover the whole field of customer services. A service could be fair without much attractiveness, or attractive without much fairness—sometimes the service model could be even intentionally vague. In any case, it seems that to be successful there must be some basic attractiveness in the service.

4.3.1 Fulfilling Consumer Expectations

One practical issue to be addressed by service providers is how to build a network service that can fulfill consumer expectations. The following statements are relevant for an ISP providing Differentiated Services:

- Most users are not particularly interested in technical details of network service (that is, bit rates and milliseconds), but in the contents of the application. Those users are either incapable or reluctant to spend time appraising the selections of complex services.

- On the contrary, technologically oriented people may appreciate the detailed service offering with perhaps 100 different bandwidth and quality classes.

- One important aspect for an ordinary end user is the freedom to select the destination (or the source of information flow) without considering anything, such as price or the geographical location of the other end. A service model with these characteristics can be called *unscoped* service.

- On the contrary, big organizations may definitely want to limit the number of destinations, or the scope. The separation of traffic streams improves the possibility to offer virtual private networks with special characteristics, such as security and high quality.

> **Note**
>
> A *virtual private network (VPN)* is a network established for the exclusive use of a single organization with an emphasis on privacy and reliability. The main advantage of a VPN compared to leased lines is that it can exploit the statistical gains and scale advantage provided by large public networks.

These examples illustrate some of the difficulties faced when a service provider wants to fulfill the expectations of all customers. The expectations and preferences could be totally opposite, but still the service provider should use the same infrastructure to provide all kinds of service. A lot of versatility is clearly needed to make the total offering attractive for different type of customers.

4.3.2 Pricing Models and Predictability of Quality

What are the main service characteristics that users are paying for? High bandwidth, low packet-loss ratio, and small transmission delay are the first issues that come to mind, and certainly they are important issues. Then there is one additional aspect that is not always evident: predictability of quality. The essence of predictability of quality, or lack of it, is that even though the average quality could be high, users might be dissatisfied if they cannot predict the quality level in advance.

You have called your friend abroad using IP telephony service, for instance, and the quality of the connection is excellent during the first minute. Then, suddenly, the quality drops below satisfactory for some seconds and then returns to an excellent level. Although the average quality is probably good by most measures, you may feel uncomfortable because you don't know in advance what will happen in the next minute.

It seems likely that users are willing to pay for a clearly predictable result. To get a preliminary insight of this complex issue, consider two situations: one with time-dependent pricing, and another with flat-rate pricing. Let's try to assess predictability requirements at different points of time.

One Month in Advance

You want to be assured that you can get a certain service at a certain price in the future. You need this assurance to rationally select your service provider. In case of time-dependent pricing, both quality of service and price are predictable: You can get quite reliable information from the Web pages of service providers.

In a flat-rate case, the price is definitely predictable, but service level is not. You need some kind of understanding about the service offered by different providers. You may select the provider just based on price, but more likely you compare service levels of different providers by discussing with your friends or by reading articles about the issue. Still, you want to obtain reliable information that makes it possible to predict what you will really get.

A Few Days in Advance

You make a decision whether to reserve time for something probably one or a couple of days in advance. For instance, you decide to have an interactive meeting with voice and video over the Internet tomorrow.

In case of time-dependent pricing, you know the price, and you likely can be sure that you will get the service. Your decision could be quite straightforward: If you think that the meeting is useful enough compared to the price of the service, you and your colleague allocate time for it.

The flat-rate case seems to be more difficult, because you might not be as sure about the availability of quality. You have some experience, and suppose that things are going in the same way as earlier, and make the decision based on those experiences. The main cost of this decision is not directly money, but time. Wasted time could actually be very expensive, particularly when it means that several persons have allocated time for the meeting days in advance: It could be extremely irritating if five persons have managed to reserve two hours for a meeting and then it must be cancelled because of a technical reason.

Decision to Buy

In many cases, you make the decision to use a service, such as a telephone call, just before you try it. You want to know, at least approximately, how expensive a service is before you make a decision whether to use the service (or at least to test it). With time-dependent pricing the procedure is quite clear: Because you know both the quality and price, you have the ingredients for a rational decision.

In case of flat-rate pricing, this decision does not seem to be relevant because the actual use of the service is free of charge. The main issue probably is whether you make some kind of reservation for the use of the service. The reservation could be soft in the sense that you just have an idea that you want to discuss with your friend about the program of next weekend. Even in this case, an unsuccessful result would be annoying, although you are not spending any money for trying the service.

Decision to Continue

The final decision of whether to spend time with the service happens some time after you have started to use the service. The worst situation from your perspective is when the quality drops below acceptable in the middle of the service, so that you have spent your time (and possibly money) without a satisfactory result. Predictability is, again, needed for a reasonable decision.

With time-dependent pricing, your anticipation probably is that the quality is constant; so you can quit soon after the start, assess whether the quality is high enough for your purpose, and determine whether it corresponds to the price.

Then with flat-rate pricing, your expectations may be somewhat different. A natural model for service usage is that you test the service first, and then decide whether you want to use it. You may perhaps not need to be sure that the quality is always available, but you definitely want to avoid situations where the quality drops suddenly after a while.

4.3.3 Provisioning High Predictability

This section assesses the possible advantages of having guaranteed services with advanced admission-control mechanisms. Two possible answers are as follows:

- The availability of quality could be better during overload situations with guaranteed services. (This issue is discussed later in section 4.4.4, "Improving Statistical Multiplexing.")

- In certain cases, there is a need to keep the service quality of an individual connection more predictable than what it inherently is without any additional mechanism.

It seems that in the case of pricing of individual flows, it is right and fair that the existing flows get some level of priority over new requests. The primary argument for doing this is the advantage attained by the user of the service: Higher predictability of quality makes the service more useful and more attractive. The problem is that although this reasoning is valid with those applications that definitely require a certain minimum bandwidth, it seems to be questionable with the majority of data applications. Therefore, that kind of priority should not be applied to all flows in the Internet.

In cases where pricing is based on a flat rate for individual users, and where applications can be adjusted easily to a different load condition, it is not at all clear that existing connections deserve any priority over any new connection request. Think, for instance, of a situation in which you cannot get a connection to the Internet because your neighbor has a permanent high-bandwidth connection through the same access link. What could be a justification to give priority for that existing connection?

One interesting question is whether it is possible to provide high predictability in a Differentiated Services network without capacity reservation for individual flows. It seems difficult to do anything inside the network if the boundary node is not giving appropriate information. (Remember that flow states are not kept in core nodes, which makes it impossible to keep track of the duration of each flow.) Basically, this situation leaves two alternatives:

- New connections are accepted only if it is certain that there is enough capacity throughout the network and for the whole duration of the flow.

- Packets belonging to existing flows get higher preference than new flows—or more generally, the preference may depend on the time the flow has been active.

Although it could be possible to implement both approaches using the Differentiated Services system, it is not clear whether either of them is useful in practice.

4.4 Operation and Management

As discussed earlier, a prevalent view seems to be that an ideal QoS provision means that every flow is protected from all external effects in a way that the quality always satisfies the predefined requirements. The situation from one application viewpoint is 1 versus $n-1$, where n is the number of all active flows, and n could be millions. From an operator viewpoint, the situation is that of N times (1 versus $n-1$). That means that the network management can hardly be based on an approach where every individual flow is protected from the effect of every other flow. Something more systematic is needed, and this chapter tries to meet that target.

4.4.1   Predictability of Load and Destination

Let's start with an overview of network services. As stated in the beginning of this chapter, the differentiation may concern nature, form, or quality. What do these aspects mean in the case of Differentiated Services? This issue can be divided into three parts: issues related to destination, traffic, and quality.

The service may differ in the extent users are allowed to select the destination. At one extreme, widely adopted in Internet, the user can freely select and change the destination whenever he wants, and without extra charge. The other extreme is that the destination is always the same during a service contract—an example of this approach is a point-to-point, leased-line service. There is an apparent possibility for differentiation from the freedom to select the destination without considering anything particular to a strictly defined scope of destinations, and there are several levels between these approaches.

Although the freedom to select the destination is an important property, it is of minor concern if there is not enough transmission capacity available for the user's purpose. This capacity issue consists of two aspects: what the user is allowed to send into the network, and the quality level that the network can provide. Here is again a good opportunity for differentiation: Users may have significantly different needs concerning both the bit rate and other quality parameters. Consequently, better service can mean freedom to select and change the destination, bit rate, or quality. The counterpart of the freedom is that it makes the network operation and management more difficult.

Two of these aspects, destination and bit rate (or traffic load), are illustrated in Figure 4.4 (from the operator point of view). The main effect of both freedom to change destination and freedom to change bit rate is that the predictability of traffic load inside the networks becomes more difficult.

Predictability of traffic load sent into a network means essentially the accuracy of information about the load in a boundary node related to the future load situation. That is, 100% means that the bit rate is exactly known far into the future—a requisite that very seldom can be met in reality. The lowest predictability means that traffic load is totally unpredictable, something like self-similar traffic with high variability on all timescales. The middle level of predictability may correspond to a traffic process with relatively small traffic variations.

Figure 4.4   Predictability of traffic and destination.

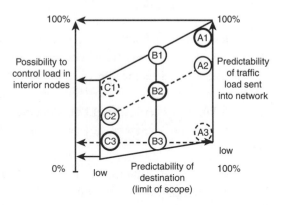

The high predictability could either be inherent due to the original traffic characteristics, or it could be attained by traffic-control actions in boundary nodes with proper mechanisms in interior nodes. It seems that in the Internet environment, high predictability can be attained only by traffic control.

Predictability of destination means how much information about the destination and route of the flow is available for traffic-control purposes. A figure of 100% means that the route to the destination is exactly known; a low predictability means that there is not much reliable information about the destinations. Although there are inherent differences in the extent of scope between end users, the network can "predict" the destination with high probability only if the number of permissible destinations is small.

4.4.2 Service Models

This section briefly outlines some possible service models, marked in Figure 4.4 from A1 to C3. In model A1, a CBR connection is established to a fixed destination for a long duration. This service model requires that the traffic sent to every destination be tightly controlled at the boundary node in a way that no excess traffic is allowed (that is, the service provider applies the guaranteed-service model described in "Implementation of Integrated Services" in Chapter 2). This kind of approach is possible if the bit-rate and destination changes are so rare that the capacity can be updated by the network-management system, or if the changes are more frequent, a signaling system is needed to inform all intermediate nodes about all changes.

The main difference between A2 and A1 is that there are traffic variations that cannot be informed effectively to the intermediate nodes, either because of quickness of the changes or limited capability to transfer load information through the network. An example could be a network with a full-meshed topology and with controlled load service. Because the service is based on predefined traffic parameters, there are some inherent limits of traffic load, and, consequently, the network can predict the traffic load to a certain extent, but not completely.

In the service model A3, the destination and path are fixed, but the user is allowed to send as much traffic as needed and to change the bit rate whenever he wants. Because the access rate always has an upper limit, the main difference between A3 and A2 is that the average load sent by users is much less than the maximum rate, but occasionally the user is using the whole capacity of the access link. This service could be something like best effort to a fixed destination; as concluded later in this chapter, however, this model does not seem to be feasible from the operator point of view.

The service models B1, B2, and B3 are basically the same as A1, A2, and A3, respectively, with the exception that the traffic destination is not totally fixed, but consists of a group of allowed destinations. Within this virtual network, it is possible to provide all kinds of services: guaranteed, controlled load, and best effort. It should be noted that if the destination of individual connections is fixed, the service belongs to A1, A2, or A3 in this methodology. Therefore, the middle group in the figure is not a synonym for virtual private network (VPN).

In service model B1, suppose that the traffic flow from a source is both constant and strictly policed, but that the destination may change within the virtual network. Although this approach may sound reasonable, the assumption that traffic is constant and strictly policed usually entails that the quality is highly assured. These requirements together with unknown destinations make network dimensioning quite difficult unless it is possible to keep the load level low. Even though B1 is not a reasonable model as the only service in the network, it might be used with some other services that can better exploit the network resources. Service model B2 can be somewhat better in this respect, and the remaining capacity can be left for best-effort service (B3).

In general, it seems that from the traffic-management viewpoint it is of minor significance whether the number of allowed destinations is 10 or 10 million. As a result, the previous consideration of B1, B2, and B3 are largely valid with models C1, C2, and C3 as well.

The fundamental problem to be solved—if the operator tries to maintain high utilization—is how the relevant information is transmitted to all nodes along the path. The accuracy of traffic prediction inside the network depends, therefore, significantly on the capability of the network to adapt to permanent or semi-permanent traffic changes, in addition to the traffic characteristics that makes it difficult to predict the traffic at the edge of the network. In the following pages, a mathematical model is used to evaluate this issue.

4.4.3 *A Model for Evaluating Statistical Multiplexing*

For those who prefer mathematical formulation, the preceding service model discussion is illustrated in the following pages by aid of a relatively simple mathematical model. It should be stressed, however, that the following model, although mathematical in form, is a simplified depiction of a convoluted phenomenon. Therefore, the model should be considered as a mathematical illustration of the service model presented in the preceding section rather than a strict mathematical reasoning. The evaluation is relatively long, but some of the conclusions are so fundamental that only a brief glance will be necessary for most readers. Moreover, numerous figures are used to make the reasoning comprehensible even without considering the mathematical formulae.

The main target of this investigation is to assess the effect of different service models on the efficiency of statistical multiplexing or, in other words, the attainable utilization level. It is always important to keep in mind that there are other, possibly more important targets in addition to efficiency, however, such as fairness, versatility, and robustness.

The Target of Modeling

Consider the network illustrated in Figure 4.5. Your task is to dimension the link from the central hub to one of the other nodes. What you know for certain is the load situation at the beginning of a dimensioning period (t=0). Based on this information, you estimate the capacity required at the end of the period (t=T) that provides sufficient QoS level.

Figure 4.5   A network model.

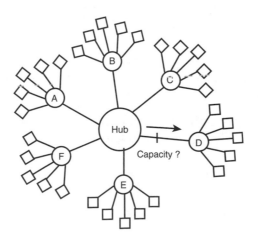

Basically, the length of the period (T) is the time needed to update the capacity. In case of a completely switched network with an efficient signaling system, the entity under dimensioning is the link capacity needed to support the connection. If it is not possible to alter the capacity reservation during the connection, the length of the period is a typical duration of a connection (for instance, some minutes). In a very efficient system where every change in required capacity of every connection is transmitted through the network, the length of the prediction period could be seconds. In the case of a virtual private network managed through an O&M center, the period could be some days (the maximum time needed to update link capacities). Finally, if the only way to manage network capacity is to increase physical capacity, the length of the period could be months rather than days, minutes, or seconds.

Nevertheless, the most significant issue concerning this simplified dimensioning model is how well it is possible to predict the load situation at the end of the period (t=T) provided that it is known at the beginning of the period (t=0). One of the principal questions is the meaning of load situation. Load level is relatively easy to define for an arbitrary instant of time: The load could be said to be the average bit rate over a period that is needed to empty a full buffer. The reasoning behind this definition is that the buffer can filter variations that occur at shorter timescales, whereas there is no guarantee that the buffer can filter longer variations. Therefore, this example attempts to predict the bit-rate distribution in a timescale of milliseconds or tens of milliseconds.

Estimation of the Load Situation at the Beginning

You are probably wondering how to know the load situation at the beginning of the period. The fundamental problem here is that mathematical models usually require that all parameters are somehow known in advance. You can use as a basic assumption that the load at the beginning is the momentary load at a certain point of time. This is a somewhat pessimistic assumption, because a longer measurement can provide more information about the actual load situation.

To keep the calculations tractable, you can further suppose that all connections are similar on/off sources. In that case, the load situation at the beginning of the period can be presented by two parameters: the total load, $M(0)$; and the capacity used by one flow, B (kbps). Respectively, the load situation at the end of a period can be described by a conditional probability distribution $Pr(M(T)=x|M(0))$. If you can attain a reasonable estimate for this probability distribution, you can decide how much extra capacity is required.

Dimensioning Principle

To avoid the tedious calculations of complex probability distributions, you can suppose that the needed capacity (C) depends only on the average (M) and variance (V) of the distribution, as shown in Formula 4.1.

Formula 4.1

$$C = M + g*V^{0.5}$$

The principle of Formula 4.1 is illustrated in Figure 4.6. Although this issue is discussed more thoroughly in section 5.4.3, "Network Dimensioning," in Chapter 5, "Differentiation of Customer Service," some basic explanations are worthwhile here. First, basically any probability distribution with two or more free parameters can be fitted to given mean and variance, and there is no way to determine what is exactly the right distribution in this case or for the intended purposes.

Figure 4.6   Dimensioning rule based on mean (M) and variance (V) of a prediction distribution.

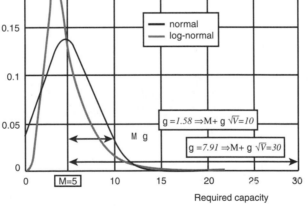

A normal distribution is a natural starting point, supposing that the distribution is formed as a sum of a large number of independent random variables. Formula 4.1 has a very clear interpretation in case of normal distribution: For any given factor g, there is a corresponding probability that the required bit rate exceeds the capacity C. If the capacity is sufficient with probability of 99.9%, for example, you select g = 3.09 regardless of the mean and variance of the distribution.

You may be inclined to suppose that this is exactly the situation in this case: There are usually a large number of more or less independent flows. Unfortunately, this is only a small part of a complicated issue. A significant part of the inaccuracy (that is, the variance of the distribution) does not stem from the variations in individual flows but from the general uncertainty concerning load levels, traffic processes, and so on. You have no specific reason to suppose that this kind of uncertainty can be modeled by normal distribution in particular when the deviation of the distribution is large compared with the mean value. In that case, log-normal distribution (shown also in Figure 4.6) could be a more realistic choice. In some cases, the results provided by normal and log-normal, or some other distribution, differ remarkably although you keep mean, variance, and exceeding probability the same. In summary, you can apply Formula 4.1; but be aware of its limitations.

Estimation of Variance at the End of the Period

If you suppose that there is no systematic change in load situation during the prediction period, the expected load $M(T)$ at the end of the period is equal to the measured load at the beginning of the period—that is, $M(T) = M(0)$.

The primary question now concerns the variance of the distribution. The variance depends crucially on the probability that a connection is active at the end of the period on the condition that it was active at the beginning of the period. If the period is longer than the average duration of an activity period, this probability is approximately the same as the probability of activity of a customer, denoted by a. (Note that this straightforward reasoning is valid only in a homogeneous case.)

Based on this probability, you can make a rough estimation, as shown in Formula 4.2. If you knew the exact value of a, the size of population N (the number of customers in all other nodes), and the bit rate needed by an active connection, B, the variance of the distribution can be calculated from a binomial distribution.

Formula 4.2

$$V = (1-a)*\ a*N*B^2$$

It should be stressed that all the parameters, N, a, and B, are theoretical measures that can be known only in practical situations and, moreover, Formula 4.2 is based on a fictive case that is much more homogeneous than what could be expected in reality. Because of these reasons, a realistic variance is likely to be larger than what Formula 4.2 gives. In the following evaluation, an extra factor of e is used to take this into account (where e is usually larger than 1).

If you further take into account that $M(0)$ can be used as an estimate for the product a*N*B, you obtain the estimation for the variance of load distribution, as shown in Formula 4.3, at the end of the period on the condition that the load were $M(0)$ at the beginning of the period.

Formula 4.3

```
V(M(T)¦M(0)) = e*M(0)*(1-a)*B
```

It should be stressed that Formula 4.3 is a rough estimation for the inaccuracy of the traffic prediction, and it should not be considered as an exact method to calculate the variance of any concrete distribution. In practical cases, several factors can either deteriorate or improve the accuracy of the prediction. In particular, parameters a and B are usually unknown and not the same for all users.

Effect of Destinations Changes

From the viewpoint of one link, it is not important whether the reason for the certain value of a is that an active user becomes idle or whether the user remains active but changes the destination in a way that the connection changes to another link. Consequently, the final value of a, from the perspective of the link between the hub and node D, depends both on the activity of the customer at the boundary node (a_b) and on the perseverance of destination (a_d). It should be noted that parameter a_b may cover both traffic variations during a connection (whenever the term is applicable), and variations due to the beginnings and endings of connections.

Figure 4.7 illustrates the situation. Parameter a_b = 1—that is, the bite rate at the boundary node is constant—and a_d = 1/3—that is, traffic is evenly distributed among nodes B, C, and D. Now from the viewpoint of the last link to node D, it is insignificant how a customer attached to node A uses the idle periods that occur on the link to D: she may be either totally idle or she may always send traffic to another node. This separation of a_b and a_d is necessary because there is an essential difference between these two factors at the boundary node, although from the inner link viewpoint they are usually not distinguishable.

Figure 4.7   Traffic from node A and to three nodes B, C, and D.

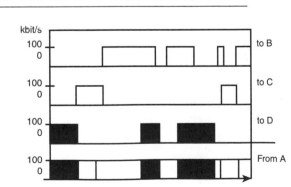

In the estimation of variance (see Formula 4.3), it was required that the connection be both active at the end of the period and remain on the same link as at the beginning of the period. If these two occurrences are independent, you obtain a simple estimation for a, as shown in Formula 4.4.

Formula 4.4

$$a = a_b * a_d$$

Finally, if you combine Formulas 4.1, 4.3, and 4.4, you obtain an estimation for the needed capacity at the end of the period, as shown in Formula 4.5.

Formula 4.5

$$C(T)|M(0) = M(0) + g*[e*(1-a_b*a_d)*B*M(0)]^{0.5}$$
$$= M(0)*\{1 + g*[e*(1-a_b*a_d)*B/M(0)]^{0.5}\}$$

Although this example has made a lot of simplifying assumptions, you may be able to draw some preliminary conclusions:

- It is possible to attain high load level only if both destination and traffic variations are under tight control. That is, no extra capacity is necessary if and only if $a_b = a_d = 1$ (expect, if you are a clairvoyant, with $e < 1$). Although this is an apparent conclusion, and it is somehow an attractive idea to apply it in reality, notice that these requirements can hardly be achieved without significantly reducing the attractiveness of the service.

- The most crucial issue in Formula 4.5 is the B to M(0) ratio—that is, what is the share of one individual connection of the total traffic load? If this ratio is large, efficient statistical multiplexing is not possible. (This is a commonly known phenomenon of statistical multiplexing.)

- If a_b is small, it is practically useless to control the destination of the connections—that is, to increase a_d!

- Respectively, if the destination is not controlled at the boundary node, and destinations vary significantly, it may seem that there is no benefit to controlling the amount of traffic variations (burstiness)—that is, a_b.

The last conclusion is somewhat misleading, however, because a change of a_b evidently affects the momentary capacity needed by a flow (B). Actually if you keep N and M(0) fixed, it is possible to present Formula 4.5 in a somewhat different form, as shown in Formula 4.6.

Formula 4.6

$$C(T)|M(0) = M(0)*\{1 + g*[e*(1- a_b*a_d)/(a_b*N)]^{0.5}\}$$

Now even if a_d is 0, a decrease of a_b may have a significant positive effect on the allowed load level.

4.4.4 Improving Statistical Multiplexing

The target of this chapter is to evaluate how an operator can improve network utilization by traffic-management actions. The available possibilities are traffic shaping, limitation of destinations, improved knowledge about traffic processes, resource reservation, and quality differentiation. The evaluation is based on Formula 4.6.

Definition of Starting Point

The usual starting point of modeling is to fix the necessary parameters—that is, a_b, a_d, N, and B in this case. Now take a somewhat different approach and suppose that you have the following knowledge:

- Current load: M(0) = 5Mbps

- The number of users in a node: N = 500

- Based on practical experience, the average load level should be below 20% of the link capacity to allow sufficient quality when there is no limitation of destination or traffic burstiness, and when some of the flows need high quality.

Formula 4.6 has basically four free parameters: a_b, a_d, e, and g. Because only the production of $e*g^2$ is significant (not the individual values of e and g), however, you can give e a reasonable value (for instance 2). Then you can choice parameter a_d according to the general insight about the probability that the destination remains the same over a relatively long period even though there is no actual restrictions to change it. A guess of 0.25 could be sensible for this parameter. (On the one hand, it is probably not near 1; on the other hand, however, every user probably uses a couple of destinations much more frequently than all other destinations.)

As to the two other parameters, the third assumption of a 20% load level means that either a_b should be smaller or g should be larger than one would primarily expect. As a reasonable compromise, you can suppose that a_b is 0.005 and g is 4.48. This starting situation could be valid with the best-effort service model with few or no restrictions concerning the traffic pattern at the edge of the network or the destination of packets.

If you are dissatisfied with the load level of your network, you basically have five possibilities to improve the situation:

1. *Limit variations in the traffic process at the edge of the network.* For instance, limit the peak bit rate of every user. In mathematical terms, you can increase a_b while keeping M(0), a_d, and N constant.

2. *Limit the transitions from link to link during the prediction period.* Mathematically this means that you increase the value of a_d.

3. *Keep the traffic as such intact, but improve the traffic prediction.* Acquire a more advanced management system that provides better knowledge of traffic processes. Mathematically this means decreasing factor e.

4. *Shorten the prediction period.* This may have an effect on parameters a_b, a_d, and e and by that means improve network efficiency.

5. *Decrease factor g.* You must be aware that the service quality may deteriorate.

As to the context of Differentiated Services, items 1 and 2 seem to be promising because they do not require any changes in the core network. Item 3 is possible as well, but it can only have quite a limited effect if nothing else is done. Item 4 is somehow a natural way to improve the network efficiency, and is widely used (for instance, in ATM networks). It seems that to be really effective, however, you need a resource reservation for every individual flow, which makes this approach expensive to implement. Finally, although item 5 is not necessarily a good idea as such, it can be applied if the total traffic can be divided into several classes with different quality requirements.

Next you can check which kind of improvements are attainable by any of the preceding items in the case of the numeric example. The figures given previously try to illustrate the reasonable limits of every approach.

Traffic Shaping

If you apply Formula 4.6, a moderate change of a_b from 0.005 to 0.01 improves the load figure to 0.26, whereas a considerable change to 0.05 improves the load figure from 0.20 to 0.44. It should be noted that in the latter case, the length of every on-period is 10 times longer than in the original case, which causes a corresponding increase of delay. Figure 4.8 illustrates this phenomenon.

The acceptability of increased delay depends crucially on the original length of on-period and on the application. With a typical data application, it could be acceptable to decrease the traffic burstiness at the expense of additional delay—for instance, if the effect is that you get a Web page in 3 seconds rather than 2 seconds. On average, however, a higher change than that from 0.005 to 0.05 is likely to result in serious deterioration to quality of service.

Figure 4.8   The effect of traffic shaping.

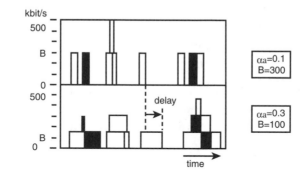

Destination Limitation

A change of a_d from 0.25 to 1 improves the original load level by a tiny amount of 0.15%. What actually happens, however, if a_d is increased to 1, but everything else is kept constant? As regards the mathematical model, that means that the traffic process at the ingress node is kept intact, but the destination of packets coming from one customer is always the same. You keep the average load on every link and the average number of customers per link unchanged. (This is an apparently somewhat theoretical assumption.)

According to the model, if all other facts remain the same but customers are not allowed to change their destinations, the possible increase of load level seems to be negligible. Only if something else is done as well, would it be worth limiting the destinations. You can, for instance, check the effect of a_d when a_b is already increased to 0.05. The result is that allowed load level can be increased by 1% if a_d is changed from 0.25 to 1—not a remarkable achievement.

The overall benefits are quite small compared to the disadvantages of having strong limits for packet destinations. Under normal statistical assumptions (in particular, destination changes are statistically independent of each other), and with typical Internet traffic, limiting the destinations does not seem to be a practical approach. There can always be other reasons to limit the destination of packets belonging to a certain customer, such as security, but those issues are beyond the scope of this evaluation.

If you make a more realistic assumption in which restricting the possibility of destinations decreases the load, you get even worse results. In the worst case—namely, when the load decreases by the same factor as a_d increases—the allowed load decreases down to 11% because of the impaired statistical multiplexing.

As you can see, this is a complicated issue. If the only service model is a pure constant bit rate without any variability in the load generated by any source, destinations definitely are of real importance. If there are exactly 50 CBR connections in the ingress node and the destination is selected randomly from two possibilities ($a_d = 0.5$), for example, Formula 4.6 gives an allowed load of 0.61. Moreover, even if the destination is selected from a huge amount of different possibilities, the allowed load is as high as 0.52. Therefore, it seems that the destination should be limited totally, if you are pursuing high utilization only, or not at all, if you prefer a more attractive service model with freedom to select destinations.

Therefore, in the case of CBR traffic, it is useful to strictly limit the destinations to attain higher utilization. This inference could be valid in general only if two conditions are true at the same time: (1) CBR traffic forms the majority of the traffic, and (2) destination limits do not essentially deteriorate the attractiveness of the service. It seems quite improbable, however, that both conditions can be fulfilled on the Internet.

Knowledge Improvement

A change of e from 2 to 1 improves the load figure from 0.20 to 0.33. In the case of the Internet, however, it is likely that factor e can be decreased by 50% only with very laborious effort (if ever) because of the intrinsic unpredictability of Internet traffic. The main difficulty of traffic prediction is related to two inherent control loops:

- The bit-rate regulation of TCP/IP is based on the number of lost packets—that is, on the load level inside the network.

- The decisions made by end users depend on the perceived quality. For instance, the time needed to download a figure through the Internet may have a significant effect on the number of figures to be downloaded later.

These issues together make it extremely difficult to evaluate Internet traffic with any mathematical model. Therefore, the possibility to essentially improve the accuracy of traffic prediction may require a huge effort, including modeling of human behavior. See, for instance, "Where Mathematics Meets the Internet," which discusses the difficulties of understanding Internet traffic (Paxson and Willinger 1998).

Resource Reservation

It is important to consider this approach more thoroughly, because it seems that we very easily return to this model even though it is somewhat opposite to the basic philosophy of Differentiated Services.

If a resource reservation system is applied to every individual flow, you can fix the destination—that is, increase a_d up to 1 and decrease e down to 1, and perhaps increase a_b from 0.005 to 0.5. This means that a customer is supposed to be totally idle 99% of the time and during the 1% of the time he has a connection to a certain destination, and the connection is active 50% of the time. But then there are only five active connections at the beginning of the period, and five is so small a number that there is no room for any realistic statistical multiplexing, and therefore, the average load cannot be higher than a_d (0.50).

That is a notable improvement compared to the original value of 0.20. There is, however, a big concern related to this seemingly good result. Although this "packet-layer" utilization can be high, this approach introduces an additional "connection layer." If there is no change in the actual traffic process, an additional control layer may deteriorate the whole situation rather than improve it.

The basic reason is that you cannot expect that exactly five users are needing a connection at all times. The traditional way to evaluate this situation is to apply the Erlang blocking formula discussed in section 5.4.3, "Network Dimensioning," in Chapter 5. Basically, the Erlang formula gives the probability that a call attempt will fail due to lack of resources. If the Erlang blocking formula and the 0.1% call-blocking standard is applied, you must reserve room for 14 contemporary connections. The final result is an average load of 0.18. Moreover, this is the result even though you supposed that the average load (five connections) was exactly known.

In short, if and when there is intrinsic uncertainty in the future traffic demand, an additional control layer cannot solve the network-dimensioning problem. In addition, because a service model with a predefined bit rate and destination could be less attractive, the outcome is not very promising from an efficiency point of view. Yet, there certainly are some clear benefits, such as more advanced pricing and the fact that resource reservation favors existing connections over new connection requests. (This issue is discussed in section 4.3.2, "Pricing Models and Predictability of Quality," earlier in this chapter.)

As to the pricing, although it is promising way to smooth traffic (that is, to increase a_h), it can be argued that you can use a similar tariff structure without any reservations inside the network. If the favoring of existing flows is an important service characteristic, and the probability of a conflict is not very small, resource reservation could be a reasonable solution. On the contrary, if the probability of a conflict is negligible, the actual result apparently is similar both with and without reservations. The following example, "CBR Service Versus DiffServ," illustrates the situation.

CBR Service Versus DiffServ

Assume that the fictional service provider Fairprofit wants to offer guaranteed services based on constant bit-rate connections, mainly for real-time applications. Fairprofit defines the customer services in a way that users are not allowed to exceed a bit-rate limit even occasionally. The service provider assumes that this service is used only by applications that really need high quality.

Under these assumptions, customers always have to select the bit rate in advance, although it is possible that they do not exactly know the necessary bit rate. Therefore, customers usually need to reserve more capacity than what they need on average. From the customer viewpoint, there seems to be two practical solutions:

- The user reserves extra capacity in addition to the best prediction of the required mean bit rate.

- The user starts with a bit-rate level somewhat less than what he expects to be necessary, and then increases the reserved bit rate until the quality is sufficient. The need and meaning of a guarantee for the user in this case is that when a sufficient level is reached, it remains sufficient for a relatively long period.

In both cases, the reserved capacity is more than the average bit rate. You can apply Formula 4.1 to approximate the relationship between required capacity (C), mean bit rate (M), and variance of the bit-rate distribution (V). Assume the following numeric values for an individual user:

$M = 100\text{kbps}$

$V = (10\text{kbps})^2$

$g = 4$

As a result, the bit-rate reservation for one flow is 140kbps, and according to normal distribution the probability that 140kbps is not sufficient is approximately $3*10^{-5}$. If the total capacity available for this service class is 10Mbps, there can be altogether 71 connections at the same time, if you suppose that Fairprofit offers a true CBR service without statistical multiplexing on the packet level.

From customer viewpoint, the availability of quality is defined by the probability that the connection request is accepted. That probability can be estimated by the Erlang blocking formula as a function of average load level. Figure 4.9 shows the result. Note that an average load level of 7.1Mbps means that the offered load on the connection level is almost 100%.

The service provider may determine the allowed load level based on this curve, and on the target value for availability of quality. For instance, availability of 99.9% is achieved by an average load level of 5Mbps. (The corresponding average reserved capacity is 7Mbps.)

This could be acceptable for Fairprofit, provided the total cost of the system is not too high. However, the CBR service with reservations for every connection is somewhat hard to implement and manage. Therefore, Fairprofit may be interested in other options as well. The other alternative provided by Differentiated Services is that Fairprofit keeps the service model exactly the same (in particular, user are paying for a virtual reservation the same tariff as for a real reservation), but accepts all connections and even all packets into the network.

What then is the availability of quality as a function of load level? You can start with the fact that bit-rate variations occur because of two basic reasons: connection-level variations, and packet-level variations of individual connections. You can assume that enough quality is available for a connection if (and only if) the momentary load level both at the beginning and at the end of the connection is low enough to make certain that quality is sufficient.

You can estimate the sufficiency by a simple algorithm: If $\{M + 4*V^{0.5} < 10\text{Mbps}\}$, then there is enough capacity; otherwise the quality is supposed to be unavailable for all connections. The result of this model is also shown in Figure 4.9. Although this model is a rough evaluation of a complicated issue, it may allow some practical conclusions.

From the service provider viewpoint, there are four load regions:

- *Region A*: In region A (from 0 to 4.4Mbps in the example), both systems provide excellent performance—that is, higher availability than 99.99%.

- *Region B*: In region B, the performance of the reservation system is deteriorated because some connection requests are discarded, whereas the sharing system still offers excellent performance.

- *Region C*: In region C, both systems yield deteriorated performance, but the sharing system still provides better performance than the reservation system.

- *Region D*: In region D, the reservation system works better because it can provide good service for some of the connections; equal sharing, on the other hand, leads (at least in theory) to a situation where no one can obtain sufficient quality.

Fairprofit may conclude that the reservation system is not the optimal one, if the network-management system can somehow limit the possibility of an overload situation.

Moreover, Fairprofit can improve the overall performance of both systems. The reservation system can be enhanced by applying statistical multiplexing by applying controlled load service rather than guaranteed service (or VBR rather than CBR in ATM networks). Capacity sharing can be improved by priorities that can guarantee high quality for some flows even during overload situation—that is, by Differentiated Services.

Figure 4.9   Availability of quality with and without reservations.

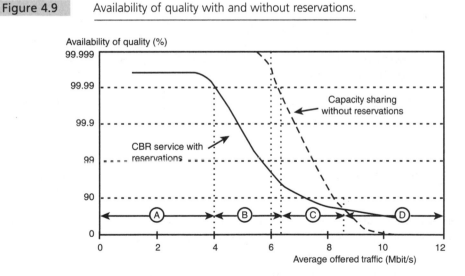

Quality Differentiation

Suppose, for example, that 20% of the traffic really needs high quality, and 80% can cope with a moderate quality. If you have a tool to protect high-quality traffic from the harmful effects of low-quality traffic, you can significantly increase the load level.

Suppose further that high-quality traffic requires a safety factor of 8. (As high a value as 8 could be required mainly because you cannot be sure that normal distribution is valid in real cases.) Therefore, higher-quality traffic can attain a load level of 0.077, if the other traffic parameters are kept the same, except that a_b is changed to 0.001. Consequently, the total load could be 5*0.077 = 0.385. This is quite a conservative evaluation, because high-quality connections are usually controlled more tightly than typical Internet traffic, which makes it possible to reduce the prediction variance.

If you suppose that the other part of the service is pure best effort, you can suppose that TCP or some other protocol adjusts the bit rates if necessary. Thus a quite low safety factor could be acceptable (for instance, 1.5). According to Formula 4.6, the total load could be approximately 0.42. Because the first limit is tighter, the total load could be enhanced from 0.20 to 0.385 purely because of the service differentiation. Note, however, that this improvement is possible only at the expense of decreased quality of service for some customers.

4.4.5 Conclusions About Statistical Multiplexing

From an efficiency point of view, the following conclusions are reasonable:

- Traffic shaping is recommendable when it is feasible, taking into account the possible reduction of service attractiveness.

- The real benefit of destination limitation is unclear, but it seems to be usually small.

- Improvement knowledge about traffic processes should always be used when there is a reasonable possibility without too high a cost.

- Resource reservation does not usually improve the network utilization; the benefits are elsewhere, such as in the better predictability of quality.

- Traffic classification surely provides promising results.

The concrete objectives for Differentiated Services based on this mathematical evaluation are as follows:

- Network service should encourage traffic shaping made either by the applications in customer equipment or by the network operator at the network edges. Encouragement means that the customer benefits from smoother traffic either by obtaining lower price, lower packet-loss ratio, higher throughput, or shorter transmission delay.

- Service differentiation is the key tool to improve cost efficiency.

4.5   *Traffic Handling*

Although network utilization is an important target when designing a network, it is definitely not the only one. This section discusses some other goals that are not directly related to network utilization, but are still important for the overall usability of the network service.

The two main aspects of traffic handling are *urgency* and *importance*. These terms may need some clarification, because a lot of similar terms are used in the literature. All combinations of urgency and importance are possible: A packet can be urgent and important, urgent but not important, important but not urgent, or not urgent and not important. In practice, high urgency means that a packet should be delivered as quickly as possible—in other words, with as small delay as possible. Thus urgency is a characteristic needed by a packet, and delay is a characteristic of packet handling.

The term *importance* is used here rather than the more technical terms *drop precedence* or *drop preference* because of two reasons:

- Drop precedence is somewhat troublesome to use because higher drop precedence means lower service class (or lower priority if you prefer that term).

- Importance is a more general term. Although importance of a packet and drop precedence can often be used as synonyms, drop precedence is not necessarily the only way to implement importance differences between packets.

In addition to these aspects, packet handling may take into account some other issues, such as bandwidth division, routing, and support for adaptive applications. The main issue from the Differentiated Services viewpoint is whether any of these issues requires special packet handling in interior nodes, or has any significant effect on the implementation of a Differentiated Services network.

> **Note**
>
> In this book, importance level refers to information about the relative importance of a packet to be used for traffic management.

4.5.1   *Urgency*

From an application point of view, two main requirements for network service are that available bit rate is high enough and that packet-loss ratio is low enough. For some applications, however, these are not sufficient requirements because the packets should be delivered within a certain period of time; otherwise, the packet is not more useful than a totally lost packet. This requirement can be called *urgency*. It seems that with the current level of network performance, a special urgency service is needed only for interactive applications, such as IP telephony or videoconferencing.

The rate at which an IP telephone generates packets is usually constant. These packets are played back at the same constant rate to make the audio signal comprehensible. Basically, there are two ways to realize this: (1) to design the network service in a way that the delay through the network is strictly constant; and (2) to use a buffer in the receiving equipment in a way that the packets can be used at the same rate as they were generated. A telephone network is based on the first option, but packet networks are usually based on the second option.

Even if you take into account the effect of playback buffers, however, there is a clear need to control delays inside the network. Although the unavoidable delay components (packetization and transmission delays) are out of the network's control, queuing delay is the controllable part. Because the basic unit for delay analysis is one buffer, it is possible to make a rough estimation for the availability of quality in one buffer. The result could be something like presented in Figure 4.9 by the S-shaped curve. For instance, a delay criterion of 10 milliseconds may theoretically yield availability of 99.993%.

With a relatively high probability (for instance, 70%), the queue is empty or almost empty and the packets do not encounter any significant queuing delay or delay variation (region A). In the middle region (B), the queuing delay increases, and a high availability can be reached if the quality requirement is increased and traffic load is under control. Finally, with certain probability, the instantaneous load level becomes too high in a way that even a very large buffer cannot prevent packet losses (region C).

This type of curve can be obtained in one buffer and controlled circumstances in which the load levels are relatively stable. The reality is again much more complex. In particular, if all flows share the same service (best-effort service in the current Internet), a majority of the traffic is likely using TCP. One straight consequence is that delay variation is usually high. Figure 4.10 presents two likely scenarios: one with a high load level and another with low load level. Although the picture does not represent any real measured situation, it seems unlikely that any tight delay requirement can be obtained with one service class unless the average load level is very low.

Figure 4.10 Availability of quality with delay criterion.

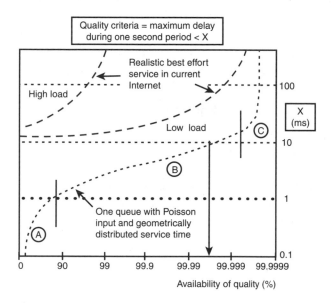

Quality criteria = maximum delay
during one second period < X

Realistic best effort
service in current
Internet

High load

Low load

X
(ms)

100

C

10

B

1

One queue with Poisson
input and geometrically
distributed service time

A

0.1

0   90   99   99.9   99.99   99.999   99.9999

Availability of quality (%)

4.5.2 *Importance*

It is crucial to attain some level of consensus about the importance; otherwise, the result could be as in *Alice's Adventures in Wonderland*:

> "Unimportant, of course, I meant," the King hastily said, and went on to himself in an undertone, "important—unimportant—unimportant—important—" as if he were trying which word sounded best. Some of the jury wrote it down "important," and some "unimportant" (Carroll [1865] 1970).

If some nodes assess the packets of one aggregate as important and other nodes as unimportant, the final result is a total mess. But why do the nodes, after all, need to know the importance of every packet? To make, when necessary, a reasonable decision as to which packets can and should be discarded if all packets cannot be forwarded.

Several aspects of importance have been discussed in this chapter, such as the differences in availability of quality can be considered as the main target of marking packets less and more important. Now the key issue is whether there is truly several kinds of importance, in a way that the interior nodes have to be aware not only of the level of importance but also of the type of importance.

An issue is the need to mark some packets belonging to a flow as more important than some other packets of the same flow. This aspect of importance could perhaps be essentially different from other importance aspects. Should the interior node make a different decision if the packet is marked important by the customer or by the boundary node? It seems apparent that sometimes this is the case. This is a somewhat misleading viewpoint, however. The right question is, is there a reason why the boundary node cannot map the user desire in the same importance scale as all other relevant issues? From that perspective, it is much harder to identify any need to have two independent importance scales.

Important Versus Less Important

The system promoted in this book is based on the assumption that it is better to map all kinds of importance issues into the same general structure, if possible. In particular, interior nodes should see only one importance dimension, and the boundary nodes should map different importance aspects to that one-dimensional scale. This is done mainly to guarantee a consistent and simple decision-making system inside the network. It may be argued, however, that this is a favorable system also from an individual flow viewpoint, as illustrated in Figure 4.11.

Figure 4.11   Selection of packets to be discarded.

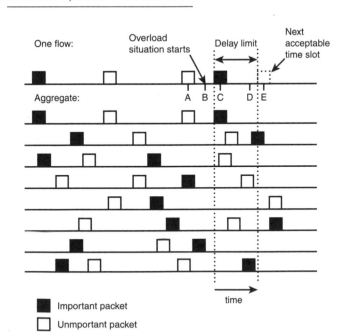

Assume, for the sake of argument, that an individual flow consists of two types of packets: important and less important. The network node encounters a situation where it needs to limit the rate of the flow, because of an overload situation (instant B in Figure 4.11). The preceding packet of the flow has been accepted at instant A because there was no overload situation at that time.

The problem when the node makes the decision individually for every flow is that there are usually not available several packets from which the node can select the least important packet to be discarded. In Figure 4.11, there is only one packet within the time limit when the discarding decision is made. An important packet could perhaps be delayed for some time, but if the next acceptable time slot for the packet is not within the delay limit, the packet has to be discarded. It is easy to say that less important packets are discarded, but in reality there could be only one packet available during the time on which the decision is made. In that case, there is no other possibility than to discard that packet regardless of the importance.

If the discarding decision is made for an aggregate stream, the possibility to make a reasonable decision is much better because there are probably both important and less important packets. As a result, important packets do not need to be discarded. In general, the more packets available, the better the possibility to make a reasonable discarding decision. This is one more reason to avoid unnecessary bandwidth fragmentation.

Urgency Versus Importance

The main question here is whether importance and urgency (or delay requirement) are essentially different things—that is, whether an important packet is always an urgent one, and whether a less important packet is always a less urgent one. As discussed previously, interactive applications create the need for real-time service in IP networks; most of the other applications can cope with the delay characteristics of the current best-effort service.

Therefore, the explicit need is for a network service that provides low delay but relatively high packet-loss ratio. If one of the main targets of importance differences is availability differences, as this book has supposed, then that kind of service could be as reasonable as a service with low delay and low loss ratio. A service with low delay and low importance could be exactly what is needed to provide inexpensive but applicable global IP telephony service. In summary, it is necessary to clearly distinguish *importance* and *urgency* in such a way that operators can freely combine different levels of importance and urgency.

> **Note**
>
> In this book, importance level refers to information about the relative importance of a packet to be used for traffic management.

4.5.3 Bandwidth Division (Virtual Private Networks)

A virtual private network (VPN) is something that a large customer or enterprise wants to use for his own purposes. The enterprise typically has multiple locations and wants to interconnect them using an IP backbone network. The VPN is defined by the collection of the locations and traffic-management rules within that VPN.

VPNs can be roughly classified into three categories, as shown in Figure 4.12. In category A, each VPN has its own dedicated resources (bandwidth and buffer space) on every link in the network. On the one hand, the bandwidth is reserved for it all the time regardless of the actual use of the capacity; on the other hand, the flows belonging to the VPN are not allowed to use any spare capacity reserved for other traffic streams in the network. In a way, this scheme is fair and comprehensible, because the customers get exactly what they have paid for. If there are large numbers of parallel VPNs, however, this approach could be very inefficient because the capacity fragmentation may seriously deteriorate the positive effects of statistical multiplexing.

Figure 4.12 VPN categories.

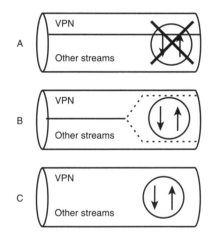

Approach B allows limited statistical multiplexing between different VPNs. The rules of capacity sharing are an essential part of the service contract. It is possible, for instance, to define that a VPN always gets a certain minimum bandwidth on each link regardless of all other traffic streams; and that it can use any free capacity on the link (perhaps up to a certain limit); and that, correspondingly, other streams can use resources unused by the VPN. These rules may also take into account the importance levels of the packets, provided that the service provider has some level of control of the importance marking of the packets.

This kind of system could be more complicated to manage than approach A, and it may induce some fairness problems, if the load levels of different VPNs vary considerably. Nevertheless, the statistical gains are so significant that they presumably exceed the drawbacks.

Approach C is an extreme case of the preceding approach with very flexible statistical multiplexing between VPNs inside the network. Although this approach may look, at first glance, inappropriate, it could be feasible if the packet marking were done carefully in the boundary nodes. It should be noted, in particular, that the packets with highest importance should be discarded with minimal probability. From a packet point of view, it is totally irrelevant whether the reason for successful transmission through the network is capacity reservation or marking to a high importance PHB. If the network is properly dimensioned and the number of high importance packets is kept relatively low, the overall result could be both appropriate from the customer point of view and efficient from the management point of view.

One fundamental matter should still be stressed: Even though the traffic of one VPN can be under strict control in the first link, the control cannot be strict inside the network without a very dynamic provision system (that is, signaling and per-flow reservations). In Figure 4.13, for instance, even though the traffic entering the network in nodes 1, 2, and 3 is within the defined limits, there is a realistic possibility to exceed the VPN capacity in the link between nodes 8 and 9 if all the traffic from 1, 2, and 3 is directed to node 9.

Figure 4.13   A VPN network with a possible conflict.

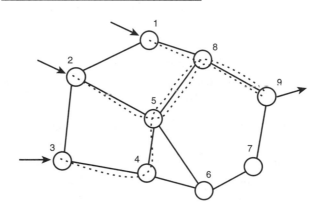

Four ways to avoid excessive packet loss can be identified:

- *Limit the traffic between every pair of nodes.* The extreme case is a full mesh of constant bit-rate channels between all nodes.

- *Limit the total traffic leaving each node low enough to guarantee that there is no packet losses inside the network.* In an extreme approach, the maximum traffic is the lowest capacity divided by $(n-1)$, where is n is number of nodes.

- *Use adaptive routing and direct some of the traffic through nodes 6 and 7.* This approach is discussed briefly in the next chapter.

- *Use either VPN types B or C, as presented in Figure 4.12.*

Even though the last approach seems to lack the guarantee provided by the three other approaches, the significantly better efficiency makes it a much more attractive solution. But then, once again, you need a systematic differentiation and control of packets and flows to attain an appropriate result that is fair, robust, and versatile.

4.5.4   Routing

As mentioned in the preceding chapter, routing is one tool to alleviate congestion situations. Nevertheless, routing is not discussed extensively in this book because of three reasons. First, the standardization of Differentiated Services mainly concerns packet forwarding, not routing. Second, adaptive routing can only have a limited effect on the overall utilization: It is not necessary in lightly loaded networks, and the effect could be even harmful if the network is highly congested and the routing mechanism is not designed carefully. On the contrary, in the middle region of a moderately loaded network, adaptive routing could be useful.

And finally, in case of a complex PHB structure, the rerouting system must be aware of the relationships among different PHBs. Two PHBs belonging to the same PHB class, for example, should not use different routes. (PHB class is used in the meaning explained in the section titled "Terminology" in Chapter 3, "Differentiated Services Working Group.") In summary, adaptive routing that takes into account PHB information cannot be the main tool for controlling network traffic or for quality provisioning.

Another issue to consider is that when the network-management system composes the routing table, it can take into account the average load level of different PHBs with different weights. The network operator may decide to maximize the availability of service for the most important PHBs, and then perhaps take into account the expected load levels of some moderately important PHBs with smaller weight, while totally ignoring the lowest level PHBs.

Finally, there are some special cases in which the route may depend on the PHB of the packet, such as satellite links. PHBs with good real-time characteristics should use satellite links with long transmission delay only if there is not other alternative with better delay characteristics. Also, if a link occasionally has a high bit-error ratio, it can be used for PHBs without high-quality expectations. Although these are possible scenarios, they have no significant effect on the requirements of the PHB architecture.

4.5.5 *Support for Adaptive Applications*

As already emphasized several times, all systems relying on signaling are mostly beyond the scope of the Differentiated Services standardization and this book. This choice means that it is usually impossible to make any admission control for individual flows, let alone to inform interior nodes about changes in traffic parameters of individual flows. Another approach, in a sense reverse, is that the network informs senders about the available capacity inside the network.

There are two different aspects related to this congestion-notification approach. The first aspect is the need to have a mechanism to inform network nodes that the flow is willing to adjust its bit rates during a congestion situation, and to inform about the actual congestion situation. The current view seems to be that the 6-bit field currently under standardization process is not used for these purposes.

The second aspect is more interesting in this connection: The question is, what is a proper consequence in an interior node if a packet is marked to belong to an adjustable flow? There are basically two approaches. The system is used merely to inform the sender of a congestion situation without any effect on the treatment of the packet. Because this system does not have any effect on the implementation of Differentiated Services inside the network, it is chiefly beyond the scope of this evaluation.

Another possible approach is that the packets obtain better treatment because the flow (or application, or finally customer) promises to reduce the bit rate if the network informs about congestion situation. In reality, this system means that the packets of those flows should have higher importance than corresponding packets belonging to nonadjustable flows. It seems that this system can and should be realized in the boundary nodes, without any need to change the general structure of PHBs (except that an additional importance level could be necessary). One possible way to tackle this problem is that packets with a low importance level could either be sent into the network or dropped, depending on congestion monitoring as suggested in "A One-Bit Feedback Enhanced Differentiated Services Architecture" (Arora *et al.* 1998).

The general conclusion is that the traffic-condition function can take into account information related to congestion notification, but there is no need to modify the PHB system. It should be stressed that a mere promise to take the congestion notification into account cannot be sufficient reason to improve the importance of the packets, because there is an apparent possibility that the customer will mark all flows as adjustable.

4.6   Framework for Per-Hop Behaviors

Now it is time to build the technical framework for designing per-hop behaviors. From the lengthy discussion about importance, delays, availability, and predictability, it is fair to conclude that three fundamental dimensions are necessary for the framework: importance, urgency, and bandwidth. This statement entails that the specification of each per-hop behavior should somehow address each one of the three aspects: What is the importance of the packets? What is the urgency of the packets? And what is the bandwidth that should be allocated to the aggregate (if any)?

4.6.1   Essence of Quality

The first question is, What form is used to define each quality aspect? Basically, there are three possibilities: quantitative, qualitative, and relative. This is the same categorization as presented in section 4.3 of the framework document (Bernet *et al.* 1998). (See section 3.3.4, "A Framework for Differentiated Services," in Chapter 3 of this book.) For instance, with a PHB class that has a moderate packet-loss ratio, provided that this is a proper measure for importance, these service categories can be depicted as follows:

- *Quantitative service*: Packet-loss ratio should be less than 10^{-4}.

- *Qualitative service*: Packet-loss ratio should be moderate, which could mean that it is less 10^{-4} most of the time, but during busy hours it can be higher; and during idle hours it is usually zero.

- *Relative service*: Packet-loss ratio of this PHB should be smaller than that of any PHB with lower importance.

There seems to be a strong temptation to quantify all issues and to suppose that quantification itself makes the system somehow better. To a certain extent, this may be true—for instance, the verification of the system or service provision is easier if there are definite numeric specifications. The operator may explicitly choose to apply that approach. It seems that the framework of Differentiated Services does not provide enough tools for implementing truly quantitative services, however, with the possible exception of one service class with high quality.

Nevertheless, the quantitative service model is still the only acceptable target for many system developers. Therefore, it is highly probable that there will be a lot of effort to direct Differentiated Services toward the quantitative service model.

On the contrary, this book recommends that if a service provider wants to *extensively* apply the quantitative service model, another technology with complete specifications (such as ATM or Integrated Services with RSVP) should be used rather than Differentiated

Services. This issue, of course, depends on the exact meaning of quantitative and qualitative. Although quantitative services likely use more advanced control methods with admission control and per-flow reservations, the perceived quality may sometimes be higher with qualitative service than with quantitative service.

This statement leaves two alternatives, the quantitative model and the relative model. Laying aside the numeric formation of the services, the overall structures of these two approaches seem to be similar, because low and high mean essentially the same as lower and higher. In particular, it is hard to distinguish any difference between these two models on the packet-handling level in interior nodes. What are the difference in packet-level implementation of two systems, one consisting of low and high importance classes, and another one consisting of lower and higher importance classes?

4.6.2 Relative Scales for Importance and Urgency

Therefore, a system with relative scales can be a good basis for a Differentiated Services framework. Therefore, if a service provider wants to apply qualitative scales, he can bind the scales to certain fixed points by appropriate operation and management functions (but that does not necessarily yield any changes to the actual packet-handling actions). Figure 4.14 shows the result. You can think of this structure as a cobweb, with the capability to stretch and shrink according to the burden without essentially changing its logical structure.

Figure 4.14   Relative scales of importance and urgency.

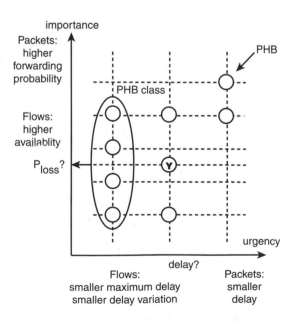

Every PHB has a definite position in relation to all other PHBs: The delay and packet-loss ratio of one PHB are either smaller, higher, or approximately the same as that of another PHB. Therefore, the definite values for delay and packet-loss ratio of a PHB depend on the load level in the network. In a relative system, service providers do not necessarily say much about the expected values of quality parameters.

It is fair to expect that the number of delay classes is limited, probably to not more than four, because each delay class requires its own queue in every node, and a large number of delay classes increases the network-management burden. The delay of individual PHBs belonging to the same PHB class cannot vary significantly, because the service provider is allowed to re-mark packets within a PHB class from a PHB to another one, and different delays may yield packet reordering. Therefore, even though the structure is somewhat elastic, the PHBs within one PHB class should be kept on the same vertical line.

A less clear issue is whether the other scale (importance) should behave in the same way. Figure 4.15 shows a situation in which the importance order of PHBs X and Y is changed from the original situation depicted in Figure 4.14. Whether this kind of change is allowed depends on the overall service model, and on the available mechanisms in network nodes. With certain mechanisms, the packet-loss ratios can be controlled only within a PHB class. On the contrary, with some other scheduling and buffering mechanisms, it is possible to keep the packet-loss ratio of two PHBs belonging to different delay classes approximately the same, even though the loads of the two classes vary in different ways. The question of which one of these approaches is better can be left for the service provider.

Figure 4.15   Changing the order of two PHBs in relation to packet-loss ratio.

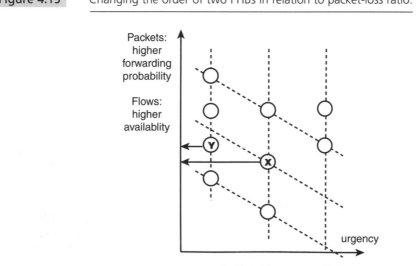

The main difference between a relative and a qualitative service system is that in a qualitative system the service provider makes some additional effort to stabilize the quality of PHBs, whereas in a pure relative system the service provider does not make such an effort. The most reasonable way to stabilize the quality levels is to somehow control the offered load level of each PHB. There are apparently a wide variety of possibilities between minimal control (relative service model) and maximal control (qualitative service model).

4.6.3 *Relative Scales for Bandwidth*

Although the relative structure shown in Figure 4.15 seems to be valid with importance and delay scales, that it is valid with the bandwidth scale as well is not evident. What do you really want to accomplish with the separate bandwidths? There are definitely different ideas and answers. The main approach adopted in this book is that bandwidth can be a useful tool to separate user groups that inevitably will be separated. That kind of group can be called a VPN group (although the purpose of the separation is not necessarily a VPN).

In this case, a quite natural approach is to apply within each VPN group a similar system, as shown in Figure 4.14. In that case, there is no need to determine the relationships among PHBs in different VPN groups. The main problem of this approach is that because the amount of PHBs is very limited, there cannot be a large number of VPNs within one PHB domain. Of course, some other mechanisms such as MPLS can be used to inform network nodes about the VPN of each packet, but the network nodes must provide appropriate mechanisms for every VPN group (for instance, separate queues for each PHB class in every VPN).

The second possibility, also mentioned in the framework document (Bernet *et al.* 1998), is that each PHB class gets a relative amount of bandwidth in every link (for instance, in proportions of 1, 2, and 4). Each PHB class may then have a number of PHBs with different importance. There is no procedure for determining the relationship between two PHBs belonging to a different PHB class. A more serious concern is that it is impossible to infer much about the information that a PHB group has larger bandwidth than another one, in particular, it does not tell much about the situation from the perspective of an individual flow or individual packet. These issues depend crucially on the traffic-conditioning function in the boundary nodes and the traffic-management functions that regulate the resources given to different aggregates.

Figure 4.16 A PHB system with importance and bandwidth scales.

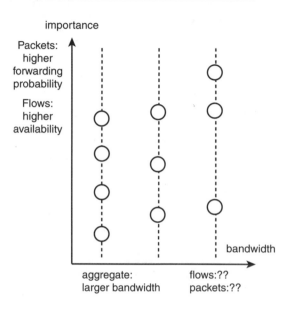

These three dimensions seem to be sufficient for depicting most of the PHB proposals and most of the integral characteristics of any service based on PHB. Some aspects may need further assessment, however.

4.6.4 Predictability of Quality

Based on the evaluation in the first part of chapter, the main concern is the predictability of quality in a short timescale—that is, the need to keep the quality of individual flows more predictable or more constant than is possible in the basic Differentiated Services system. The main application of this kind of system is to give a priority to existing flows during emergence of congestion, in particular to IP telephony calls. One straightforward approach is to make a resource reservation for every individual flow. Because that kind of system is beyond the scope of Differentiated Services, we need another approach.

The essential nature of a system to give priority to existing flows seems to be that the packet of existing flows should have somewhat higher importance than the packet of starting flows. Although it is not clear how to implement this in reality, the required procedures should evidently be done in the boundary nodes. Therefore, this issue seems to require only traffic-conditioning functions without any need to introduce new PHBs.

Summary

This chapter addressed three fundamental issues:

- *Availability of quality:* A tool to compare service models, from guaranteed services to relative services with one universally applicable measure

- *Efficiency of statistical multiplexing:* An evaluation that takes into account predictability of load and destination

- *Predictability of quality:* The need to provide constant quality for existing flows

The common objective of all these considerations has been to provide a framework and tools for fair and extensive evaluation of all service types from pure best-effort service to highly guaranteed service.

The most concrete result of all the considerations is a simple and consistent framework for per-hop behaviors. The framework consists of three dimensions: importance, urgency, and bandwidth. This framework is used extensively in Chapter 7, "Per-Hop Behavior Groups," to evaluate and compare different PHB proposals.

Thus endeth the afternoon's talk of Raphael Hythoday concerning the laws and institutions of the island of utopia.

—Sir Thomas More

5

Differentiation of Customer Service

In general, this book strongly emphasizes the wholeness of the system rather than the separate parts of the system. And although the potential forms of Differentiated Services are endless, the most relevant issue is its purpose: All parts of Differentiated Services have to support the building of an attractive and lucrative network service. This objective, closely related to customer service, is the topic of this chapter. Three specific issues are addressed:

- Overall service models

- Ways to request specific service

- Pricing structure

Customer expectations related to different services may vary remarkably. The same users who expect their telephone company to provide consistent high quality may content themselves with variable quality when it comes to the Internet. Various reasons may account for this. One reason may be the different pricing schemes. A customer can usually obtain an Internet service to any destination for a set monthly fee. Telephone calls (except local calls), on the other hand, are usually incrementally priced, increasing with the distance to the destination and the duration of the call.

In the future, as Internet customers begin to exploit new technology to make telephone calls and to use the many other services that the Internet infrastructure makes possible, the expectations of different customers will also change (making those expectations much more difficult to predict, from a service provider's perspective). The general service model, closely related to the marketing of the service, is a key tool to handle this intricate issue. The service provider may promise a guaranteed service with definite quality characteristics, or it may merely sell shares of network resources without any explicit guarantees.

The dynamic nature of service requirements is another critical consideration that providers must keep in mind. A service level can be either permanent (that is, guaranteed) or the provider may allow the customer to inform the network when service requirements change (perhaps even every second). These two levels of service, guaranteed and dynamic, help to define the four basic service models discussed in this book:

- The guaranteed-connections model

- The leased-line service model

- The dynamic-importance model

- The resource-sharing model

Another key issue when building a viable business model is *pricing*. From an ordinary customer's viewpoint, the main requirements for pricing are simplicity and fairness. But can simplicity and fairness really be reached in a multiple-service environment? If and when various parameters related to bandwidth, quality, and destination must be taken into account, pricing systems can become inherently complex and even incomprehensible. This chapter addresses various aspects related to pricing in multiple-service networks. A general model that takes into account bandwidth, quality, and availability is also introduced.

Before jumping into specifics, some general remarks on possible service models are in order. One question to consider is whether definite conditions are necessary concerning acceptable behavior. You may think that some terms, or conditions, are absolutely necessary. For instance, all TCP implementations shall be appropriate, or real-time service shall be requested only when needed. This definitely makes sense if the service model is based on the requirements of applications and on the cooperation of all end users.

On the other hand, if the service model is based on the price paid by the customer, the operator shall be more cautious when setting any conditions for the customers. There can surely be some restrictions, however; for instance, the provider might enforce conditions related to excessive or inappropriate use of email systems or other clearly undesirable behavior. From a traffic control viewpoint, however, it is up to the user to decide the actual purpose of the network service. If the customer sends more packets than his or her fair share, the network can simply discard some of the packets.

5.1 Service Level Agreement

Although the main aspects of a service level agreement (SLA) were introduced in earlier chapters, it might be helpful to review the basics. (The definition of SLA was presented in Chapter 3, "Differentiated Services Working Group.") An SLA is a contract between a customer and a service provider that specifies the forwarding service.

An important distinction between static and dynamic SLAs was also mentioned in Chapter 3. Static SLAs are based on a negotiation between human agents—that is, between customer and service provider; dynamic SLAs, on the other hand, change usually without human intervention and therefore require an automated agent (Bernet *et al.* 1998). A second distinction can be made among quantitative, qualitative, and relative service models. (See the section "Service Models" in Chapter 3 and section 4.6.1, "Essence of Quality," in Chapter 4, "General Framework for Differentiated Services.")

As for the SLA between the customer and service provider, it is essential to define how the customer and network services are situated on these two scales, determined by dynamics and the service category. Figure 5.1 shows the following four primary approaches:

- Guaranteed connections (dynamic bandwidth)

- Leased-line service (permanent bandwidth)

- Dynamic importance (dynamic precedence)

- Resource sharing (permanent share)

Each primary term (such as guaranteed connections) illustrates the main application of the service models. The secondary terms (such as dynamic bandwidth) are more related to the technical implementation. The following sections discuss these models.

Figure 5.1   Four basic approaches for SLA.

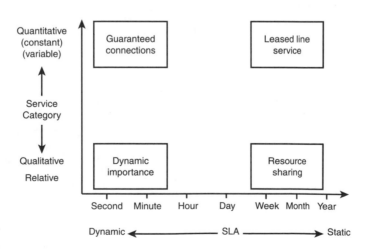

5.1.1 *Guaranteed Connections*

The *guaranteed-connections model* is the traditional model of multiple-service networks, such as ATMs. Although this model often requires quite a lot of effort to implement, it is just as often considered to be the "right" target of service provision. Because some service providers will likely apply this approach despite the inherent difficulties, it is relevant to briefly describe how an SLA with guaranteed connections can be designed.

> ### Note
>
> The term *guaranteed connection* refers here to a service used by an individual application with specific quality requirements and duration. In addition to this service model, there are other service models in which a customer buys a connection for aggregate traffic streams. In those cases, however, the connection is more permanent than what this section is assuming.
>
> The feasibility of guaranteed connections was discussed earlier in this book: See section 2.4, "Integrated Service Model," in Chapter 2, "Traffic Management Before Differentiated Services," and the section, "Resource Reservation," in Chapter 4.

The SLA can be based on a model shown in Figure 5.2. The model is basically the same as the customer model presented in section 4.2.2, "Levels of Aggregation," in Chapter 4. The main actions of this model are as follows:

1. The customer decides to use an application.

2. The application informs the end user about required service characteristics.

3. The service provider offers the requested service at a certain price.

4. If the end user makes the decision to buy the service, the network provides a service based on the price paid by the customer rather than the requirements of the application.

5. The application begins to use the available network service as well as it can.

Figure 5.2   Service model for guaranteed connections.

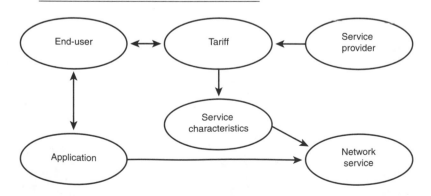

It is assumed that the end user will select a network service that will meet the requirements of the application; however, there is no guarantee that this will happen. If a user reserves a 500kbps connection for an IP telephony call that actually requires only 20kbps, for instance, he may pay a lot of extra money without any notice from the network. (Although that is not directly a problem of the service provider, it may indirectly deteriorate the relationship between customer and operator.)

Although part of these actions can be automated, the basic process remains the same: The service provider sells network services based on individual connections, and the customer makes the decision based on the price and what the service offers. From the network service viewpoint, this means in essence that end users buy a fixed capacity more or less (usually more) from the network to a fixed destination, and applications then exploit that capacity as well as they can.

The main advantage of this model is that the customer is paying for definite service at definite price. It is a fair, clear, and consistent service model. The disadvantages of this model are the lack of scalability and its unfitness with adaptive applications. Consequently, this model is not realistic as the only end-to-end service model in IP networks.

5.1.2 Leased-Line Service

Unlike the dynamics of the guaranteed connection model in which the end user pays for a fixed amount of services for a fixed price, the leased-line service model is more permanent and less binding on the individual end user. Although this model can be used by and for individual end users, it is better used in an organization with a large number of end users—you are probably not eager to buy a permanent connection to all the places within the Internet you want to have a connection.

In this context, the main differences between these service models—leased-line and guaranteed connection—are the dynamic natures of the service(s) and the customer category. Leased lines are usually permanent, whereas guaranteed connections can be established within seconds. You can think of the guaranteed connection model as an abbreviation of switched guaranteed connections; leased-line service, on the other hand, represents all permanent guaranteed connections independent of the actual use of the service. When the term *virtual leased line* is used, it indicates that the level of guarantee is not as high as with "real" leased-line service.

Figure 5.3 presents one possible leased-line model. (See also section 4.2.2, "Levels of Aggregation," in Chapter 4 for an explanation of the differences among an application model, a customer model, and an organization model). An organization pays for a set of leased lines between its sites, and a number of end users then utilize the available network resources. Usually each end user starts an application, which then uses some network resources from the organization's common pool.

In a basic model, no congestion occurs inside the provider's network and, correspondingly, there is no need to define any mechanism for congestion. (Those mechanisms might be useful, however, in the private networks of the organization or at the interface between private and public networks.)

Figure 5.3   Service model for leased-line service.

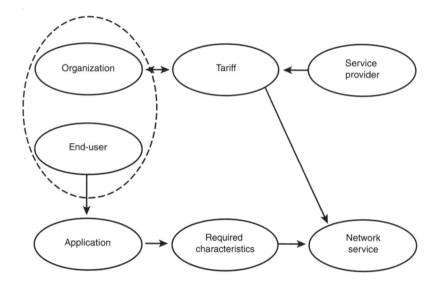

There is a real demand for this type of service model. A large part of the traffic in Frame Relay networks is based on this type of service model. This model could even be relatively efficient provided that the load levels are stable enough to enable efficient network dimensioning. In practice, this could be possible if the number of active users is very large and the traffic process of one user is not very bursty. Based on the evaluation made in the section, "A Model for Evaluating Statistical Multiplexing," in Chapter 4, it seems that it is not possible to satisfy this condition without controlling the traffic sent by end users.

Because this is not necessarily a realistic possibility, the use level of the leased-lines model remains low (or very low). This assumption is supported by some studies made on real networks. According to Andrew Odlyzko, "The greatest inefficiency in data networking today is that thousands of corporations are running their own private networks" (Odlyzko 1998). Whether this is an actual problem is an unclear issue because bandwidth is not necessarily the most expensive resource. Nevertheless, the situation provides an opportunity for more efficient use of resources.

Although resource reservations can be considered to be against the fundamental principles of Differentiated Services, a couple of reasons make it possible to realize simple reservations inside Differentiated Services networks. The most obvious reason is that if the capacity reservations are permanent enough, they can be managed without any signaling system. The other, perhaps just as important reason, is that although the service model was based on the idea of reserving capacity, the traffic control inside the network does not necessarily rely on reservations for every individual connection but, for instance, on appropriate packet marking.

5.1.3 Resource Sharing

It is easy to proceed from the preceding leased-line model to the *resource-sharing model* by adopting the idea of using packet marking rather than real reservations. This model makes it possible to improve statistical multiplexing, but also necessitates the use of additional mechanisms to solve conflicts.

Figure 5.4 presents one practical service model for resource sharing. End users buy a share of network resources permanently. Applications exploit the available (variable) bandwidth as well as possible. In principle, there is no direct connection between application and network service besides the packets sent by the application.

Figure 5.4   Service model for resource sharing.

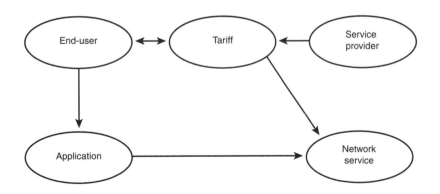

The main advantage of the resource-sharing model is that it provides a simple and consistent service: Each user gets the share that he pays for (provided that the underlying mechanisms can divide the network resources in a fair manner). Moreover, this model is inherently suitable for adaptive applications because there can be significant differences in the available share from time to time and from destination to destination.

This model (in its purest form) does not adapt well if the needs of the user and application change quickly and considerably. In particular, a real-time service can be necessary to make the overall service model attractive for a majority of users. Then an open issue is how to take real-time requests, or some other special requests, into account. If there is no incentive to request special service only when really needed, the result can be unfavorable for the service provider because everyone can ask for better treatment.

Another drawback to this model is the difficulty of verifying the performance and fairness of the service. There is no way for an individual user to verify whether he gets a fair share of the resources. It is, therefore, probable that the formal SLA is based on a somewhat different model from the actual service structure inside the network. The operator may, for instance, apply the qualitative service model within customer service, although the real implementation inside the network is based purely on a relative service model.

5.1.4 Dynamic Importance

The simple resource-sharing model described in the preceding section can provide acceptable basic service for most users and applications. Some needs cannot be satisfied with this model, however, because of its simplicity at the most basic level. Any one of the three major quality aspects—delay, importance, and bit rate—can be insufficient for a specific purpose. High-quality IP telephony needs better delay properties than those properties provided by the basic service. Some applications may need more bandwidth or higher assurance of packet delivery. Finally, some demanding applications, such as video meetings, may require all these characteristics at the same time. Some additional tools can be used to increase flexibility of static resource sharing, however.

The key characteristic of this model (shown in Figure 5.5) is that a mechanism informs the network nodes that the current flow needs somehow better treatment than that which the user usually gets. These mechanisms are presented in the figure by broken lines.

Although this adjunct appears to be similar to that of the guaranteed-connections model, there is an essential difference: In the model of dynamic importance, you explicitly suppose that the network infrastructure is based on the resource-sharing model. Because of this, the dynamics should be based on changes in packet marking rather than reservations inside the network.

Note that this is in accordance with the basic philosophy of Differentiated Services. The most difficult issue in this system, provided that the basic resource-sharing system is available, is the price of extra quality. Basically, there are at least two options: a direct time price that depends on the required quality and a system price in which each user may utilize the monthly flat rate somewhat unevenly. If a user wants to momentarily send packets with high bit rate, for instance, a smaller share during some other period can compensate for such a momentary "upgrade." (It is possible to apply a large variety of rules.) In the case of real-time service, an option is that if real-time service is requested, the share measured in bit rate is smaller than that of non–real-time service.

Figure 5.5   Service model for resource sharing with dynamic importance.

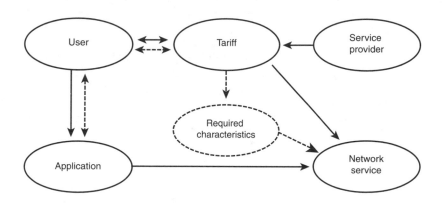

In all cases, the SLA should contain reasonable incentives for the user to request supplementary characteristics only when really needed. Moreover, the system should be as simple as possible, particularly if you suppose that the majority of traffic can be handled without these additional mechanisms. This seems to be the hardest part of this scheme: how to build an effective pricing system without too complex management and customer care.

5.1.5   Comparison Based on Availability of Quality

The preceding section covered four service models that describe different kinds of SLAs. One of the fundamental questions of any quality of service offering is how the service provider can market it to customers. Two models—guaranteed connections and resource sharing—possess essentially different characteristics, whereas the customer's needs might be quite similar in both cases. What common aspect do both of these models share that makes it possible to market and compare both of these services? Availability of quality, which is discussed in more depth in Chapter 4, can be an appropriate tool for this purpose.

Suppose that a service provider has a customer who wants a 200kbps connection with high quality, for example. If the service model and the SLA are based on the guaranteed-connection model, the availability of quality can be depicted by the graph shown in Figure 5.6. The customer attains the desired characteristics by buying a 200kbps connection through the network. A limit to availability exists, however, depending on the dimensioning of the network: With a finite probability, the connection request has to be rejected because of exceptional load level. Figure 5.6 illustrates the situation. Point A defines the availability of the quality in this case. For any bit rate higher than 200kbps, the availability is 0%; for any lower bit rate, the availability is 99.99% (or whatever the call blocking is).

Figure 5.6   Quality function for guaranteed service and resource-sharing service.

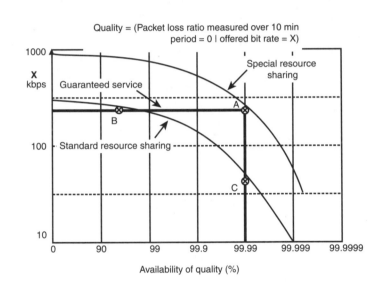

The other option for the service provider is to build the customer service on the basis of shared resources. In this case, the service provider has a more complicated task when trying to define the availability of quality. Based on traffic and performance measurements and general experience, the operators of the network may be able to moderately distinguish the availability of different quality levels. Figure 5.6 shows an approximate availability function for a standard resource-sharing service.

Although this service may provide the 200kbps most of the time (point B in the figure), that may not be enough for demanding users and applications. On the other hand, the availability target can be met by a lower bit rate (point C in the figure). Still, that property is of minor value if the application definitely requires a connection of 200kbps.

The service provider has two main options to solve this dilemma. First, it can provide the possibility to buy a guaranteed service in addition to the resource sharing. Second, the service provider can merely provide different levels of resource-sharing services. It is even possible to base the service sold to the customer on the guaranteed-service model while the implementation is done by means of a larger share inside the network. Figure 5.6 also shows a special resource-sharing service that meets this target.

5.2 Requesting Specific Service

The preceding section addressed issues relating to the contract between the customer and a service provider. Now the discussion takes one step toward technical matters, specifically how to request a certain service. Again, it is important to remember that the service can be based either on the resource-sharing model or the requested-quality model, and the dynamics of the request can vary from seconds to months.

5.2.1 Dynamic Quality or Bandwidth for Guaranteed Connections

The combining of dynamic allocation and guaranteed connections seems to be a difficult task. First, it requires some kind of signaling throughout the network. Because per-flow signaling inside the core network is beyond the scope of Differentiated Services, that possibility is not addressed further here. Notwithstanding, it is possible, as discussed earlier, that even though the customer makes a definite request by using RSVP, the request is converted to an appropriate Per-Hop Behavior (PHB) without any actual reservation for individual flows.

5.2.2 Permanent Bandwidth Reservation Versus Permanent Share

If the dynamic of reservation is days rather than minutes, the resource allocation task is essentially easier. Reservations can be made through the management system if the requirements do not change frequently. Of course, the management system and network nodes must be able to appropriately support the reservations.

From the requesting point of view, permanent share is similar to permanent bandwidth. The only fundamental requirement is that the management system and network nodes support the system; the issue of requesting a definite share seems to be simple.

The main difference may relate to the concept of *share*: One possible definition is merely to say that a customer obtains one share if he buys the basic service, and that all other shares are defined in proportion to this basic share. From a marketing perspective, however, this type of definition can be too abstract. For instance, a basic share may mean—under normal load conditions to most destinations—an available bandwidth of 50kbps with small packet-loss ratio.

More concretely, the service provider can use a description similar to that presented in Figure 5.6. The disadvantage of doing this is that the customer might consider the numbers as guaranteed performance. If the service provider understands the situation in the same way, the number will be very low. For instance, the real available bandwidth frequently can be 10 times larger than the promised one.

Finally, the service provider can leave out all numbers and just state that certain service classes have lower and higher quality. Nevertheless, the realization of the service can be based on fixed shares. These three ways of requesting a service are possible; only hands-on experience can tell which is the best one.

5.2.3 Dynamic Share

With dynamic share, three different ways of messaging can be identified. (You should assume that the basic service model is resource sharing.) The customer may explicitly request a certain service, such as a 200kbps connection to somewhere using appropriate RSVP messages. In the Differentiated Services network, this message is translated into a proper PHB. In addition, the boundary node must have proper mechanisms to control the incoming packet flow, and probably a system to charge for the special service.

Another messaging possibility is when a customer does not request any definite quality characteristics but rather a bigger share, if the standard share appears to be insufficient. The advantage of this approach is that it does not necessarily yield any action outside the boundary node. Particularly, there is no need to change the PHB class, but only the thresholds that determine the importance levels within the PHB class. In this case, it is probable that an extra charge is needed to limit the requests of bigger shares. Various approaches do not include any additional prices—for instance, the monthly flat rate may include the right to use extra shares at certain times. Pricing is discussed later in this chapter, in the section "Pricing as a Tool for Controlling Traffic."

The third option is to use the DSCP field to inform the network about any special treatment needs. Packets belonging to an IP telephony service, for instance, can be marked as real-time packets with a suitable DSCP value. The boundary node then selects a proper PHB class for those packets. In addition, the system must have an incentive for the user to select real-time service only for those applications that really need that property. One incentive is to charge extra for real-time service. A more feasible solution, however, is to make the "real-time share" smaller than the default share while keeping the pricing the same. This latter solution is described later in section 5.3.6, "The Relationship Between Quality and Bandwidth."

5.2.4 Summary of Service Requests

These three alternatives for service requests are summarized in Table 5.1. Notice that although it is more convenient to use the term *user* (as the final entity making a decision), in many cases the requests can be done automatically by the application without any human interaction.

Table 5.1   Alternatives for Service Requests

Way of Messaging	Content	Example	Boundary Changes Functions	PHB Change from PHB_default
RSVP message	Requesting quality parameters	Bandwidth = 200kbps	Traffic control and pricing	=> PHB_high
Share message	Requesting to change the share	Share_new = 2*share _old	Pricing and threshold	No change of PHB class
DSCP indication	Requesting special treatment	Low delay service	Pricing or threshold	=> PHB_rt

The main three quality aspects that can be requested are bandwidth, importance, and delay. An RSVP message is basically suitable for all of these. A customer can use an increased share either to increase bandwidth or to improve the importance level of the packets (that is, the availability of the service). These two changes can be presented in Figure 5.6 as horizontal or vertical shifts. A change of share does not necessarily have any effect on the delay characteristics, although that is possible.

DSCP indication is a particularly useful tool to inform the network about the need for real-time service, because most customers are not willing to choose permanently either real-time or data service. DSCP can also be used to indicate the relative importance of different packets, although it seems quite difficult to combine the resource-sharing model with the requirement to have different importance levels for different packets belonging to one flow. One reasonable scheme could be that packets marked as the lowest importance level have no effect on the PHB calculation mechanisms of any other packets; thus the user can effectively send a large amount of unimportant packets without deteriorating the treatment of other packets. Finally, DSCP indication is not the right mechanism to inform the network about bandwidth requirements.

Moreover, a network can use another alternative to prompt the user to select the right service. As discussed in section 6.2.3, "Feedback Information," in Chapter 6, "Traffic Handling and Network Management," networks can give information about the current load and quality inside the network. Because only a limited number of applications and users can use the information, however, it is perhaps unreasonable to disseminate the information without an explicit request. Yet, it is possible to design a protocol by which the end users can inquire as to the current state of a path to a certain destination. The information could be related either to an individual PHB, a PHB class, or all PHBs.

Table 5.2 summarizes the characteristics of different approaches related to different applicability aspects. The additional aspects addressed here are scope of service, interdomain issues, and status of standards. Reservation mechanisms, such as RSVP, are suitable for connections with fixed endpoints—that is, for scoped services. (It is somewhat hard to imagine a real reservation without fixed endpoints.) The Differentiated Services–oriented approaches (share message and DSCP indication) are primarily appropriate with unscoped services; however, there is no technical obstacle to using DSCP indication with scoped services as well. Quality inquiry seems to require a fixed destination to be really useful. It may also be practical to certain a extent, however, even if the destination is not defined (just to get information about the general condition of the network).

Table 5.2 Applicability of Different Messaging Approaches

Way of Messaging	Quality Aspects	Scope of Service	Interdomain Flows	Status of Standards
RSVP message	Bandwidth, importance, delay	Scoped	Possible if available in all domains	Available
Share message	Bandwidth or importance	Unscoped	If the same service model is applied	Not available (useful, but not obligatory)
DSCP indication	Delay, importance	Unscoped or scoped	If possible to map PHBs	Standard PHBs can be used
Quality inquiry	Delay, packet-loss ratio (bandwidth)	Scoped (perhaps unscoped)	If support available	Not available, necessary

One general problem of any service provision within the Internet is that different domains may apply different service systems. RSVP could be used in some domains, for example, but probably never in all Internet domains. It should also be noted that if a user requests a certain service with RSVP, that does not mean that RSVP should actually be used in all domains (see the section "Interoperability with RSVP/Integrated Services" in the framework document [Bernet *et al.* 1998]). The advantage of RSVP is that complete standards define the formats of all necessary messages.

In a region with the resource-sharing model, standardization could be quite minimal. The main requirement of practical implementation covering a wide Internet region is that the resource-sharing model should be applied in some form by most of the service providers. The details of implementation can vary from operator to operator. Particularly, the communication between service provider and customer equipment can be based on proprietary messages, although some level of standardization would be useful.

5.3   *Pricing as a Tool for Controlling Traffic*

As mentioned several times in the previous sections, pricing is one of the key issues with any Differentiated Services model. This is an extremely complex issue and only some aspects can be addressed in this book. The main viewpoint in this section is Differentiated Services; for a more extensive discussion about Internet pricing, see "Internet Economics" (McKnight and Bailey 1997).

The main issue to be addressed is how a pricing scheme can help users maximize the ratio of user benefit to service cost. There are basically two options to tackle this issue:

- To somehow influence user behavior so that users do not waste network resources

- To give a fair service compared to the price paid by the customer (regardless of how the user is using the network service)

Within an organization, the first target is relevant and the solution is usually not based on actual pricing but rather on rules or recommendations concerning the use of network resources. Therefore, this chapter concentrates on the second case in which the price paid by the customers should somehow reflect the service provider's actual cost.

The framework addressed in this chapter consists of four main elements:

- Bandwidth

- Quality

- Availability of quality

- Price

If one factor is presented as a function of another factor, and the remaining two factors remain constant, six different cases result (as shown in Table 5.3).

Table 5.3	Basic Relations Among Main Elements Of Network Service		
Case	Element	As a Function Of	For Constant
1	Price	Bandwidth	Available quality
2	Price	Quality	Available bandwidth
3	Price	Availability	Quality bandwidth
4	Availability	Bandwidth	Price quality
5	Availability	Quality	Price bandwidth
6	Quality	Bandwidth	Price availability

Cases 1 and 2 are the standard functions of pricing in reservation-oriented networks. The price of the connection is calculated as a function of bandwidth and quality, and the service provider usually tries to keep the availability constant—that is, the call-blocking probability should be approximately independent of bandwidth and quality requirements. There could be, nevertheless, a hidden availability aspect even in this case. When the price is higher for busy hours than for idle hours, it could be said that the price actually depends on the availability.

To get a relevant insight into all these relations, a simple but somewhat realistic mathematical model may be helpful. The following exemplifying figures are based on one formula of the form, as shown in Formula 5.1:

Formula 5.1

$$\log(P) = c_B * \log(B) + c_Q * \log(Q) + c_A * \log(1-A) + c_P$$

In Formula 5.1, P = price, B = bandwidth, A = availability, and Q = quality (delay variation in the following examples, but it can be another quality parameter as well). Formula 5.1 is selected here mainly because of simplicity. The logarithmic form makes the effect of each parameter systematic. If bandwidth is increased by a factor of 2, and c_B is 0.5, for example, the price is increased always by 41% regardless of the other parameters.

It should be strongly emphasized that this is just one example of the many possible pricing schemes, and particularly that the selected constants for c_B, c_Q, c_A, and c_P are arbitrary (although they try to be realistic). Further, the position of this book is that the basis of pricing should be as consistent as possible, even though the actual tariffs may deviate from any simple mathematical formula. (There are many opportunities for inconsistent tariff structures.)

5.3.1 *Price of Bandwidth*

Figure 5.7 depicts one fundamental problem associated with the pricing for network services related to the relationship between bandwidth and price. On the one hand, practical experience shows that when bandwidths differ significantly, a linear relationship is not a practical approach. According to "Dynamic Behavior of Differential Pricing and Quality of Service Options for the Internet," for example, if the price of a 56kbps connection were $595, the price for a 1.5Mbps connection would be $1,795, and the price for a 45Mbps connection would be $54,000 (Fishburn and Odlyzko 1998). In this case, the relationship between bandwidth and price is far from linear.

These figures strongly support a model in which parameter c_B is significantly smaller than 1. This phenomenon can be explained by the following example. Assume that the average bit rate required by a customer is R_{ave}, and the total cost of providing service for all customers is $C_T(R_{ave})$. If the average bandwidth requirement is increased tenfold in a way that all other factors are kept unchanged (as far as it is possible), the total cost of service provision is evidently more than $C_T(R_{ave})$, but most probably significantly less than $10*C_T(R_{ave})$.

On the other hand, if you consider the dimensioning problem of a given network, you might come to a totally different conclusion. One connection with a constant bit rate of 1Mbps consumes basically as much resources as 10 connections with a constant bit rate of 100kbps. If a very large number of tiny connections are made, however, the management costs could induce the major costs. Therefore, the main issue may be the charged unit measured in bit rate rather than the average bit rate of a connection. Consequently, for a given network the result can be something like that shown in Figure 5.7.

Figure 5.7 An approximate relationship between charged unit and costs.

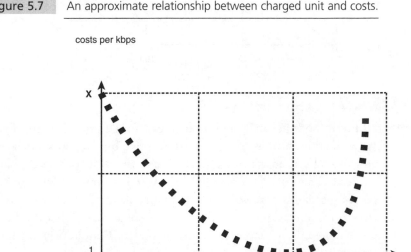

costs per kbps

bit rate requirement per charged unit

So there are two opposing phenomena: The total cost tends to be high if the charged unit is very small, and the effects of statistical multiplexing tend to deteriorate if the number of independent units is small (perhaps less than 20). In the middle region, the cost per bit rate could be relatively constant. It should be stressed that the right ascent in the figure is relevant only if you suppose that the total network capacity is fixed and cannot be easily updated and that the operator's intention is to use the network for public network services.

In reality the situation is not static, but highly dynamic. Network capacity is updated all the time according to demand, and in high-capacity public networks one customer is seldom so dominant that the effect of statistical multiplexing considerably deteriorates. Therefore, despite the significant opposing arguments, it is possible to tentatively apply Formula 5.1 with a C_B smaller than 1. A value of 0.6 is used in Figure 5.8, as well as in other figures related to pricing. Service providers may, of course, build real services based on totally different approaches.

Figure 5.8 A tentative relationship between bandwidth and price.

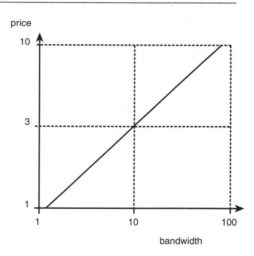

5.3.2 Price of Quality

Quality is an ambiguous term both generally and particularly from a pricing point of view. This attempted concise evaluation, however, concentrates on one quality aspect: delay variation. (Note that bandwidth aspects are already discussed, and the next topic, availability, contains aspects related to different packet-loss ratios.) Because real-time network service requires additional control mechanisms as well as additional management actions, it is justified to suppose that the price of real-time service should be somewhat higher if other aspects remain constant. Figure 5.9, for example, supposes that a 100-fold decrease in delay variation means a double price.

The main point seems to be that real-time support makes traffic control more complicated. However, it is difficult—even practically impossible—to give any clear rule for the price difference. In some cases, for instance, when the traffic flow sent by the user is exactly constant, it is not clear whether there is any significant difference from a statistical-multiplexing or traffic-control viewpoint as to whether a flow uses real-time or data service.

Figure 5.9   A tentative relationship between delay variation and price.

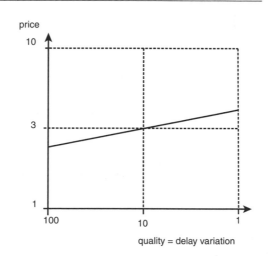

5.3.3   *Price of Availability*

The relationship between availability and price may appear somewhat artificial (if you suppose that the availability is a common characteristic for the whole network). One possible interpretation is that availability is related to the availability of a service at a certain price at different times. When availability is high (say, 99.999%), the service is available even during the busiest times of the year. An intermediate availability means that the service is available at that price on a typical busy hour. Finally, low availability means that the price is valid on idle hours. A value of 0.15 is used for constant c_A in Figure 5.10.

A similar model can be used if availability is interpreted as the probability that a packet is successfully forwarded through the network. For this, however, you must suppose that availability means primarily the probability that all packets are forwarded during a moderately long period for reasons discussed in section 4.2.1, "Availability of Quality," in Chapter 4.

Figure 5.10   A tentative relationship between availability and price.

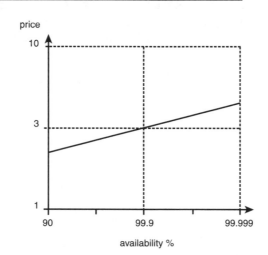

5.3.4   *Relationship Between Bandwidth and Availability*

All the previous evaluations were based on the assumption that price is a variable quantity. This is a reasonable assumption if the operator applies service models with reserved connections. On the contrary, with some other service models it is not realistic to expect that a different price can be attached to all differing situations. Particularly if the service provider uses flat rate pricing, the price is basically fixed whereas all other parameters can change.

Figure 5.11 shows the relationship between bandwidth and availability for fixed price and quality, for example. It is easy to draw the figure, because the same parameters as in the earlier sections can be used. Yet, the reality is much more complex because with many service models the relationships between different aspects, such as availability and bandwidth, are results of a complicated process that is not totally controllable by the service provider. Therefore, all the figures are definitely illustrative, but may be used to check whether the parameters chosen earlier are realistic.

Essentially, the relationship between bandwidth and availability depicts the differing demands on busy and idle hours (and minutes). If the target is to share the bandwidth equally on times with differing busyness, the availability-bandwidth relationship directly reflects the relationship between demand and time of day. It is apparent that there is a significant difference between available bandwidth during busy and idle moments, perhaps of the order of 10 as in the tentative model. This difference encourages end users to use less bandwidth during busy hours, or to change the time of use from busy to idle times if the application is not adaptive.

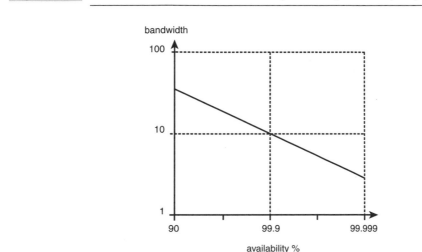

Figure 5.11 Bandwidth as a function of availability for fixed price and quality.

5.3.5 Relationship Between Quality and Availability

If the application cannot adapt to available bandwidth, it may be possible to degrade the quality in case of insufficient bandwidth. If we again apply Formula 5.1, we get the relationship between quality and availability shown in Figure 5.12. It seems that there is usually only a limited possibility to apply this approach. If, for instance, a real time application requires definitely small delay variation, it is probably not reasonable to allow much larger delay variation during the busiest hours.

Consequently, the main effect of this relationship could be that there is an incentive for customers not to use high quality service for less demanding applications in particular during busy hours, that is, when network resources are scarce.

5.3.6 The Relationship Between Quality and Bandwidth

Finally, it is possible to assess the relationship between quality and bandwidth. It seems that this relationship is relatively weak in the sense that even a substantial change in quality may cause a relatively small change in available bandwidth. (However, that statement is valid only if the general model is valid, which is not at all sure.) Nevertheless, it is important that users can attain more bandwidth if the quality requirements are looser, if it is not possible to attach additional pricing for higher quality.

Figure 5.12 Quality as a function of availability for fixed price and bandwidth.

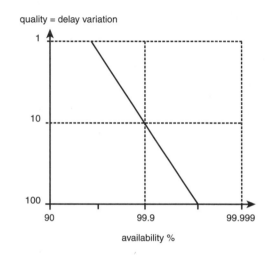

The available bandwidth is approximately three times larger for non–real-time service than for real-time service in the model shown in Figure 5.13. One interpretation of this tentative result is that the average load level of real-time service classes can be one third of the load level of non–real-time services in cases where the whole traffic uses only one service class. Note again that this specific relationship between available bandwidth and delay characteristic is a result of selected parameters in Formula 5.1, whereas in reality the relationship could be totally different.

Figure 5.13 Bandwidth as a function of quality for fixed price and availability.

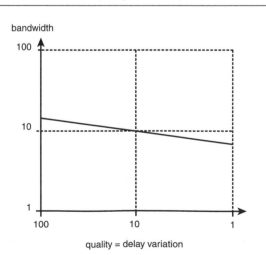

5.3.7 Effect of Variable Destinations

One important aspect that was not addressed in the tentative pricing model is the effect of destinations. The Internet is obviously a very heterogeneous network. Some parts of the network are equipped with high-capacity links and routers that can handle all the incoming flows without any losses most of the time. Then there are low-capacity access networks with a permanent lack of resources. Finally, some links, most prominently those between main continents, are expensive and heavily used.

If the resource-sharing model described in the beginning of this chapter is applied, the real available share depends strongly on the destination. The fair share for an ordinary customer on a local link may be 200kbps. The fair share over an Atlantic link may well be fraction of that, however, say 20kbps.

A fundamental consequence is that either the pricing will depend somehow on the destination or, alternatively, a higher importance level is needed to transmit packets over expensive and highly loaded links. In any case, the customer has to pay for the availability of the service, where availability is related not only to point of time but to destination as well. Therefore, the model presented in Figure 5.11 might also be applicable to this case. By decreasing the bit rate enough, the customer obtains the "right" to use even the most expensive links. From the network-control perspective, that means that those packets must get a high-importance marking.

5.3.8 Levels of Pricing

There are two basic levels of pricing. In residential markets, each individual customer is paying for his or her service. In the case of organizations, however, the whole service is usually paid for by the organization. Then there are sometimes additional needs related to the intermediate levels of the organization. Even though the contract between an organization and the service provider can be based on the total service, there is often a need for internal pricing of departments, based on resources they have used. The organization can accomplish this in one of three ways:

- The simplest approach is just to collect information about the use of network resources and make internal charges based on the information. This system has to take into account the requested quality levels, for instance, by measuring separately the load on each PHB in a Differentiated Services network.

- In a more sophisticated system, the whole organization may have a common resource pool, departments may buy a share of that pool and, finally, each end user may have a share of the department's pool. Although this appears to be a desirable system, it may increase considerably the complexity of traffic control and the burden on management personnel.

•In an intermediate approach, the management system has a large pool for the whole organization, and departments can reserve or buy a definite share for each end user. When the total pool is increased, each customer immediately recognizes a similar increase of available capacity.

5.3.9 Variable Bit Rate

This chapter assumes that the bit rate of each flow is more or less constant. That is, of course, an unrealistic assumption because Internet traffic is a highly variable entity. Many recognized studies relate to the optimal pricing of variable bit-rate connections (Roberts, Moggi, and Virtamo 1996).

An elegant approach, proposed by Frank Kelly, is based on the concept of effective band-width (Kelly 1996, 141–168). In Kelly's method, pricing of a connection depends on the following three parameters:

•Peak rate

•Mean rate declared by the customer

•The real (measured) mean rate

The better the customer is able to predict the real mean rate, the lower price she gets. An example of this is in cases where a service provider offers reserved connections for a price depending on the quality and bandwidth requirements. This method is, therefore, difficult to apply in Differentiated Services networks. (Yet the fundamental idea that the user gets a certain advantage if she can accurately predict her bit-rate requirement can be useful if a network operator wants to use network resources very efficiently and all the required mechanisms are available.)

What can the service provider do in the case of the resource-sharing model? A direct relationship between traffic variations (or the user's ability to predict mean rate) and pricing seems to be impractical. In contrast, the available average bandwidth may depend on the amount of traffic variations. This kind of relationship can actually be relatively easy to realize. If the resource sharing is done purely based on the bit rate measured over a short period, constant bit-rate flows may attain significant advantage over variable bit-rate flows.

This relationship can be, to some extent, adjusted by changing the measuring period. A short measuring period strongly favors constant bit-rate sources, whereas a long measuring period results in a more equal share between constant and variable flows as shown in Figure 5.14. Note also that a very long measuring period yields the same result as usage-based pricing that is insensitive to traffic variations.

The optimal length of a measuring period depends both on the service model and on the requirements of traffic control. A short period could provide better means for effective traffic control, if you suppose that the main task of traffic control is to alleviate congestion. From that perspective, it seems reasonable to penalize those flows that have the most significant effect on congestion—that is, flows with highest momentary bit rate. This is particularly important with real-time services with small buffers that can be filled with short, but intense, traffic bursts.

On the contrary, because non–real-time services with larger buffers can better tolerate traffic bursts of short duration, the measuring period could be longer for those services. Consequently, the two lines in Figure 5.14 can also illustrate the pricing difference between real-time and non–real-time services.

Figure 5.14 A tentative relationship between traffic variability and available bandwidth.

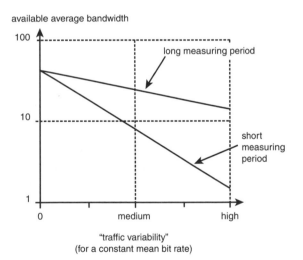

Summary

This chapter discussed primarily two main aspects related to the customer contract, or service level agreement: the service model and the pricing model. Four service models were identified in the first section of this chapter. The models differ both in the dynamics and in the level of guarantees:

- *Guaranteed connections.* This is a general term for a service model in which a customer can request a connection with specific quality requirements. The service provider either offers a connection with the required characteristics or, if there are not enough resources, rejects the connection request.

- *Leased-line service*: This is a general term for a service model in which a customer, usually a large organization, buys a permanent connection with a constant bit rate through the network. The quality, including security aspects, should always be high enough for critical business needs.

- *Resource sharing*: This is a general term for a service model in which the customer buys a share of network resources instead of specifying the requirements of individual flows. The actual amount of resources the user can obtain depends inherently on the network's load level. In this model, the assumption is that the size of the share is relatively permanent.

- *Dynamic importance*: This is a general term for a resource-sharing model with improved dynamics. In this model, each user is allowed to request dynamically higher importance classification, either for individual packets or for all packets during a short period of time.

The main conclusion related to pricing is that *the overall pricing model has to be very consistent*. One specific pricing model was introduced, mainly for illustration purpose. The main property of this tentative model is that it defines the relationship between any two aspects if all other aspects are kept constant. If a customer is paying a constant bill every month, for example, it is still possible to have quality differentiation if the bit rate is changed at the same time.

Nonetheless, the real implementation of service makes it often impossible to realize a given pricing model. Therefore, it is necessary to design the service and pricing models jointly with the development of traffic-handling mechanisms used inside the network.

6

Traffic Handling and Network Management

This chapter discusses the constituent parts of Differentiated Services. In *Philosophical Investigations*, Ludwig Wittgenstein asked, "But what are the simple constituent parts of a chair?" Then he commented, "It makes no sense at all to speak absolutely of the 'simple parts of a chair'" (Wittgenstein 1953).

The definition of the leg, as a simple part of a chair, is better expressed by defining the leg's purpose rather than by describing the forms or characteristics of a leg. A leg of a chair can take many forms: It can be straight or crooked, wooden or metallic, red or blue, and so on. The purpose of a leg is to support something against gravity. The system of Differentiated Services is a logical structure—in the sense that the inherent logic of the system and the relationships of the various parts make the service differentiation, not the characteristics of the individual parts.

Nevertheless, the parts must be designed as well. As with a chair, after the manufacturer has clarified the purpose of the chair, appropriate form and material for the legs and back must be chosen. The main technical parts of the network service are as follows:

- Tools for traffic handling in boundary nodes

- Tools for traffic handling in interior nodes

- Network operation and management systems

This chapter discusses all these aspects.

6.1 *Traffic Handling in Boundary Nodes*

The role of boundary nodes as they relate to traffic management was discussed in the section "Traffic Classification and Conditioning" in Chapter 3, "Differentiated Services Working Group." This section now takes a closer look at the mechanisms needed for proper traffic control. There are four basic phases of traffic handling:

1. Setting the target, or goal

2. Collecting information

3. Making the decision

4. Executing the decision

Defining the target could be the most difficult task. You could say something general, such as that the result of traffic handling should be fair, efficient, and robust; or something specific, such as that each flow should obtain predefined quality requirements. Many important questions are situated in the middle ground between these extremes, actually they consist as both general and specific aspects. This chapter focuses on the aspects of the middle ground that may associate the general targets to specific mechanisms of Differentiated Services.

It is useful, once again, to recall that several service models with different requirements exist. Many, although not necessarily all, models can be mapped in the structure shown in Figure 6.1. A customer, or actually an application, sends a flow of packets to the network. Customers and applications do not, however, observe the network directly; instead, they observe a service structure specified by the service provider.

In a genuine Differentiated Services network (in the sense that not only the traffic control inside the network but also the customer service is based on the Differentiated Services model), service structure may be composed of a couple of service classes. The fundamental characteristic of a class is that it offers *reasonable* service for a packet flow, where reasonable means that someone has made a reasoned selection for each flow. But who makes that selection? The possibilities range from a pure application model in which the application automatically selects a preferable service class to a customer model in which the network selects an appropriate service class based on the customer contract regardless of the application.

Figure 6.1 Differentiated Services from a customer's perspective.

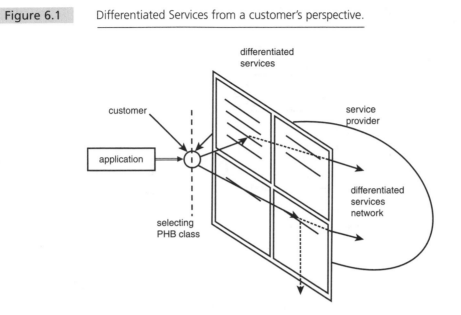

The overall system should allow simultaneous use of different models. Figure 6.1 presents an approach in which the PHB class is selected based primarily on the requirements of the application. Each class consists of several importance levels, emphasizing the need to have one unambiguous importance dimension inside the network, as described in section 4.5.2, "Importance," of Chapter 4, "General Framework for Differentiated Services."

Although the selection of the PHB class is based mainly on the requirements of the application, the selection of the importance level has more to do with the customer contract. The customer contract, or SLA (see the section "Architecture Model" in Chapter 3), defines the relationship between the incoming traffic stream and the importance level for every service class: The higher momentary load, the lower importance. Furthermore, packets belonging to the lowest importance level might be discarded immediately. Although this structure does not cover all possible service models, it forms a good basis for evaluating traffic-control mechanisms. It should also be noted that because the selection process can be dynamic, as described in the section "Service Models" in Chapter 3, this model is actually quite comprehensive.

The implementation of the system illustrated in the figure can be based on the model presented in the architecture document titled "An Architecture for Differentiated Services" (Black, Blake, Carlson, Davies, Wang, Weiss 1998). You can use Figure 3.8 in Chapter 3 with slight modifications. In Figure 6.2, *classification* means the selection of PHB class, and *marking* means the selection of the importance level. Note that here importance refers to the situation inside the network, and does not usually directly relate to the relative importance of different packets of one flow.

Figure 6.2   The main building blocks of traffic handling.

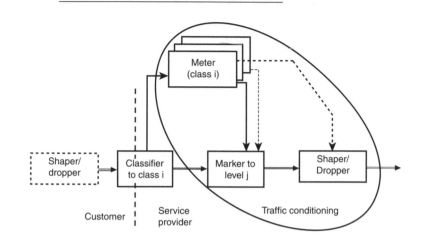

Moreover, based on the classification and marking result, the network can either delay some packets (that is, shape the traffic flow) or even drop packets. Nevertheless, it often seems more reasonable, for reasons discussed later in this chapter in section 6.1.4, "Traffic Shaping," to shape the traffic flow before metering and marking, perhaps in the customer's network.

In summary, the main elements of traffic handling in boundary nodes are classifier, meter, marker, shaper, and dropper. The main purpose of the whole system is to support the service model applied by the service provider, and therefore, the characteristics of the mechanisms cannot be assessed without defining the service model to some extent.

6.1.1   Classifiers

A *classifier* is a mechanism used to select the PHB class for a traffic flow. Although this is quite a straightforward task technically, some scalability problems could result if a large number of issues are taken into account. Because this question depends on the service model adopted by the service provider, it is necessary to refine the issue. The following models, differing in the classification method, can be identified:

1. The user selects a definite service class from the available classes.

2. The application automatically selects a preferable service class for each flow or packet.

3. The network selects an appropriate service class based on information about the application.

4. The network selects an appropriate service class based on the customer contract regardless of the application.

5. A combination of the first four approaches.

Note, in particular, that the classification should not depend on the result of traffic metering, because all packets belonging to a flow should be classified in the same class.

The main requirement of the first approach is that there should be a method to transmit classification information between customer and network. If the customer is not satisfied with one service class for all flows, a sufficient dynamics of signaling is required. This method, without additional mechanisms, does not allow the simultaneous use of several classes—for instance, one class for an IP telephony application and another one for data transfer.

Therefore, the second approach in which the application informs the network seems to be more practical. In a Differentiated Services framework, a sensible scheme is to use the same DS codepoints between the customer and network as inside the differentiated network. Then the classification problem can be solved in such a way that the application selects a DSCP codepoint that it expects to be the most appropriate for the application. A videoconference application, for example, may select the highest importance level of the realtime PHB class for all packets. Thus, if the customer is not allowed to use the selected class, the network operator can use the default service for those packets.

One problem with the second approach is that it requires the capability to set an appropriate DSCP codepoint in the customer's equipment. If that kind of mechanism is not available, the only reasonable choice is to classify the packets in the boundary node (third approach). It is likely that a standard mapping is available for all widespread applications.

It is also possible that each customer has access only to predefined PHB classes. In the extreme case (the fourth approach), each customer can use only one PHB class. Then the classification problem is trivial: All packets of one customer are classified in one PHB class.

Finally, it is possible to combine different approaches. For instance, the boundary node usually selects the PHB class based on the identified application, but if the application has already marked packets with a predefined DS codepoint, the boundary node does not make any change of codepoint.

6.1.2 Meters

The main purpose of traffic metering, with regard to Differentiated Services, is to make it possible to sort the classified packets into the right importance level. The primary approach is that the ensuing decisions (marking, shaping, and dropping) are based on the measuring result of the class to which the packet belongs. It also is possible that the packet marking takes into account several measuring results. If there are two classes—real-time and data, for example—the user can either divide his capacity (permanently) between the classes or use the whole capacity continuously for both classes. In the latter case, the marking of each packet depends on the measuring result of both classes. Therefore, it is usually necessary to measure every PHB class separately. The rest of this section addresses the issue of traffic metering of one PHB class.

The Target of Metering

The combination of traffic metering and traffic marking is a very critical issue for the general characteristics of the network service. Therefore, it might be useful to recall the four aspects defined in Chapter 1, "The Target of Differentiated Services," used to assess the target of traffic metering:

- Versatility

- Cost-efficiency

- Fairness

- Robustness

Whatever method the service provider decides to use for measuring traffic, it has to work properly in all situations even with a mixture of strange traffic patterns. This does not mean, however, that the method should work optimally in every imaginable case.

Cost-efficiency dictates that the method should be as simple as possible, but with the appropriate level of flexibility. Even though someone may invent a theoretical model that promises a perfect result, it is useless if the model is too complicated for any practical implementation. For instance, a model with 10 different mechanisms for 10 time scales could be, in theory, much better than a scheme with only one or two mechanisms with four parameters. The simple model could be much more practical, however, if it provides a satisfactory result. Consequently, the primary goal is a simple, but versatile enough model.

The other two aspects, fairness and robustness, should be used to further assess the measuring methods. Again, it should be stressed that the overall target is the key. Simply put, the target is to provide a fair share of network resources in a robust manner.

One interpretation of *fair share* is that for a given quadruple of {PHB class, importance level, point of time, link}, the price of a packet is approximately the same (here the term price should be understood very generally). Unfortunately, because of the inherent complexities of pricing issues, this interpretation is not such a clear statement as is it may appear. It might be clearer, therefore, to express the target in another way:

A fair share means that for a given quadruple of {PHB class, importance level, point of time, link}, the price of a packet reflects appropriately the service model applied by the service provider. (This statement ignores the fundamental question of what is a fair service model.)

You may even be able to make some inferences from this statement. Figure 6.3 shows two possible service models with essentially different targets. In the guaranteed-service model, the packets under a predefined bit rate obtain the best possible treatment (related to delay and loss probability); all excessive packets, on the other hand, are either marked with lowest importance or dropped immediately. In the resource-sharing model, a (virtually) continuous importance function is needed to inform the interior nodes about the relative amount of resources used by customers. Apparently, different characteristics are needed for these two service models.

In the guaranteed-service model (as well with several other service models), it is only necessary to know whether a limit is exceeded. In the case of the resource-sharing model, the metering gives information about the instantaneous bit rate, or more generally, about the amount of resources needed to transmit the packet flow through the network.

Figure 6.3   Desired measuring principle for guaranteed service and resource-sharing service.

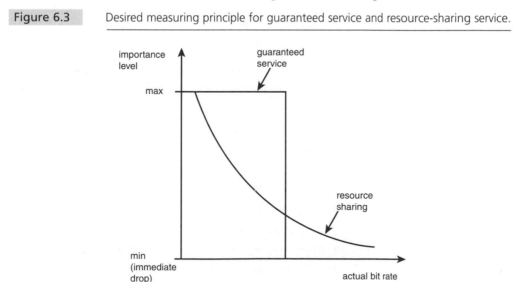

Note also that not only bit rate, but also packet rate can sometimes be an important factor. For a given link speed, the number of packets that the router has to handle each second depends on the packet size: The smaller the packets, the harder the processing requirement. Therefore, it can sometimes be reasonable to give more weight to small packets by using an extra term (B_0), as shown in Formula 6.1.

Formula 6.1

$$B_j = c_M * B_{j,real} + (1-c_M) * B_0$$

The component c_M is a constant between 0 and 1; $B_{j,real}$ is the real size of the IP packet; and B_0 is the "standard" packet size. If c_M is 1, the result is the real amount of bytes, and $c_M = 0$ means that only the number of packets is taken into account, not the packet sizes. Note that this is only one example of many possible schemes to take this requirement into account.

Measuring Principles

A long tradition of traffic measurements (well, at least *long* in a network-specific sense) means that there are many ways to manage traffic. This brief introduction to this complex issue concentrates on only a few typical models. As to the first goal (to evaluate whether a limit has been exceeded), the prevalent standard is to apply a token bucket scheme. See, for example, "General Characterization Parameters for Integrated Service Network Elements" (RFC 2215) and "An Architecture for Differentiated Services" (RFC 2475).

The Token Bucket Principle The basic principle of *token bucket* is that a bucket of capacity *b* is emptied by a constant rate of *r*. (Note that *leaky bucket* is often used as a synonym for token bucket.) The result of this formula measures whether the bucket is empty (or more accurately, whether there are enough tokens available for the incoming packet).

Token bucket is a reasonable and prevalent way to classify packets into two classes that can be called *in profile* and *out of profile*, where the profile is defined by the two parameters, *r* and *b*. Consider a simple example with an on/off source. This kind of source can be defined by three parameters:

- Average bit rate (A)

- Peak bit rate (P)

- Burst size (B)

For a given pair of *b* and *r*, each source defined by a triple (A,P,B) can be classified either as conforming or nonconforming flows (that is, some packets do not get a token). For instance, if

P = 10*A

b = 5KB

and r = 100kbps

the classification shown in Figure 6.4 results. The clarity of the token bucket principle stems from the fact that for every source with A ≤ r and B ≤ b, the packets of the flow are classified as conforming. Furthermore, if P ≤ r, all packets are conforming regardless of burst size.

Figure 6.4   Conforming and nonconforming flows measured by token bucket and by exponential moving average.

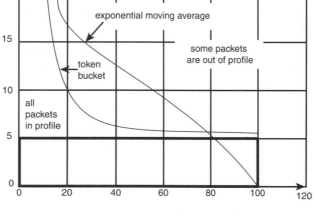

Measuring Bit Rates   Another simple alternative is to measure the momentary bit rate at the arrival time of packet j, $M(t_j)$, by using the exponential moving average, as shown in Formula 6.2.

Formula 6.2

$$M(t_j) = M(t_{j-1})*\exp\{[t_j-t_{j-1}]/\tau\} + B_j/\tau$$

In Formula 6.2, B_j is the size of the packet size in bytes, and defines the measurement period. An alternative simple method is based on windows (see Formula 6.3).

Formula 6.3

$$M(t_j) = \text{sum}(B_j \mid t \ge t_i > t_j - \tau)/\tau$$

This bit rate is the average bit rate over a period τ. It should be noted that the window method requires more memory because all the arrival times and packet sizes during the measuring period should be kept in the memory.

Both formulas produce a minimum bit rate for each value of packet size: B_j/τ. If the packet size is 500 bytes and the measuring period is 10 milliseconds, for example, the smallest measuring result is $500*8/0.01 = 400$kbps. This is a quite high value for an individual flow and, therefore, the measuring period should be longer if possible.

It is not clear why the measuring period should be short in general. What would happen if you applied an essentially longer period (for example, 10 seconds)? As to the fairness, the question can be asked in the following way: If each customer (i) is promised to obtain bit rate R_i, or a share S_i of network resources, what is the period on which the share or bandwidth should be determined? You may have different answers, ranging from one millisecond to one month. If your answer is relatively long (say, one hour), totally different traffic processes are considered equal.

A flow (F1) with constant bit rate of 10kbps is considered equal to another flow (F2) with one 10-second burst once an hour with a bit rate of 3.6Mbps, for example. This result seems to be inappropriate. If the period is 10 seconds, flow F2 is considered equal to a flow F3 with a permanent constant bit rate of 3.6Mbps. This result also seems to be inappropriate.

One solution to this dilemma is that instead of one measuring period, there are two (or even more). The total measuring result can be of the form shown in Formula 6.4.

Formula 6.4

$$M(t_j) = c_1 *\{M(t_{j-1})*\exp\{[t_j - t_{j-1}]/t_1\} + B_j/t_1\} + (1-c_1)*\{M(t_{j-1})*\exp\{[t_j - t_{j-1}]/t_2\} + B_j/t_2\}$$

Whether this additional complexity provides enough advantages is hard to assess without practical experience. With flat-rate pricing, the answer can be positive; with time pricing, however, the answer is most likely negative.

6.1.3 Packet Marking

Packet marking has two basic targets, as described in the preceding section. The first is to mark packets below and above a given threshold for bit rate. This can be generalized to a system with several thresholds. The second target is to somehow reflect the smoother function in Figure 6.3—that is, how much below or above the measuring result is compared to a standard value. From the perspective of Differentiated Services, the main objective in both cases is to map packets into one of the available importance levels of the PHB class used by the flow. When the measuring results are available, the actual marking is a mere technical issue.

There is a degree of freedom to build different models if the system provides measuring results on different levels of aggregation. The actual marking may depend on the measuring result of the particular PHB, of total traffic sent by the customer, and of the total traffic load of the end user's organization. Very complicated models are not recommended because of the additional management burden and higher probability of erroneous configurations.

Furthermore, an additional issue may have a significant effect on the robustness of the system. There are two marking principles:

- When a packet exceeds a threshold, it is marked as low importance, but it is not used to determine the load level of the following packets. Effectively, the allowed bit rate of the higher importance level is totally independent of the load of lower importance level. This principle is usually used with the token bucket system.

- When the momentary load level exceeds a threshold, every packet is marked with lower importance. This principle seems to be more reasonable with several importance levels, in particular, if the intention is to offer different availability levels.

The following example illustrates the fundamental difference between these principles. Suppose, for example, that there are three importance levels with packet-loss ratios 0, 0.01, and 1, and thresholds between the levels are 1 and 2. In marking method M1, the system marks as many packets as possible with the highest importance level, or with the intermediate importance levels if there are packets that cannot be put into the highest level.

In method M2, all packets are marked with the same importance level based on the bit rate of the flow: If the threshold is below 1, all packets attain highest importance; if the threshold is above 2, all packets get the lowest importance.

Now the final effect of packet losses depends crucially on the application that needs the network service. With certain applications, such as videoconferencing, the value of the service does not only depend on the successfully transmitted packets, but the negative value of a lost packet can be remarkable, because even one lost packet can generate significant disturbance in the application. Suppose that the value of a successfully transmitted packet is 1, and the value of a lost packet is -1000. (That means that a packet loss ratio of 0.001 or higher yields a worthless service.) In this case, the result from the user's perspective is quite similar with both marking principles, marked by (M1, -1000) and (M2, -1000) in Figure 6.5.

Alternatively, if the application is not at all sensitive to packet losses, there is no negative value for the lost packets. That is, in principle, the case if the application can retransmit lost packets, and only the total amount of successfully transmitted packets is an important factor. In this case, there is a significant difference between the two marking methods. After the bit rate exceeds the second threshold (2), the value for the customer basically remains constant with marking method M1, whereas marking method M2 results immediately in zero value for the customer. Therefore, the method M2 induces much stronger incentive for the customer to control its bit rate and not send excessive packets.

Figure 6.5   Two marking principles (M1 and M2) with two values for lost traffic (0, −1000).

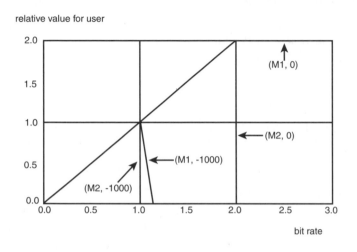

6.1.4 Traffic Shaping

The basic idea of shaping is that if a packet should be re-marked to a lower importance level, an alternative could be to shape the traffic process in such a way that re-marking (or dropping) is not necessary. Then you would obviously need another metering to determine whether the result is acceptable, however. In the case of several importance levels, it can be quite hard to decide when shaping is reasonable and when it is not, because this issue depends also on the delay constraints.

The user is, of course, allowed to shape the traffic before it is sent to the network. In general, that is probably a more reasonable scenario than shaping inside the network. If the only alternative for shaping is immediate dropping, the shaping option inside the public network might be reasonable. It is fair to conclude that shaping is usually better to do before metering and marking, or alternatively, in an integrated unit that could be able to make an optimal decision.

Therefore, you may consider shaping as something that is done for a given traffic process to reduce traffic variations, and by that means to improve the treatment inside the network. This is relatively simple action if there is a known target bit rate (or packet rate) and a known limit for additional delay. In contrast, it is not at all clear whether it is practical to delay packets to smooth a traffic process for achieving some benefit in some other part of the network. The two main points seems to be that shaping at the edge may decrease the delay variations inside the network for some other flows, and statistical multiplexing can be improved inside the network. It should be noted that traffic shaping leads to a non–work-conserving service discipline because even though there are packets to be transmitted they are not sent.

If the traffic process includes frequent high peaks, the multiplexing target could be realistic. An MPEG type of video coding could generate the traffic in Figure 6.6. In this case, it surely is reasonable to smooth the regular high peaks if the additional delay is not too long for the actual purposes of the application.

Figure 6.6   Traffic shaping for an MPEG-coded video stream.

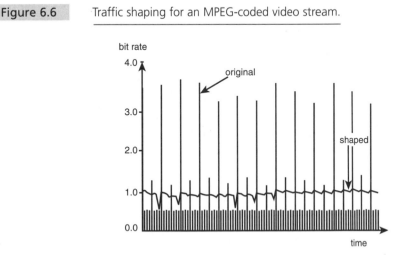

In that case, Figure 6.7 shows a case in which the traffic process is more irregular and has significant variations on different time scales. Although the traffic process could somewhat be smoothed, it is not feasible to even variations on time scales longer than some tens of milliseconds. If middle- or long-term variations are dominant, the real effect of traffic shaping on statistical multiplexing is likely insignificant. It is actually better to drop some packets rather than delay them excessively, because that could be the only way to reduce the load level.

Figure 6.7   Traffic shaping for traffic process with variation on all time scales.

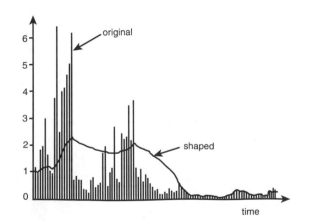

As to delay target, the main conclusion could be that if there are different flows with dif-fering delay requirements multiplexed in the same aggregate stream, it could be advanta-geous to shape streams with loose delay requirements at the boundary nodes as much as allowed. The main point is that traffic control inside the network is in practice easier with a smooth traffic process than with high variable traffic, even though in theory the drop and delay characteristics could be quite similar with and without shaping. A more recom-mended solution is always to use different delay classes on the one hand, for flows requir-ing low delay, and on the other hand, for flows with high bit-rate variations.

In particular, if and when traffic control is based on momentary load rather than on long-term average load, some packets may get essentially better treatment after shaping. In Figure 6.7, for instance, the boundary node may mark the packets belonging to the high-est peaks by low importance if it interprets the situation in such a way that the traffic load is high during the peaks—that is, it does not take into account that the peak rate is used very briefly.

Figure 6.8 further illustrates the situation. For instance, the decision of packet dropping may depend on the numbers of packets sent during a control window in a relatively short period (W). Suppose, for this example, that there are two flows on a link, an on/off flow (A) and a constant bit-rate flow (B).

If congestion emerges at time T1, the control system notices that there have recently been more packets in flow A than in flow B. In consequence, the node discards packets from flow A rather than from flow B. Because the average bit rate of flow B is much higher than that of flow A, it is more likely that flow B is more responsible for the congestion than flow A. Depending on several issues, however—such as other traffic flows and buffering capacity—the situation could be considered the other way around as well.

Figure 6.8   Effect of shaping on the metering result.

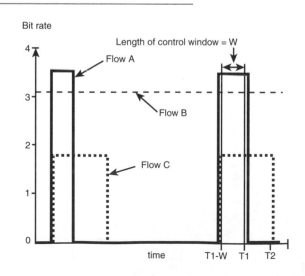

Then if you replace flow A by a smoother flow C with the same average bit rate, the result could be that the point of congestion is moved from T1 to T2 and the same amount of packets are discarded as in the original case. The difference is that, in this case, the control system expects that flow B is more responsible for the congestion than flow C, and as a result, discards packets from flow B. In this case, the discarding decision seems to be the right one. In summary, the effect of shaping can be quite dramatic for the application, although it is possible that the real effect from the network operator point of view is insignificant (for instance, the total amount of discarded packets remains the same).

6.1.5   Packet Dropping at Boundary Nodes

The last option is to drop packets before they enter the network. Certain services, particularly those using guaranteed connections or leased-line services presented in Figure 5.1 in Chapter 5, "Differentiation of Customer Service," may require that nonconforming packets be discarded immediately. Clear and unambiguous rules and algorithms should be used with these services, because erroneous packet drops violates the service model.

Although immediate packet dropping based merely on the traffic process sent by the customer is somewhat opposite to the fundamental principles of the resource-sharing model, an additional threshold for every user may restrict the total traffic sent by the customer. The problem of a straightforward system that controls only the total traffic is that it does not take into account the differences in packet importance. Customers would surely accept that some of the least important packets are dropped at the network boundary; whereas they probably would not approve if any of the most important packets were dropped immediately. A more complicated dropping system might solve this problem.

6.2   Traffic-Handling Functions in Interior Nodes

Basically the same tools are available both in boundary and interior nodes. There are, nevertheless, certain differences with regard to the main tasks. Boundary nodes are mainly responsible for packet marking and classification, but the main tasks of internal nodes are buffering and discarding. In addition, interior nodes may give information about the load or congestion to traffic sources.

In principle, the same classification as in the boundary nodes can apply to interior nodes as well. According to the main principles of Differentiated Services, however, interior nodes classify packets based on the DSCP field of the packet. In that sense, the situation is very clear. You may still ask whether some other information can be used as well (for example, the information provided by MPLS). This is surely a possible scenario, but it is not discussed further here because it is somewhat beyond of scope of Differentiated Services.

6.2.1 Buffering

A lot has been written about different queuing systems. For an in-depth analysis of the different systems, refer to *Queueing Systems, Volume 1, Theory* (Kleinrock 1975), *Queueing Systems, Volume 2, Computer Applications* (Kleinrock 1975), and *Broadband Network Teletraffic* (Roberts 1996). This section does not try to explain every queuing system in exhaustive detail. The main goal is to give an overview of the most reasonable queuing system, particularly from a Differentiated Services perspective.

First In, First Out (FIFO)

The primary model of queuing is *first in, first out* (*FIFO*). Because the simplicity is one of the key goals of Differentiated Services, it can be always considered as the default choice. A more complicated queuing system should be applied only if a FIFO system cannot offer appropriate characteristics.

In FIFO the packets that want to use an output link are placed into a queue in the order in which they were received. In the basic form of FIFO, every packet accepted into the queue is also transmitted forward, and moreover, packets are discarded only if the queue is so full that there is not enough space for the incoming packet.

As to the four attributes used for assessing Differentiated Services in this book (fairness, cost-efficiency, versatility, and robustness), the FIFO system provides certain clear advantages.

Cost-Efficiency FIFO can offer high cost-efficiency because the output link and buffer capacity are utilized very efficiently (although not necessarily in the absolutely optimal manner) with a simple mechanism. In that respect, there is not much to be gained with a more complicated mechanism. On the other hand, there are some significant problems with the other three attributes.

Fairness As long as all users behave in the same way—that is, they send packets according to an identical traffic process—FIFO appears to be quite fair. The delay and packet-loss properties are similar for every flow. That is, however, not a sufficient criteria for fairness, because a versatile system must also be able to offer fairness among customers with different behavior patterns. One of the fundamental problems of FIFO is that the system provides the same treatment for flows with a very high bit rate and a very low bit rate. That is, of course, not a problem if the customer is charged according to the bit rate; if the customer is charged a flat rate, however, this can be a significant problem.

Robustness Although a part of the fairness problem can be solved merely by providing appropriate traffic control in boundary nodes, even in the case of pure FIFO buffering inside the network, it seems that a high level of fairness requires a more complicated queuing. The same statement is largely valid for robustness as well. A basic FIFO relies completely on the traffic-control functions in boundary nodes, which may make the overall system too vulnerable to misbehaving users.

Versatility Moreover, the most critical shortcoming of FIFO from a Differentiated Services viewpoint is that it definitely does not support quality differentiation, because every flow going through a FIFO queue recognizes the same delay and packet-loss characteristics. Particularly, delay differentiation is practically impossible to achieve without a more advanced queuing system in interior nodes.

The main approach applied in this chapter and following chapters is to solve the versatility, fairness, and robustness problems of FIFO queuing. The following list summarizes the goals:

- It must provide reasonable tools for differentiation related to delay and loss characteristics.

- It must provide reasonable fairness even in cases where customers have totally different behavioral properties.

- It must work appropriately even in cases where the traffic control at boundary nodes does not work perfectly.

Priority Queuing

The first consideration is the issue of delay differentiation. This target can be met by using one queue for every delay class. In the simplest case, there are two queues with a strict priority discipline; that is, the lower-priority packet is served only if the higher-priority queue is empty (when the packet is starting the service).

A basic performance evaluation for the higher class is quite straightforward. If the link speed is C, the size of the higher-priority buffer is S_H, and the maximum size of packet is B_{max}, the maximum delay for a higher-class packet is $(S_H + B_{max})/C$. For instance, if link speed is 100Mbps, buffer capacity is 10KB, and maximum packet size is 1KB, the maximum queuing delay is approximately 0.9 milliseconds.

On the contrary, it is difficult to declare much about the delay of the lower-priority class, because that issue depends crucially on the traffic load and variations of the higher class. Yet, if the network operator can guarantee that the load level of the higher class remains always below a certain value, an evaluation of maximum delay for the lower class can be made. If the load level of the higher class measured over period T is always less than ρ_H, the maximum delay for lower class is bounded by the limit shown in Formula 6.5.

Formula 6.5

$$D_{max,L} < \rho_H * T + (S_L + S_H) / [(1-\rho_H)*C]$$

In Formula 6.5, S_L is the buffer size of the lower class and S_H is the buffer size of the higher class. This approximation is based on the assumption that when a lower-class packet arrives, the queue of the higher class is full, and in the lower queue there is space exactly for the incoming packet. To formulate an approximation, you must keep in mind two factors:

- The time that the higher queue can remain full because of the higher-class traffic

- The time needed to empty both buffers if you suppose that the load of the higher class remains on the level of $\rho_H * C$

If $S_L = 10KB$, $S_H = 1000KB$, $\rho_H = 0.5$ and $T = 0.1$ seconds, for instance, the maximum delay for the lower class is less than 212 milliseconds.

The practical problem is how the operator can effectively control the load level of a service class in interior nodes. It seems apparent that there is not any strict method because the load on every interior link is not controllable in a pure Differentiated Services networks. Nevertheless, something can be done for better control of delays as shown in the next sections. It should be stressed that in all practical implementations, the load level of the low-delay class should be somehow controlled to keep the packet-loss ratio at an acceptable level. This is particularly important because small buffers mean that the nodes cannot absorb a large burst of packets in the same way as larger non-real-time buffers.

Weights for Controlling Delays

The fact that traffic loads cannot be tightly controlled inside a Differentiated Services network makes the delay control problematic. Although the incoming packet stream in an interior node is largely uncontrollable, the outgoing stream of each service class can be rigorously controlled. Suppose, for example, that a PHB class i gets a proportion w_i of the whole link capacity when every queue is non-empty. Moreover, if one or several queues are empty, the link capacity is divided in proportion to the shares. If you ignore the problems to realize perfect weights with variable size packets, the maximum delay for class i is that expressed in Formula 6.6.

Formula 6.6

$$D_{max,i} = S_i / (w_i * C)$$

The main disadvantage of this approach is that although the weights seem to solve the delay-control problem, the target is attained at the expense of increased problems related to packet losses.

You may ask whether there is any fundamental difference between the approach based on weights and the approach that seeks to directly control the incoming load of each service class. In a certain sense, there is not much difference, because the weights together with finite buffer sizes actually control the incoming bit rates after the packet discarding (that is, R12 and R22 in Figure 6.9). For instance, the maximum average rate at point R12 over a period of length t is that expressed in Formula 6.7 if the buffer S_2 is not empty during the period t.

Formula 6.7

    R₁₂,max(t) = w₁*C + S₁/t

Therefore, if the load of Class 2 is high, the incoming flow to the Class 1 is controlled basically in the same way as in the delay-control system based on direct control of incoming traffic presented in the preceding chapter.

Figure 6.9   Bit rates before (R_{11} and R_{21}) and after (R_{12} and R_{22}) packet discarding.

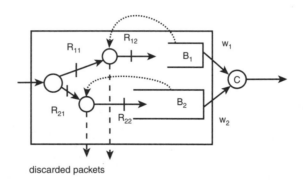

discarded packets

Weights are, however, better in the sense that they allow the use of total link capacity for one class when there is no traffic demand in the other class(es). Two key things make the weight approach better. First, weights yield a control loop from the buffer to the packet-discarding mechanism. The second key thing is the controlled sharing of the network capacity. Even the straightforward method to discard packets only when the buffer is full is definitely better than to discard packets merely based on the incoming bit rates of each class (R_{11} and R_{12} in Figure 6.9) regardless of the load in the buffers. This system, by itself, cannot manage packet-loss ratios if the incoming bit rates (R_{11} and R_{21}) are not regulated. Therefore, both fairness and robustness of this system depend crucially on traffic control at the boundary nodes.

Table 6.1 shows some numeric values that illustrate the delay characteristics of a queuing system connected to a 100Mbps link. The buffer size of the real-time class is so small compared to the typical packet size in IP networks that load level has to be low to obtain a small packet-loss ratio. Other tools to control packet-loss ratio in case of small buffers are to limit the maximum packet size and to limit traffic variations. This is the main reason why the metering function at boundary nodes should be different for real-time classes (as discussed in Chapter 5 in section 5.3.9 "Variable Bit Rate").

The maximum delay for the other two classes calculated by Formula 6.6 can be quite conservative, because the formula supposes that Class 1 utilizes its whole share all the time. If and when the average load level of Class 1 remains low—for instance, below 0.3—the real bandwidth share of the other classes is significantly higher than the theoretical minimum share. For instance, the capacity used by classes 1 and 2 during a 100-milliseconds period very seldom exceeds 50%. It should be stressed the figures in the rightmost column are valid only if the network-management system and the traffic control related to classes 1 and 2 can appropriately limit the load levels of classes 1 and 2.

Table 6.1   Maximum Delay for Three Traffic Classes

Delay Class	Share	Buffer Size Kb	Theoretical Maximum Delay (ms)	Realistic Maximum Delay (ms)
Class 1	0.75	10	1.07	0.5
Class 2	0.20	50	20	10
Class 3	0.05	500	800	100

Equal Queuing

As discussed in the preceding section, the basic mechanisms that can be used to control delays are often inappropriate for controlling bit rates or packet-loss ratios. This section offers an overview of a simple system that can be used to improve the fairness and robustness of FIFO queuing. This discussion uses the general term *equal queuing* for those systems that try to divide the link capacity evenly among some entities. The entity can be an active flow or an aggregate traffic stream—it is up to the service provider to specify the entity and to use an appropriate system to classify packets according to the specification.

This discussion avoids using the term *fair queuing*, because equal share is not necessarily synonymous with fair share. (Note that according to RFC 1254, "Gateway Congestion Control Survey," fair queuing is the policy of maintaining separate gateway output queues for individual end systems by a source-destination pair [Mankin, Ramakrishnan 1991].)

From the Differentiated Services viewpoint, the fundamental difficulty is that interior nodes are not supposed to keep any per-flow records. Further, even though an equal share for every individual user could be considered fair, the same approach is not usually applicable to aggregate streams. What then would be the use of equal queuing in a Differentiated Services network? One tentative answer is robustness. Although equal share is not necessary an optimal result, and it is not easy to classify packets accurately into meaningful groups inside the network, even an inaccurate classification may significantly improve the robustness of the total service system.

Several proposed queuing systems can be classified into this group of queuing systems. A brief outline of two of them is offered here: Stochastic Fairness Queueing and Fair Buffer Allocation.

Stochastic Fairness Queueing (SFQ) McKenney suggested Stochastic Fairness Queueing (SFQ) as a technique to solve the implementation problems of more complicated fair queuing systems (see *Stochastic Fairness Queueing* [McKenney 1990] and RFC 1254, "Gateway Congestion Control Survey" [Mankin, Ramakrishnan 1998]). SFQ classifies packets according to the source-destination address pair in an incoming packet. SFQ uses a simple hash function to map the packet with an address pair to one of the available queues. The hash function means that the assignment of an address pair to a queue is probabilistic. Therefore, it is possible that packets belonging to different flows are classified into the same queue. To improve the long-term fairness, SFQ periodically changes the hash function in a way that the same address pairs do not collide continually.

According to McKenney, you may need to have up to 5 to 10 times more queues than the number of active source-destination pairs. Note that the activity has in this case a very limited sense: Only those flows that have at least one packet in the buffer are active. It is possible to assess the effect of stochastic sharing by a simple mathematical model. The probabilities that a flow has its own queue or that it has to share the queue with one or several flows can be calculated from binomial distribution. Table 6.2 shows the result in a case with 1,000 queues and either 100 or 200 active flows. You can further calculate a theoretical value for the available bit rate, if you suppose that SFQ can divide the bandwidth exactly among all active queues and that the bandwidth of a queue is divided exactly evenly among flows directed to it.

Table 6.2 SFQ Queuing System Sharing a 10Mbps Link

Sharing of Queue	100 Active Flows		200 Active Flows	
	Probability	Bit Rate (kbps)	Probability	Bit Rate (kbps)
Alone	0.9057	105.0	0.8195	55.1
With 1 flow	0.0898	52.5	0.1632	27.6
With 2 flows	0.0044	35.0	0.0162	18.4
With 3 flows	0.0001	26.3	0.0011	13.8
With 4 flows	0.0000	21.0	0.0001	11.0

It should be noted that although SFQ clearly increases the bit-rate variation compared to a perfect system (that is, equal sharing of bandwidth), the number of active flows is in practice a variable as well. The user cannot, therefore, expect that the available bit rate for a flow remains constant in any resource-sharing system. Therefore, the essential issue is whether the increase of bandwidth variation is acceptable or even noticeable. The final assessment of SFQ depends on the service model adopted by the service provider: The more guarantees promised, the more queues needed. Further, because of the stochastic nature of SFQ, it seems very difficult to use different weights for different flows.

Fair Buffer Allocation In the Fair Buffer Allocation, the interior node keeps track of the number and/or size of packets in each buffer. When the occupancy level of the buffer exceeds a certain limit, the queuing system starts to discard incoming packets belonging to those streams that have the most packets in the buffer. The decision formula proposed in "A Fair Buffer Allocation Scheme" was originally intended for ATM networks with constant size packets (Heinanen, Kilkki 1995). If you modify it to IP networks with variable-sized packet, the rule shown in Formula 6.8 results.

Formula 6.8

Discard an incoming packet belonging to stream i

if $x > c_2$ and
$$S(i)/E\{S(i)\} > c_1 *[1 + (1 - x)/(x - c_2)]$$

for which

$S(i)$ = buffer space used by stream i

$E\{S(i)\}$ = average buffer space used by all active streams

x = occupancy level of the buffer—that is, the amount of used buffer space divided by the total buffer size

c_1 should be smaller than 1 to keep the probability of a totally full buffer small

c_2 defines the lowest occupancy level on which the FBA is active

An obvious result of this system is that the packet-loss ratio of streams with a high bit rate (or burstiness) is higher than that of smooth streams with a low bit rate. With TCP it tends to equalize the bit rates of different flows.

Class-Based Queuing (CBQ)

According to Ferguson and Huston, in the book *Quality of Service, Delivering QoS on the Internet and in Corporate Networks*, the fundamental goal of CBQ is to prevent complete resource denial to any particular class of service (Ferguson, Huston 1998). (See also "Link-Sharing and Resource Management Models for Packet Networks" [Floyd and Jacobson 1995].) Hence, the objective of CBQ is to solve the starvation problem of strict priority queuing. The basic assumption of CBQ is that traffic is classified into relatively large aggregates according to a principle that depends on the service model. (See section 4.2.2, "Levels of Aggregation," in Chapter 4.) The three main principles are as follows:

- Requirements of applications

- Price paid by customers

- Organization of the user

Requirements of Applications As to the CBQ, the first option means that flows are grouped according to the application, and one class can be used simultaneously by a large number of users. What is the fairness (or robustness) problem that CBQ tries to solve in this case? Apparently users are grouped according to the application they are using. If a group is too active or too large compared to other groups, it is considered fair to limit the available bandwidth for those users. If a user then changes the group—for instance, from IP telephony to a data application—he may obtain better service because the latter group happens to be smaller at that moment.

So the fundamental idea is that a group of users should not utilize the whole capacity even though the application they are using may need higher quality than another application. What does this statement actually imply? One interpretation is that the importance of an individual packet depends on the aggregate load level of the class. The more users there are in the same service class, the less important individual packets are, and vice versa.

Because the relative importance of packets from different classes depends both on the load levels and on the weights of each class, it is practically impossible to make any useful predictions for the quality of individual flows. It is not possible to state that the packet-loss ratio in a class is always lower in Class 1 than in Class 2, for instance. In particular, without any additional traffic-control mechanisms, this system is vulnerable to misbehaving users. This application model could, however, be reasonable in certain cases—for instance, in private networks.

The following evaluation of other approaches is based mainly on the pricing model—that is, on the assumption that the main classification criteria is related to pricing.

Higher Price, Better Quality A common claim related to CBQ is that lower relative load level somehow automatically means better service quality. You can attempt to attain different relative load levels either by regulating incoming traffic or by changing the weights dynamically. Static weights without traffic control, on the other hand, seems to be an unrealistic approach.

A simple approach is to just give different prices for different classes (see, for example, the Paris Metro pricing discussion in "A Modest Proposal for Preventing Internet Congestion" [Odlyzko 1997]). Another approach could be that each user is allowed to send more traffic if he selects a lower class. (Note that there is actually not much difference between these two approaches.) Regardless of the mechanism used to induce load differences, one question remains: In what way is the service of the higher class better than the service of the lower class? The answer might be more bandwidth or smaller packet-loss ratio or lower delay, or possibly even a combination of these.

It seems apparent that the loss ratio of every flow within a class is approximately the same if there is only one importance level in every class. If the load level is the only significant factor, it seems obvious that both delay and loss characteristics are better in Class 1 than in Class 2 or 3, if the relative load level is highest in Class 3 and lowest in Class 1. Figure 6.10 shows a possible target of this system.

Figure 6.10   A target for quality differentiation of a CBQ system.

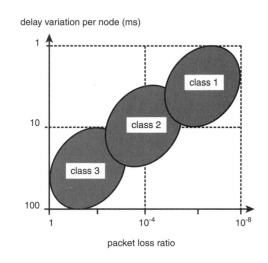

If the average load level is the only controlled factor, however, the relationship between delay and loss is not as clear as can be expected. Both low delay and low loss ratio can be achieved only if the traffic load is somehow controlled within a relatively short period, as described in the section "Priority Queuing" earlier in this chapter.

A short control period actually means that traffic must be smooth (or the load level must be extremely low). Unfortunately, high price does not, by itself, encourage smooth traffic. On the contrary, the first assumption of some customers may be that high price means freedom to send whatever they want. It is not recommended, in general, to mix delay-sensitive and bursty data traffic in the same class, even in the case of a low load level. An additional mechanism is needed to prevent users from sending highly variable traffic to a low delay class.

Higher Price, More Bandwidth The general problem with trying to associate high price with high quality is that the system should also define how the quality depends on the traffic sent by the customer. It does not appear reasonable just to have three classes without defining the relationship between sent traffic and quality. A CBQ system could have a more advanced goal, such as within each class, higher bit rate means higher packet-loss probability. The difference between the classes could then be in the available bit rate. Figure 6.11 depicts this target system.

Figure 6.11   Target "higher price, more bandwidth" for a service model using CBQ.

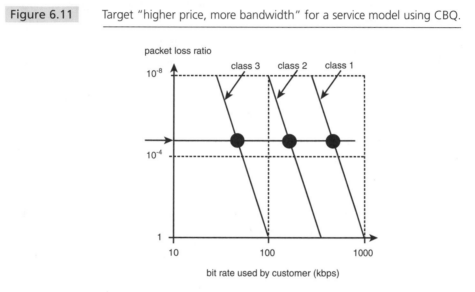

Although this target, or goal, could be achieved by means of CBQ with some additional mechanisms (discussed later in section 6.2.2, "Discarding," it is important to ask whether CBQ is the best tool for trying to attain this goal. Suppose, for example, that flow 1 with a bit rate of 500kbps uses Class 1, flow 2 with a bit rate 150kbps uses Class 2, and flow 3 with a bit rate 50kbps uses Class 3. According to Figure 6.11, the packet-loss target for every flow is approximately the same, 10^{-5}. In this case, the fundamental issue is how the treatment of these three flows will differ inside the network. The importance of the packets belonging to each flow is the same, and the bit rate should be controlled in the boundary node.

Delay is the remaining basic service characteristic. It is not, however, clear why the operator should associate low delay with high bit rate. Once again, a feasible low delay service cannot be realized without a mechanism that controls the traffic burstiness.

Summary of CBQ Although Class-Based Queuing is technically a reasonable approach, it is somewhat difficult to define a feasible purpose for its application. The three targets identified here are the requirements of the applications; higher price and better quality; and higher price and more bandwidth. Each of these could be met with CBQ, and CBQ might even be practical in some cases. Nevertheless, the fairness criterion of the Internet is that customers get service proportionate to the price they pay. CBQ doesn't seem to meet this expectation; if it did, CBQ is difficult to apply efficiently.

Weighted Fair Queuing (WFQ)

You can find overviews of Weighted Fair Queuing (WFQ) in *An Engineering Approach to Computer Networking: ATM Networks, the Internet, and the Telephone Network* (Keshav 1997) and *Broadband Network Teletraffic* (Roberts 1996). According to Keshav, the intuition behind WFQ is to compute the time a packet would complete a service had a General Process Sharing (GPS) server been used to service the packets and then to serve packets to these finishing times. GPS is a theoretical scheduling discipline that shares the bandwidth exactly in proportion to the weight of the connections.

Three facts make WFQ itself not an attractive approach in Differentiated Services networks. First, it is difficult to utilize WFQ without per-flow queuing. Second, WFQ systems need to know the weight of each flow, and if the requirement changes, a signaling system is needed to transmit relevant information. Third, WFQ requires quite a hard computational effort. All these three factors—per-flow queuing, signaling, and complex computation—are avoided in Differentiated Services networks.

Several variations of WFQ may reduce the computational complexity. These variations include Self-Clocked Fair Queuing (SCFQ) and Start-Time Fair Queuing (SFQ). (Note that the abbreviation SFQ is applied in this book usually to the Stochastic Fairness Queuing). Because all these disciplines require per-flow computations inside the network, they are not discussed further in this book.

If the principle of WFQ is used to offer fair service between aggregates, there remains the fairness problem between flows inside the aggregate. Therefore, it is not necessarily useful to implement complex systems to guarantee optimal fairness between aggregate streams if there is not any mechanism to provide reasonable fairness within the aggregate. This issue depends, however, on the service model applied by the service provider. If the service provider wants to separate the traffic streams among organizations, a variant of WFQ can be a reasonable solution.

6.2.2 *Discarding*

Various methods have been developed to discard packets better than the basic FIFO queue. In this instance, basic FIFO refers to a queuing system in which packets are discarded only if the queue is so full that there is not enough space for the incoming packet. Usually the decision to discard is based on the current load level: The higher the load level, the higher the probability of discarding a packet. There are various ways to implement this simple idea:

- The load can be measured in several ways. The main approaches are based on the buffer occupancy level and on the bit rate. Although it is also possible to take into account the trend (rate of load change), more complicated algorithms may increase the risk of unstable behavior. Therefore, the starting point should be a simple system based on an average load level.

- Different time scales can be used from momentary occupancy level to a bit rate measurement over a long period.

- The load can be related merely to the PHB class used by the incoming packet, or it could be related to the total load.

- Either hard thresholds or smooth probability functions can be applied to make the discarding decision.

The following sections provide an overview of some discarding principles. The target is not to explain all possible principles, but to emphasize realistic applications for Differentiated Services networks.

Hard Thresholds

The simplest step from a basic FIFO queue is to classify packets into two importance groups. Packets with high importance are accepted whenever it is possible, and packets with low importance are accepted only when the load level is below a certain threshold. Obviously, this kind of system provides a simple tool to realize two importance levels within a class (where all packets of a particular class use the same queue).

Although this is a well-known and elaborately studied system, it is difficult to give any general rule for dimensioning the system—that is, to determine the proper buffer size and the proper threshold for given quality requirements. Nevertheless, you can take the higher importance level as a starting point and suppose that it needs a buffer of size B_H to guarantee sufficient quality. In this case, the worst case scenario is that the traffic load on the lower level is not controlled at all and, therefore, keeps the buffer occupancy level steadily near the threshold. Therefore, the total buffer capacity would be $B_H + B_L$, where B_L is the buffer space available for packets with low importance. The only significant effect of low importance packets to the high importance packets is the increased delay component.

Although this system can be easily generalized to several levels of threshold, an accurate analysis of the system becomes very complex. In particular, one fundamental question has to be answered before any real implementation with several importance levels can be made. Although a two-level system may work even without any significant traffic control for the lower-importance level, a network with several importance levels certainly requires a systematic control mechanism that makes the use of the system logical.

In principle, the system can rely either on the application model or on the customer model. (See section 4.2.2, "Levels of Aggregation," in Chapter 4.) One plausible reason for the opposition of several importance levels in the Internet is that more than two levels are hardly justified if the service model is based on the different requirements of applications. Therefore, the purpose of several importance levels has to be sought from the customer model instead. And even in that case, the target is not to provide a large number of distinguishable levels of packet-loss ratio, but rather levels of availability (see section 4.2.1, "Availability of Quality," in Chapter 4).

Therefore, the system should support the provision of availability levels in a consistent fashion. One possible target could be the realization of function presented in Figure 5.10 in Chapter 5 (see section 5.3.3, "Price of Availability," in Chapter 5). There could be, for instance, three levels of availability with different prices aimed to cover idle, normal, and busy hours. In addition, the service provider should take into account the effect of different destinations, because the available resources may greatly vary in different parts of the global Internet. These two dimensions, time and destination, together may yield a need for several levels of availability, even though at times two levels of importance could be enough on a certain link for all practical purposes.

Random Early Detection (RED)

Although the previous discussion emphasizes to the need to support customer service with differentiated pricing, there is one clearly identified need to improve the performance in case of a pure application model. The problem relates to the interaction between the congestion control of TCP and the "tail drop" principle, where the tail drop means that packets are dropped only when the queue is full.

The core of the problem is that although certain properties of a TCP control mechanism are definitely necessary, they result in problems with a pure FIFO queuing. TCP effectively increases the bit rate of a flow until a packet is dropped. Because the control mechanism allows the sender to transmit several packets in a burst, a full buffer may generate a situation in which numerous flows encounter several packet drops. As a result, all these flows decrease their bit rate sharply, and then start again to increase their bit rate. In the worst case, this may result in a global synchronization where the overall load oscillates between overload and low load levels. For a more detail account of this issue, refer to RFC 2309, "Recommendations on Queue Management and Congestion Avoidance in the Internet" (Braden *et al.* 1998).

Large buffers in IP networks are primarily needed to handle bursts of packets appropriately, not to increase utilization. Note that, in general, the link utilization depends only on the probability that a queue is non-empty, not on the average number of packets in the buffer. Therefore, it can be reasonable to drop some packets even before the buffer becomes full to control the incoming bit rates. In addition, it is desirable that only one packet per flow is dropped and that drops do not occur exactly at the same time. This kind of system, Random Early Detection (RED), was first proposed by Floyd and Jacobson in an article titled "Random Early Detection Gateways for Congestion Avoidance" KC (Floyd, Van Jacobson 1993, 397–413).

Figure 6.12 illustrates the principle behind RED. Under a certain load level, all packets are accepted. In such as case, on the middle region the packet-loss probability depends on the load level. Finally, if the queue, after all, becomes full, all packets are discarded.

Figure 6.12   The principle behind RED.

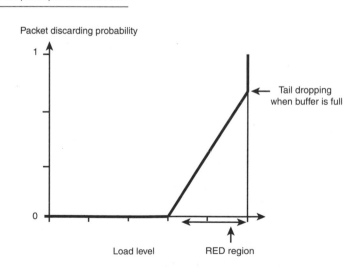

RED can be evaluated by using the four attributes guiding this discussion: fairness, cost-efficiency, robustness and versatility. RED solves certain problems very effectively due to its simplicity. The increase in complexity compared to FIFO is so small that it does not seem to be an obstacle even in very high-speed routers.

Although RED attempts to solve only specific problems, if (and when) it is used in real networks, network operators and service operators have to be sure that it works appropriately with all applications and services that use queues with RED. In case of large buffers, an appropriately configured RED probably does not have any significant harmful effect. On the contrary, it may both reduce average delay and provide a more even packet-loss ratio among flows than a pure FIFO queue.

In a sense, RED is very fair: The packet-loss ratio is similar with all flows, which means that flows with a higher bit rate encounter a larger number of losses. But then, once again, the real fairness depends crucially on the target, or on the service model. If the target is to share the capacity equally and efficiently, RED serves that purpose well. If the target is more complicated, as it likely is in Differentiated Services networks, a mere RED could be a useful, but not a sufficient, tool.

Because RED seems to decrease the probability of some harmful effects, such as global synchronization, it clearly is more robust than a FIFO system. RED can work effectively only if the majority of flows apply an end-to-end congestion control, however, such as TCP. Therefore, it does not solve the fairness and robustness issues related to nonadaptive flows.

Besides, any system with several free parameters requires additional management effort. To be really efficient, RED parameters should be properly adjusted to each situation with a specific traffic process, link capacity, and buffering scheme. Without a profound understanding of these issues, the parameters could be incorrectly selected; if that happens, system performance could deteriorate.

RED with Several Levels of Importance

The previous chapters separately discussed the need of several importance levels with hard thresholds, and the need of one soft threshold. If and when both needs are justified in real networks, you should be able to combine these two into the same system. Technically, this is a simple issue: Every hard threshold can be replaced by a soft, probabilistic discarding function. However, a couple of practical issues are not totally clear. Should the RED regions overlap each other, and should you use RED for all thresholds?

It seems that the primary situation is that RED regions of different importance levels should not overlap with each other, as shown in Formula 6.9.

Formula 6.9

```
If 0 < Pr_drop(x,p) < 1,
then Pr_drop(x,p-1) = 1 and Pr_drop(x,p+1) = 0
```

The component x is load level, and p is an importance level, and higher numeric value of p means higher importance, and $Pr_{drop}(x,p)$ is the packet-discarding probability. In addition, the probability function should be a nondecreasing function, such as this:

$Pr_{drop}(x,p) \geq Pr_{drop}(y,p)$ if x > y

$Pr_{drop}(0,p) = 0$ (for every p, unless the service provider wants to discard all packets of lowest importance levels)

$Pr_{drop}(1,p) = 1$ (because 1 means full system)

If the service provider, after all, decides that RED regions should overlap, that means a weaker separation between adjacent importance levels. Because this is not usually a desirable effect, it could be better to separate the RED regions, and even to leave an additional region between the areas as shown in Figure 6.13.

Figure 6.13   Random Early Detection with two importance levels.

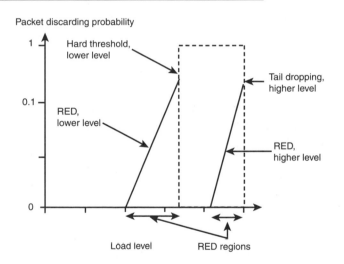

Moreover, it is not clear whether a RED mechanism is useful with the highest levels of importance. With high service levels, the expectation is that packet losses are very rare, and consequently, it is not reasonable to suppose that the bit rates are adjusted based on packet losses. If TCP or another control mechanism is not used to adjust the bit rate, there is not necessarily any significant difference between hard threshold and RED. Yet, there could be some advantages to using RED also with higher importance levels; for instance, it may distribute the packet drops more evenly among active flows, and it may give a warning signal about imminent quality degradation to the users.

Finally, it is possible that in some cases TCP flows that normally use lower importance levels may exploit higher importance levels by decreasing their bit rate below a certain threshold. Therefore, even though under normal circumstances higher importance levels are used to transmit something other than TCP flows, under abnormal conditions a significant portion of the traffic could be TCP flows.

In summary, RED is certainly recommended for the dominant service class of the Internet—that is, for best-effort service with a majority of flows using TCP congestion control. On the other hand, it is not evident whether RED is advantageous with nonadaptive services, although it doesn't seem harmful.

6.2.3   Feedback Information

The Differentiated Services model is based primarily on the assumption that each user sends packets into the network according to a traffic process that is essentially independent of the network service. Packets may request a PHB class based on the requirements of the application, and the importance level of the packet is set mainly by the boundary node according to the service level agreement. However, the network does not require that a PHB class be used only if the traffic process complies with certain rules. The definition of PHB may, of course, include that when the incoming bit rate exceeds a certain limit, some packets are discarded immediately. Thus the PHB rules and incoming traffic process together determine how the packets are treated inside the network—but basically the network service does not dictate the incoming traffic process.

This primary principle appears logical as long as the service is based on the customer model. (See section 4.2.2, "Levels of Aggregation," in Chapter 4.) If the service model is based on the requirements of applications, however, with the assumption that users behave appropriately, the network operators may use a different approach in which they try to directly control the incoming traffic process based on the load inside the network.

TCP flow control is one example of this kind of approach (see section 2.3.2 "Basic Best-Effort Service Based on TCP," in Chapter 2, "Traffic Management Before Differentiated Services," and the previous section in this chapter related to the RED mechanism). Although TCP relies on the fact that some packets must be dropped during (severe) overload, some other schemes are based on softer congestion indication. Further, it is possible that the network tries to inform the source about the exact available bit rate (see the section "Available Bit Rate, (ABR)" in Chapter 2). Because that kind of service model requires per-flow calculation inside the network, it is chiefly beyond the scope of Differentiated Services and this book.

Although the current Differentiated Services framework does not include the application of congestion indication, it may be used later with some PHB classes as proposed by

Kalyanaraman, *et al.*, in "A One-Bit Feedback Enhanced Differentiated Services Architecture" (1998). Therefore, this discussion provides a brief overview of two possible approaches: DECbit and congestion avoidance in Frame Relay.

DECbit

The fundamental idea behind the DECbit approach is that the packet header carries a bit that can be set by a network node when the node is experiencing congestion, as discussed in "A Binary Feedback Scheme for Congestion Avoidance in Computer Networks with Connectionless Network Layer" (Jain, Ramakrishnan 1988). The receiver copies the bit to the acknowledgment packet, and sends it back to the source. Finally, the source is supposed to reduce the sending bit rate when more than 50% of the packets have the congestion bit set; if less than 50% of the bits are set, however, the sender is allowed to increase the bit rate.

In the basic DECbit scheme, the network nodes make the decision of setting the congestion bit depending on the bit rate of each connection. The nodes set bits first on those connections that are using more capacity than their fair share. This system apparently does not comply with the fundamental philosophy of Differentiated Services because it requires per-flow calculations inside the network. In a simpler scheme, the network node measures only the aggregate queue length and sets the congestion bit when the average queue length exceeds a threshold.

The main flaw of the DECbit approach is that it requires that both senders and receivers cooperate and be able to adjust their bit rate. If one sender decides to ignore the congestion bit, for example, it may have a harmful effect on all other flows. In such a case, if the operator tries to control the behavior of all customers, complicated mechanisms are needed at boundary nodes. This hard problem has to be solved before a DECbit or another similar scheme can be applied to the global Internet.

Congestion Avoidance in Frame Relay

The congestion avoidance scheme of Frame Relay is similar to that of DECbit (see, for example, the FRForum Web site at www.frforum.com). The main difference is that in a Frame Relay network, nodes may inform both sender (Backward Explicit Congestion Notification, [BECN]) and receiver (Forward Explicit Congestion Notification [FECN]) about upcoming congestion. In the Internet environment, backward congestion indication appears impractical, if not impossible, because there is no guarantee that packets in the reverse direction use the same path.

Although there is no specification as to how the user should react when receiving congestion notification, the basic idea is that end users alleviate the congestion by reducing the bit rate somehow. From a fairness point of view, this is obviously a problematic situation because when some users react and other do not, the final result is an uneven share of resources.

Moreover, Frame Relay specification also introduces a *discard eligible* bit. Essentially, this means that frames can be classified into two importance groups as described earlier in the section "Hard Thresholds". In summary, a Frame Relay node may have four states, depending on the load:

- Low load, where all frames are accepted and no congestion indication bit is set.

- Moderate load, where all frames are accepted but congestion indication bits are set.

- High load, where frames with a discard eligible bit are discarded, and congestion indication bits are set.

- Full buffer means that all incoming frames have to be discarded.

A similar system is surely possible in Differentiated Services networks—actually, the discard eligible bit is a natural part of Differentiated Services. On the other hand, the role of congestion indication is not very clear: The network may, of course, set the bit, but what is the customer supposed to do when he receives a congestion notification?

One approach is to make the congestion notification just extra information provided by the network; users can use the information or ignore it totally. It seems that to be useful in Differentiated Services networks, the congestion notification should somehow indicate on which service (or importance) level the congestion notification is valid. Then, for instance, if the network informs that some packets on the lowest importance level of a PHB class must be discarded, the user can reduce the bit rate in such a way that all packets attain better importance level. Some users, on the other hand, may prefer to use a high bit rate even at the risk of losing some packets. Both behaviors should be equally acceptable.

6.3 Functions Related to a Network Domain

Most of the standardization effort of Differentiated Services relates to the function inside network nodes. In addition to these important aspects, a successful service provision requires a systematic way to manage the whole effort. This section briefly introduces three key issues related to the operation of a network domain: routing, resource reservations, and network dimensioning.

6.3.1 Routing

Routing is an integral part of IP networks. Although it is totally clear that routing a system is necessary, the issues related to the dynamics and QoS aspects of routing are less clear.

According to the fundamental rules of both IP networks, in general, and Differentiated Services, in particular, it is not reasonable to apply adaptive routing to individual packets based on the load in the network (that is, within the packet-forwarding function).

In contrast, it could be reasonable to balance the load of different links on longer time scales. Consider, for example, the simple network with six nodes shown in Figure 6.14. Usually the primary route is that with the shortest path. If you calculate the length between each node pair in the network, you get a result of 1.4 hops. In most cases, the secondary route is longer than the primary route. The primary route from A to D consists of two hops, for example, although any other route consists of at least three hops. Although in some cases the number of hops could be the same, such as between nodes B and F, the average length of a secondary route is significantly longer, 2.2 hops, than the average length of the primary route.

As a result, if the load level when using only a primary router is 0.7, and half of the traffic is shifted (randomly) to the secondary route, the average load level is increased to 0.9. Of course, random decision is not rational, and the situation could be much better if the decision is based on some level of optimization. The point is that optimization, or at least feasible reasoning, is necessary when making the decision to use secondary routes.

Figure 6.14   Primary and secondary routes.

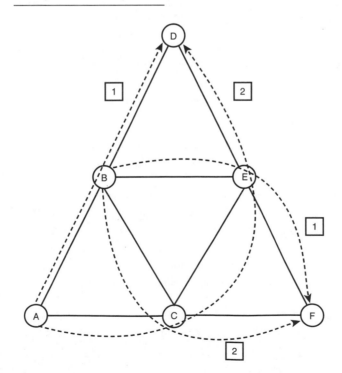

The main reason to use alternative routes is *load balancing*, which is a part of the larger problem of long-term network planning, in which the operator tries to optimize the use of network resources. Load balancing can be defined as the capability to decrease the maximum load by changing the traffic from links with high load to links with lower load. Remember, however, that the average load level is increased.

It is possible to decrease the load on links with the highest traffic, for example, but at the expense of a higher average load in the network. Based on a constricted evaluation of the network presented in Figure 6.14, it seems that the maximum load among the links can be decreased by 25% at the expense of a somewhat higher average load level (for instance, 5%). Figure 6.15 shows one example in which the load level of the most loaded link (D-E) can be reduced from 16 down to 12 by using secondary routes. At the same time, the load level of most other links is increased.

This useful, albeit moderate, result is more a theoretical possibility than an achievable proposition in real networks, however, because of the following reasons:

- It is supposed that the average load levels were exactly known. That is, of course, possible with past traffic processes, but that does not mean that the future traffic levels are known.

- It is not necessarily possible to divide traffic streams arbitrarily among different routes; for instance, in the case of AF service, different routes for PHBs within one PHB class cannot be used.

- There is no obvious and simple common goal for optimization; in the example, the goal was just to minimize the maximum load among all links. In Differentiated Services networks, that is not necessarily the right objective because it does not take into account the relative importance of packets.

- In a large network, it is very hard to solve the complex optimization problem (particularly, if the effects of the first three items are taken into account).

To summarize, even though alternative routes can be useful, especially during extraordinary situations (for instance, if a cable is broken), they probably do not essentially improve the network performance during normal situations. Load balancing is reasonable, but only with other appropriate planning and management tools. One possibility in Differentiated Services networks is to use load balancing mainly for the highest importance levels and to ignore the effect of the lowest importance levels.

| Figure 6.15 | Load balancing using secondary routes. |

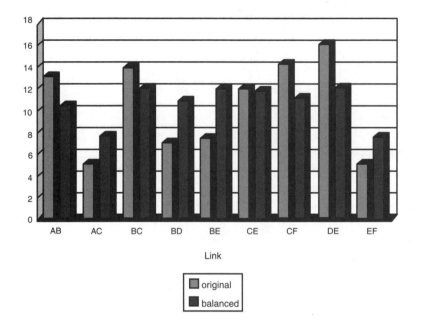

6.3.2 Resource Reservation

The general argument of this book relating to resource reservation is that it should be used only when really necessary, not as the only standardized solution to all quality problems.

Note

The basic characteristics of resource reservation are discussed throughout this book. For instance, see section 2.4, "Integrated Service Model," in Chapter 2; the section "Resource Reservation" in Chapter 4; and the section "Service-Level Agreement" in Chapter 5.

Considering resource reservation from the perspective of Differentiated Services, the most practical level of resource reservation is the PHB class. In addition, it could sometimes be necessary or reasonable to make capacity reservations for large organizations. In both cases, the rationality of the reservation should be assessed carefully, because reservations tend to complicate networks and their management and deteriorate statistical multiplexing.

The technical part of resource reservation is mostly beyond the scope of this book. It can be done either by using an IP protocol, such as RSVP or MPLS, or by using some other technology, such as virtual paths and virtual connections in ATM networks.

One way to implement resource reservation is with a bandwidth broker, as discussed in "A Two-Bit Differentiated Services Architecture for the Internet" (Nichols, Van Jacobson, Zhang 1997). The idea of a bandwidth broker is, in itself, clear. Rather than using a signaling system to separately ask every node through the path whether there is enough available resources to support a new flow, the request is handled primarily by one or a couple of bandwidth brokers. Consequently, an efficient bandwidth broker must have real-time information about the load within a network domain, and about the prices of all types of flows.

Although this approach is clearly unsuitable for all short-duration flows in the Internet, it may offer a reasonable solution for those (rare) cases in which a significant amount of resources are required through the network and where additional pricing is needed to control the use of such resources. A bandwidth broker can also be used solely to inform users about the characteristics and prices of different service classes.

6.3.3 Network Dimensioning

Dimensioning a network that is used to transmit Differentiated Services is an intricate task. The traffic processes and quality requirements vary almost infinitely—how is it possible at all to determine appropriate capacities in this kind of situation? It is fair to say that dimensioning is an almost impossible, albeit inevitable, task for any network operator.

This chapter briefly outlines two starting points for dimensioning. The first one is based on the methods and models used in connection-oriented network. The second one is mainly based on the idea that practical experience is your only guide when dimensioning packet networks with variable traffic processes and quality requirements. Certain other possibilities exist as well, but they are left to a more specific book.

Connection-Oriented Networks

Quite a lot of theoretical research has been conducted in the area of dimensioning connection-oriented networks; the history of this research can be traced back to the studies of A. K. Erlang. What Erlang achieved was a simple, but efficient formula for call-blocking probability under certain statistical assumptions. If the inter-arrival time between successive call attempts is an exponentially distributed random variable with mean λ, the average holding time is h, and the number of channels is S, the call-blocking probability is that shown in Formula 6.10.

Formula 6.10

```
Pr(blocking) = [(Aˢ)/S!]/{sum [(Aⁱ)/i!]}
                             i=0...S)
```

A = average offered load = λ/h. If the network operator has a rational approximation for average load level (A) and a target for blocking probability, he can just use the Erlang's formula to define the required number of channels.

Although all the theoretical assumptions are not valid in reality, telephone networks have largely been planned using this formula. Why can't this be applied to the dimensioning of packet networks as well? Actually it is possible, supposing that dimensioning is based on the requirements of reserved connections. Nevertheless, some modifications are needed because the assumption of equal connections is apparently not valid in multiple-service networks. Several approaches can be followed—some approaches provide either an accurate result with complex calculations; other approaches provide a less accurate result with simpler calculations. (See Chapter 18 in *Broadband Network Teletraffic* [Roberts *et al.* 1996].)

Dimensioning of Differentiated Services Networks

The expectation in Differentiated Services networks is, however, that the great majority of traffic is not using reserved connections (instead, that they are using best-effort kind of service). Evidently, the whole problem of network dimensioning is then completely different. There are no calls, no real holding times, and no call-blocking probabilities; instead, there are just variable streams of packets. Therefore, the traffic models must rely on a totally different approach that somehow takes into account the peculiar characteristics of data traffic.

Dimensioning of a packet network is such a complex task that it cannot be addressed extensively in this book. Yet, it is one of the primary tasks of any network operator. To get some level of insight regarding this issue, consider (as a starting point) the evaluation in section 4.4.3 "A Model for Evaluating Statistical Multiplexing", in Chapter 4. In that framework, the main target of efficient network dimensioning is to reduce the parameter ε. So what is the essence of parameter ε in Formula 6.11?

Formula 6.11

```
C(T)¦M(0) = M(0)*{1 + γ*[ε*(1-α_b*α_d)/(α_b*N)]^0.5}
```
Recall the meaning of the other parameters:

$M(0)$ defines the known, current load level

Parameters α_b, α_d, and N are used to describe the characteristics of traffic process on the link.

γ defines the desired quality level

The laborious task of parameter ε is to take care of all difficulties and inaccuracies related to the real task of making real predictions. In particular, even though M(0) can be, in a certain sense, measured accurately, a lot of practical difficulties exist with the other parameters and the whole model. First of all, it should be stressed that α_b, α_d, and N are fictional parameters without any right values in real situations. Basically the same concern is valid with parameter γ; it is only a tool that can be used to satisfy a certain quality target without any guarantee that a certain value of γ leads to the same quality level in practice. Therefore, parameter γ tries to give a realistic estimation of effects related to all these factors.

In general, the better you understand the real process, the smaller ε is, and consequently, the better prediction you can make. In theory that is clear, but what can be done in reality to decrease ε Suppose, for example, that you have 10 links to be dimensioned with an original load of 50Mbps. Without an advanced information system, you must rely on your earlier experience with link dimensioning and traffic growth. You may suppose that the expected load of every link at the end of a half-year period is 100 higher than at the beginning of the period.

Further, based on previous experience, you may assume that the typical variance of the prediction ("error") is proportional to the mean value, $V(t) = [M(t)/2]^2$. Moreover, you know that you need a safety factor ε = 4 to keep your customers satisfied. A simple calculation shows that you must reserve a capacity of 300Mbps for every link.

Note that you did not make any assumption about specific traffic parameters in this simple, but seemingly practical method. Now, you can just change the relation between V(t) and M(t) if the result is not satisfactory—that is, you reserved systematically too much or not enough resources. But that information, however useful, cannot essentially improve your ability to make traffic predictions.

You can, on the contrary, improve your prediction by acquiring more information about the load on individual links, because some part of the inaccuracy of prediction is probably caused by the differences in different links. You can classify the links into two groups according to the expected growth rate. If the expected load of the first group at the end of the prediction period is 70Mbps, and the expected load of the other group is 130Mbps, the variance related to this difference is $(30\text{Mbps})^2$. The remaining part of the variance, $(40\text{Mbps})^2$ (note that, $40 = (50^2 - 30^2)^{0.5}$), can then be supposed to be a result of statistical traffic variations. In this case, the required capacities are as follows:

Group 1: C(1) = 70 + 4*40 = 230Mbps

Group 2: C(2) = 130 + 4*40 = 290Mbps

This result is certainly promising, but also somewhat surprising because even the links in Group 2 require less capacity than what was originally estimated. The explanation is that additional information about the two groups increases significantly your knowledge of the situation.

The improvement can be achieved, however, only if the link classification is reasonable in the sense that the variation inside each group is actually smaller than that of the original group of all links. On the contrary, if the classification is a random process, the outcome is probably worse than the original situation without any grouping.

This phenomenon is actually easier to be thought of in the reverse order: First you have the situation with two groups, and then you lose information about the classification links according to the growth rate. Then if you know that there are these groups, but you do not know which group each link belongs to, you can use the value of 290Mbps. Finally, without any information about the groups, you need 300Mbps capacity for every link.

This example supposed that you could improve the knowledge about growth rates on individual links. Similar evaluation is valid with other parameters, α_b, α_d, N, or whatever parameters your model includes. The values of the parameters may vary from link to link, and if the differences are significant, traffic prediction could be improved by evaluating individual links or specific groups of links in specific ways rather than evaluating all links in the same way.

6.3.4 Boundary Nodes Between Network Domains

Differentiated Services provide different quality levels for packets, flows, or aggregate streams, and these levels may significantly affect the customers' perception of quality level. The basic assumption of Differentiated Services is that the use of the quality levels is controlled at the boundary node between customer and service provider. Yet the real situation is that a packet may traverse through network domains managed by different service providers.

Should the end users have an SLA with every service provider that ever conveys packets sent by the end user? No, that is not a realistic approach in the global Internet. The primary rule has to be that each user has a contract with one service provider (or perhaps with a couple of them), and that the service provider makes contracts with other service providers and network operators.

The primary issue is the form of the service contract between different service providers. Because this is relatively new territory—that is, not many "real" service providers are offering Differentiated Services yet, and therefore the future business models are still largely unknown—it is prudent at this point in time to just briefly consider some realistic scenarios.

There seems to be three main options for the contract between two service providers:

- *Pricing*: A device measures the traffic of each PHB in each direction. Based on the information gathered, either of the providers may pay the other provider compensation.

- *Re-marking*: An automatic system re-marks packets based on the load level on of all PHB aggregates.

- *Per-flow marking*: A similar marking as at the first boundary node between customer and service provider is also marked at the boundary nodes between network domains.

The last option could be feasible in some special situations, but it cannot be a common solution among all service providers. In addition, the approach needs a reliable signaling system to transmit relevant information among all boundary nodes. Therefore, it is not discussed further in this chapter

Pricing Approach

In essence, this approach means that the aggregate traffic of each PHB is measured in both directions. Let's denote the amount of bytes transmitted in PHB Class i on importance level j by X(i,j) in one direction and by Y(i,j) in the other direction. The compensation (Z) can be calculated from these factors—for instance, by a linear model such as that shown in Formula 6.12.

Formula 6.12

```
Z = sum[c1(i,j)*X(i,j)]  -  sum[c2(i,j)*Y(i,j)]
    i,j                     i,j
```

In case of two backbone operators, it is possible that c1(i,j) = c2(i,j) for all i's and j's. Moreover, the operators may agree that no compensation is made if the traffic loads are approximately in balance.

On the contrary, when a small Internet service provider (ISP) is connected to a large backbone operator the situation could be totally different. The pricing could be based only on the traffic sent from the small ISP to the backbone network, for example. It should be stressed that all these issues relate to business models of service providers and network operators; they are beyond the scope of any standardization process.

Re-Marking Approach

As with the pricing model, the traffic load of each PHB should be measured individually. Instead of pricing, the network may re-mark the packets if certain thresholds are exceeded. Although there are numerous alternatives, some rules seems to be relevant across the board:

- Under normal situations, re-marking should be avoided, because it may negatively affect the overall service.

- Re-marking should be done, if possible, only within a PHB class.

- If a PHB class has only one importance level, and re-marking is needed, the default service (used to transmit best-effort traffic) is the secondary choice.

- If there are enough importance levels, it is better to re-mark all packets systematically (one step up or down) than to re-mark packets here and there; the systematic approach helps keep the network service as consistent as possible.

- Although re-marking a packet can be based on the load level of the PHB class used by the packet, it is sometimes more reasonable to use the total load level with appropriate weights for each PHB.

It should be stressed that these rules are tentative, and without practical experience it is impossible to state what is the most practical approach.

You can also combine the pricing and re-marking approaches in several ways. If the pricing model is your primary approach, for instance, you could also apply load limits to the highest PHB classes to limit the possible problems related to PHB marking within a network domain.

Summary

This chapter discussed several integral issues related to Differentiated Services. The implementation of traffic classification, metering, marking, shaping, and dropping essentially determine the service structure. Correspondingly, the requirement of consistent, fair, flexible, and efficient service makes it necessary to carefully design traffic-handling functions.

Section 6.2, "Traffic Handling Functions in Interior Nodes," dealt mainly with the different buffering systems, including FIFO, priority queuing, SFQ, and CBQ. In Differentiated Services networks, the main constraint for the application of queuing systems is that individual flows are not supposed to be discernible; instead, all the mechanisms should use the DS codepoint in the packet. For this reason, the discussion focused mainly on the application of simple queuing systems in a Differentiated Services environment.

FIFO is the basic choice because of the plain implementation; priority queuing and Class-Based Queuing (CBQ) provide quite straightforward means to solve some of the fundamental problems of FIFO systems. This book recommends always avoiding complex systems with a large number of adjustable parameters, however, because although they can be realized, they tend to require additional management and are prone to configuration errors.

The main dropping disciplines are to drop packets just when the buffer is full, have several thresholds for different importance levels, and RED. Different combinations were also discussed.

The first, simple dropping, is not a sufficient mechanism for implementing Differentiated Services. A threshold for every importance level is an apparent and feasible approach to provide quality differentiation. Moreover, RED seems to be the recommendable mechanism to further improve the service performance when the TCP protocol is used in customer equipment. The usefulness of RED in a queuing system with several importance levels is not totally clear, however.

Finally, some elementary functions related to traffic management were discussed in Section 6.3, "Functions Related to a Network Domain." These discussed functions included network dimensioning and contracts between service providers.

7

Per-Hop Behavior Groups

The traits and characteristics that define a Per-Hop Behavior (PHB) consist of the rules used to treat packets in specific ways inside the network. The rules should be indisputable in the sense that they can be used for practical (human) discussions among different parties, particularly service providers, backbone operators, and vendors. Otherwise, the whole concept of PHB can be harmful rather than useful—PHB itself is situated somewhere in the nebulous space between mechanisms and services.

The term *hop* also needs some clarification. A path between two end systems consists of a number of hops. From a Differentiated Services viewpoint, a hop is a subpath between two network nodes that does not have any significant effect on the characteristics of traffic flows. An ATM virtual path (VP) between two routers is one hop, for instance, although the VP goes through several ATM nodes, if those nodes keep the traffic process virtually unaltered. If a node makes decisions related to statistical multiplexing (such as which packets or cells should be discarded), the incoming and outgoing links evidently belong to different hops.

One of the fundamental ideas of DiffServ is that the treatment of flows should be similar in every node and over every hop to provide reasonable network service. This chapter makes an earnest effort to define the following four PHB groups:

- Class selector PHB

- Expedited forwarding PHB

- Assured forwarding PHB

- Dynamic RT/NRT PHB

The search is based on information covered in the previous chapters, which provided various perspectives on Differentiated Services from service and quality models to packet marking and queuing. (Refer to Chapter 4, "General Framework for Differentiated Services," and Chapter 5, "Differentiation of Customer Service.")

7.1 Systematic Basis for PHB Evaluation

This section introduces the system used to evaluate PHB groups. First, I give a clear insight into each PHB group. The description of PHB should be something that can be used for practical discussions among different parties. The description does not, however, make any reference to either any particular implementation or to any particular end-to-end service.

Although Per-Hop Behavior is not a service in the traditional sense, PHBs cannot be analyzed without considering services. Service is the ultimate purpose of defining and implementing PHBs. One of the main difficulties of designing PHBs is that there are various different ideas on what the service build from the PHBs should be. Table 7.1 summarizes the main service aspects from fairness criteria to VPN type.

> **Note**
>
> Although the importance of each individual aspect of service depends on the business model of the service provider, in general, all aspects are relevant and should be considered. Each PHB group differs on both the relevance of different aspects and the applicability to different service models.

Table 7.1   Service Models

Aspect of Service	Service Models	Chapter Section	Figure
Fairness criteria	Application Customer Organization	4.2.2	4.3
Dynamics and degree of guarantee	Guaranteed connections Leased-line service Dynamic importance Resource sharing	5.1.1	5.1
Control of load and destination	Constant bit-rate (CBR) connection "VPN with VBR service" Best effort	4.4.1	4.4
VPN type (multiplexing)	No capacity sharing Limited sharing Total sharing	4.5.3	4.13

One key aspect of a PHB group is how it establishes a feasible quality structure. Without a consistent and comprehensible quality structure service, providers cannot build reasonable services within their own domain (and even fewer services extending several domains). Urgency (or delay), importance (packet-loss ratio), and bandwidth (bit rate) are the main quality aspects. Every extensive PHB should somehow cover all these aspects, and a confined PHB should define how it can be located in a broader framework covering all aspects. Predictability of quality is an aspect that can have an autonomous importance in some cases. Table 7.2 shows the main quality options and references to earlier chapters.

Table 7.2   Quality Models

Aspect	Main Options	Chapter Section	Figure
Urgency and importance	Fixed order of import. Flexible order of import.	4.6.2	4.14 4.15
Bandwidth and importance	Bandwidth partition Proportional bandwidth	4.6.3	4.16
Predictability	Marking depending on duration of flow Guaranteed service	4.3.2, 4.6.4	n/a

Service differentiation is defective without sophisticated pricing. Although there is not always any direct relationship between a PHB group and a pricing model, you can often assess which quality aspects are easy to realize and which ones are either difficult to realize or unrealistic. Table 7.3 presents the main relationships between quality aspects and price.

Table 7.3   Relationships Related to Pricing

Aspect	Versus	Chapter Section	Figure
Bandwidth	Price Availability Quality	5.1.3	5.8 5.11 5.13
Availability	Price Bandwidth Quality	5.1.3	5.10 5.11 5.12
Quality (delay)	Price Availability Bandwidth	5.1.3	5.9 5.12 5.13

Technical implementation is the other main part of network service in addition to the general structure. Tables 7.4, 7.5 and 7.6 summarize the main implementation alternatives. The most central part of any PHB implementation is related to the interior nodes—remember that PHB refers to the treatment of the packets inside the network. Nonetheless, because boundary node functions are essential parts of service provision, they have to be addressed when evaluating the whole system build by a given PHB group.

Table 7.4   Implementation Options for Boundary Nodes

Aspect	Main Options	Chapter Section	Figure or Table
Service request	RSVP message DSCP indication Quality inquire	5.1.2	Table 5.1 Table 5.2
Classifying	Based on service-level agreement (SLA) Based on application	5.2.1	n/a
Metering	Recognition of excess load Metering of load level	5.2.2	Figure 5.17
Marking	Only excessive packets All packets based on momentary load	5.2.3	Figure 5.19
Shaping	Before or after other conditioning functions	5.2.4	Figure 5.20 Figure 5.21 Figure 5.22
Discarding	No/yes	5.2.5	n/a

Table 7.5   Implementation Options for Interior Nodes

Aspect	Main Options	Chapter Section	Figure
Buffering	FIFO, Priority queuing, CBQ, WFQ	5.3.1	5.23 5.24 5.25
Discarding	Hard thresholds RED	5.3.2	5.26
Feedback information	Congestion indication Available bandwidth	5.3.3	n/a

Table 7.6	Implementation Options Related to Network Domain		
Aspect	Main Options	Chapter Section	Figure
Routing	Static, adaptive	4.5.4	5.4
Resource reservation	Static or dynamic per flow or aggregate	4.4.4 5.4.2	4.9
Network dimensioning	Mathematical model Practical experience	5.4.3	n/a
Contracts between domains	Based on charging Based on marking	5.4.4	n/a

7.2 Class Selector PHB Group

According to the RFC 2474, the main motivation of Class Selector PHBs (CS PHB) is backward compatibility with present uses of bits 0–2 of the IPv4 TOS octet. The history of these bits is somewhat convoluted. According to the original Internet Protocol specification, the precedence can mean that only traffic above a certain precedence at the time of high load is accepted (Postel 1981).

In 1989, "The Requirements for Internet Hosts—Communication Layers," stated that the precedence field (three first bits of TOS field) was intended for the Department of Defense applications of the Internet protocols (Braden 1989). The RFC even recommended that vendors should consult the Defense Communication Agency for guidance on the precedence field. It seems that the main use of the bits has been to separate packet related to network control from best-effort packets.

Because the use of these bits is similar to that of PHBs, it is reasonable to adapt the deployed uses of the bits into the Differentiated Services framework. Therefore, the perspective of the Class Selector PHB group is special: Although the other PHB groups are used to build new services, the definition of the CS-PHB group tries to encompass various, in worst case contradictory uses, in existing networks. Because of this background, the specification of CS PHBs primarily gives limits of acceptable use of the bits, but not any unambiguous exact rules.

7.2.1 Description

RFC 2474 states the following:

A Class Selector PHB should give packets a probability of timely forwarding that is not lower than that given to packets marked with a lower Class Selector PHB, under reasonable operating conditions and traffic loads.

This can be called the *timely forwarding* requirement. A further clarification is that a discarded packet is considered to be an extreme case of untimely forwarding. Moreover, a network node can limit the maximum resources used by each PHB. CS PHBs might be used to provide delay, importance, or bandwidth differentiation.

All three aspects can be obtained at the same time only if the traffic load within each PHB is tightly controlled—which is an unrealistic assumption in Differentiated Services networks. Particularly, *timely forwarding* and *bandwidth enforcement* objectives can conflict during a congestion situation. If a higher PHB class is using an excessive amount of resources, the node cannot comply with both the timely forwarding requirement and the bandwidth enforcement requirement. The interpretation used in this chapter is that bandwidth enforcement is an acceptable tool to realize the timely forwarding behavior, but it is not an independent target of the CS-PHB group itself. This leaves two aspects, delay and importance.

The fundamental question is, what does higher probability of timely forwarding primarily mean? Figure 7.1 illustrates this dilemma. The figure shows two PHB behaviors:

- *PHB1*: Provides excellent delay characteristics most of the time—that is, less than 1-millisecond delay per node. However, the probability that a packet has to be discarded (0.01%) could be unsatisfactory for some applications.

- *PHB2*: Provides worse delay characteristics for forwarded packets, but the packet-loss ratio is significantly better than that of PHB1.

Figure 7.1 Criteria for higher probability of timely forwarding.

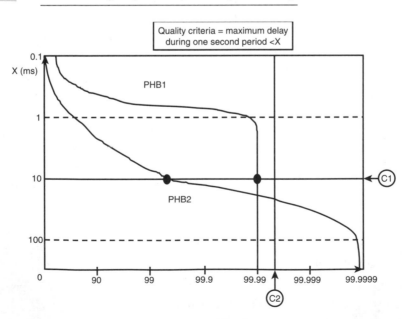

As a result, the requirement of *higher probability of timely forwarding* is ambiguous. Only in cases where the delay characteristics are systematically better for one PHB than for another one should it be stated that the probability of timely forwarding is higher for the first PHB. Basically, there are four approaches to solve this problem:

- Both the delay and loss ratio of a CS PHB must be at least as good as any of the lower CS PHBs.

- The probability of timely forwarding is defined for fixed-delay characteristics—for instance, for a 10-millisecond delay (criterion C1 in Figure 7.1).

- The availability value is fixed. For instance, the "timeliness of forwarding" is defined for availability of 99.995% in Figure 7.1 (criterion C2).

- The question is intentionally left vague; each operator is allowed to define its own criterion (if any).

Although the two middle approaches are somewhat attractive because they give, in principle, a tool for systematic assessment of any PHBs, they could be hard to apply because the final conclusion depends essentially on the traffic processes within each PHB. Therefore, either the first tight approach or the last loose approach should be applied. The compromise used in this chapter is that the requirement of consistent ordering based on packet-loss ratio should be met, and there could be small deviations in the ordering for different delay criteria.

Returning to the original goal of CS PHB, backward compatibility, the application of CS PHBs is limited by the mechanisms available in the interior nodes. Therefore, the main advantage of CS PHB is that the service provider can avoid upgrading interior nodes but still attain some level of differentiation by upgrading boundary nodes.

If the interior nodes of a service provider have only a couple of importance (or delay) levels without any supporting tools, however, the application of the CS PHB system remains inevitably limited. Actually that kind of system deserves only a brief discussion in this book. On the contrary, the approach of this section is to consider the full possibilities of the CS-PHB system with all eight individual PHBs, although it is not certain that current equipment supports this system.

7.2.2 *Position in the Framework*

This section identifies the location of the CS-PHB group in the framework(s) introduced in the first section of this chapter. The extensive framework consists of service models and quality models, whereas *pricing* is an issue that is hard to assess in case of CS PHB because boundary behaviors are a totally open issue.

Service Models

Let's start with delineating the three main service models according to the most relevant fairness targets:

- In the application model, fairness issues are considered from an application viewpoint.

- In the customer model, they are considered from the viewpoint of the paying customer.

- In the organization model, the viewpoint is an organization that wants to provide an appropriate service to a large number of end users.

Because of its special background, the CS-PHB structure is primarily an application service model rather than a customer or organization model. Another possible approach is that each person or other entity has a right to use specific PHBs. In that sense, CS PHB could be a tool to regulate the use of network resources among end users.

Yet, the basic nature of CS-PHB is a pronounced lack of any traffic-conditioning specifications. Therefore, the main fairness issues to be considered are those among applications: F1, F2, and F3 in Figure 7.2. Of course, the CS PHBs can be used to build customer services with appropriate traffic conditioning at boundary nodes. Although that is possible, it appears more reasonable to use other PHB groups for that purpose, because there is no common understanding of the proper condition for the CS-PHB group.

Figure 7.2   Fairness criteria for Class Selector PHBs.

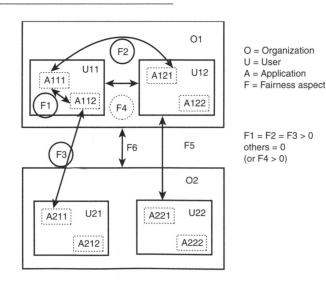

O = Organization
U = User
A = Application
F = Fairness aspect

F1 = F2 = F3 > 0
others = 0
(or F4 > 0)

The issue of service categories is somewhat irrelevant to CS PHBs, because the original target of the bits was not to build services. Nonetheless, in a future environment with specific services for customers, even CS PHBs will have a proper location—they cannot merely float over other PHBs and services without any relationship with them.

One way to define a *class selector service* is to eliminate those service models that are not reasonable. The guaranteed-connections model is apparently excluded because it does not have traffic-control functions in boundary nodes. Dynamic importance is excluded because it doesn't have a signaling system to transmit information about changes in packet classification. Leased-line service is excluded because it seems irrational to define different leased lines in the order of probability of timely forwarding. (Leased lines are more about bandwidth separation.) Therefore, as for the service classification presented in Figure 7.3, the only relevant model is the resource-sharing model. In other words, the system behavior is static and the service description is either qualitative or relative.

| **Figure 7.3** | Most relevant service category for Class Selector PHB group. |

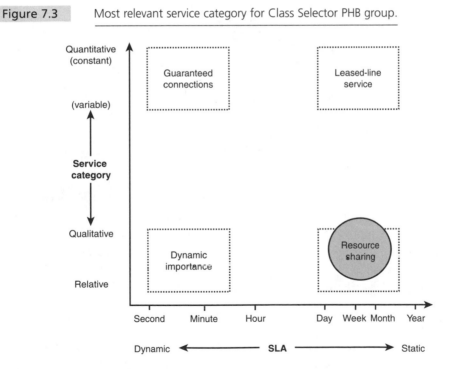

The origin of Class Selector PHBs is deep in the traditional IP networks. The fundamental assumption in IP networks has been that there is only limited traffic-control mechanisms inside the network. The best-effort model includes the principle of not controlling the destination or the traffic sent into the network. That statement concerns mainly the lowest PHB, not the other levels, because several levels of importance can hardly be used without any clear limits of use. Although this issue is difficult to assess without any systematic mechanism in boundary nodes, it seems that the CS-PHB group does not fix the destination of packets. Because some level of load control is inevitable, the region of CS PHB is extended in Figure 7.4 somewhat in the moderate level of traffic control.

Figure 7.4   Predictability of load and destination for the Class Selector PHB group.

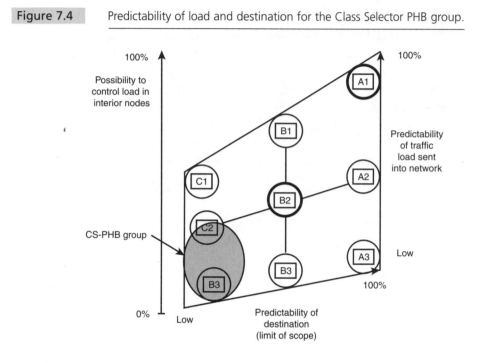

No fundamental obstacle stands in the way of combining the Class Selector system with appropriate mechanisms at boundary nodes, and thereby extending the application of CS PHBs into the areas of more advanced control of load and destination. This remark is valid also with the last customer-service aspect in Table 7.1, virtual private networks; although the Class Selector PHB group is perhaps not directly applicable to building VPNs, the CS PHBs might be used to control traffic within a VPN.

Quality Models

As discussed in the preceding section, "Service Models," the requirement of higher probability of timely forwarding can be realized in different ways. Figure 7.5 shows some of the possibilities. The first option is that only the importance, but not urgency, is a significant factor. In this case, there are several (at most eight) importance levels within one PHB class. This straightforward scheme is unacceptable, however, because there has to be two independently forwarded classes of traffic according to RFC 2474, "Definition of the Differentiated Services Field (DS Field) in the IPv4 and IPv6 Headers" (Baker *et al.* 1998).

The alternative 2 in Figure 7.5 means that there are eight different delay classes with the *same* importance. This seems technically acceptable and realizable, but apparently this is not the original purpose of the Class Selector PHBs. A pure delay differentiation without any differences in packet-loss ratios is not a viable approach if the packet-loss ratio is as high as can be expected in the Internet.

The third option in Figure 7.5 is that every CS PHB differs both in delay and importance. Although this is definitely acceptable according to the Class Selector PHB specification, a system with eight discernible delay classes is not necessarily a practical goal. Approach 4 could therefore be more realistic: six (or perhaps five or seven) lowest importance levels share the same delay class, but both of the two highest importance levels have their own delay class. The highest class can be used for transmitting packets related to internal traffic such as traffic-control messages and routing messages. The second highest class can be used for demanding real-time applications. Finally, a more complicated structure 5 is possible as well.

Figure 7.5   Delay and importance relations of Class Selector PHBs.

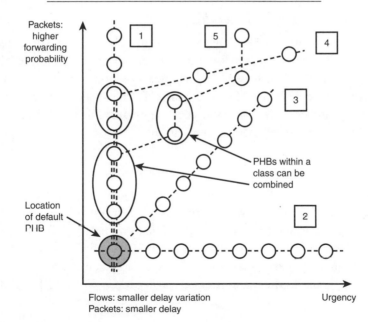

The other fundamental quality-control target presented in Table 7.2 is bandwidth management. Although there is no obstacle to dividing the network into separate parts and to use CS PHBs for quality management, the main purpose of the Class Selector PHBs is most likely in other quality aspects.

What, therefore, is the role of *predictability* in the case of the Class Selector PHB group? This is a somewhat artificial question—there is no direct relationship between the duration of flow and packet-loss ratio with any of the CS PHBs. (Note that predictability of quality means here that a flow with high quality in the beginning gets the same quality for the duration of the flow). The main aspect of predictability in case of CS PHB seems to be that, for instance, routing information *always* gets high probability of timely forwarding. (In the terminology used here, however, that is an importance aspect rather than a predictability aspect.)

7.2.3 Required Technical Tools

This section mainly addresses approach 4 in Figure 7.5. The assumption is that the operator wants to implement three different classes: Each of the two highest classes consists of one PHB, and the lowest six PHBs share the same PHB class. Although there surely are other reasonable approaches as well, the implementation requirements do not differ significantly from those presented in this section.

Implementation Options for Boundary Nodes

Again, the problem of obscurity arises. When no clear idea about the general objective of the system is available, it is impossible to say much about the mechanisms needed in boundary nodes. The only evident issue is that a logical marking system is required, in the minimum, based on the rights of use of certain PHBs. Packets with inappropriate marking can be either dropped immediately or marked with the default PHB. In addition, a logical scheme is to provide classification based on applications.

Implementation Options for Interior Nodes

Option 4 in Figure 7.5 requires three queues. The highest queue has strict priority over all other queues, the second queue has strict priority over the lowest queue, and the lowest queue is served only if the other queues are empty. The two higher queues accept packets as long as empty space exists. The lowest queue is divided into three regions. If the occupancy level is low enough, all packets are accepted; in the middle region, default packets (PHB=0) are discarded; and in the highest region, only packets with PHB=4 or PHB=5 are accepted.

As usual, the default PHB, which is used to implement the best-effort service, clearly benefits from RED. The other thresholds for the lowest queue can also use RED, whereas the higher queues most likely apply a hard threshold. Figure 7.6 presents a possible implementation of Class Selector PHB.

Figure 7.6   An example of Class Selector PHB implementation.

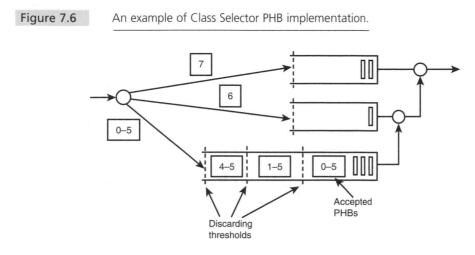

Implementation Options Related to the Network Domain

It is difficult to identify any specific requirements for routing, network dimensioning, and contracts between domains related to the Class Selector PHB group. Appropriate routing and network dimensioning are surely necessary components. Then contracts between different domains need to define the rules related to the use of CS PHBs.

Finally, the issue of explicit reservation for some of the CS PHBs must be addressed. Considering all the options presented in Figure 7.5, it seems that explicit bandwidth reservations are harmful rather than useful. In general, reservation leads to a situation in which the packet-discarding decision may depend more on the momentary load level of the class than on the importance level of the packet. Why should this be done? Two reasons can be identified:

- *Increased robustness against faulty situations:* If a defective device sends a large amount of packets with a certain PHB, for example, other PHBs still obtain some network resources.

- *Avoiding starvation of the lowest PHBs:* In particular, the default PHB should obtain a moderate amount of resources even during overload situations.

It could be useful, therefore, to have some level reservations that have no significant effect on the network behavior under normal load conditions but that may improve the network performance, robustness, or fairness under high load conditions.

7.2.4   *Evaluation of Attributes*

Now it is time to apply the list of attributes to check whether all relevant aspects have been considered. It is fair to assume that the main reason to apply Class Selector PHBs is enhanced traffic management within a domain without any significant effect on customer services. In this case, the main fairness requirement is that the default service should provide a moderate service quality, at least without considerable interruptions. If the network can be provide this characteristics, the better quality of other PHBs could be fair and acceptable.

Because the implementation and management of CS PHBs seem to be relative straightforward, cost efficiency is probably not a major concern. One of the primary ideas behind the use of CS PHB is improved robustness. If the classification of packets is appropriate, the prioritization of packets could significantly better the network performance under abnormal situations. The main deficiency of the Class Selector model is versatility. There is one clear customer service, best effort, but not any other commonly accepted service level. If service differentiation is necessary, other PHB groups should be used instead of, or in addition to, the Class Selector PHB group.

7.3 Expedited Forwarding PHB

Expedited Forwarding PHB (EF PHB) has a clearly defined target similar to the guaranteed-services model addressed in Chapter 2, "Traffic Management Before Differentiated Services." The main merit of EF PHB is the adaptation of the guaranteed-service model into the framework of Differentiated Services.

7.3.1 Description

The objective of *Expedited Forwarding Per-Hop Behavior* (EF PHB) is to provide tools to build a low loss, low latency, low jitter, assured bandwidth, end-to-end service through DS domains. The essence of EF seems to be in the following requirements for the treatment of an EF PHB traffic stream (Jacobson, Nichols, and Poduri 1998):

> The departure rate *must* equal or exceed a configurable rate. EF traffic *should* average at least the configured rate when measured over any time interval equal to or longer than a packet time at the configured rate.

What does this actually imply? Apparently, if packets of the same size come exactly according to the configured rate, the node should send the packets forward with exactly the same rate. Although the situation is not as clear with variable size packets, the basic idea is to avoid any excessive delay and jitter if possible. The other side of this model is that it requires tight traffic control in boundary nodes.

Figure 7.7 illustrates the principle of EF PHB. Note that marking is not available in case of EF PHB because there is only one importance level. Consequently, if a packet arrives before its scheduled time, there are three options both in boundary and interior nodes:

- To forward the packet immediately

- To forward the packet at the scheduled time

- To discard the packet

Before scheduled time means here that the stream would exceed its configured rate if the packet were sent immediately.

There is a clear difference between boundary and interior nodes. Traffic control in a boundary node should apply either the second or third option to prevent the source from exploiting excessive bandwidth. In contrast, the wording of the RFC indicates that the first option is strongly recommended inside the network. The second, shaping option, also appears to be possible inside the network. Packet B in Figure 7.7 depicts why shaping is not necessarily a reasonable alternative. If packet B has encountered additional delay inside the network, the next packet (C) may come too soon after packet B compared to the con- figured bit rate. The shaping option means that packet C, and possible all the following packets, will encounter excessive delay because of the problems of one packet in the mid- dle of the stream. That behavior seems to be against the principles of EF PHB.

In summary, EF PHB means a strict bit-rate control in the boundary node and as quick forwarding in the interior nodes as possible. The fundamental assumption is that traffic is controlled in boundary nodes in a way that each packet inside the network can be deliv- ered immediately without risking that the flows get excessive bandwidth.

Figure 7.7   Shaping and discarding in EF PHB.

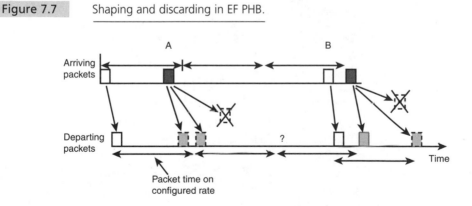

Moreover, one principle of EF seems to be that an excess rate of EF aggregate inside the network is an erroneous condition; and for protecting other services, EF packets can be dis- carded rather than packets belonging to the other PHBs (usually with lower importance). This might or might not be a rational rule. Nevertheless, if the excess is a result of a config- uration error inside the network, packets belonging to other PHBs should apparently be discarded first. On the contrary, if the reason is that a traffic source can send an excessive amount of EF packets because of a defective traffic control in the boundary nodes, it could be justifiable to discard EF packets before some other packets. Note in this case, however, that several innocent EF flows may perceive deteriorated quality.

7.3.2 Position in the Framework

Expedited forwarding is one of the clearest specifications within Differentiated Services. It has a comprehensible target and a large part of the implementation is relatively easy. This section attempts to further clarify the model, and in particular, to address those issues not profoundly addressed in the EF specification.

Service Models

The primary EF service model is based on the customer contract. Therefore, the main fairness issue considered by EF PHB is the fairness between different customers, as shown in Figure 7.8. In addition, it is possible to apply EF PHB to separate organizations. The usefulness of EF PHB for that purpose is still somewhat questionable, because it does not offer any tool for traffic control inside the bit pipe (because there is only one importance class).

Figure 7.8   Relevant fairness issues for expedited forwarding.

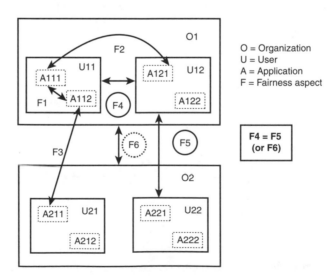

EF PHB specification mentions one service, virtual leased line (Jacobson, Nichols, and Poduri 1998). Therefore, there is no problem in defining the main region for EF in Figure 7.8. With a static service-level agreement, EF PHB can provide a leased-line service. In addition, if the network can support dynamic SLAs and dynamic capacity reservations, the EF region can be extended to the area of *guaranteed connections.*

Note

The term *guaranteed connection* in this book refers to a service used by an individual application with specific quality requirements and limited duration.

It should be further noticed that EF does not support variable bit-rate reservations, although the real bit rate may, of course, be variable provided that the peak rate remains below the policed rate. Figure 7.9 shows the principal service models that can realized by Expedited Forwarding PHB.

Figure 7.9   Primary and secondary service models for EF PHB.

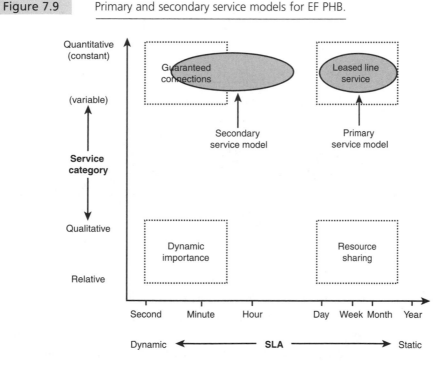

The fundamental principle of EF PHB is to provide very high quality, related to both delay and loss characteristics. Essentially, the aim of EF PHB is to provide a connection that appears as a physical link with very low delay and bandwidth variations. As extensively discussed in section 4.4.1, "Predictability of Load and Destination," in Chapter 4, real assurances can be given only if traffic is controllable, and controllability requires that load be controlled in boundary nodes and that the destination be fixed.

Although EF PHB provides a strict traffic control in boundary nodes, fixing the destination or route is not explicitly required. Yet, a successful provision of EF type of service likely requires that the destination be known, because an EF service to an arbitrary destination appears to be an impractical approach. Consequently, the applicable region of EF PHB is in the upper-right corner of Figure 7.10.

Figure 7.10 Predictability of load and destination for Expedited Forwarding PHB.

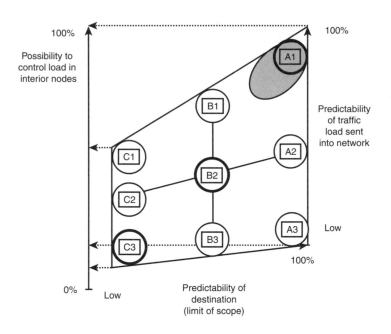

As mentioned earlier, the primary target of EF is to provide a reserved connection between two locations. Those connections can be used to build virtual private networks, but primarily without any capacity sharing between VPNs. The main problem of EF as a VPN technology is that a full mesh of reserved connections could be a complex and inefficient way to build VPNs, if the number of sites is large. This issue is discussed further in section 9.3, "Virtual Private Networks by Using an EF-PHB," in Chapter 9, "Implementing Differentiated Services."

Quality Models

The location of EF PHB in the scale defined by delay and importance is apparent, at least in relation to the best-effort service (default PHB). EF PHB should provide much better delay as well as much better loss characteristics, as shown in Figure 7.11.

Figure 7.11   Expedited Forwarding versus default PHB in delay-importance scale.

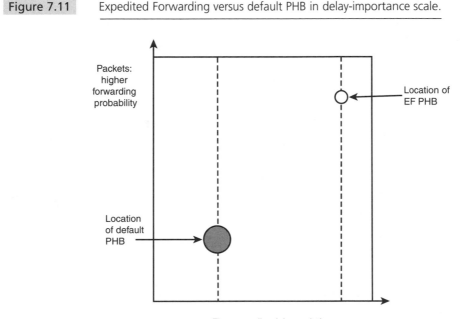

Predictability is the essence of the whole EF service model. A high level of assurance means largely a predictability of quality realizable only with the following:

- High-quality standard

- Constant bit-rate traffic model

- Fixed destination

These characteristics are exactly what EF PHB provides. If *real* predictability of quality is needed, therefore, the model adopted by EF PHB appears appropriate.

The service provider must also consider several other issues. Pricing is one of the most important issues. Table 7.7 summarizes the main approaches supported by EF PHB. Some kind of pricing related to the amount of bandwidth is necessary to avoid uncontrollable use of EF PHB. Another relevant aspect is the relationship between availability and price, in the sense that price should likely depend on the time of day and on the destination. Because there is only one quality class, there is no true quality differentiation within the EF PHB. (The situation changes when the operator simultaneously uses several PHB groups.)

Table 7.7   Charging Options for Expedited Forwarding

Differentiation of	As a Function of	Remark
Price	Bandwidth	Necessary
Price	Quality	Only one quality class
Price	Availability	Charging may depend on the time of day and day of the week
Availability	Bandwidth	Possible in limited sense (course granularity)
Availability	Quality	Not a probable approach
Quality	Bandwidth	Not a probable approach

7.3.3   Required Technical Tools

Because the EF PHB, as such without anything else, is quite a trivial issue on the packet-handling level, this section considers a combination of EF PHB and default PHB. The assumption is that default PHB is used to transmit all packets using the best-effort service, and all flows with higher-quality requirements use EF PHB.

Implementation Options for Boundary Nodes

The first issue is how the user should request an EF PHB, or actually a virtual leased-line service. If the primary model is based on static reservation, the request could be implemented in almost any imaginable way—for instance, by calling the service provider that makes the required configurations in network nodes through the management system. If a more dynamic system is needed, RSVP could be a suitable tool for capacity reservations. Bandwidth brokers, discussed in section 6.3.2, "Resource Reservation," in Chapter 6, "Traffic Handling and Network Management," can also be a part of the solution.

One possible scenario is for the user to inform the service provider that packets using certain port numbers and/or with certain destination addresses should be classified into the EF PHB, and all other packets use the default service. This seems to be necessary because users will probably want to use their network connection for several applications at the same time, and buying a separate EF connection for all flows is an impractical approach.

The workability of EF PHB requires that the boundary node strictly control the bit rates of each incoming flow. A token bucket type of mechanism is one possibility to identify excessive packets that should be dropped immediately instead of being marked as lower importance. Traffic shaping can be used to improve the loss characteristics perceived by end applications.

Implementation Options for Interior Nodes

The main principle of EF seems to be that EF packets deserve the best possible service. EF-PHB specification mentions as possible alternatives a simple priority queue, weighted round-robin, and CBQ (Jacobson, Nichols, and Poduri 1998). Figure 7.12 illustrates one simple realization with two queues: a relatively small EF queue with strict priority, and a larger default queue with the RED mechanism. The main additional requirement is that the available bit rate be high enough at point A regardless of other possible traffic streams.

Figure 7.12   One possible implementation of Expedited Forwarding with default PHB.

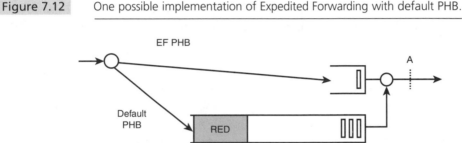

Implementation Options Related to the Network Domain

All the matters so far related to EF PHB have been clear and reasonable. The most critical area of EF implementation has not yet been discussed, however. The fundamental issue is how to make the resource reservations inside the network with possibly hundreds of nodes and millions of flows, without generating the same scalability problems that are the main concern of RSVP.

On a principle level, the answer provided by Differentiated Services and explicit forwarding is that reservations are not done for individual flows but for traffic aggregates. Unfortunately, this is not a perfect solution: If there are not per-flow reservations, boundary nodes cannot accurate decide whether to accept new EF connections. Therefore, without per-flow reservation, the destination is not fixed from the viewpoint of the interior nodes. That essentially deteriorates the controllability of EF traffic inside the network. (Note that if the aggregate reservation is always updated when a new flow is established, that *is* per-flow reservation.)

Network dimensioning is an alternative tool to manage the service. That is, the overall load level of the EF connection is kept low enough to virtually guarantee that there is enough capacity on every interior link within the network domain. In the extreme approach, each interior link would transmit all existing EF connections. As long as there is no robust and clear solution to this problem, the surplus value of EF PHB compared to the more traditional guaranteed-service approaches is questionable.

7.3.4   *Evaluation of Attributes*

Expedited forwarding has the same advantages and disadvantages as all other CBR services. Cost efficiency is a somewhat arguable issue in a large network with a limited number of EF connections; however, the additional mechanisms could be acceptable from an implementation and management perspective.

Fairness depends significantly on the pricing structure. The main issues are the relationship between price and reserved bandwidth and the pricing difference between services provided by EF PHB and default PHB. If the price gap is too large, the demand for and use of high-quality service could be negligible, whereas a very small difference may complicate the network dimensioning.

EF PHB by itself is not versatile. Note, however, that the purpose of EF PHB is not to provide the only basis for Internet services but rather to complement service provision. If EF PHB is built properly and the number of EF connections is limited, the robustness is not a big concern. In contrast, despite the intrinsic robustness of the EF model, the management of a large number of connections using a centralized OAM system could be prone to human errors.

7.4   *Assured Forwarding PHB Group*

Assured Forwarding PHB (AF PHB) group is an integral part of Differentiated Services. AF PHB seems to reflect some of the inmost ideas of the Differentiated Services model. In particular, there is much freedom to implement different behaviors within the AF specification (although not necessary all at the same time). The other side of freedom is that the inherent logic of the AF system appears somewhat weak. This section discusses the diverse possibilities of the AF-PHB group as well as the difficulties in achieving consistent end-to-end services.

7.4.1   *Description*

In principle, the AF-PHB group can have a number of PHB classes (N), each with a number of drop precedence levels (M). The current specification defines that N = 4 and M = 3, but more classes or levels can be defined for local use (Baker *et al.* 1999). This section discusses only the basic AF structure with four classes and three drop precedence levels, as shown in Figure 7.13. Note that the wording of the AF specification indicates that it is not obligatory to implement all four AF classes. In addition, if the operator expects that congestion situations will be rare, an implementation with only two drop precedence levels is acceptable.

Figure 7.13   Structure of AF-PHB group.

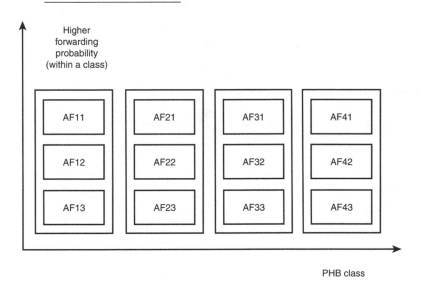

The additional essential characteristics of the AF model are that a Differentiated Services node

- *Must* allocate a configurable, minimum amount of buffer space and bandwidth to each AF class

- *Must not* aggregate two or more AF classes together

- *Must not* reorder AF packets of the same flow when they belong to the same AF class, regardless of their drop precedence

It should be stressed that the target of AF is not any end-to-end service model, but an assemblage of tools to build services.

7.4.2   *Position of AF-PHB Group in the Framework*

The evaluation of the AF-PHB group is based on this author's best understanding, and tries to be as realistic as possible. Nevertheless, AF PHB, and particularly its applications, is such an ambiguous area that it is hard to make absolutely certain or clear statements.

Service Models

The inherent freedom of AF makes it possible to realize different service models based on applications, individual customers, or an organization. However, it seems that the relevance order is as follows:

1. Customer model, in which the fairness considerations are based on the service-level agreement between customer and service provider

2. Organization model, in which organization makes the contract with a service provider, but the end user is basically free to use the bought bandwidth

3. Application model, in which flows are classified into different PHB classes based on the information about applications

The corresponding fairness issues presented in Figure 7.14 are summarized in Table 7.8; where X means primary fairness issue, Y means secondary fairness issue, and the hyphen (-) means inapplicable fairness issue.

Table 7.8   Relevance of Different Fairness Issues for AF-PHB Group

Service Model	F1	F2	F3	F4	F5	F6
Customer	-	-	-	X	X	-
Organization	Y1	Y1	-	Y2	-	X
Application	X	X	X	Y1	Y1	Y2

Figure 7.14   Relevant fairness issues for Assured Forwarding PHB group.

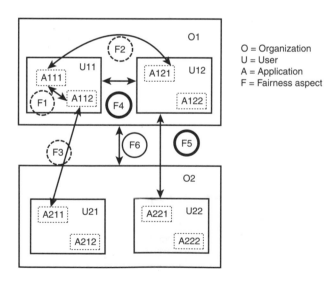

One of the practical problems of the AF-PHB system is that the fairness targets positively depend on the service model, and because different service models may coexist, even within one network domain, the overall system tends to become either complex or ambiguous (or both). Hopefully, this evaluation will help to clarify the situation.

The next issue is the relevance of different service models. This issue is, once again, open to various interpretations; Figure 7.15 shows two of them. In both options, the highest importance level provides a relatively high assurance of quality, and the lowest level is basically a best-effort service. In the first option, the middle level provides a somewhat lower assurance, but still the expectation is that the packet-loss ratio is small most of the time. In the second option, the two lowest importance levels together provide a better than best-effort service (for instance, with higher fairness than a basic best-effort service). Actually, "Assured Forwarding PHB Group" mainly promotes the second option because it requires that if a node supports only two drop precedence levels, two lower importance levels must be combined (Baker *et al.* 1999).

Figure 7.15   Possible service model for an AF-PHB class.

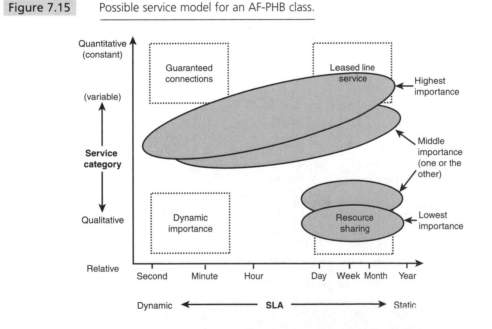

Supposing that the weight of each AF-PHB class is permanent, the level of assurance (vertical axis in Figure 7.15) depends on the dynamics of the SLA. The more permanent the SLA, the more likely that the network operator will have to provide truly assured service. In contrast, if customers can request short-lived assured connections, the network must be prepared for rapid and significant changes of load levels. If the weights cannot be adjusted according to the variable demand, the only possibility is to permanently reserve capacity of more than the average demand.

The lowest importance level of each PHB class forms a best-effort service that has essentially the same characteristics all the time, although the available capacity can change. It is hard to identify any need to request a change of best-effort service. As a result, the dynamic importance of an AF-PHB system could mean that some parameters of the marking algorithm change based on user request. In other words, the threshold between best effort and better service can be changed for an individual customer, although the service itself remains the same. It is not clear, however, whether there are enough importance levels in an AF-PHB system for this purpose.

Moreover, note that Figure 7.15 primarily depicts the situation of one AF-PHB class; a natural question is how PHB classes may differ from each other. The main answer seems to be that PHB classes differ in the following ways:

- In the assurance level of highest importance level

- In the dynamics of the highest importance level

- In the role of the middle importance level

- In a quality aspect not presentable in Figure 7.15

Figure 7.16 shows one possible approach with three AFD classes. PHB1, PHB2, and PHB3 differ in each of the three first aspects. This figure mainly illustrates the possibilities; however, a system covering all possible aspects could be impractical to manage in real networks.

Figure 7.16   Possible service model for three AF-PHB classes.

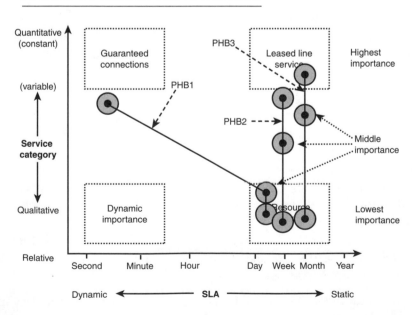

figure 7.17 further evaluates the same issue. In contrast to EF PHB, Assured Forwarding is likely operated without per-flow reservations and without taking explicitly into account the route through the network domain. This assumption limits the scope of AF to cases where the interior nodes cannot have strong control over traffic process even on the highest importance level. Consequently, the AF area in Figure 7.17 extends from best effort (C3 in Figure 7.17) to strictly controlled load with limited destination (B1).

Strictly controlled incoming load without any destination limits (C1) appears to be somewhat impractical, as does the limitation of destination without any load limitations (A3 and B3). Moderate destination and/or load control (C2 and B2) could be a suitable area to make experiments related to the applicability of the middle importance level. In practice, model B2 may mean a network domain with a small number of nodes and traffic control that is not as loose as with best-effort service but which still allows relatively large traffic variations.

Figure 7.17	Predictability of load and destination for AF-PHB group.

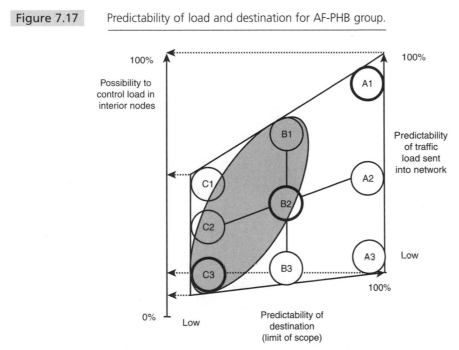

The last service-oriented issue is the applicability of AF-PHB groups to realize VPNs. Table 7.9 presents some preliminary considerations about this issue. The most relevant approach seems to be a combination of VPN-A2 and VPN-C, which means that the load level of the highest importance level is kept very low, and a limited capacity sharing is provided by using the other two importance levels.

Table 7.9   Suitability of AF-PHB Group for Different VPN Types

VPN Type	Main Tool to Manage Congestion Inside Network	Remark Considering AF-PHB Group
VPN-A1	Full mesh of CBR connections	Technically possible, but somewhat opposed to the principles of AF PHB.
VPN-A2	Strict limit for traffic sent to the network ($< C/(N-1)$)	Possible approach, but relevant only with the highest importance level.
VPN-A3	Alternative routing for load balancing	Not a primary approach.
VPN-B	Limited capacity sharing between VPNs	Perhaps the most realistic in principle, although the exact rules are unclear.
VPN-C	Total capacity sharing between VPNs	Three levels of importance could be insufficient for this approach.

Quality Models

Without defining the goal of the AF PHB, it is practically impossible to say anything about any quality issue. Therefore, it is necessary to select some service goals to evaluate the possibilities of an AF-PHB scheme, as follows:

- Delay differentiation

- Bit-rate differentiation

- Importance differentiation

- Improved predictability

- Pricing differentiation

The following sections discuss these service goals.

AF PHBs for Delay Differentiation   The first idea is to suppose that each AF class represents a delay class with its own importance scale. Unfortunately, it is extremely difficult in practice to attain four discrete delay classes merely by regulating weights for aggregate streams. Why? Although any real proof is hard to provide, several issues support this statement in the case of Differentiated Services:

- Delay, especially maximum delay, is very sensitive to the traffic process. Even if two traffic processes have exactly the same average bit rate, the difference in maximum delay could be several orders of magnitude.

- The traffic process inside the network depends essentially on the intrinsic control mechanisms that regulate the incoming traffic. These mechanisms are largely (although not totally) out of the control of interior network nodes.

- The traffic process on different importance levels could be totally different. If this is the case, because the delay characteristics are common to all importance levels, the overall result could be an intractable problem.

- If the traffic on a certain class is tightly controlled (that is, smooth even on short timescales), there are significant delay differences only on high load levels. Consequently, if delays are controlled by regulating load levels, the process will be very accurate because tiny changes in load level—for instance, from 98% to 101%—may change the delay and loss characteristics abruptly.

In summary, even if the operator has advanced tools to control the weights, the characteristics of the four delay classes most probably will overlap each other most of the time. In contrast, it seems possible to realize two PHB classes with consistently different delay characteristics. Figure 7.18 illustrates this structure. But even in this case, it is somewhat difficult to identify any simple tool for determining the proper values for weights, or proper control mechanism to regulate the weights.

As a general rule, the relative load level compared to the bandwidth defined by the weight should be lower for the better importance class. This approach probably leads to a situation in which the packet-loss ratio of both the highest and the middle importance levels of the low-level PHB class are negligible. On the contrary, the packet-loss ratio of the lowest importance level could even be higher for the low delay class (PHB class 1 in Figure 7.18) than for the normal delay class 2.

The reason for this somewhat counter-intuitive result is that low delay class has to use relatively small buffers that probably cannot cope with the large burst of IP packets. Yet, it should be stressed that this reasoning is based on the assumption that the traffic on the lowest level is not tightly controlled; whereas with a proper traffic control, the situation could be totally different. If the traffic control at the boundary nodes keeps the packet size in PHB class 1 small and the bit-rate variations minimal, the packet-loss ratio can be insignificant even with small buffers. (Actually, the CBR service category in ATM networks demonstrates this property quite well.)

Figure 7.18 Two delay classes made by two AF PHBs.

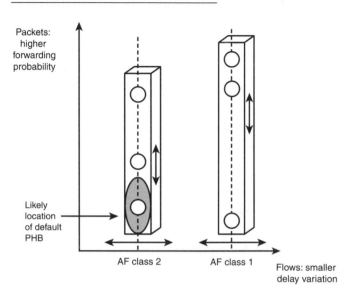

AF PHBs for Bit-Rate Differentiation The second idea for using AF PHBs meaningfully is to provide bit-rate differentiation. In a way, this is an attractive idea because bandwidth is one of the most important aspects of service differentiation.

For simplicity's sake, assume only two classes, one for customers with an expected bit rate of 50kbps and another class for customers with an expected bit rate of 250kbps. So far fine, but what do these bit rates really mean? The answer cannot be the bit rate of the highest importance level, because that bit rate is controlled in the boundary node and there is no evident reason to restrict the bit rate into one value per PHB class. The same reasoning is valid for the middle importance level as well. The only remaining class is the lowest one.

Then what is the purpose of knowing the expected bit rate for a flow inside the network? The primary purpose cannot be that the capacity of the lowest importance is divided proportional to the expected bit rate because that requires per-flow measurements in interior nodes. One, at least partly reasonable answer is that the information about the expected bit rate is used for management purposes. The network operator attempts to regulate the load levels and weights in a way that customers on average attain bandwidth proportional to the expected bit rates. If all four PHB classes are used for this purpose, it means four different expected bit rates for management purposes at the expense of nine extra code-points. (Note that an arbitrary amount of assured bit rates can be achieved merely by one PHB class.)

AF PHBs for Importance Differentiation The third imaginable option is to apply the PHB classes for additional importance levels. Figure 7.19 shows the target system. Even though the target itself can be justifiable, however, the implementation of this system could be a tricky task if you comply with the basic rules of AF—that is, the relationships among AF classes are regulated by the weights. Besides, because it is allowed to change the order of packets belonging to different AF classes, the whole range of importance values are not properly available for one individual flow. Therefore, it seems apparent that if more than three importance levels are needed, an AF class should be extended instead of using several AF classes.

Figure 7.19   Six importance levels made by two AF PHBs.

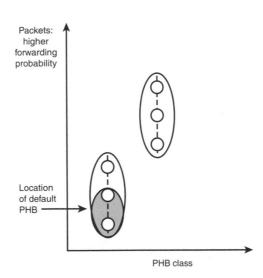

AF PHBs for Improved Predictability The former three approaches related to delay, bandwidth, and importance did not provide any evident purpose for all four AF classes. The fourth option is predictability. Perhaps one AF class is reserved for high predictability. What does that really mean? The target could be to keep the quality changes as slow as possible in such a way that the following occurs:

- The highest importance level permanently provides high quality (but that is expected anyway).

- The middle importance level permanently provides moderate quality (but that will be really difficult to realize in practice).

- The lowest importance level permanently provides the best-effort quality without starvation (but that is expected anyway).

The main conclusion of this preliminary assessment is that some level of predictability is a rational target for any AF class, although a useful differentiation seems difficult to realize. In particular, the predictability on the middle level likely requires an artificial deterioration of quality (excessive packet discarding or additional delays).

AF PHBs for Pricing Differentiation Finally, maybe it is necessary to omit all the previous considerations and just declare that AF classes are for pricing differentiation. Unfortunately, it is not possible to totally avoid the quality or bandwidth issues, because there must be a reason for customers to pay more for one service than for another one. As section 5.3, "Pricing as a Tool for Controlling Traffic," in Chapter 5 discussed, there is no prominent differentiation aspect that can be used as a basis for pricing. Even so, Table 7.10 presents some preliminary ideas about the possibilities of the AF-PHB group being used for pricing differentiation.

Table 7.10   Preliminary Pricing Considerations for AF-PHB Group

Differentiation of	As a Function of	One AF Class	Four AF Classes
Price	Bandwidth	Necessary at least for the highest importance level and perhaps for the middle level.	It does not seem reasonable to have different prices for purebandwidth in different AF classes if all other aspects are constant.
Price	Quality (delay)	Not relevant.	Two delay classes with different prices is a reasonable approach.
Price	Availability	Pricing may depend on the time of day and day of the week.	Different AF classes may have different pricing structures (for instance, because class 1 is for residential users and class 2 is for business users).
Availability	Bandwidth	Possible in a limited sense (more bandwidth with the same price during idle hours).	As above.

Differentiation of	As a Function of	One AF Class	Four AF Classes
Availability	Quality	Not relevant.	Possible to a limited extent because customers are allowed to change AF class.
Quality	Bandwidth	Not relevant	As above.

7.4.3 Required Technical Tools

Once again, the problem of uncertainty arises. When no clear idea about the general objective of the system is available, it is impossible to strictly evaluate the required mechanisms. The following evaluation is based on certain assumptions that are deemed relevant, but that may be proved erroneous in real networks.

Implementation Options for Boundary Nodes

Suppose that there are two reference bit rates: a lower one for controlling the traffic on the highest importance level, and a higher one for controlling the traffic on the middle importance level. Another possible difference between the two importance levels is that the measuring period for the middle class is longer than the measuring period for the highest importance class. If there is no premarking made by the customer, the boundary nodes mark as many packets as possible into the highest importance level according to the rules defined in the SLA. Correspondingly, if the packets cannot attain the highest importance level, the middle importance level is used, if possible. Only if both of these are impossible is the packet marked on the lowest importance level.

In summary, the philosophy of AF seems to be that only excessive packets are marked, which means that regardless of the used bit rate on the highest importance level, the user is allowed to send as many packets on the lowest importance level as wanted. However, the SLA may also include restrictions to send an excessive amount of packets on the lowest importance level. All these properties can be implemented, for instance, by three token buckets with different bucket rates and bucket depths.

Implementation Options for Interior Nodes

Although the AF specification "Assured Forwarding PHB Group" does not mention any specific queuing system, the AF-PHB structure resembles the class-based queuing (CBQ) system (Baker *et al.* 1999). In particular, a configurable amount of buffer space and bandwidth must be allocated to each of the four AF classes—this can hardly be done without four real or virtual queues. Bandwidth allocation for different queues is exactly what CBQ is supposed to do. Nonetheless, vendors are allowed to use any queuing system that satisfies the AF-PHB requirements.

The other integral part of AF-PHB implementation is the algorithm used to decide which packets have to be dropped during overload situations. The specification states that an AF implementation must attempt to minimize long-term congestion within each class. This seems to require an active queue-management algorithm, such as *Random Early Drop (RED)*. An open issue is whether RED or a similar algorithm should be used for all thresholds or only for the lowest importance levels. Figure 7.20 shows an implementation with four queues and different combinations of hard thresholds and RED regions.

Figure 7.20 AF implementation based on four queues and three importance levels.

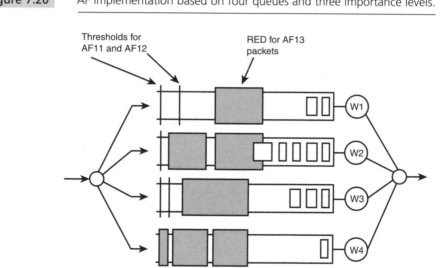

Implementation Options Related to Network Domain

Table 7.11 presents a preliminary assessment of the management aspect related to the AF-PHB group. The main concern is related to the network dimensioning in general. If the use of AF-PHB classes is more or less unclear, it is extremely difficult for the vendors to develop appropriate supporting systems for network operation and management.

Table 7.11 Preliminary Management Consideration for AF-PHB Group

Aspect	Main Options with AF
Routing	Primarily static routing.
Resource Reservation	The primary idea of AF is to use permanent or semipermanent reservation of traffic aggregates.

Aspect	Main Options with AF
Network dimensioning	Because mathematical modeling seems to be very difficult, network dimensioning will probably be based instead on practical experience.
Contracts between domains	The primary option is to apply appropriate packet marking, but some level of compensation could be needed if the load is not balanced.

7.4.4 Evaluation of Attributes

The traffic-handling part of the AF-PHB system is relatively simple, and hardly results in high implementation costs. Moreover, if properly managed the statistical multiplexing could be efficiently utilized with a couple of clearly defined AF-PHB classes. However, the costs related to network management and customer care are difficult to predict when the service model is not known. The same concern is valid also with fairness—an AF system may provide tools to offer good fairness, but that is not an evident situation.

In a sense, the AF system provides considerable versatility because a large variety of service models can be implemented. It is even fair to say that there is too much versatility, because there is no commonly accepted service model for AF that makes it possible to design useful end-to-end services. Robustness also depends on the general effectiveness of the AF system; a systematic approach is definitely needed to avoid ambiguous situations that endanger the robustness of the system.

7.5 Dynamic RT/NRT-PHB Group

The main target of Dynamic RT/NRT (DRT)-PHB group is to provide a consistent and clear framework for building Differentiated Services (Kilkki, Loukola, and Ruutu 1998). Although the DRT-PHB specification is an independent document, the roots of the specification are in the more extensive Simple Integrated Media Access (SIMA) model (which can be found at http://www-nrc.nokia.com/sima/).

7.5.1 Description

The DRT-PHB group defines a system with two PHB classes and six PHBs in each of the classes depicted in Figure 7.21. PHB classes offer two distinctly different delay characteristics: RT class is for flows needing real-time service, and NRT is for flows without strict delay requirements. Six importance levels offer wide dynamics for various traffic-control and pricing schemes. The framework can be extended in both directions if necessary; there could be more than two delay classes and more than six importance levels. The values 2 and 6 are considered as the minimum to provide appropriate characteristics for various needs.

Figure 7.21   Structure of DRT-PHB group.

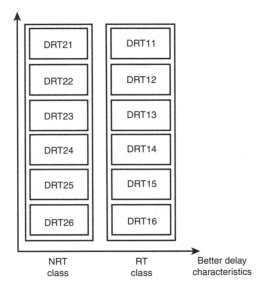

7.5.2 Position of DRT-PHB Group in the Framework

The evaluation the DRT-PHB group is based on this author's opinion and on the original idea behind the DRT-PHB group. That basis is both an advantage and disadvantage. On the one hand it makes the assessment, in a way, easy; on the other hand, there is risk that the assessment of the PHB group is somehow partial (or subjective). In particular, it is comprehensible that the DRT-PHB group fits better in the framework presented in earlier chapters than the other PHB groups, because the PHB model and the framework are based on the same insight of Differentiated Services.

This section tries to give, after all, a relatively impartial assessment of the DRT-PHB model. Nonetheless, personal preferences always have substantial effects on the conclusions, unless something can be strictly proven (and unfortunately, mathematical proofs are not possible in this case). Therefore, the conclusive comparison of different PHB models remains open as far as there is no extensive experiments of different PHB models.

Service Models

The DRT-PHB group is essentially, as all PHB groups should be, a specification of packet treatment inside the Differentiated Services network. Yet, to assess the possible services, it is necessary to specify the boundary functions to some extent. The original system behind the DRT-PHB model—that is, Simple Integrated Media Access (SIMA)—includes specifications for both the boundary functions and the interior functions, and even for the pricing structure (found at `http://www-nrc.nokia.com/sima/`). Although the DRT-PHB group is not limited to the SIMA system model, it is used to assess the possible services build on the basis of the DRT-PHB group, because the SIMA model comprises in a systematic manner all the aspects from customer services to packet-level mechanisms.

One of the key concepts of the SIMA model is *nominal bit rate (NBR)*. NBR defines the relative amount of resources that a certain entity is supposed to achieve from the network. The entity can be anything: a part of a flow, flow, customer, group of customers, or a large organization. In that sense, the DRT-PHB group can be applied to any of the three service models: application, customer, or organization model. Yet, the basic philosophy of the DRT-PHB group mainly supports the customer model (in which each customer buys as big a share of the network as she wants and is ready to pay for). Therefore, the primary fairness relations addressed by the DRT-PHB group are those between users—that is, F4 and F5 in Figure 7.22.

Figure 7.22   Relevant fairness issues for the DRT-PHB group.

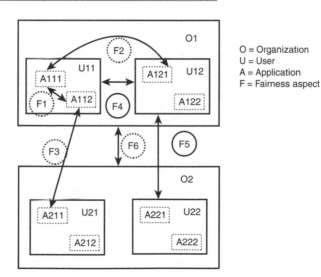

The next issue is the SIMA service in relation to dynamics and level of assurance. The primary model of SIMA—and this is generally valid with the DRT-PHB group as well—is resource sharing, as illustrated in Figure 7.23. NBRs (that is, the shares of customers) should usually be as static as possible to facilitate the network management.

Nevertheless, the DRT-PHB framework can support other models as well: Leased-line service basically needs a high enough importance level (perhaps beyond the six importance levels of DRT PHB). A constant bit-rate connection could have a special traffic control in the boundary node similar to that of EF PHB. Furthermore, if NBRs are dynamic rather than static, the service provider can use a dynamic importance model. Note, however, that increased dynamics make load prediction and network dimensioning more difficult. Guaranteed connections need additional mechanisms that are not covered by the specification of the DRT-PHB group. It is, therefore, likely that increased dynamics will be used in real networks only after significant experience is gathered about static quality differentiation.

Figure 7.23   Primary and secondary service models for DRT-PHB group.

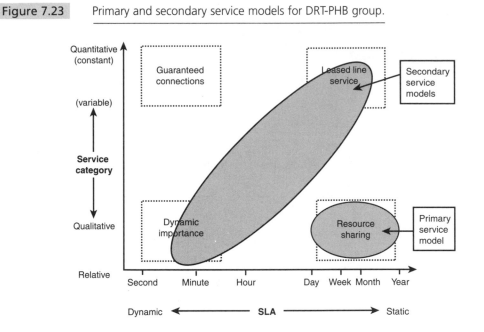

One of the basic assumptions of the DRT-PHB group is that most of the traffic on the Internet consists of short-lived flows to variable destinations. The predictability of destination is intrinsically low for that kind of traffic, and there is not much to be done to improve the situation. The architecture of DRT PHB is adapted to that situation. There is no obstacle to using DRT PHB with long-lived flows, however, such as IP telephony and video streams.

The six (or more) levels of importance cover the scale from very low predictability of load to high predictability. Even on the highest level, the assumption is not a constant bit rate, but rather the reasoning is that the higher price keeps the use of the highest level limited (particularly if the NBR is static). On the contrary, the lowest importance level could be available without any restrictions, which makes it difficult to predict load level and traffic process inside the network. Figure 7.24 shows both primary service models and the most important region that is not covered directly by DRT-PHB group.

Figure 7.24 Predictability of load and destination for DRT-PHB group.

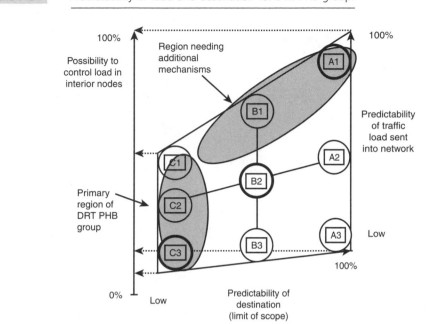

The main VPN model for the DRT-PHB group is VPN-C in Table 7.12. That is, all relevant marking is done at boundary nodes, and the interior nodes are not aware of the VPN itself. The actual result depends on the marking rules implemented in the boundary nodes, and in some cases the result could be is similar to VPN-B. Moreover, some simple additional rules can be used in interior nodes to increase the separation between different VPNs (model VPN-B in Table 7.12). VPN-A is also possible, although it clearly requires additional tools that are beyond the scope of the DRT-PHB group.

Table 7.12 Suitability of the DRT-PHB group for Different VPN Types

VPN Type	Main Tool to Manage Congestion Inside Network	Remark Considering DRT-PHB Group
VPN-A1	Full mesh of CBR connections	Not relevant with DRT-PHB group.
VPN-A2	Strict limit for traffic sent to the network ($< C/(N-1)$)	Could be used, but presumably not a useful model.
VPN-A3	Alternative routing for load balancing	Not a likely model.

continues

Table 7.12   Continued

VPN Type	Main Tool to Manage Congestion Inside Network	Remark Considering DRT-PHB Group
VPN-B	Limited capacity sharing between VPNs	Can likely be done by combining NBR management in boundary nodes and weights for VPNs in interior nodes (but implementation is not trivial).
VPN-C	Total capacity sharing between VPNs	Can be done by appropriate managing of NBRs in boundary nodes. (This model is in accordance with the basic philosophy of DRT PHB.)

Quality Models

If there is something really original in the DRT-PHB group it is the idea to fasten the importance levels of two PHB classes together. Figure 7.25 illustrates this. Although the actual packet-loss ratio of an importance level depends significantly on the load level and traffic processes, the instantaneous value for an importance level is independent of the service class. Consequently, the whole package of 12 PHBs moves in the scale defined by delay and loss ratio in a way that relations of each PHB pair remain the same regardless of the load situation in the network. This is the target model of the DRT-PHB group.

Figure 7.25   Quality model of the DRT-PHB group.

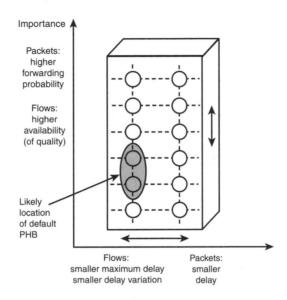

Predictability with DRT-PHB Group

Because of the basic principles of the DRT-PHB group, the predictability of quality can be limited, in particular on all intermediate importance levels. If high predictability is positively needed, it seems that some additional mechanisms are necessary. On the highest quality level, that could mean an EF type of PHB model.

The other relevant predictability target is that default PHB should not be starved even in the case of a high load level. This issue can be divided into two parts: the treatment of traffic flows *with* and *without* the possibility to obtain a higher importance level by reducing the bit rate of the flow. The first case with the possibility is trivial: Every flow can avoid starvation just by reducing its bit rate. If the application cannot adjust the bit rate, it should use a higher importance level rather than suppose that the default PHB provides permanently high enough quality.

The other case without the possibility is more difficult. The primary approach is to avoid mapping those streams into PHBs with a high possibility of starvation. (For this reason, default PHB is not the lowest importance level in Figure 7.25). Another approach is to guarantee that the importance level used by the default best-effort service always attains a minimum bandwidth. Because this kind of system violates the fundamental logic of the DRT-PHB system, however, it should be avoided whenever possible. Finally, default service may use its own queue with a more or less permanent weight. In that case, the importance relationship between packets belonging to default PHB and DRT PHB can be defined only approximately.

Pricing Models

One of the potential advantages of a consistent PHB architecture is that it makes it possible to design comprehensible relationships between different service aspects and price. Table 7.13 gives a short overview of some of possibilities provided by the DRT-PHB group.

Table 7.13   Preliminary Pricing Considerations for the DRT-PHB Group

Differentiation of	As a function of	DRT-PHB Group
Price	Bandwidth	The price of NBR defines the relationship between bandwidth and price. (Note that the price of NBR has no effect on the mechanisms inside the network.)
Price	Quality (delay)	For a constant packet flow, there is no explicit pricing difference between the two delay classes. On the contrary, for a given variable bit-rate flow, higher NBR (that is, higher price) is needed to attain the same importance level if the customer uses the RT class rather than the NRT class.
Price	Availability	This is one of the inherent relationships of the DRT-PHB system: The availability of given quality and bandwidth depends automatically on the load situation. That means that what the system provides is different between busy and idle hours without any additional management effort.
Availability	Bandwidth	Basically the same relationship as above: If the price and quality are constant, a lower bit rate automatically means higher availability, and vice versa.

| Availability | Quality | Possible in a limited sense: For a variable bit-rate flow, a change from RT PHB to non-RT PHB may improve the availability. |
| Quality | Bandwidth | Possible in a limited sense: For a variable bit-rate flow, a change from RT PHB to NRT PHB may allow the use of a higher average bit rate. |

7.5.3 Required Technical Tools

The following investigation of required technical tools is based on the assumption that the DRT-PHB group is mainly used to implement a resource-sharing model. If the service model is different, the requirements could be somewhat (but probably not much) different.

Implementation Options for Boundary Nodes

The main, and almost the only requirement for boundary node functions is that the bit rate of each entity with an NBR be measured; and based on the measurement result, the boundary node determines the importance level for each packet. It is also possible to use some other, totally different approaches. For instance, the boundary node can mark the packets merely based on the application. That kind of systems violates the fundamental resource-sharing principle of the system, however. If the marking does not depend systematically on the bit rate used by the customer, the interior nodes cannot divide the capacity in a fair manner among customers.

The primary marking system for DRT PHB is that the instantaneous metering result defines entirely the packet marking of every packet—that is, as long as the metering result remains the same, all packets obtain the same importance marking. Nevertheless, it seems possible to develop a more complicated system in which the marking depends also on other issues, such as the packet marking made by the customer. This kind of system makes it possible to support, for instance, a layered video coding with more and less important frames.

Finally, it should be noted that because the RT-PHB class with relatively small buffers is more sensitive to bursts of packets (and large packets as well), the marking system should somehow depend on the PHB class selected by the customer. That can be achieved in practice by a short measuring period that punishes real-time flows with high burstiness or very large packet size.

Implementation Options for Interior Nodes

Figure 7.26 presents one possible implementation for the DRT-PHB group. Two queues and six thresholds are basically inevitable system components. In addition, two important principles largely define the system behavior:

- The RT-PHB queue has a strict priority over the other queue.

- The packet-discarding decision is made independent of the PHB class.

The first principle provides an easy method to guarantee a maximum delay for the RT PHB in a way described in the section "Priority Queuing" in Chapter 6, "Traffic Handling and Network Management." A mere strict priority, however, may result in a situation in which the RT-PHB queue can use the whole link capacity while the NRT-PHB queue becomes totally starved. This is a critical problem and should be solved somehow.

One possibility is to define a minimum amount of link capacity for the NRT queue—that is, a finite weight. The main difficulty of this approach is that there is no clear relationship between the importance levels of the two queues. Depending on the load situation of the two queues, at an arbitrary point in time the system may discard RT packets of importance level 4, and at the same time accept NRT packets of importance level 6. When the load levels of the two queues change, the situation could be totally reverse after a while.

This kind of behavior is not desired in a DRT-PHB system. Therefore, the DRT-PHB system uses another alternative to avoid starvation of the NRT queue. In DRT PHB, the discarding of a packet is independent of the PHB class. In consequence, the packet-loss probability at a given point in time depends on the importance level, but it is virtually independent of the PHB class. If there is any starvation problem, it is common for a certain importance level of both RT and NRT classes.

Figure 7.26   An implementation of the DRT-PHB group.

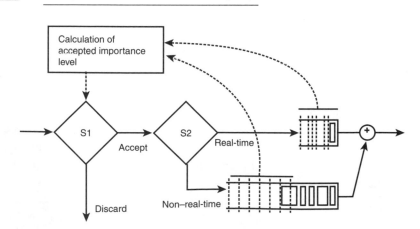

Implementation Options Related to the Network Domain

Table 7.14 presents a preliminary assessment of the management aspect related to the DRT-PHB group. The main concern is related to the network dimensioning. Without appropriate network dimensioning, the services build on the basis of the DRT-PHB group cannot the consistent. If the load level in one part of the network is much higher than that of another part, for instance, the average share attained by the same price could vary significantly. That could deteriorate the fairness of the service among customers in different parts of the network. Moreover, customers will probably expect that the available share be at least somehow predictable, if not constant. Large and quick variations can also be defective for customer services.

Table 7.14　Management Considerations for the DRT-PHB Group

Aspect	Main Options with DRT-PHB Group
Routing	Primarily static routing. If adaptive routing is used, it should take into account separately the load level of every individual PHB (not only the average load level).
Resource reservation	The fundamental idea of the DRT-PHB group is to avoid explicit resource reservation whenever possible.
Network dimensioning	This is the most critical part of the DRT-PHB model, because the customer service relies on the assumption that the share bought by the customer provides a predictable and stable bit rate even for arbitrary destinations.
Contracts between domains	Both pricing and re-marking of packets are possible approaches. In particular, pricing should take into account the importance levels of each packet. Re-marking should be as stable as possible—for instance, the importance level of all packets coming from a network domain are decreased by one step for a relatively long duration.

7.5.4　*Evaluation of Attributes*

A simple and consistent system such as the DRT-PHB group is likely to provide highly efficient implementation on a traffic-handling level. The main concerns are traffic control and network management. The control mechanisms must be able to effectively prevent the misuse of high importance levels. The management system should support a workable network dimensioning and operation system that appropriately takes into account the requirements of both PHB classes and all importance levels.

The fairness of the service provision depends decisively on the NBR management and pricing structure. The logical structure of the DRT-PHB system itself gives tools to realize a fair service based on the resource-sharing model. Versatility is achieved by both delay classes and by wide dynamics that make it possible to apply exquisite pricing schemes. Robustness is appropriate if the network operation and management gives appropriate support for customer care and network management.

Summary

The introduction to this chapter defined the essence of PHB—that is, the rule that determines the treatment of packets inside the network. The rule should be useful and comprehensible to make it possible to build practical services. But the rules should not necessitate a specific implementation nor should they exactly specify the service model. This discussion reviewed four PHB models: Class Selector, Expedited Forwarding, Assured Forwarding and Dynamic RT/NRT. Did they meet the fundamental targets?

The Class Selector PHB group lacks clear rules because it is mainly intended to provide backward compatibility for current, various uses of the DS octet. Expedited Forwarding appears to be a service specification rather than a PHB. This is in a sense a significant advantage; on the other hand, however, the EF specification does not considerably advance the development of the general-purpose framework for Differentiated Services.

Assured Service defines requirements for mechanisms in interior nodes rather than a clear PHB structure from a packet or flow perspective. Although the AF-PHB model may allow the operator to introduce numerous new services, it does not give much guidance for interoperability. Different service providers may understand the (largely hidden) AF rules in different ways.

The Dynamic RT/NRT-PHB model satisfies the goal better; the essence of the DRT specification is about the relationships among packets belonging to different PHBs. Logical behavior of the PHB system requires that the boundary mechanisms comply with certain rules, however. In particular, if the importance level of each packet does not depend systematically on the bit rate of the flow, the whole system model is somewhat questionable.

It is apparent that the current PHB specifications as such do not provide one clear way to the utopia of Differentiated Services. It seems that the reality is too complicated and too many matters resist any significant, quick changes in the Internet technology and service models. Because there is such strong pressure on service evolution, however, some significant changes will certainly happen within the next few years. This chapter's evaluation of PHBs offers some tools to direct the evolution toward reasonable goals.

PART III

Building Global Networks Based on Differentiated Services

CHAPTER

Interworking Issues

This chapter contains four main parts. The first part discusses interoperability issues among the Class Selector PHB (CS-PHB) group, the Expedited Forwarding PHB (EF-PHB) group, the Assured Forwarding PHB (AF-PHB) group, and the Dynamic RT/NRT PHB (DRT-PHB) group. The second part addresses other IP quality models from the viewpoint of a Differentiated Services framework. The QoS evolution of the Internet will largely depend on the smooth interworking of different technologies, particularly Integrated Services (IntServ), RSVP, MPLS, and Differentiated Services (DiffServ).

To further widen the scope, some non-IP technologies are discussed in section 8.3, "Interworking with Non-IP Networks." ATM networks are widely used in high-capacity backbone networks. The capability of ATM to offer quality differentiation for IP networks is, however, somewhat questionable because of the differences in service models. A significant part of the Internet traffic goes through local area networks (LANs). Contemporary LANs have limited QoS mechanisms, but IEEE 802.1p could mean a pivotal change in that respect. The QoS capabilities for data services are also under strong development. Section 8.3.3, "Wireless Networks," discusses some general wireless issues with a closer look at General Packet Radio Service (GPRS). Finally, some issues related to multicasting services are discussed.

8.1 Interworking Among Differentiated Services Models

One of the conjectures of the Differentiated Services effort is that when the working group has designed a number of building blocks, the natural evolution process generates a reasonable combination of network services. Perhaps something like that will happen, although it is hard to identify any network service that has merely emerged without an explicit design process. The prevalent ISP business model based on flat-rate pricing comes perhaps closest to that evolutionary process. But even that is an example of a business model rather than an example of a network service. Network service based on the best-effort model has been used throughout the history of the Internet.

Regardless of the form of evolution, those service providers that can either predict the next step of evolution or define it have a great advantage compared to other service providers. The evolution of Differentiated Services starts with the selection of PHB groups. "The competition will generally be most severe between the forms which are most like each other in all respects," Charles Darwin noticed already 150 years ago (Darwin 1972). What does this mean in the case of PHB groups, or the forms of Differentiated Services? At length only a few PHB groups can survive; moreover, each of the surviving PHB groups will have to find a distinct place or application. One niche cannot maintain several species.

This section assesses the prospects of four PHB groups—the Class Selector PHB group, the Expedited Forwarding PHB group, the Assured Forwarding PHB group, and Dynamic RT/NRT PHB group—with respect to the following topics:

- Class Selector PHB group with other PHB groups

- Expedited Forwarding versus Assured Forwarding

- DRT-PHB group compared with AF- and EF-PHB groups

- Summary of PHB groups

8.1.1 *Class Selector PHB Group with Other PHB Groups*

The first topic is the general usability of the Class Selector PHB group if the service provider uses one or several other PHB groups. Figure 8.1 shows the applicability areas for different PHBs:

- AF-1 = Main area covered by the highest importance level of Assured Forwarding PHB

- AF-2 = Main area covered by the middle importance level of AF-PHB

- AF-3 = Main area covered by the lowest importance level of AF-PHB

- BE = Best-effort service (default PHB)

- CS = Main area for Class Selector PHB group

- DRT-p = Primary area for DRT-PHB group

- DRT-s = Secondary area for DRT-PHB group

- EF-p = Primary area for Expedited Forwarding PHB group

- EF-s = Secondary area for EF-PHB group

Figure 8.1 Applicability areas for PHB groups.

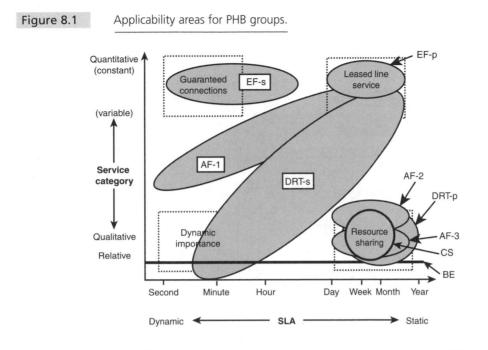

In the framework of Figure 8.1, there is apparently no empty space to be filled by the Class Selector PHB group. Only if the operator decides to use merely an EF-PHB group is it reasonable to apply a CS-PHB group either for providing better than best-effort service or facilitating traffic management inside the network. The conclusion of Figure 8.2 is very similar: Although a CS-PHB group may enlarge the succinct area of best-effort service, AF and DRT groups do the same job, but better, mainly because of more systematic approach for traffic conditioning in boundary nodes.

Finally, Figure 8.3 shows that AF- and DRT-PHB groups can, at least in principle, cover almost the whole range of importance and urgency levels. It is therefore reasonable to assume that CS is used merely to provide backward compatibility.

Figure 8.2 Predictability characteristics of the CS-PHB group compared to other PHB groups.

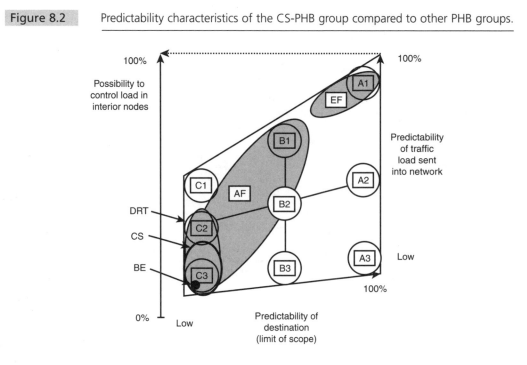

Figure 8.3 The CS-PHB group compared to other PHB groups with regard to importance and urgency scales.

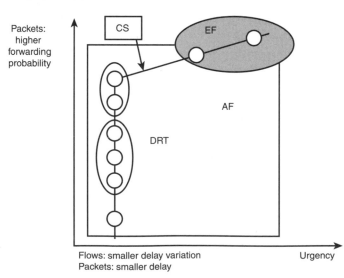

8.1.2 Expedited Forwarding Versus Assured Forwarding

The Expedited Forwarding PHB and the Assured Forwarding PHB group have some clear similarities. The target and implementation of the highest importance level of AF could be similar to those of EF-PHB. Therefore, if both Assured Forwarding and Explicit Forwarding are used in the same network domain, it is important for the operator to identify distinct roles for both PHB groups. In general, Figures 8.4 and 8.5 show that the application regions for EF and AF are mainly separate, which indicates that they can be used in a reasonable manner within one network domain.

| Figure 8.4 | Service model comparison of the EF-PHB and AF-PHB group. |

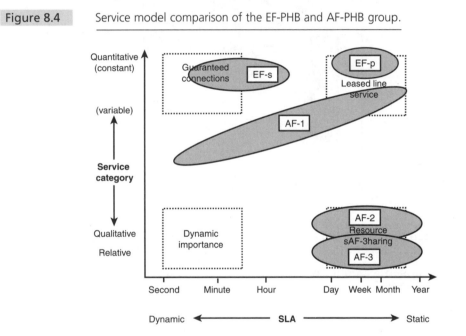

The operator may, nevertheless, want to minimize the number of PHBs to facilitate network management. The primary idea behind most PHB proposals is to provide specific treatment for packets that have passed certain traffic-conditioning actions at boundary. Now you may ask whether *every* different conditioning action requires its own DS codepoint. The viewpoint of this book is that the logic and structure of the PHB system should be chiefly independent of the boundary functions. That means that a new codepoint should be introduced only if there is a compelling reason, and even then it should be fitted in the existing system of PHBs.

Figure 8.5 Comparison of the EF-PHB and AF-PHB group with regard to importance and urgency scales.

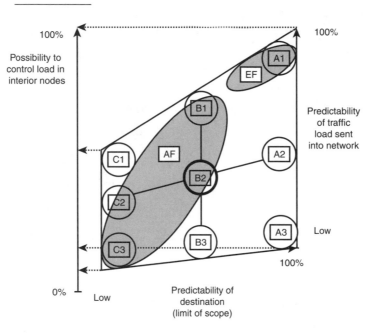

In this case, when you are assessing the interoperability of the EF-PHB and AF-PHB groups, the key question can be derived from Figure 8.5. Is a higher predictability of destination a good enough reason for reserving for EF-PHB its own codepoint? It might be, although the basic idea of both EF and the highest importance level of AF is that the network can somehow make certain that the packet-loss ratio will be minimal. In addition, because the relationship between different AF classes is an open issue, it is hard to map EF into any specific AF class.

It is fair to conclude then that a distinct EF-PHB could be useful. The next issue is to specify the proper relationship between AF and EF. It is easy require that a certain PHB be treated in a certain way (usually very well) regardless of any other traffic streams in the network. But how can anything truly be independent in such an environment as the Internet? An attractive solution to this problem is that the network gives each PHB class certain link and buffer resources. Yet it seems that systematic quality differentiation and strict separation (true independence) are hard to achieve at the same time.

Consider now a system with only one AF class and an EF-PHB, as illustrated in Figure 8.6. From the service provider viewpoint, there has to be a reason for having both AF- and EF-PHBs. In particular, the relationship between EF and highest AF-PHB (AF11) is critical. Should EF be better regarding delay or loss ratio, or perhaps another unidentified aspect? It is possible to investigate this is from the perspective of the fictitious service provider, Fairprofit.

Figure 8.6   The location of an AF class and EF-PHB in the scale of urgency and importance.

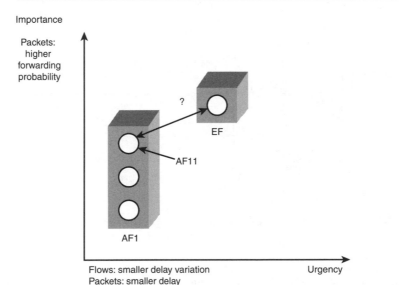

Implementing AF- and EF-PHBs in the Same Network

Consider first the loss ratio in a situation where Fairprofit has links with a capacity of 20Mbps for AF- and EF-PHBs together. The managers of Fairprofit have identified four possible models to divide the link capacities inside the network:

• *Model A*: Both AF and EF classes have a 10Mbps capacity without the possibility to utilize any free capacity left unused by the other PHB class.

• *Model B*: This ensures that the available capacity for each of the classes is at least 10Mbps. If one of the classes uses less than 10Mbps, however, the other class can use the remaining capacity.

• *Model C*: AF and EF are sharing the whole capacity of 20Mbps with equal importance for AF and EF packets.

• *Model D*: AF and EF are sharing the whole capacity of 20Mbps in a way that EF packets have higher importance than all AF packets.

The problem encountered by Fairprofit is that despite the incoming EF or AF traffic streams being under tight control on the first link, such as the one from node 1 to node 4 in Figure 8.7, it does not necessarily guaranteed the there is no conflicting situation in any interior node. Nevertheless, it is expected that over-load situations caused by pure EF traffic are very rare.

Figure 8.7 Possible location of overload situation with EF- and AF-PHB groups.

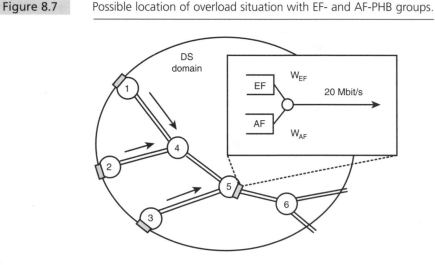

Table 8.2 summarizes the main characteristics of the four models. The table shows the general behavior of the models in five traffic cases, from a case without any overload to a case where both service classes are overloaded.

As long as everything is going well and nothing unexpected happens, there is no discernible difference between AF and EF (no packets are lost). In reality, Case 1 in Table 8.2 should be valid most of the time, say 99.99%, to provide high enough quality. Because there is no difference between different models in Case 1, the only relevant issue is how the system works in exceptional Cases 2, 3, 4, and 5.

Table 8.2 Division of 20Mbps Link Between EF- and AF-PHBs, (For Instance, 12 + 8 Means 12Mbps for EF and 8Mbps for AF)

Case	EF Mbps	AF Mbps	Model A: Strict Separation (at most 10Mbps)	Model B: At Least 10Mbps Available for Both	Model C: Sharing of 20Mbps with Equal Importance	Model D: Sharing of 20Mbps with Higher Importance for EF
1	8	8	8 + 8	8 + 8	8 + 8	8 + 8
2	12	8	10 + 8	12 + 8	12 + 8	12 + 8
3	16	8	10 + 8	12 + 8	13.3 + 6.7	16 + 4
4	8	16	8 + 10	8 + 12	6.7 + 13.3	8 + 12
5	12	12	8 + 10	10 + 10	10 + 10	12 + 8

It seems that there is no clear advantage to applying strict separation (Model A), because it wastes resources in a case where one service class exceeds its capacity while there is free capacity in another class. If there is any justification for using Model A rather than Model B, it might be the assumption that a looser model encourages users to send excessive traffic in the network. That reasoning seems questionable, particularly with EF-PHB, because end users cannot send any excessive packets into the network. Therefore, any excessive EF traffic inside the network is most likely a management fault rather than a result of end-user misconduct.

Fairprofit may consider Model B as practical because the result in every overload case (3, 4, and 5) is justifiable. Still, Models C and D could be worth of further evaluation. Model C means essentially that the packet-loss ratio is the same for AF and EF, whereas Model D gives a clear advantage for EF in all situations. Which one is the best model depends on the objective of Fairprofit—that is, on the end-to-end service model. That is not the only issue to be assessed, however, because Table 8.2 does not take into account the three importance levels of each AF class. Even though Model B appears to be justified in Case 5, that conclusion is not clear if a significant part of the AF traffic is on the lowest importance level.

Table 8.3 shows four different versions of Case 5. In Case 5a, all AF traffic is marked on the highest importance level; in Case 5d, the AF traffic is marked on the lowest importance level. In Cases 5b and 5c, load is divided between the highest and the lowest importance level. Even though Model B is justifiable in Case 5a, it is much harder to justify it in Cases 5c and 5d. Why should AF13 packets be transmitted rather than EF packets in any case? If the answer is that EF packets always have higher importance than AF13 packets, Fairprofit should use either Model C or Model D. The EF specification mainly promotes the application of Model D.

Table 8.3 Division of 20Mbps Link Among EF, AF11, and AF13 (For Instance, 10 + 4+6 Means 10Mbps for EF, 4Mbps for AF11, and 6Mbps for AF13)

Case	EF Mbps	AF 11 Mbps	AF 13 Mbps	Model B: At least 10Mbps Available for Both	Model C: Sharing of 20Mbps, Importance: EF=AF11>AF13	Model D: Sharing of 20Mbps, Importance: EF>AF11>AF13
5a	12	12	0	10 + 10+0	10 + 10+0	12 + 8+0
5b	12	8	4	10 + 8+2	12 + 8+0	12 + 8+0
5c	12	4	8	10 + 4+6	12 + 4+4	12 + 4+4
5d	12	0	12	10 + 0+10	12 + 0+8	12 + 0+8

Fairprofit should consider also the delay characteristics of the services. If EF requires better delay properties than the best AF class, Model C could be quite hard to implement within the AF framework, whereas both Model B and D are possible. An ultimate version of Model D means that EF can reserve the whole link capacity. But that is against the Assured Forwarding specification requiring that certain buffer and link resources be reserved for each AF class.

If Fairprofit decides that EF can be content with the delay characteristics of AF class 1, EF and AF11 may share the same PHB (Model C in Table 8.3) or share the same class but with a higher importance level for EF (Model D in Table 8.3). Unfortunately, also these models seem to be against the AF and EF specifications because the treatment of EF traffic should be independent of the other traffic streams.

A virtual rescue from this dilemma could be that the behavioral requirements are strictly valid only under reasonable operating conditions and traffic loads. Fairprofit may conclude that because any excess of EF traffic inside the network means unreasonable operating conditions, the specification does not give any strict rules for those situations. In summary, Fairprofit may consider both Models B and D to be acceptable. Moreover, Fairprofit may claim that traffic control and the network-management systems are able to totally avoid overloads within EF PHB.

8.1.3 DRT-PHB Group Compared with AF- and EF-PHB Groups

The fourth PHB proposal evaluated here is made by the author of this book. This section, however, offers an objective comparison between it and other proposals as far as that is possible. Figures 8.8 and 8.9 illustrate the position of DRT-PHB group compared to EF- and AF-PHB groups. It is important to first concentrate on the relationship between AF and DRT, and return to the EF issue at the end of this section.

Both Figures 8.8 and 8.9 show that the application regions of AF and DRT are similar. For instance, AF drop levels 2 and 3 can be used to implement the resource-sharing model that is the primary area of DRT-PHB group. Therefore, it is reasonable to ask whether there is any good reason to use DRT- and AF-PHBs at the same time.

Figure 8.8 Service model of the DRT-PHB group compared with the EF-PHB and AF-PHB groups.

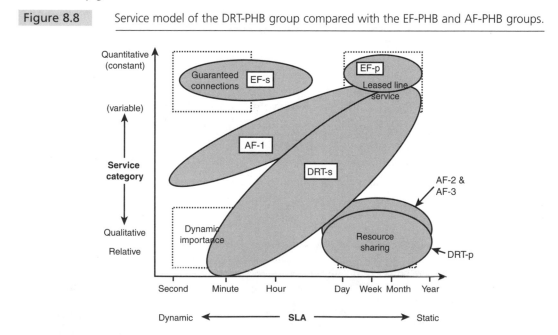

Figure 8.9 The DRT-PHB group compared with EF and AF with regard to predictability of traffic and destination.

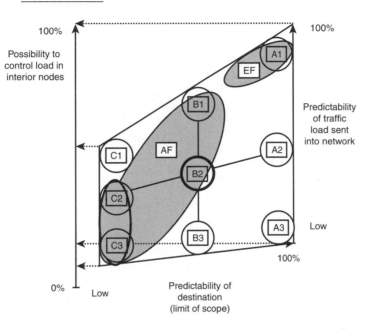

The Assured Forwarding PHB group appears to have the largest area of application. Although this supposition may usually be valid, it is unclear whether the whole area can be covered at the same time by any real implementation. Note that unlike AF the other two PHB groups, EF and DRT, both have their primary implementations that clearly define the application region in Figures 8.8 and 8.9. Hence it is difficult to further evaluate AF without specifying the AF service model or implementation to some degree.

As long as the primary separation between AF-PHB classes is bandwidth (or weight), the actual result related to delay and loss remains unsure. Although a table similar Table 8.3 could be devised for one DRT-PHB group and several AF classes, the result would be too complex. It is better, therefore, to let a figure illustrate the situation. Figure 8.10 presents a system with one DRT-PHB group and three AF-PHB classes. It is supposed that each class has a permanent share of bandwidth (weight) and the relative share is on average larger for AF class 1 than for AF class 2, and so on. Yet, the attribute *on average* means that not much can be said about the instantaneous importance and urgency orders. Although this system can be realized, the design of consistent end-to-end services could be too difficult if both a DRT-PHB class and several AF classes are used in parallel.

Figure 8.10   Three AF classes (each with three PHBs) and a DRT-PHB group (2*6 PHBs).

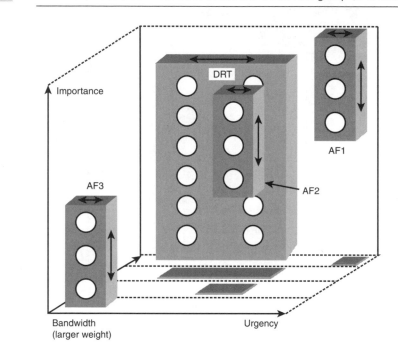

As to the combination of EF and DRT, the most logical approach is that an EF kind of PHB be added to the DRT structure. Figure 8.11 shows four possible locations for a virtual EF-PHB. Adjunct *virtual* is used here because the result does not necessarily comply with the EF specification.

Because of the strict requirements of actual EF, it seems that only approach 1 represents an actual EF-PHB. Without its own buffer (approaches 3 and 4) or without distinct importance level (approaches 2 and 4), the characteristics of virtual EF could be inappropriate in some cases. Yet, approach 2 in Figure 8.11 could be suitable for all practical purposes provided that the traffic control can keep the packet-loss ratio of the highest importance level minimal. The main disadvantage of approaches 1 and 2 (with EF having its own buffer) is that they necessitate very strict traffic control for EF traffic to guarantee appropriate delay characteristics for the real-time DRT class.

Figure 8.11   Three AF classes (each with three PHBs) and a DRT-PHB group (2*6 PHBs).

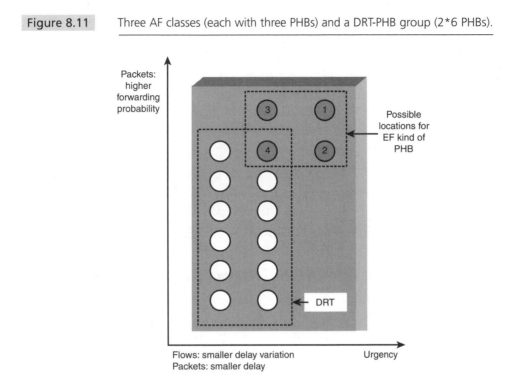

8.1.4   *Summary of PHB groups*

The main conclusion that can be drawn from this PHB evaluation is that the service provider needs to clearly define the target and then to select a proper system for that purpose. It is unlikely that any rational target will require all PHB groups because the result would be too complex to be managed in a reasonable way. The other conclusions are as follows:

- The main use of CS-PHB can be that the service provider introduces service differentiation by upgrading boundary nodes and applying some CS PHBs in existing interior nodes. In the long run, however, the Class Selector PHB group should be left for backward compatibility, mainly because the system does not provide enough information for proper traffic conditioning in boundary nodes.

- The application of Expedited Forwarding should be limited to cases where both the destination and traffic volume of every EF stream are tightly controlled. Any excess of EF traffic inside the network can be interpreted as an error of traffic management rather than actual misbehavior of any end user. Therefore, even in rare cases of excessive EF traffic, EF packets may have a higher importance than any other PHB used to transmit traffic between end users.

- The main difference between the AF-PHB group and the DRT-PHB group is related to importance order of PHBs. The goal of the DRT-PHB group is to keep the importance order fixed, even between two PHBs belonging to different PHB classes. A proponent of an AF system can claim that the AF structure provides more flexibility in importance ordering; on the other hand, an opponent of AF may claim that it lacks a systematic approach to importance ordering. Because both claims are somewhat justifiable, the final conclusion depends on the service and business models adopted by the service provider.

- Finally, end users encounter the hard task of deciding which one of the numerous service models designed by service providers is the most reasonable for their purpose. Customers should actually be alert because some services are designed more for marketing purposes than for meeting the real needs of customers.

8.2 Interworking with Other Internet Schemes

Differentiated Services is an effort to improve the quality of the Internet service. Yet Differentiated Services cannot just instantly replace the current best-effort network. The evolution toward richer differentiation should be as smooth as possible and in such a way that the users of current services do not experience noticeable degradation of quality. Section 8.2.1, "Best-Effort Service," addresses this issue.

The first approach to offer advanced quality for the Internet was based on Integrated Services (IntServ) and RSVP. The evolution of this IntServ model has been uneven; the original prospects were promising, but the reality has revealed lots of obstacles in the path toward widespread application. Still the IntServ model has not been vanquished, and there is an inescapable need to define the interoperability between IntServ and DiffServ models. Five primary interoperability models are discussed in section 8.2.2, "Integrated Services and RSVP."

The third important specification process within IETF related to QoS issues is Multiprotocol Label Switching (MPLS). The original target of MPLS was to facilitate the routing in high-speed networks. The scope of the MPLS working group has, however, also extended to the region of QoS provision. If MPLS will be widely used on the Internet, it is necessary to clearly define its role with regard to the QoS area to avoid needless overlapping of mechanisms and inconsistent QoS models.

8.2.1 Best-Effort Service

It seems that there is one relevant problem regarding best-effort traffic in a network with service differentiation: how to avoid momentary starvation of best-effort service. This may be considered a fairness issue. To avoid unfairness between "old" best-effort users and "new" DiffServ users, the service level of the current best-effort traffic should not be degraded significantly when new services based on PHBs are introduced.

A service based on EF-PHB should not yield any significant problems because the service provider should keep the load level of EF-PHB relatively low compared to best-effort traffic. The situation could be different with AF- and DRT-PHB groups because in both cases part of the traffic could be quite loosely controlled. In DRT the lowest importance level is intended for lower than best-effort traffic with very few constraints of use, and consequently without any quality guarantees (for instance, during the busiest hours all packets could be lost). The most apparent solution with the DRT-PHB group is that that best-effort traffic is mapped to the DRT system, as discussed in section 7.5.2, "Position of DRT-PHB Group in the Framework," in Chapter 7, "Per-Hop Behavior Groups." The mapping may depend on the load level in the network domain.

As for the Assured Forwarding PHB, a table similar to Table 8.3 can be devised. The main difference between Table 8.3 with EF and AF and Table 8.4 with best-effort and AF is that in the latter case overloads are not unlikely—quite the opposite, both best-effort traffic and the total AF traffic can regularly exceed the reserved capacity. Therefore, the consideration of importance ordering might be more relevant here than in the case of EF-PHBs. Again, for the sake of simplicity this discussion considers only one AF class (AF1) and ignores the middle importance level (AF12).

Table 8.4   Interoperability Models for AF-PHB and Best-Effort Service

Case	AF 11 Mbps	AF 13 Mbps	BE Mbps	Model B: At Least 10Mbps for Both Classes	Model C: Sharing of 20mbps, Importance: AF11>AF13=BE	Model D: Sharing of 20Mbps, Importance: AF11>AF13>BE
6a	12	0	12	10 + 0 + 10	12 + 0 + 8	12 + 0 + 8
6b	8	4	12	8 + 2 + 10	8 + 3 + 9	8 + 4 + 8
6c	4	8	12	4 + 6 + 10	4 + 6.4 + 9.6	4 + 8 + 8
6d	0	12	12	0 + 10 + 10	0 + 10 + 10	0 + 12 + 8

Each of the three models shown in Table 8.4 has some drawbacks. Model B appears somewhat questionable in Case 6a because AF11 packets should normally be more important than best-effort packets. On the other side, Model D is not a good solution if the traffic load on the lowest importance level is unlimited. Model C raises implementation problems because equal importance for two PHB belonging to different PHB classes is impossible to obtain by permanent weights. (Note that if AF class 1 is used for real-time applications, best-effort traffic cannot use the same PHB class.)

One practical approach could be that the service provider applies Model B and keeps the load level of the two highest importance levels below the capacity reserved for the AF class with very high probability. The momentary ordering of the lowest AF packets and best-effort packets is then totally arbitrary. If that result is acceptable from the customer-service viewpoint, however, Model B could be a feasible approach.

8.2.2   Integrated Services and RSVP

Because the authors of "A Framework for Use of RSVP with Diff-Serv Networks" are among the most important ones with regard to the development of DiffServ, that document should be considered as integral specification for Differentiated Services (Baker *et al.* 1998). Although the authors stress that there are different possible scenarios, the only one that they address in detail is a network in which customers use Integrated Services with RSVP for invoking end-to-end service and Differentiated Services is used mainly in the core network (Case 1 in Figure 8.12). The fundamental expectation is that important applications, and users as well, require dynamic high-quality service, and that this demand is the driving force for QoS provision. It is easy to locate this service model in Figure 8.13.

Figure 8.12   Five alternatives for interoperability between Differentiated Services and Integrated Services.

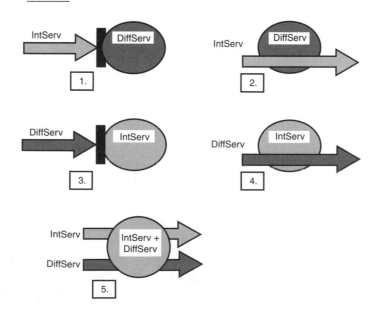

Figure 8.13 The primary service model for Integrated Services.

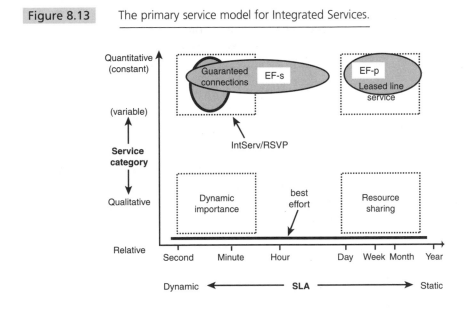

The opinion presented in "A Framework for Use of RSVP with Diff-Serv Networks" seems to be that the *guaranteed-connection* model is the evident target model, and the main reason why RSVP is not yet used throughout the network is the lack of scalability. The only positive addition of Differentiated Services is that it may provide a looser level of quality—but that is acceptable only because strict quality guarantees are often too difficult to realize. Accepting those opinions, the system described in "A Framework for Use of RSVP with Diff-Serv Networks" makes a lot of sense. To summarize it briefly, a RSVP flow can be implemented by the following seven steps:

1. The sending host generates an RSVP PATH message.

2. In the IntServ network, the PATH message is handled in a normal manner.

3. In the DiffServ network, the PATH message is transmitted transparently through the network.

4. The receiving host generates an RSVP RESV message.

5. In the IntServ network, the RESV message is handled in a normal manner.

6. At the edge between the IntServ and DiffServ networks, the RESV message generates an admission control action in the DiffServ network.

7. If there is enough capacity available, the RESV message is sent toward the sending host.

The critical item is the sixth one, which necessitates an admission control system for the Differentiated Services network. The minimal admission control system consists of a permanent threshold for the PHBs used by Integrated Services. A more complicated system may include the use of bandwidth brokers. An extreme system means that an accurate admission control procedure is made for every RSVP request. (In such a case, a fair question arises: What is left of the simple idea of Differentiated Services?)

As shown in Figure 8.12, there are several other scenarios. Five basic scenarios to combine Differentiated Services and Integrated Services are shown, as follows:

- Integrated Services are used as a customer-service model and Differentiated Services are used in a core network as discussed previously. Integrated Services is mapped to the appropriate PHB within the DiffServ domain. Possible conflicting situations in interior nodes are resolved by means of DiffServ mechanisms.

- The main difference between the first two scenarios is that in the second one the DiffServ network does not provide any statistical multiplexing for IntServ connections. In other words, the DiffServ network is merely used as a transmission medium.

- In the third scenario, Differentiated Services are used as a customer-service model and Integrated Services are used in a core network. Differentiated Services is mapped to the appropriate service within the IntServ domain. Possible conflict situations in interior nodes are resolved my means of Integrated Services mechanisms. This could be problematic, however, because the IntServ model expects that congestion situations are rare core networks.

- The fourth scenario requires tunnels with fixed capacity between each pair of edge nodes, in such a way that a Differentiated Services packet is discarded before it enters the Integrated Services network if necessary. In other words, the IntServ network is merely used as a transmission medium for Differentiated Services. Best-effort traffic can likely be transmitted in a normal manner inside the IntServ domain.

- In the fifth scenario, both Integrated Services and Differentiated Services are implemented throughout the network. This possibility is assessed further in the following paragraphs.

In general, the relationship between EF and Integrated Services is interesting. Figure 8.13 presented the main difference between EF and Integrated Services: EF primarily relies on static reservation, whereas IntServ with RSVP provides dynamic reservations. In contrast, it is somewhat difficult to recognize any significant difference in predictability aspects (see Figure 8.14). EF may, however, allow looser limits for destination according to the principles of Differentiated Services (ingress node does not necessarily know the exact destination of every EF packet). Finally, Integrated Services, particularly controlled-load service, may to a certain extent exploit the variability of the incoming traffic process.

The key issue now is whether these relatively small differences justify clearly different treatment of EF and IntServ packets inside the network. A preliminary answer is that in most cases EF and IntServ packets can share the same PHB inside a DiffServ domain, as long as IntServ flows require real-time service. There are four main reasons for this statement:

- Redundant management and control systems tend to waste some resources, both human and technical.

- Because both services expect an insignificant packet-loss ratio, only very rarely should EF and IntServ packets have to be discerned.

- The importance ordering between EF and IntServ packets is not clear; although the more advanced dynamics of IntServ provides, in theory, better control of the IntServ traffic, the complexity of IntServ may also induce more malfunctions.

- If any kind of statistical multiplexing is utilized, it is better to aggregate as much traffic as possible under one PHB.

Therefore, it is not reasonable to implement specific IntServ mechanisms in a core network using Differentiated Services. Instead, IntServ flows should be mapped to a suitable PHB, such as an Expedited Forwarding PHB.

Figure 8.14 Integrated Services compared with the EF-PHB and AF-PHB groups with regard to predictability.

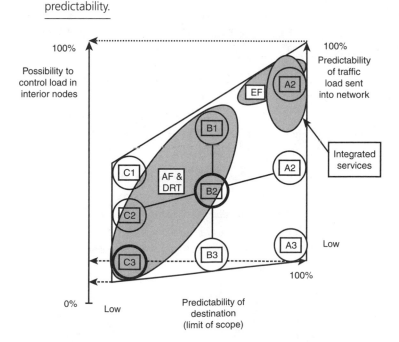

8.2.3 *Multiprotocol Label Switching*

The problem statement of the Multiprotocol Label Switching working group(MPLS) identified four relevant problem areas that can be improved by MPLS:

- Scalability of routing

- Flexibility of routing

- Network performance

- Integration of routing and switching

These are very general goals. However, MPLS actually promises to facilitate almost everything stated in "A Framework for Multiprotocol Label Switching": MPLS makes use of common methods for routing and forwarding over packet and cell media, and potentially allows a common approach to traffic engineering, QoS routing, and other aspects of operation (Callon *et al.* 1997). Although this approach could be successful, history has shown that too ambitious and extensive goals may misguide the development process and conceal the real benefits of the technology.

Because the MPLS working group has recently spent most its effort on traffic management, there is a considerable overlap between DiffServ and MPLS. MPLS has introduced a concept called Forwarding Equivalence Class, for example, which is a group of packets forwarded in the same manner—for instance, over the same path with the same forwarding treatment (Callon, Rosen, and Viswanathan 1997). The purpose of the Forwarding Equivalence Class is basically the same as that of PHB.

Table 8.5 presents a comparison of MPLS, RSVP, and some Differentiated Services approaches to identify the main strengths of MPLS. Routing is clearly an area not covered by RSVP or Differentiated Services. (This discussion does not further address the question about the best way to provide efficient routing in IP networks; there could well be other better approaches than MPLS.)

Network management in general and capacity reservation in particular might be a suitable area for MPLS. If a network operator utilizes MPLS, however, it must be done in close cooperation with other technologies, because it is irrational to make a reservation with several, perhaps inconsistent mechanisms. If any kind of statistical multiplexing is applied inside the network, overlapping reservation systems could be very harmful.

Table 8.5 Targets of MPLS Compared to RSVP and Differentiated Services (X = main target, o = secondary target)

Aspect	Option	MPLS	RSVP	EF	AF	DRT
Facilitating:	Network management	X			o	X
	Routing	X				
Reserving capacity for:	Flows	o	X	o		
	Aggregates	X	o	X	X	
Provided service models:	Guaranteed	o	X	X	o	
	Relative	o			o	X
	Best effort	o			o	o

Building the end-to-end service models on the basis of MPLS does not seem a good idea, because there is no unequivocal MPLS quality model. MPLS might certainly be used with guaranteed and best-effort service, but so far there is no clear insight about general quality or service differentiation. "A Framework for Multiprotocol Label Switching" states that a provision for a class of service (CoS) field in the MPLS header allows multiple service classes within the same label (Callon *et al.* 1997). Later, the authors clarify that the CoS mechanism provides a simple method of segregating flows within a label. The architecture document recognizes that routers may analyze a packet's header to determine a packet's "precedence" or "class of service" to apply different discard thresholds or scheduling disciplines to different packets (Callon, Rosen, and Viswanathan 1997). Unfortunately, the document does not elaborate on this issue except to the mention that MPLS allows (but does not require) the precedence or class of service to be fully or partially inferred from the label.

Consequently it could be better to abide by the service rules of Differentiated Services and to try adjusting MPLS to that framework. The recommendation of this book is that if MPLS is used in a DiffServ network, the MPLS label should refer to a PHB class and the CoS field to the importance level of the packet. This statement requires substantiation because it is not necessarily the most prevalent opinion:

> MPLS should not deteriorate the service differentiation available without MPLS. Therefore, if MPLS is used for traffic-management purposes inside the network, it should provide basically the same functionality as Differentiated Services.

> All packets of a PHB class should be transmitted using exactly the same route and buffer. Hence, different PHBs belonging to one PHB class should use the same MPLS label.

The CoS field is the only available tool for quality differentiation within an MPLS label. If it is not used to inform about the relative importance of the packet, the network node has to look at the IP header for that information. Because of the small size of the CoS field, it can hardly be used for several purposes simultaneously.

One of the main targets of MPLS labels is to facilitate the management of link resources. Because this target is basically the same as that of the AF-PHB classes, it is reasonable to avoid overlapping and inconsistent systems. If both AF and MPLS are used, they should (at a minimum) apply consistent logic.

In summary, the future of MPLS is still unclear, but the main role of MPLS seems to be to facilitate routing and network management on a general level. Because MPLS cannot offer a clear service model, it has to rely on other approaches to provide the service structure. The division of functions between MPLS and Differentiated Services may be based on the principle that MPLS is used to make capacity reservation for aggregate streams and Differentiated Services provides quality differentiation related to delay and loss characteristics.

8.3   Interworking with Non-IP Networks

This concise analysis addresses the most fundamental problems of cases where the implementation of Differentiated Services depends on networking technologies other than IP. Asynchronous Transfer Mode (ATM), IEEE 802.1p, and wireless networks are the technologies addressed in this section. Although this is definitely not a complete list of networking technologies, these three networks provide clearly different viewpoints to QoS issues. ATM has developed for high-speed networks with a large variety of services. IEEE 802.1p is the first real effort to specify quality differentiation for all kind of local area networks. Wireless networks have several specific problems related to the limited bandwidth and the characteristics of a radio channel.

This discussion focuses on the possibility of implementing Differentiated Services in the diverse environment of networking technologies. Unfortunately although many fundamental issues have been identified thus far in this book, perfect solutions to many issues have remained elusive. Remember, however, that the main objective is to identify problems and propose some *possible* solutions.

8.3.1   Asynchronous Transfer Mode

Asynchronous Transfer Mode (ATM) is widely used in the Internet backbone mainly as an intermediary layer between optical transmission and IP packet forwarding. The application of ATM is quite straightforward as long as the IP service is based on best-effort model. The situation is more problematic with Differentiated Services. The original idea of ATM was crisply based on guaranteed-service models; UBR, ABR, and GFR service categories have been added to solve ATM's inability to offer efficient service for connectionless data applications. Because of this background, it is unlikely that CBR and VBR services can provide an appropriate basis for Differentiated Services apart from PHB intended for (nearly) guaranteed service, such as Expedited Forwarding PHB.

The service model of EF is so close to the CBR model that there is hardly any significant obstacle to using the CBR service to implement EF-PHB. In addition, the UBR service category seems well-suited for implementing best-effort service, as the present Internet has verified. Yet, EF and best effort are not enough to provide real quality differentiation—for real differentiation, something more is needed. This issue is illustrated in the following implementation example of the fictitious service provider Fairprofit.

Implementing AF PHB on the Basis of an ATM Network

Fairprofit wants to use ATM as the core network technology for building advanced Internet service. The targeted service model is based on two AF classes with three importance (drop preference) levels: one class for real-time applications and another one for data applications. The desire is to avoid packet-level processing in the core network, and instead use only high-capacity ATM switches.

First, Fairprofit can consider an approach with a full mesh of virtual paths (VPs) between each node pair. That approach provides only a transport network for IP without any real service differentiation, however, and Fairprofit wants to exploit the network resources and ATM capabilities as efficiently as possible.

Even a larger number of CBR paths, however, do not provide much quality differentiation when the delay and loss characteristics are the same for every path connection. Two quality levels, best effort and high, are certainly more than one level. Nevertheless, this kind of bipolar system does not improve the service offering for a majority of the traffic; best effort is still the same best effort as in the present Internet. Although VBR service allows better statistical multiplexing, the fundamental expectation of VBR service is that cell-loss probability is kept minimal by a proactive traffic-control mechanism. In contrast, VBR service may provide delay differentiation in the form of real-time and non–real-time VBR service categories.

Therefore, to provide equal service for all flows and packets within each AF class, Fairprofit should only use one VP for each AF class between two adjacent network nodes. The reasoning is that packet-loss differentiation within one AF class cannot be built on the basis of several VPs with different theoretical packet-loss ratios. Therefore, Fairprofit has one VP for AF1 and another VP for AF2 on each link. Is this really an implementation of an AF system? I would not say so, although the cell-loss priority (CLP) bit that provides a rudimentary two-level importance differentiation is available. Still, two VBR VPs may provide a moderate solution with the following characteristics:

- Two delay classes, the better one suitable for real-time applications.

- Two levels for loss differentiation; that is, the middle and the lowest PHBs use the same CLP marking in the ATM network.

- Cell-loss ratio for the lower CLP marking should (probably) be kept relatively small to provide sufficient quality for the middle AF level.

- Best-effort service should use a separate UBR VP.

Figure 8.15 illustrates this system. Fairprofit may suppose that the average load level of real-time service can be maintained lower than that of non–real-time service. Consequently, the relative importance of real-time cells is usually higher than that of non–real-time cells, but this relationship depends essentially on overall traffic management in the network.

Can Fairprofit and its customers be satisfied with this model? Definitely it promises some advantages. But the final result appears something other than a true AF—if anyone really knows what that means. The differentiation provided by ATM seems to be limited to two delay classes and two importance levels. If that is a sufficient service model, Fairprofit should devise and implement a capable network-management and customer-care system to support the guaranteed services.

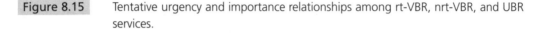

Figure 8.15   Tentative urgency and importance relationships among rt-VBR, nrt-VBR, and UBR services.

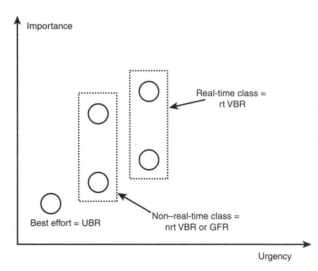

A curious fact is that any service provider has been able to build this kind of system for the past several years using ATM switches. Yet there are not many practical implementations. Although the reason may well be something other than an inferior service model, the lack of concrete use of this model makes it somewhat doubtful. If it is so simple and useful, why there is not yet any real business? The full answer is surely convoluted, but one important aspect is the fundamental service model of ATM that makes real quality differentiation quite difficult to attain.

It is important to finally investigate the issue of what ATM nodes can do with two virtual paths with different packet-loss ratios. It seems that they cannot do anything if they are using the same queue in every network node. The function of the whole system in grounded on the assumption that packet-loss ratio is small, so that there is no need for importance differentiation inside the network. The only clear exemption is the UBR category, which closely resembles best-effort service in IP networks. ABR does not include any genuine quality differentiation, because packet-loss ratio is supposed to be insignificant and the overall system is primarily intended for non–real-time applications.

The new GFR service category appears to be most similar to Differentiated Services. Actually, when GFR service is available, it is likely to be a more practical choice for data services than nrt-VBR service. From the quality differentiation viewpoint, there is not much difference, however. GFR itself provides two importance levels and only one delay level. Another relevant issue with GFR is the appropriateness of an additional level of best-effort service. The most reasonable approach might be that the lower level of GFR be used to improve the fairness of traditional best-effort service.

GFR is also similar to the service model of Frame Relay, which is comprehensible because the objective of GFR is to offer service similar to Frame Relay. In Frame Relay, the ingress node controls the traffic sent to the network; and if the committed information rate of a flow is exceeded, the node marks packets with lower importance. Frame Relay is also similar to GFR with respect to delay differentiation; there is only one delay class. The congestion-avoidance mechanisms of Frame Relay were discussed in section 6.2.3, "Feedback Information," in Chapter 6, "Traffic Handling and Network Management."

8.3.2 IEEE 802.1p

Many end users are attached to a corporate IP network or to the public Internet via a local area network. Traditionally, local area networks, such as the Ethernet, have not supported any quality differentiation. IEEE 802.1p is the first comprehensive effort to extend the scope of local area networks in that respect (802.1p 1998). IEEE 802.1p specification provides a technique to give some packets (formally frames) preferential queuing and access to network resources. IEEE 802.1p offers a consistent method to transport priority information through the local area network regardless of the underlying network layer. To be useful, the network nodes have to be upgraded to understand and utilize the priority bits of packets.

The current specification defines eight levels of user priority, with seven being the highest value. Similar to Differentiated Services, the specification leaves the implementation as open as possible. However, the fundamental assumption is that each level of user priority will have its own queue—in some parts of the document, queue and priority are used almost as synonyms. In contrast, the informative annex of IEEE 802.1p does not mention drop thresholds or similar techniques at all. In contrast, the following short evaluation of IEEE 802.1p does not hold to this viewpoint but takes as the starting point the reasonable motivation of each additional priority level. The steps from one priority level upward are as follows:

1. Time-critical traffic, such as voice and video, is separated from bursty best-effort traffic.

2. Controlled-load traffic is separated from voice traffic.

3. Best-effort traffic is divided into two parts with different business importance. The lower part is called background traffic.

4. Controlled-load class is divided into two parts in a way that the higher one can be used by video applications.

5. Excellent effort is separated from best-effort traffic.

6. Network-control traffic is separated from voice traffic. It is mentioned, however, that the network-control traffic is probably less delay sensitive than voice but it is of higher importance.

7. The eighth user priority can be used to support bandwidth sharing of data applications.

It is easy to notice that these steps and goals are largely consistent with those of Differentiated Services. There are basically three goals: to separate time-sensitive traffic from bursty data traffic, to provide different importance levels for data traffic, and finally to separate extremely important network-control traffic. If you consider the traffic management of a given network that has altruistic end users, the list of issues is appropriate. The main viewpoint of IEEE 802.1p is the requirements of applications; in Differentiated Services, on the other hand, the main purpose could be to provide building blocks for chargeable services—that is, to facilitate ISP business.

The preceding list of steps makes a good outline for mapping the user-priority system into a scale defined by importance and urgency. Figure 8.16 shows the result of doing just that. Is it possible to map this interpretation of IEEE 802.1p to Differentiated Services? Yes indeed, it might be possible to convert the system to its own PHB group. What is needed is to define reasonable traffic-conditioning actions and clear relationships between the PHBs belonging to the group. A more viable approach is to map the user-priority system to a more general PHB framework.

Another key question is whether there is any significant interoperability problem between IEEE 802.1p and the current PHB proposals. Expedited Forwarding PHB can apparently be mapped into the voice or video user-priority value. A conservative approach is for both voice and video traffic from the local area network to be transmitted in a Differentiated Services network using EF-PHB, and for EF-PHB traffic to be primarily located into voice user priority when transmitted into the local area network.

Figure 8.16   Urgency and importance relationships of IEEE 802.1p.

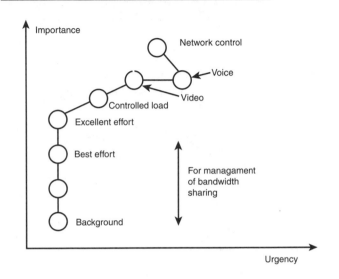

Assured Forwarding is not as clear a case as EF. A possible interworking scenario with AF and IEEE 802.1p is to use three AF classes, as follows:

- Best PHB class might be used together with voice and network control in a way that network control uses the highest importance level.

- Controlled load and video may share a middle PHB class in a way that video uses the highest importance level, and controlled load uses the two lowest importance levels.

- Lowest PHB class is used to provide a mechanism for bandwidth sharing—that is, for the four lowest levels of user priority. (The two lowest levels of user priority may share the same PHB.)

This tentative approach leaves the fourth PHB class for some other use (for instance, for building virtual private networks).

Figure 8.17 presents a possible mapping of IEEE 802.1p priorities to the DRT-PHB group. The mapping of the four lowest priority levels is apparent: They occupy the four lowest importance levels of non–real-time PHB class. The remaining four priorities bring about more difficulties. Controlled load might be on the same importance level as excellent effort, but with better delay properties, or it may share the same PHB as video. The location of video is clear in the sense that it must have both better delay and loss characteristics than excellent effort.

Voice is the hardest matter. It is quite possible in a high-speed core network that voice shares the same delay class as video and controlled-load traffic. Nevertheless, because voice may need distinct delay characteristics in a low-speed access network, a separate PHB class is reserved for voice in Figure 8.17. Although voice may be very delay sensitive, it does not imply that it is very loss sensitive as well. Actually, the prevalent view is that video is usually more sensitive to loss than voice. A packet-loss ratio of 1% could be acceptable with voice, for example, whereas the same loss ratio is likely to make a video application totally useless. Voice is therefore marked with better delay but lower importance characteristics than video. Network control requires the highest importance level, but it does not necessarily need the best delay class.

Figure 8.17 IEEE 802.1p adjusted into the DRT-PHB structure.

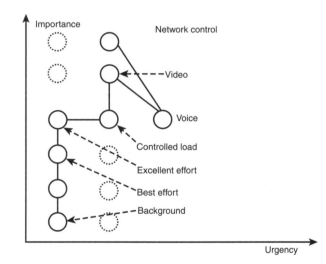

8.3.3 Wireless Networks

The current Internet is chiefly based on wireline links—that is, the network nodes are connected either by electrical or optical cables. Two additional cases are of certain importance and have some special characteristics: satellite links and wireless networks. The most prominent property of satellite links is long transmission delay, particularly if geostationary satellites are used. Although it is reasonable to suppose that real-time flows avoid satellite links whenever possible, they probably do not have any significant effect on the quality model of IP networks.

The situation could be different with wireless networks. The number of wireless terminals with data applications is growing rapidly. Therefore, it is important that the quality model in wireless networks be consistent with that of the Internet. Several aspects make it difficult to reach this target. Certain assumptions that are usually valid in wireline networks—

such as large capacity links and virtually errorless transmission—are not necessarily valid in wireless networks. The main problems of wireless technology relate to the following issues:

- Small bit rates

- Large overheads

- Delay

- Jitter behavior

- Error behavior

- Optimization of packet size

In wireless networks, bit rates vary from 9.6kbps to 20Mbps, which means several orders of magnitude smaller bit rates than in the Internet backbone. Table 8.6 depicts the effect of the bit rates to the transmission delay of one packet. The delay control tends to be very difficult below 64kbps. To attain useful real-time service, the packet sizes should be as small as possible; however, small packet size usually means large overhead. Because bandwidth is a scarce resource in wireless networks, the optimization process related to delay, packet size, and efficiency becomes very complex. The situation is further aggravated by the fact that wireless networks have large overhead because of issues such as encryption information, power-saving signaling, and error-control coding.

Table 8.6   Transmission Delays in Wireless Networks

Packet Size in Bytes	9.6kbps	64kbps	2Mbps	20Mbps
40	33 ms	5.0 ms	0.16 ms	16 ?s
100	83 ms	12.5 ms	0.4 ms	40 ?s
500	417 ms	62.5 ms	2.0 ms	0.2 ms
1500	1250 ms	187.5 ms	6.0 ms	0.6 ms

A further problem is that automatic retransmissions may considerably increase the delay variations or jitter. In addition, because wireless networks are shared mediums, the prediction of delay characteristics is a much more difficult task than in a wireline network where each node has a tight control over every outgoing link.

Consequently, in wireless networks it is practically impossible to give any delay guarantees below 100 milliseconds if the bit rate is, say, less than 100kbps. The only realistic way to considerably improve the situation is to increase the bit rate. Even then, the delay control in wireless networks requires special attention. For instance, it is not reasonable to divide the relatively small capacity permanently between quality classes. That would deteriorate both the efficiency of statistical multiplexing and the possibility to efficiently manage delays. In addition, because the buffer sizes cannot be as large as in high-speed networks, the queue management may encounter problems when selecting which packets should be discarded (if necessary). Note that the number of incoming packets is much smaller during a given period of time, which makes it more probable that there is no unimportant packet to be discarded.

QoS of General Packet Radio Service

Global System for Mobile communication (GSM) is the most widespread cellular network today. Although the popularity of GSM is based mainly on the versatile telephony service, GSM supports short message service and transmission of circuit-switched data. There is strong demand for developing more efficient service data transmission. General Packet Radio Service (GPRS) is the most important service specification that provides efficient support for typical data applications with bursty and unpredictable traffic. From a Differentiated Services viewpoint, the most essential part of GPRS specification is the QoS profile found in "Digital Cellular Telecommunications System (Phase 2+); General Packet Radio Service (GPRS) Service Description—Stage 2," which defines the following attributes (GPRS 1998):

- Peak throughput class

- Mean throughput class

- Precedence class

- Delay class

- Reliability class

Peak throughput class specifies nine values from 8kbps to 2Mbps. Mean throughput class defines 19 values up to 111kbps. The closest points in common with Differentiated Services are the bit-rate values used for traffic-conditioning purposes. The logic of GPRS, however, seems to be that every attribute can be derived from the requirements of the application and that all the attributes are primarily independent of each other. Because there is no traffic-conditioning model in GPRS, the QoS attributes are the same for all packets of a flow. On the contrary, the DiffServ model makes possible a flexible packet marking even within a flow. This discrepancy between the models may yield problems even though the other three attributes—precedence, delay, and reliability—appear to be similar to those used in Differentiated Services.

Unfortunately, a further evaluation of these attributes reveals some additional problems. In principle, three precedence classes of GPRS could be quite similar to those of Assured Forwarding precedence levels if the precedence level of GPRS were not permanent for a flow. Although there are for delay classes, there is no class suitable for real-time applications because the delay specifications are upward from 0.5 second. Five reliability classes enable the user or application to define whether the application is more loss sensitive or delay sensitive. The GPRS network uses this information to decide which kind of error-control mechanism is appropriate for the flow.

Figure 8.18 shows one possible interpretation of the GPRS system. In this framework, it is somewhat hard to understand how all three attributes could be orthogonal. In one possible scheme, reliability means that if the network cannot simultaneously fulfill both delay and importance requirements for a flow, the reliability attribute is used to decide how much effort the network should use to transmit the packet at the expense of longer delay. This mechanism relates to the fact that wireless networks cannot offer small packet-loss ratio and small jitter simultaneously because of the fundamental characteristics of radio channels.

Figure 8.18   GPRS quality attributes.

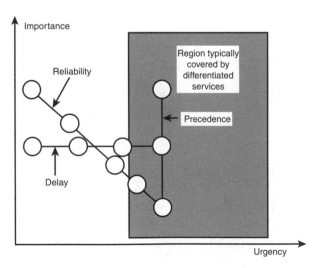

The overall system, with 10,260 (=3*4*5*9*19) possible combinations of attributes, is so complex that it is very unlikely that vendors and network operators will be willing to implement the whole range of attributes. Quite the reverse, it is possible that the first GPRS implementations will support only best-effort service without any quality differentiation.

8.4 Multicast Services

Multicast service could be used by various applications, such as streaming public radio stations, software updates, and highly demanding real-time engineering applications. From the DiffServ perspective, two main aspects make multicast special:

- A significant amount of traffic on the future Internet may use multicast services.

- The requirements of traffic management with multicast services could be significantly different from traffic management with ordinary point-to-point flows.

From a technical perspective, multicast streams consume network resources differently than do point-to-point streams. In a Differentiated Services network, the boundary node that classifies and marks packets cannot exactly know how many resources a packet uses later. Therefore, even though the traffic pattern could be constant, the traffic control inside the network is not necessarily able to predict traffic loads on every link. This could be a serious problem if the service model is based on guaranteed quality; with quantitative or relative-service models, however, the situation does not differ significantly from normal non-multicast traffic. Figure 8.19 illustrates this phenomenon.

Figure 8.19   Predictability of load and destination for multicast streams.

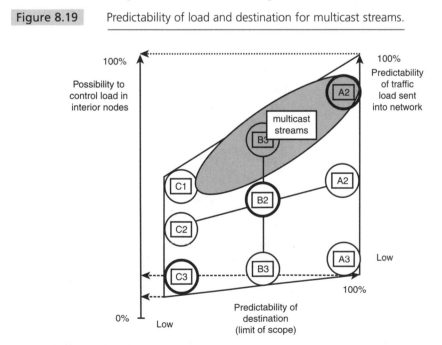

As stressed several times, the only relevant situation in a Differentiated Services network is when there are too many packets to be transmitted immediately. Then the system has to be able to make a rational decision about which packets should be discarded or which should be queued. What is the effect of multicast packets to this decision process? This is largely a matter to be resolved by each service provider. It is possible, however, to present some preliminary ideas about the fairness issues related to multicast streams.

Note

It should be stressed that the multicast business and services models are still largely uncertain, which makes it difficult to make any strict evaluation of different technical approaches.

Consider, for example, a service model that primarily takes into account the requirements of each application. Some may think that multicast applications are just used for entertainment purposes and are less personal than applications that use point-to-point connections. (Ignore, for a moment, the fact that these assumptions are apparently incorrect in many cases.) Someone may, for instance, listen to a radio station through the network without paying any attention to the contents of the program. If both *entertaining* multicast packets and *serious* point-to-point packets are present during a congestion situation, we may be inclined to think that multicast packets should be discarded first.

Before concluding too quickly, however, it is important to recognize some significant defects in the preceding reasoning. In public networks, any model that relies on the assessment of applications is prone to raise difficult conflicts. Who can be the final judge for assessing the value of different applications? Even in corporate networks, that would be hard issue; and it is not clear that network-management personnel are always able to make appropriate decisions. Therefore, it might be better to apply a more general approach that is largely independent of the applications using the network services.

The other, perhaps more tractable issue is that although a multicast packet might be judged to not be very important for an individual receiver, there might be thousands of simultaneous receivers. Actually, the number of receivers for one individual packet could vary from one to millions, depending on the location of the packet. In this respect, a multicast packet near the sender could be very important, whereas near the receiver it is unimportant. It is, at least in principal, possible to limit this problem by decreasing the importance level of a multicast packet at some branch points.

One practical question is whether there should be a special PHB or special PHB group for multicast services. Four basic reasons justify this approach:

- Special delay requirements

- Special requirements related to importance marking

- The need to isolate multicast streams from other traffic streams

It is not probable that multicast streams have such unique delay requirements that multi-cast streams need their own PHB for that purpose. The previously mentioned possibility—to remark multicast packets inside the network—could be a reason to reserve a PHB group for multicast purposes-—but the usefulness of this approach is uncertain.

The main justification for a multicast PHB could be to facilitate network management. If the receivers of multicast streams form a distinct customer group, it could be useful to have multicast PHB with fixed resources to protect other users from unexpected quality degradation during high demand of multicast applications. However, the same result might be achieved without a separate PHB group as well.

According to "A Framework for Differentiated Services," the Differentiated Services architecture deals only with unidirectional flows and therefore each source that wants to send to the multicast group needs a separate SLA (Bernet *et al.* 1998). An additional problem of SLA is that an incoming packet may exit the network domain at multiple points. The contracts between other domains could be different in a way that requires different treatment for basically the same packet going to different destinations. This matter may also promote the use of a special PHB for multicast traffic.

Summary

This chapter addressed interoperability issues on three levels:

- Between PHB groups

- Between DiffServ and other QoS mechanisms for IP networks

- Between DiffServ and QoS mechanisms of other non-IP networks

The main results of the evaluation were as follows:

- Class Selector PHB group does not offer a systematic enough structure to provide an agreeable overall QoS system.

- EF has a clear scope and can usually be integrated with other models, although the mechanisms to solve conflicting situations should be carefully planned.

- There is so much overlapping between Assured Forwarding (AF) and DRT-PHB groups that it is questionable to use them in the same network domain. Note that the status of AF-PHB at IETF is higher because DRT-PHB is proposed only by individual contributors.

- The need for Integrated Services and RSVP depends on the actual demand for highly guaranteed, dynamic connections. If the demand is not considerable, EF or some other PHB should be used in the core networks rather than explicit reservations for every flow.

- Despite the highly promoted QoS mechanisms of ATM, it is a problematic tool when attempting to implement Differentiated Services. All the additional management can hardly be justified by the attained advantages of ATM if Differentiated Services is used as the fundamental service model.

- The role of MPLS is still open, but it seems more suitable for facilitating resource management than for providing quality differentiation.

- The quality models for local area networks and wireless networks are still somewhat unclear, at least when assessed from the viewpoint of Differentiated Services. These issues definitely require more research and development to attain a consistent QoS structure throughout all major packet networks.

CHAPTER 9

Implementing Differentiated Services

This chapter condenses the entire discussion about Differentiated Services into four implementation examples. The main target is to evaluate as realistically as possible the applicability of the DiffServ models that were introduced in Chapter 7, "Per-Hop Behavior Groups."

Any formal evaluation of an extremely complex issue, such as Differentiated Services, in a real environment is inevitably restricted. If all possible aspects are incorporated into the evaluation, it may turn out that no useful consequences can be made: Certain aspects must be chosen while others have to be ignored. The main aspects evaluated in this chapter are as follows:

- The difference between adaptive and nonadaptive applications

- The difference in relative load levels on different links

- The long-term traffic variations between busy and idle hours

- The efficiency of statistical multiplexing.

- The effects of importance levels

These aspects are investigated in four implementation examples. Each example is analyzed in the same network using essentially the same traffic models. These models are introduced in section 9.1, "Network and Traffic Models," and described in detail in the succeeding four sections. The key elements of the four examples are as follows:

1. In section 9.2, "Improving Fairness by Using an AF-PHB Group," the target is to use one AF-PHB to provide *fair* service between TCP and UDP users within a university environment. An equal service among all end users is preferred, because it is difficult to give every end user a specific service.

2. In section 9.3, "Virtual Private Networks Using an EF-PHB," a backbone operator provides a *cost-efficient* virtual private network (VPN) service for several large organizations with a number of distributed units. The implementation is based on EF-PHB.

3. In section 9.4, "Service Differentiation with Three AF-PHB Groups," a service provider wants to offer *versatile* services for residential users. The customer service is based on three levels of quality, called here *grades*. To implement this service structure, the ISP utilizes three AF classes with three importance levels.

4. In section 9.5, "Total Service on the Basis of a DRT-PHB Group," the three first examples are put into the same *robust* network. That is the real challenge for service providers and network operators. The approach presented here is based on the DRT-PHB group expanded with an EF type of PHB.

9.1 Network and Traffic Models

The global Internet connects tens of millions of computers through a myriad of network domains. There are numerous applications with different characteristics, users with different needs, as well as service providers with different business models. Furthermore, tens of relevant aspects and numerous DiffServ proposals should be assessed. It is impossible to strictly analyze the whole network in any reasonable way with all the DiffServ models. Indeed, the art of mathematical modeling is to make feasible simplifications—simplifications that make the model tractable, but still maintain the essence of the original phenomenon.

The most important simplification made here is that only steady-state behavior is taken into account, whereas all detailed phenomenon are ignored as long as they have no distinct effect on the steady-state behavior. In essence this means that each importance level of each flow is considered as a continuous fluid flow rather than a traffic process of separate packets. Further, every flow is supposed to be constant during a relatively long period and chiefly independent of the perceived quality of the network service. The main expectation is that TCP protocol is supposed to be able to divide the available bandwidth equally between all active TCP flows on a link. Note, however, that in a real heterogeneous network the capacity division provided by TCP is often less fair. Finally, no effort is made to model human behavior when the quality is unsatisfactory.

Clearly, this bunch of simplifications may make the results arguable. But unfortunately there are not too many sound alternatives. An application of an advanced simulation tool might be applied, but hardly with very large number of users. Besides, to obtain essentially more relevant results than in the following examples, human behavior should be modeled as well. That laborious task is left for further study to be done in premium universities and research centers.

Even with a simple steady-state fluid model, innumerable cases and aspects must be studied, including the following:

- Long-term traffic variations

- Significant variations in relative load between links and nodes

- Adaptive and nonadaptive applications

- Several importance levels

- Several levels of aggregation

The following examples address all these aspects.

Figure 9.1 shows the network used in the evaluation. The number of nodes, 14, is a compromise between a realistic, large network and a tractable model. The number of node pairs (91) is large enough to bring about some important aspect related to capacity reservation, but not too large to prevent straightforward analysis. Still for simplicity, the links marked with broken lines in Figure 9.1 are only for protection purposes, not to signify a primary route for any packet.

Figure 9.1   Network structure for implementation examples.

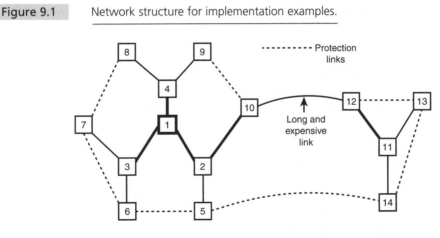

One tricky task is to define a realistic division of traffic between node pairs. Although some kind of randomization could be useful, the approach adopted here (to keep the study comprehensible) is quite systematic and homogeneous. The traffic demand between two nodes is supposed to be proportional to the number of users attached to the nodes. The number of users is constant, but the activity of each user could be different for busy and idle hours. For this discussion, *activity* means the probability that a user is *sending* traffic.

Although this traffic configuration may appear arbitrary, or even unrealistic, a more complex model would make the evaluation very difficult. It is especially important to remember that the whole system should be tractable even in the case of relative complex PHB proposals, such as Assured Forwarding with several PHB classes and importance levels. Apparently, there are various issues not addressed here that need further, more elaborate research. This chapter concentrates on some fundamental issues essential for the realization of viable service differentiation in the Internet.

Assume the following:

> Node 1: 10,000 users
>
> Node 2: 20,000 users
>
> All other nodes together: 50,000 users
>
> Probability of activity during busy hour: 0.2

In this case, the number of active users sending traffic from node 1 to node 2 is

$$0.2*10,000*(20,000/80,000) = 500$$

Note that because users in node 1 are also included in the total number of users (80,000), some of the active users are not sending traffic in the network, but only to other users in the same node. It is also easy to notice that traffic is equal in the other direction from node 2 to node 1.

If an active user sends traffic with a moderate bit rate of 25kbps, the total amount of traffic sent by the user during one hour is 11.25MB. Furthermore, supposing that 20% of the users are active during the busiest hour and that the average load level is double the long-term average load, the amount of traffic sent by an average user is 189MB in one week. Actually, that is equivalent to 6.6 hours of phone calls when a continuous 64kbps coding is applied. Therefore, although 25kbps is definitely not a high value as a peak rate for a flow, it is at least moderate as an average traffic over a longer period of time.

9.2 *Improving Fairness Using an AF-PHB Group*

The first implementation example evaluates the capability of an AF-PHB group to provide better fairness than a mere best-effort (BE) service. As long as most users are using similar TCP implementations, best-effort service can offer appropriate service for adaptive applications. Still there are some fundamental constraints in the BE service model: It is vulnerable to nonadaptive applications, and an equal share of resources is not always the preferred outcome. This implementation example addresses the first problem, vulnerability; the second problem is discussed in the third example in section 9.4, "Service Differentiation with Three AF-PHB Groups."

A university environment is used to evaluate this fairness issue concretely. The university is distributed into three sites: 20,000 users in locations near to nodes 3 and 4, and 10,000 users in a location near node 11. A network based on the best-effort model has so far worked well, but now the university has two main concerns:

- The emergence of nonadaptive applications may deprive TCP applications of a significant amount of resources.

- The growth rate of IP traffic has been so high that the university can no longer afford to provide excellent service to the remote site near node 11.

These two issues together require some improvements to the network service model used by the university. Because of the special environment, the preferred service model is still as simple as possible. Specifically, it is not reasonable to assume that each end user is charged based on the network resources he or she has used. The identification of actual end user could be quite a hard task, particularly in the reverse direction. (Note that often the primary direction of traffic is toward the actual user rather than away from the user.) To minimize management costs, each user has to have the same basic rights of use. As a result, the preferred service model is equal service for each individual flow. To meet this target, the university wants to buy better than best-effort service from the service provider Fairprofit (a fictitious ISP introduced in Chapter 1, "The Target of Differentiated Services," and used in examples throughout this book).

9.2.1 Traffic Model

Concrete information about users and traffic demand is needed before it is possible to make any useful evaluation. The following assumptions regarding the user behavior are made:

- The probability that a user is sending TCP traffic is 20% during busy hour and 5% during idle hour.

- The probability that a user is sending UDP traffic is 0.6% during busy hour and 0.15% during idle hour.

- Each active TCP user is primarily greedy, but the bit rate is properly adjusted based on the lost packets. (For this discussion, *greedy* means that an active user is always sending traffic with as high a bit rate as possible.)

- Each active UDP user is greedy up to 250kbps regardless of the packet-loss ratio.

If the university wanted to offer an available bit rate of 20kbps for each active user during busy hour regardless of the location, the required capacity would be approximately

49Mbps from node 1 to nodes 3 and 4, and 33Mbps from node 1 to node 11. Because the remote link to node 11 is more expensive than other links, however, the university decides to acquire 60Mbps from node 1 to nodes 3 and 4, and only 20Mbps from node 1 to node 11. Note that in principle there is relatively small difference between users in different sites, because the capacity out from node 3 is 3kbps per user compared to 2kbps from node 11. Therefore, the decision to favor users at nodes 3 and 4 seems acceptable.

Because the traffic load is equal in both directions and you are evaluating only a steady-state situation, it is possible to divide each link into two virtual paths (VPs) for analyzing purpose. Figure 9.2 illustrates the bidirectional auxiliary VPs: 50Mbps between nodes 3 and 4, and 10Mbps from node 11 to nodes 3 and 4. It should be stressed that despite these auxiliary VPs, no real VPs with fixed capacity are supposed.

Figure 9.2   Auxiliary VPs between nodes 3, 4, and 11.

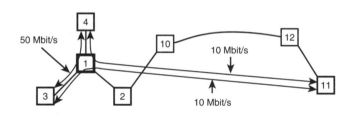

9.2.2   *Implementation*

Fairprofit may consider the following method to implement an equal service for the university, based on one AF class with the following mechanisms:

- A classification unit in boundary node distinguishes every flow.

- A metering unit in boundary node measures every flow by two token bucket devices to define whether the traffic exceeds either of the two predefined thresholds.

- The packet is marked to one of the three importance (drop preference) levels based on the metering result.

- There is only one queue for this service because there is no delay differentiation.

- In every buffer inside the network, packet dropping is based on the importance level of the packet.

In addition, it is possible that the implementation includes the use of random early detection (RED) to improve the performance of the system. This assumption does not have any significant effect on the following performance evaluation.

Because in this case there is only one PHB class, the management of the core networks is probably not much more complicated than the management of a pure best-effort network. Therefore, if appropriate mechanisms are available in all network nodes, the provision of this service could be a relative easy and inexpensive effort for Fairprofit. Correspondingly, the additional price to be paid by the university could acceptable.

9.2.3 Performance Evaluation

This evaluation begins with the best-effort service, to see whether there is any actual problem in the current service. Table 9.1 shows the situation without UPD users. An important observation is that even with moderate differences in link dimensioning and with moderate differences between idle and busy hours, there could be remarkable variations of the available bit rates. Although this is in a way a trivial issue, it is also very easy to forget. If you just consider a separate link with constant traffic demand, these variations related to different links and moments are ignored, and consequently, the results of analysis might be irrelevant.

Table 9.1   Best-Effort Service with TCP Users

Busy / Idle hour	VP from - to	Total Capacity Mbps	Active TCP Users	Capacity per Active TCP User kbps
Busy	4–3	50	1,600	31.3
Busy	11–3	10	800	12.5
Idle	4–3	50	400	125.0
Idle	11–3	10	200	50.0

Next, you add UDP users to evaluate the effect of nonadaptive applications. (For this discussion, the term *UDP* represents all nonadaptive applications.) The number of UDP users is supposed to be only 3% of the number of TCP users, yet they can exploit a significant amount of scarce resources. During busy hour, for example, on average 24 UDP users send traffic from node 11 to node 3. Consequently, UDP applications reserve 6Mbps of the total capacity of 10Mbps. The remaining capacity of 4Mbps is divided between 800 TCP users, which means 5kbps for each TCP flow while each UDP flow attains 250kbps.

Furthermore, remember that this evaluation does not take into account short-term variations. If the traffic load of UDP applications varies significantly, the available capacity for TCP users could occasionally be very small, as Table 9.2 shows. Even the average capacity available for TCP users can vary remarkably, however, while UDP users attain the same bit rate. This is the main issue that should be improved by a more advanced service model.

Table 9.2   Best-Effort Service with TCP and UDP Users

Busy/ Idle Hour	VP	Mbps	Active UDP Users	UDP Load Mbps	Capacity for TCP Users	Active TCP Users	Per Active TCP User
Busy	4-3	50	48	12	38	1,600	23.8
Busy	11-3	10	24	6	4	800	5.0
Idle	4-3	50	12	3	47	400	117.5
Idle	11-3	10	6	1.5	8.5	200	42.5

The first phase of planning an AF-PHB system is to decide the bit-rate thresholds for the two highest importance levels. According to Table 9.1, 10kbps could be assured for all flows and 30kbps could be assured for flows between nodes 3 and 4. Therefore, a packet could be marked according to following rules.

- If there are enough free tokens in the AF11 bucket with a token rate of 10kbps, the packet is marked with the codepoint of AF11.

- Otherwise, if there are enough free tokens in the AF12 bucket with a token rate of 30kbps, the packet is marked with the codepoint of AF12.

- Otherwise, the packet is marked with the codepoint of AF13.

Consequently, each flow is allowed to send AF11 packets with a bit rate of 10kbps and A12 packets with a bit rate of 20kbps.

Tables 9.3 and 9.4 present the analysis of the AF-PHB system. All packets with AF11 can be transmitted successfully. The capacity left for AF12 and AF13 varies from 1.8Mbps to 45.9Mbps. During busy hour, for instance, 1,648 active users are on the auxiliary VP between nodes 3 and 4, which means an average AF11 load of 16.5Mbps and 33.5Mbps for other importance levels.

Table 9.3   Capacity Used by AF11-PHB

Busy/ Idle Hour	VP	Cap. Mbps	Active TCP Users	Active UDP Users	Total AF11 Load Mbps	Capacity Left for AF12 and AF13, Mbps
Busy	4-3	50	1,600	48	16.5	33.5
Busy	11-3	10	800	24	8.2	1.8
Idle	4-3	50	400	12	4.1	45.9
Idle	11-3	10	200	6	2.1	7.9

The remaining capacity is used first by UDP traffic marked with AF12, and then by TCP AF12 traffic as much as there is free capacity. Table 9.4 shows the results. It turns out that all AF12 traffic can be transmitted successfully except between nodes 3 and 11 during busy hour. In that case, you may assume that UDP AF12 packets are transmitted with a bit rate of 20kbps, whereas TCP flows adjust their bit rate down to 1.6kbps to fill up the link. In practice, some UDP packets will be lost and TCP will probably not be able to fill the whole link, but these issues have only a minor effect on the overall conclusion.

Note that UDP traffic on the two highest importance levels cannot fill the whole link in this case because there are not enough active UDP users. As a result, TCP users also get a small amount of resources even though UDP and TCP flows are competing for the same resources.

A similar evaluation can be made for AF13 traffic. The result is that UDP flows can attain the preferred bit rate during idle hours, whereas the available bit rate will be only a fraction of the preferred bit rate during busy hours.

Table 9.4   Capacity Division Between UDP and TCP Flows

Busy/ Idle Hour	VP	AF12 per UDP User kbps	AF12 per TCP User kbps	Capacity for AF13 Mbps	AF13 per UDP User kbps	AF13 per TCP User kbps
Busy	4-3	20	20	0.6	11.7	0
Busy	11-3	20	1.6	0	0	0
Idle	4-3	20	20	37.6	220	87.5
Idle	11-3	20	20	3.8	220	12.5

Table 9.5 summarizes the results of the evaluation. The main conclusions are as follows:

- The results are very promising for busy hour traffic in the sense that TCP users can attain almost an equal share of resources (99% and 96%).

- Somewhat surprisingly, the AF system has no effect at all during idle hours.

The explanation for the second item is that the bit-rate thresholds were optimized for busy-hour use, and were, therefore, too low to be effective during idle hours.

| Table 9.5 | | Comparison of Best-Effort and AF Services | | | | | |

Busy/ Idle Hour	VP	Equal Share kbps	BE TCP kbps	BE UDP kbps	AF TCP kbps	AF UDP kbps	AF Real/ Equal for TCP, %
Busy	4-3	30.3	23.8	250	30.0	41.7	99
Busy	11-3	12.1	5.0	250	11.6	30	96
Idle	4-3	121.4	117.5	250	117.5	250	97
Idle	11-3	48.3	42.5	250	42.5	250	88

It is important, however, to be somewhat cautious with the results. In general, the selection of bit-rate thresholds is a troublesome task—in practice, there can hardly be as complete knowledge about traffic levels as was supposed in this example. In addition, short-term variations certainly disturb this elegant model. With realistic traffic with strong variations on all timescales, for instance, the bit-rate threshold for AF11 should be lower than 10kbps to guarantee a small packet-loss ratio.

Furthermore, you may ask how those UDP users behave—the ones trying to use 250kbps, but getting only a fraction of the desired bit rate. The answer evidently depends on the characteristics of applications. There are two main alternatives:

• UDP is used by a nonadaptive application with a specific bit-rate requirement.

• UDP is used by an adaptive application merely for getting more resources than with ordinary TCP.

In the first case, the use of AF-PHB system actually yields a high call-blocking probability during busy hours, and may effectively prevent the use of high bit-rate UDP applications during busy hours. This may or may not be an acceptable result. In the latter case with the questionable use of UDP, the effect of an AF-PHB system certainly is appropriate because well-behaved TCP users can get a significant part of the resources deprived by UDP users.

9.2.4 Possible Improvements

There are some evident possibilities to improve the overall service model based on an AF class. The bit-rate thresholds could depend on several issues such as time of day, destination, or user. If a user definitely needs connection with 100kbps, for instance, that can be implemented merely by changing the bit-rate threshold for AF11. The main difficulty of this approach is related to the management of rights and bit rates, which probably limits the applicability of this approach to relatively rare cases.

Another possibility is to improve the performance of the AF-PHB system to dynamically adjust thresholds of AF11 and AF12 according to the general load level in the network, or according to the destination of the packets. Both approaches may improve the capacity division between adaptive and nonadaptive applications under variable conditions. Nevertheless, it is not clear whether the attainable gain is large enough to justify the required additional mechanisms and management effort.

Finally, it is possible that the service provider merely has enough capacity in the core network to transmit all packets on every importance level. In that case, PHB classes and importance levels only have a significant effect during exceptional situations, and perhaps in access networks. Sometimes this is the most effective solution for the service provider.

9.3 Virtual Private Networks by Using an EF-PHB

The starting point of this implementation example is the fact that current leased lines are inefficiently used because of poor utilization of statistical multiplexing. The Internet may provide a good possibility to improve the situation, but only if there are proper mechanisms for provision of a service with high quality and reliability. The prevalent best-effort service is apparently insufficient, whereas Expedited Forwarding PHB is designed for that purpose.

The objective of Fairprofit is to provide high-quality virtual private network (VPN) service with low delay and virtually no packet losses for large, demanding customers. Because of this goal, the evaluation is mainly related to network dimensioning made by the service provider rather than traffic analysis. The fundamental assumption is that network dimensioning can keep congestion situations inside the network extremely rare.

9.3.1 Traffic Model

Fairprofit has four big customers. Each of the customer organizations has one large unit and five small units, as shown in Figure 9.3. The following figures defines the traffic demand:

- Each large unit comprises 25,000 employees.

- Each small unit comprises 5,000 employees.

- The activity level of each user is 10%. (Only busy hour is addressed in this example because network dimensioning is based on busy hour traffic.)

- Each active user generates traffic with a bit rate of 25kbps.

The total traffic generated by all 20,000 employees is 500Mbps, but only 350Mbps is actually transmitted within the network, because a part of the traffic is transmitted within each unit. The total traffic load generated by the users appears to be small enough to be handled by a relatively small system without any significant problems.

Figure 9.3   The units of four large organizations.

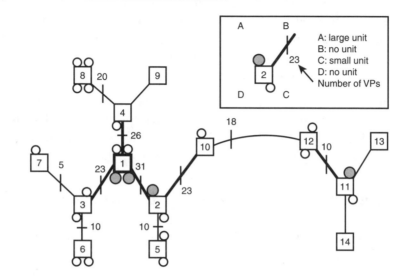

If a virtual path (VP) is established between each pair of units, there are 15 VPs in total for every organization. (Note that *VP* is used here as a general term for any aggregate that is policed as an indivisible entity without any reference to ATM technology.) The number of VPs on each link also depends on the number of hops of each VP. In this example, the number of VPs on a link varies from 5 to 31. Table 9.6 presents the number of VPs and average loads. Note that the last row shows the numbers in one direction, and that the total capacity figure can be obtained by multiplying those figures by two.

Table 9.6   Number of VPs and Load Levels on Used Links

Link	VPs					Load	Mbps			
	A	B	C	D	Total	A	B	C	D	Total
1-2	8	9	9	5	31	30.0	26.3	26.3	11.3	93.8
1-3	5	5	5	8	23	11.3	11.3	11.3	20.0	53.8
1-4	8	5	5	8	26	20.0	11.3	11.3	20.0	62.5
2-5	0	5	5	0	10	0.0	11.3	11.3	0.0	22.5
2-10	5	8	5	5	23	11.3	30.0	11.3	11.3	63.8
3-6	0	0	5	5	10	0.0	0.0	11.3	11.3	22.5
3-7	5	0	0	0	5	11.3	0.0	0.0	0.0	11.3
4-8	5	5	5	5	20	11.3	11.3	11.3	11.3	45.0
10-12	0	8	5	5	18	0.0	30.0	11.3	11.3	52.5
11-12	0	5	5	0	10	0.0	31.3	11.3	0.0	42.5
Total	36	50	49	41	176	95.0	162.5	116.3	96.3	470

On the link from node 1 to node 4, for example, both organizations A and D need eight VPs and organization B and organization C need five VPs. The average traffic transmitted by each of the total 26 VPs is either 6.25Mbps or 1.25Mbps. (In real networks, much more bit-rate variability among VPs should be expected.)

9.3.2 *Implementation*

The basic way to implement this VPN service is *Expedited Forwarding* (*EF*) PHB. The main property of EF from the viewpoint of this evaluation is that the bit rates are strictly policed. In other words, if there are exceeding packets they are dropped immediately regardless of the load situation inside the network. This characteristic makes it necessary to carefully dimension the capacities reserved for the service.

Now Fairprofit has three primary options to manage and control the VPNs:

- *No sharing*: There is an EF VP between every node pair with fixed capacity for every organization.

- *Partial sharing*: An EF VP is reserved for every organization on every link.

- *Total sharing*: There is only one EF VP for all organizations on every link.

No sharing is equivalent to leased-line service, and therefore quite a clear service model. There is a maximum bit rate from every unit to every other unit of the same organization. In *partial sharing*, each organization can better utilize the bought capacity. If an organization has four VPs of 10Mbps capacity on a link, for example, *partial sharing* means that the total 40Mbps is available for all traffic flows of the organization.

Partial sharing may induce problems inside the network, because the traffic load of an interior link may exceed the reserved capacity even though the load levels in ingress nodes are acceptable. Because EF-PHB does not provide any specific tool to solve this kind of situation, the capacity dimensioning should be quite conservative.

Total sharing provides the most efficient statistical multiplexing. The model, if applied literally, includes an inherent problem. If the traffic control is related only to the aggregate EF stream of all organizations, there is a risk that some organizations may attempt to exploit the situation by reserving less capacity than what they really need. Therefore, a more likely model is one in which the traffic sent by each organization into the network is strictly policed, even though there is only one EF stream on each link. In that case, the main difference between partial sharing and total sharing is in the network dimensioning. In the total-sharing model, the network operator utilizes network resources more efficiently by allowing statistical multiplexing between organizations inside the network.

Figure 9.4 further illustrates the situation. *No sharing* means that each small box (such as the 6.25 in the upper-left corner) is dimensioned separately. An average load level of 6.25Mbps may require a capacity of 30Mbps. *Partial sharing* means that each row with several small boxes is dimensioned separately. Finally, *total sharing* means that the whole area is dimensioned together without taking into account the detailed structure with rows and boxes. In practice, the operator adds up all traffic from all organizations and defines the required capacity based on the total average load and variance.

Figure 9.4   Average bit rates of 26 VPs on link 1-4.

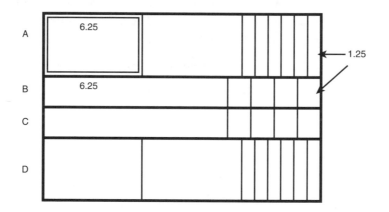

9.3.3 *Performance Evaluation*

How much does the actual result depend on the sharing principle? To answer this question, it is necessary to define the dimensioning principle applied by Fairprofit. As discussed in section 6.3.3, "Network Dimensioning," in Chapter 6, "Traffic Handling and Network Management," a simple but still feasible model is to define the required capacity (C) as a function of average load (M) and variance of the load distribution (V), as shown in Formula 9.1.

Formula 9.1

$$C = M + \gamma * V^{0.5}$$

If the average load measured on a link is 100Mbps and the corresponding amount of traffic variation (formally, standard deviation) is 20Mbps, for example, the operator needs to have much more capacity than 100Mbps to satisfy customers' requirements. The parameter γ defines the level of assurance that the capacity is sufficient to cope with momentary traffic peaks.

Now a good estimation for the average load has been arrived at, but not a practical estimation for the variance. A mathematically elegant approach would be to calculate the variance based on the activity of individual users and the bit rate used by an active user. If there are 2,000 users with a bit rate of 25kbps and activity of 0.2, the average load is $M = 10$Mbps and the theoretical variance is $(0.2$Mbps$)^2$. However, that model may significantly underestimate the real variance. Particularly, the greedy and possibly synchronized TCP flows tend to increase traffic variations in real networks. This example adopts a theoretically less elegant, but more realistic model in which the variance is supposed to be as high as $V = M*(1$Mbps$)$. Table 9.7 shows the required capacity for each link with the three sharing principles, with $\gamma = 10$.

Table 9.7 Required Link Capacity with Different Sharing Principles

Link	Offered Load Mbps	No Sharing	Partial Sharing	Total Sharing
1-2	94	592	285	191
1-3	54	380	199	127
1-4	63	436	219	142
2-5	23	162	90	70
2-10	64	418	219	144
3-6	23	162	90	70
3-7	11	81	45	45
4-8	45	324	179	112
10-12	53	337	174	125
11-12	43	237	132	108
Total	470	3129	1631	1132

The differences between sharing principles are apparent. Without any sharing, the load level would be as low as 15%; total sharing raises the load level up to 41.5%.

In practice the differences could be somewhat smaller. The first two alternatives basically leave the dimensioning task for the customers: Customers buy capacity based on the estimation they have about traffic demand in the future. They may use a similar method as was used in this example, but that is not necessarily the case. Some other methods may lead to a smaller difference between no sharing and partial sharing. As an extreme case, the operator decides that the expected EF load should exceed, say 20%, of the reserved capacity. Then there is no difference at all between the sharing principles from a dimensioning point of view.

Nonetheless, from the customer viewpoint there is usually no reason to prefer the no-sharing to the partial-sharing principle, particularly if the capacity dimensioning is conservative. Only if a unit does not rely on the reasonability of other units within the organization, it may want to reserve capacity exclusively for itself. But it is still hard to see how this approach could be beneficial for the whole organization.

Total sharing is a more complicated issue because both the customer and the service provider have significant roles. Again, the customer buys a fixed capacity, probably using partial sharing and reasonable traffic estimation. The service provider may then, based perhaps on a long experience, presume that customers actually use the whole capacity reservation very rarely, if ever. Therefore, a further statistical multiplexing could be possible without too high of a risk. Yet the figures related to total sharing shown in Table 9.7 could be overoptimistic, because the quality of this service category could be of great importance for the reputation of the service provider—therefore, even a tiny risk could be too high.

9.3.4   Possible Improvements

From a customer viewpoint the main issue is how to utilize the unused capacity. If 80% or even more of the bought capacity will be unused because some applications cannot tolerate any packet losses, there could be a strong temptation to utilize the unused capacity by more tolerant applications. A technically straightforward approach is to use a BE-PHB in addition to EF-PHB. Further, as shown in Figure 9.5, it is possible to use some other PHBs to further improve the service model.

Note that in reality the situation is very convoluted. If customers can better utilize the capacity, for instance, the network operator actually needs more resources compared to the paid capacity to provide as high of quality as earlier. In the worst case, that may cause pressure to raise prices.

Figure 9.5   EF-PHB with best-effort (BE) PHB and an intermediate PHB.

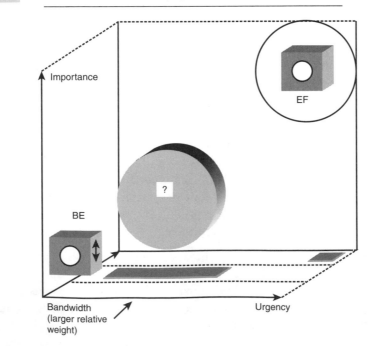

9.4   Service Differentiation with Three AF-PHB Groups

One of the fundamental aims of Differentiated Services is, of course, service differentiation. The current best-effort model, albeit technically efficient, does not offer much support for advanced business models. Yet there is significant variability in the paying capacity of residential customers. This incongruity is the starting point of this implementation example. The objective is to investigate whether an AF-PHB system can provide viable mechanism for service differentiation on the Internet.

The prevalent Internet service with flat-rate pricing and best-effort service is about as simple as possible. Therefore, it is likely that the next evolutionary step cannot be based on a complex business model. Because a majority of customers likely favor simple and inexpensive service, service differentiation should mean the introduction of a couple of better service categories. One additional service is the minimum, but likely a system with three levels is a reasonable starting point. Suppose, therefore, that Fairprofit were going to build the customer service on the basis of three service grades. (Note that the term *service class* is not usable in this context because of the apparent risk of confusion with *PHB class*.)

- *Grade A*: Intended for intensive Internet use and small business as well, including the possibility of using real-time videoconferencing.

- *Grade B*: Intended for customers willing to pay more for better than best-effort service, but these customers have basically the same characteristics as ordinary users. This grade should provide clearly better service than Grade C, but with distinctly lower assured bit rates than Grade A.

- *Grade C*: Essentially the same as the current best-effort service.

In the first phase, these service grades are relevant only within the network domain administrated by Fairprofit. In the long run, however, the aim is to expand the services to other network domains as well. Moreover, Fairprofit wants flat-rate pricing to apply to all services grades regardless of the destination within the Fairprofit domain.

9.4.1   Implementation

The implementation adopted by Fairprofit is based on three AF classes. The highest AF class (AF1) is used to realize a real-time service with two importance levels. The lowest importance level (AF13) is not used because real-time characteristics are actualized by a large weight in proportion to the offered load. (That property is needed to keep delay variation small enough for the most demanding applications.)

The two highest importance levels are used to provide two levels of availability. Although the middle importance level may offer high availability, the packets with the highest importance attain preferred service during exceptional situations, such as when a primary link is broken and traffic has to be directed to an alternative route. If the link between nodes 10 and 12 gets broken, for instance, the link between 5 and 14 should be used. It is possible that the capacity of the protection link is not sufficient for all traffic demand on the middle importance level.

The second AF class (AF2) offers a non-real-time service with a better than best-effort quality. In practice, this could mean that the two highest importance levels (AF21 and AF22) provide relatively high assurance for two bit-rate levels in the same way as AF1, but without real-time characteristics. This service class may allow the use of the lowest importance level with loose or no limits of use.

The third AF class (AF3) is used to transmit best-effort packets without any additional traffic-conditioning actions in boundary nodes. In this basic model, the special characteristics of the AF-PHB class are not fully utilized because only one PHB is used in AF class 3. Figure 9.6 shows the entire AF-PHB structure.

Figure 9.6   AF-PHB structure with three AF classes.

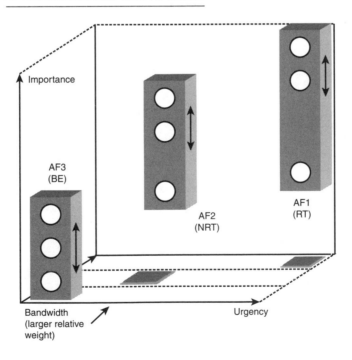

The aim of Fairprofit is to regulate the weights of each class in a way that

- The relative load level of AF class 1 is low enough to guarantee small delay variation and negligible packet-loss ratio, almost always;

- The relative load level of AF class 2 is low enough to almost always guarantee a negligible packet-loss ratio for the highest importance level, and a small packet-loss ratio for the middle importance level most of the time;

- The relative load level of AF class 3 is low enough to guarantee moderate service without significant risk of starvation for best-effort flows.

The fundamental question of the entire AF-PHB system is whether these targets are reachable by any simple management system adjusting the weights. In a real implementation, the adjusting of the weights should be automatic, without significant effort by any management personnel.

9.4.2 Traffic Model

To assess the applicability of an AF system, this section introduces a case with a large number of residential users distributed among the 14 nodes in Fairprofit's network. Each node has the following number of users:

Node 1: 100,000 users

Node 2, 3, 4, and 11: 50,000 users

Other nodes: 20,000 users

The total number of users is 480,000. This means that if every user is producing traffic with a bit rate of 100kbps, the total amount of traffic is 48Gbps. Fortunately, this number is relevant only in the access point of customers, where the possibility of statistical multiplexing is limited. In the core network, on the other hand, a significantly smaller total capacity could be sufficient.

Table 9.8 presents other traffic and service characteristics. It shows only the combined bit rate of the two highest importance levels. The middle level may represent, for instance, 80% of the total bit rate. The thresholds for real-time PHBs are systematically half of the NRT thresholds to generate incentive to use real-time service only when really needed. It is expected that Grade A and B users are not using best-effort service, although there is not necessarily any limitation of use.

For this discussion, the term *activity* means that at any point of time 5% of all possible users are active Grade C users, 0.5% are active Grade B users, and 0.05% are active Grade

A users. If a Grade A or B user is active, he or she is using real-time service with a probability of 40%. This figure may appear quite high, but notice that the duration of real-time flows are usually much longer than data flows. Moreover, real-time application may generate continuous data flows, whereas data flows often contain relatively long idle periods.

The total amount of traffic generated by a Grade A user is very high in this example. Nevertheless, that assumption could be justifiable if Grade A service is mainly used for business purposes. For instance, if all employees of a small company share one Grade A service, the traffic load could be very high during busy hour.

Table 9.8   User Profiles for Grades A, B, and C

Customer Grade	RT AF11+ AF12 kbps	NRT AF21+ kAF22 bit/s	BE (AF3x) Expected Bit Rate kbps	Activity Among All Users	RT Use	NRT Use	BE Use
Grade A	500	1000	0	0.0005	0.4	0.6	0
Grade B	100	200	0	0.005	0.4	0.6	0
Grade C	0	0	30	0.05	0	0	1

9.4.3   Network Dimensioning

The most critical task for the service provider is to dimension the network properly. The approach applied in this example is to use Formula 9.1 for three different traffic aggregates:

1. There should be enough capacity for the real-time service including both Grade A and Grade B customers. Because the load level of this service category should be low, as large a value as 20 for the parameter γ is used. (Note that parameter γ defines how much extra capacity is reserved for traffic variations: The larger the γ, the smaller the probability of an overload situation.)

2. There should be enough capacity for the non-real-time service after the capacity used by the RT service is deducted from the total capacity. Because this service should provide high quality, a relatively high value, $\gamma = 10$, is needed.

3. The last calculation is related to the total traffic, including all three service grades. It is reasonable to suppose that in this case a relatively low safety margin ($\gamma = 5$) provides sufficient quality for best-effort service.

With the given traffic predictions, the last item produces the highest capacity requirement for all links. Table 9.9 shows only five links, because the traffic on links 1-4 and 11-12 is essentially the same as on the link 1-3. Similarly, the results on link 2-5 also are valid for links 3-6, 3-7, 4-8, 4-9, 11-13, and 11-14.

Table 9.9   Load Levels and Required Capacities (Mbps)

Link Type	RT AF11 AF12	NRT AF21 AF22	BE AF31	RT γ=20	NRT+RT γ=10	All γ=5	Final Capacity
1-2	35	105	175	153	258	404	410
1-3	22	66	110	116	182	268	270
2-5	6	17	29	55	71	88	90
2-10	28	85	142	134	219	336	340
10-12	25	76	127	125	201	305	310

Next, the total link capacity of each node should be divided among the three AF classes. This example assumes that the division is equal on every link:

- RT-PHB: weight = 0.4

- NRT-PHB: weight = 0.3

- BE-PHB: weight = 0.3

The next step of evaluation is to investigate the workability of these weights. First, it is fair to assume that the weight for RT-PHB is high enough to guarantee high-quality service without noticeable packet losses. Because of the policy mechanisms of the RT-PHB, all flows using this PHB class have bit-rate limitations. Therefore, you can just subtract the expected RT load from the capacity and divide the remaining capacity evenly between NRT and BE-PHB classes because these two classes have the same weights.

The capacity within each AF class is divided between the importance levels in a manner that the highest level (for example, AF21) uses as much capacity as there is traffic demand. The middle level (for example, AF22) uses as much of the remaining capacity as there is demand. Finally, the lowest importance level (for example, AF22) can utilize the remaining capacity (if there is any).

When the network is properly dimensioned, the highest and the middle importance level of NRT flows (AF21 and AF22) cannot utilize the whole available capacity under normal circumstances. AF23 packets use the rest of the capacity available for NRT-PHB. If you suppose that all NRT users are greedy, you may assume that this AF23 capacity is divided evenly among all users regardless of the service grade. In other words, you assume that the capacity available for AF23 is divided evenly among all active users belonging to both Grade A and Grade C. An ordinary TCP implementation and basic DiffServ mechanisms probably result in that kind of division (but this issue clearly needs further studies).

The bit-rate values for NRT users are so high that all users are probably not greedy enough to use the whole available capacity. As a result, Grade C customers may in practice get a somewhat larger portion of the network capacity than what the preceding calculation indicates.

Table 9.10   Available Bit Rate per User for Grades A, B, and C

Link	Mbps	RT Mbps	share NRT=BE Mbps	NRT AF21 AF22 Mbps	NRT AF23 kbps /User	Grade A NRT kbps/ User	Grade B NRT kbps/ User	Grade C BE kbps/ s/User
1-2	410	35	188	105	214	1214	414	32
1-3	270	22	124	66	241	1241	441	34
2-5	90	6	42	17	393	1393	593	44
2-10	340	28	156	85	225	1225	425	33
10-12	310	25	142	76	236	1236	436	34

The results presented in Table 9.10 are convincing as such. It is important to note, however, that the quality of the result is largely based on the assumption that the traffic prediction during the dimensioning phase and the real traffic loads are equal. That is in reality, of course, a highly improbable situation. Table 9.11 shows a more realistic case in which the activity of customers is not known accurately. In this case, the only difference is that the number of active users at each node is supposed to be a random variable. (Actually the activity numbers have been multiplied by a random number with standard deviation of 0.3, but the total load is approximately the same as in the original case.)

On most links, the results shown in Table 9.11 do not differ much from the results in Table 9.10. It seems that flows on the lowest importance levels and on the smallest links are most vulnerable to unpredictable traffic variations. For instance, best-effort users links on link 4-8 can attain almost three times the capacity of users on link 4-9. You can also expect that the available bit rates for best-effort flows will vary widely between busy and idle hours, although this factor is not analyzed in this example.

Table 9.11   Available Bit Rate per User with Moderate Traffic Variations

Link	Mbps	RT Mbps	Share NRT=BE Mbps	NRT AF21 AF22 Mbps	NRT AF23 kbps/ User	Grade A NRT kbps/ User	Grade B NRT kbps/ User	Grade C BE kbps/ User
1-2	410	36	187	107	204	1204	404	31
1-3	270	22	124	67	235	1235	435	34

Link	Mbps	RT Mbps	Share NRT=BE Mbps	NRT AF21 AF22 Mbps	NRT AF23 kbps/ User	Grade A NRT kbps/ User	Grade B NRT kbps/ User	Grade C BE kbps/ User
1-4	270	21	124	64	261	1261	461	35
2-5	90	8	41	24	201	1201	401	31
2-10	340	29	155	87	213	1213	413	32
3-6	90	8	41	24	200	1200	400	31
3-7	90	5	43	14	587	1587	787	57
4-8	90	4	43	11	758	1758	958	68
4-9	90	10	40	30	97	1097	297	24
10-12	310	26	142	79	218	1218	418	32
11-12	270	22	124	66	237	1237	437	34
11-13	90	5	43	14	571	1571	771	56
11-14	90	7	41	22	237	1237	437	34

9.4.4 Possible Improvements

One approach to develop this AF service model is that the normal best-effort traffic obtains the highest importance level of AF class 3, while the other two levels are used for less than best-effort service. For instance, there could be a mechanism that marks packets with lower importance levels when it detects inappropriate behavior. These packets may encounter a very high dropping probability.

The main difficulty of this AF system is the management of weights. Although it is possible to provide three levels of differentiation, a consistent implementation could be difficult in large networks. Nonetheless, the assessment of this critical issue remains tentative until there is real experience with the management of an AF-PHB system.

9.5 Total Service on the Basis of a DRT-PHB Group

All the previous implementation examples were about separate issues. Yet the reality of an Internet service provider is that the same network infrastructure has to be used for all purposes. Is the right solution merely to combine the previous three approaches in the same network? That seems possible because the first implementation example required one AF class, the second one required an EF-PHB, and the last one required three AF-PHB classes.

Basically it is possible to just integrate these five PHB classes with appropriate weights. However, the management of all the weights in a way that all the differing targets are met could be a laborious effort for service providers. Therefore, the approach in this implementation example is to design a consistent framework for all services in the network. The objective is to build a network wherein one extensive service model can satisfy the various needs of different customers.

9.5.1 Implementation

The implementation of this example is based on the DRT-PHB model. It means essentially that the frame of the system is based on two PHBs classes with six PHBs. One PHB class (2) is intended for real-time applications, and the other PHB class (3) is intended for all other applications. In addition to this basic system, one PHB class with one PHB (16) is reserved for services with very high quality. It can be applied to build VPNs in the same way as EF-PHB in the second implementation example. PHB (16) needs a separate buffer and strict traffic control in boundary nodes. Another PHB (27) is reserved for network control traffic. Figure 9.7 illustrates the entire system.

Figure 9.7   DRT-PHB structure with 14 PHBs.

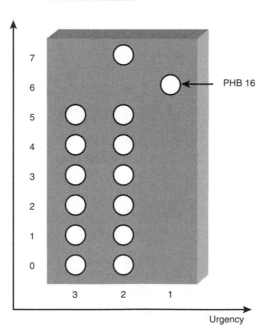

The customer service is based on the concept of *nominal bit rate* (NBR). NBR can be attached to an individual flow or aggregate stream. The primary pricing model is flat rate, which means that each customer (an individual end user or an organization) buys a permanent NBR—for instance, 50kbps for an ordinary user, or 50Mbps for a large organization.

In both cases, the boundary node measures the incoming traffic flow and compares the result with the NBR. If the measured bit rate is higher than NBR, all packets get a low PHB marking. Correspondingly, a high importance level can always be attained by sending traffic with a bit rate lower than NBR. Table 9.12 shows some examples of packet marking.

Table 9.12 Importance Level as a Function of NBR and Measured Bit Rate

NBR kbps	Measured Bit Rate, kbps	Importance Level
100	25	5
100	50	4
100	80	3
100	100	3
100	130	3
100	200	2
100	400	1
100	800	0
10000	2500	5
10000	10000	3

The same packet-marking system is applicable to both PHB class 2 and PHB class 3. There should, however, be an incentive to primarily use non real-time service. There are various possibilities to realize this kind of incentive. One simple model is that NBR is smaller for real-time service (class 2) than for normal service (class 3).

The same measuring system can also be used with PHB (16). However, the marking is entirely different. There are only two importance levels: very high (6) and immediate drop (actually less than importance level 0). The price of PHB (16) should also be consonant with the value and quality of the service, implementation especially compared to the actual price of PHB (25).

9.5.2 Traffic Model

The approach adopted here is to utilize the traffic patterns of the three previous implementation examples. Table 9.13 summarizes some key figures that define the traffic load in the network. Table 9.13 does not present the total traffic values because some users are supposed to exploit all available capacity.

The most important single figure is the NBR sum of active customers. If the NBR sum is multiplied by the average number of hops needed to transmit a packet through the network, you obtain a good estimate for the real traffic demand within the network, and thereby an estimation for the total required network capacity. In general, if that value is considerably smaller than the total network capacity, there is a good possibility for the operator to provide appropriate service.

Table 9.13   Traffic Parameters for Fourth Implementation Example

User Type	Number of Users	NBR kbps	Activity	Average NBR in Use, Mbps
University user, TCP	50000	20	0.2	200
University user, UDP	1500	20	0.2	6
Grade A users, RT	4324	500	0.022	48
Grade A users, NRT	4324	1000	0.033	144
Grade B users, RT	43243	100	0.022	96
Grade B users, NRT	43243	200	0.033	288
Grade C users	432432	30	0.056	721
Large units (VPN)	4	125000	1	500
Small units (VPN)	20	45000	1	900
In total				2903

9.5.3 Performance Evaluation

To keep the analysis simple, only the bottleneck link, 10-12, is evaluated. Because traffic figures were taken from previous implementation examples, you also can apply the link capacities from those three examples. The university reserved 20Mbps (in both directions) from link 10-12. If the partial-sharing principle with $\gamma = 10$ is applied, VPNs require together 174Mbps. Finally according to the third implementation example, residential services require capacity of 340Mbps on link 10-12. Together, this means that 534Mbps implementation is supposed to be sufficient for all services.

Table 9.14 presents the results of the evaluation. The first column shows the number of active users sending traffic going through link 10-12 (all figures are for one direction). The second column shows the traffic load used by VPNs. It is expected that VPN traffic will always use the highest importance level, either 5 or 6 depending on the system adopted by the service provider. The remaining capacity, 481Mbps, is available for other customers.

For the sake of simplicity, you can expect that real-time applications send traffic with a constant bit rate regardless of the packet-loss ratio. That means that UDP users in universities always get the lowest importance level, and therefore obtain only poor service (if any).

Grade A and B customers sending real-time traffic are assumed to use real-time NBR with bit rates of 500kbps and 100kbps, respectively. When this traffic load of 26Mbps is deducted from the total capacity, the remaining 455Mbps is available for all TCP users. The last column shows the bit rate available for each customer type based on the assumption that the system can divide the total available capacity in proportion to the NBR of each user.

Because of the improved statistical multiplexing, most of the customers attain a higher bit rate than in the previous implementation examples. The only exception is Grade B users who seem to get a considerable gain by sharing the same AF class with Grade A users in the second implementation example.

Table 9.14   Available Bit Rates on Link 10-12 with a Capacity of 534Mbps

User Type	Number of Active Users	Level 6 Mbps	Level 3 Mbps	Sum of TCP NBRs	Available Bit Rate for TCP Users kbps
Univ., TCP	1600	0	0	32	39
Univ., UDP	48	0	0	0	0
Grade A, RT	17	0	9	0	0
Grade A, NRT	25	0	0	25	1936
Grade B, RT	170	0	17	0	0
Grade B, NRT	254	0	0	51	387
Grade C, BE	4240	0	0	127	58
VPNs		53	0	0	0
In total		53	26	235	—
Remaining Mbps		481	455		

The results in Table 9.14 appear promising, although it should again be stressed that this evaluation is very limited in the sense that numerous details were ignored. For instance, the capability of the system to divide the total available capacity in proportion to NBRs should be evaluated by comprehensive simulation studies.

As a final stage of this evaluation, implementation consider a case in which link 10-12 gets broken and all traffic has to be routed through a secondary route going through the small capacity link 5-14. Table 9.15 presents a case in which the secondary route can provide only a half of the capacity of the original route. In the example system, this is no problem for the traffic with the highest importance level (VPN traffic). On the contrary, there could be significant quality differences on the lower importance levels.

Because the total capacity is less than the sum of NBRs of active customers, for example, the network cannot provide loss-free service if customers are sending traffic with their NBR. It is reasonable to suppose that because of this, real-time users of Grades A and B change to importance level 4 by reducing the bit rate to half of the original value. Still the results seem appropriate, although the situation in a real network is certainly more complex.

Table 9.15 Available Bit Rates on Link 10-12 with a Capacity of 267Mbps

User Type	Number of Active Users	Level 5 Mbps	Level 4 Mbps	Sum of TCP NBRs	Allowed Bit Rate in Proportion to NBR kbps
Univ. TCP	1600	0	0	32	17
Univ. UDP	48	0	0	0	0
Grade A RT	17	0	4	0	0
Grade A NRT	25	0	0	25	855
Grade B RT	170	0	8	0	0
Grade B NRT	254	0	0	51	171
Grade C	4240	0	0	127	26
VPNs		53	0	0	0
In total		53	13	235	-
Remaining cap. Mbps		214	201		

9.5.4 Possible Improvements

The basic model presented here implementation seems to work appropriately in most cases. Nevertheless, there are various possibilities to modify the service model. The university may decide to prefer a more advanced system with specific NBR for each end user. That kind of system makes it possible that if someone really needs a high-quality real-time connection, a high enough NBR can be allocated for the user. Actually, the customer relationship between the service provider and university could be that the university buys a large NBR and divides that NBR among the end users.

The main advantage of the VPN model with strict traffic control and high importance marking is evident during exceptional situations, such as presented in Table 9.14. In contrast, during normal situations the model seems to waste resources, at least from the viewpoint of the organization that pays a lot of money for the network service. Therefore, rather than a typical VPN a similar model as described in the previous paragraph could be used by any organization.

If the system allows the organization to allocate the network resources (NBRs) dynamically among end users, the result could be at the same time flexible and cost efficient. There may, however, be some concerns about the robustness of the system, because in this case there is not any clear separation of the VPNs with regard to the capacity division.

Note, however, that the service model based on NBRs makes it possible to use as many service grades as the service provider wants to have, because the main tool of differentiation is NBR. The main additional feature that is probably useful for building practical service differentiation is dynamic NBR. Even in cases where flat-rate pricing is the basic model, it is possible to build a system in which each customer can acquire additional NBR based on time-dependent pricing.

The main difficulty in that approach is that the majority of the residential traffic is directed toward the customers. Consequently, a dynamic NBR approach probably requires some kind of signaling to inform the sender that the receiver is willing to pay extra NBR to get better implementation service.

Summary

This chapter evaluated the applicability of three PHB systems. Assured Forwarding seems to be a feasible approach to improve best-effort service, although the advantages are diminished if load levels are highly variable. Similarly, Expedited Forwarding seems to be a feasible approach to integrate leased-line services with other IP traffic. A DRT-PHB structure could be a practical approach to integrate differing demands into one consistent model.

With all DiffServ models, as well as with any service model, a good result requires a clear target and careful designing. What more should be said about the design and objectives of Differentiated Services? Recall the six questions asked at the end of Chapter 2, "Traffic Management Before Differentiated Services." Based on the models and analysis presented in this book, you can provide the following answers.

Q: **How can you sell a service package to ordinary customers without any technical background?**

A: If the customer service is not comprehensible, even an extremely advanced system could be worthless. Therefore, all the PHB models, such as AF-PHB group, EF-PHB, and DRT-PHB, should be hidden from ordinary end users. (The inner meaning of PHB could far too difficult to explain.)

Q: What kind of billing system do you need to support your service model and to make it fair?

A: A smooth evolution from the prevalent Internet model requires that flat-rate pricing be included in the total model. It is better to start with a simple flat-rate pricing scheme and then later add a more complicated pricing scheme if necessary.

Q: Do you understand all interactions between the building blocks of services, and do they allow efficient troubleshooting?

A: Management problems are likely if the total system consists of incompatible parts. Therefore, it is highly recommendable to plan a total system that can offer acceptable service for all purposes rather than to build separate services and mechanisms optimized for differing purposes.

Q: How efficient is the model when used in a large network with millions of users?

A: Something that works perfectly with a small number of users in a small network could be unsuitable for large networks. Therefore, although dynamic provision of bit rates and quality could be useful by itself, the management of all the necessary parameters could a laborious effort and prone to errors. Whenever an equal service for a majority of users is acceptable, use that model.

Q: Is the service model robust enough to limit the effects of intentional misuse of network resources?

A: Robust and consistent behavior is one of the key requirements of DiffServ networks. The main tool against theft of network resources is that if a flow uses more than its fair share of resources, the packets of the flow should be dropped rather than other packets.

Q: Does the service model provide a realistic evolution path from the current best-effort network?

A: It is unrealistic to suppose that a new infrastructure will totally replace the current best-effort network. Therefore, the treatment of best-effort traffic should be good enough to avoid starvation of best-effort flows in DiffServ networks.

Even after the considerations in this and earlier chapters, all answers tend to be somewhat vague. Various issues are still extremely difficult to assess. On a technical level, for instance, the detailed behavior of flows using TCP in case of several importance levels is still an unclear issue. Similarly, the effect of weight adjustment of several PHB classes is an extremely intricate phenomenon. Those technical issues are relatively clear, however, compared to the phenomenon of human behavior.

It is possible that the Differentiated Services model, or perhaps another new technology or business model, will change the whole picture of Internet service provision. End-user reaction to this new paradigm can only be guessed.

Fortunately, several issues probably remain the same. Some users are seeking high quality and are willing to pay more than others. They require a service with high and predictable quality most of the time (high availability of service). Quality requirement may be related to delay, packet-loss ratio, and bit rates with various combinations. Still, most users favor moderate, but inexpensive service. The promise of Differentiated Services is that it is possible to meet various demands within one network in a consistent manner.

BIBLIOGRAPHY

References

Berger, L. "RSVP over ATM Implementation Requirements." Request for Comments 2380, August 1998.

Bernet, Y., J. Binder, S. Blake, M. Carlson, S. Keshav, E. Davies, B. Ohlman, D. Verma, Z. Wang, and W. Weiss. "A Framework for Differentiated Services, <draft-ietf-diffserv-framework-01.txt>." Internet Draft, October 1998.

Bernet, Y., R. Yavatkar, P. Ford, F. Baker, L. Zhang, K. Nichols, and M. Speer, "A Framework for Use of RSVP with Diff-serv Networks, <draft-ietf-diffserv-rsvp-01.txt>." Internet Draft (a working document), November 1998.

Blake, S., D. Black, M. Carlson, E. Davies, Z. Wang, and W. Weiss. "An Architecture for Differentiated Services." Request for Comments 2475, December 1998.

Braden, R. (Editor). "Requirements for Internet Hosts—Communication Layers." Request for Comments 1122, October 1989.

Braden, R. (Editor), L. Zhang, S. Berson, S. Herzog, and S. Jamin. "Resource ReSerVation Protocol (RSVP)—Version 1 Functional Specification." Request for Comments 2205, September 1997.

———. "Recommendations on Queue Management and Congestion Avoidance in the Internet." Request for Comments 2309, April 1998.

Bradner, S. "The Internet Standards Process—Revision 3." Request for Comments 2026, October 1996.

Callon, R., P. Doolan, N. Feldman, A. Fredette, G. Swallow, and A. Viswanathan. "A Framework for Multiprotocol Label Switching, <draft-ietf-mpls-framework-02.txt>." Internet Draft (a working document), November, 1997.

Carroll, L. *The Annotated Alice, Alice's Adventures in Wonderland and Through the Looking Glass.* New York, NY: Penguin Books, 1970.

Coudreuse, J. P. ATM Explorer, "Cable TV's Loss Is the Networking World's Gain," Data Communications on the Web, October 21, 1997.
`http://saxophone.agora.com/25years/jean-pierre_coudreuse.html`

Darwin, C. *The Origin of Species.* London: J. M. Dent & Sons LTD, 1972.

Davie, B., P. Doolan, and Y. Rekhter. *Switching in IP Networks.* San Francisco, CA: Morgan Kaufmann Publisher, 1998.

Differentiated Services (DiffServ) charter at `http://www.ietf.org/html.charters/ diffserv-charter.html`; DiffServ mail index at `http://www-nrg.ee.lbl.gov/diff-serv- arch/`.

End-to-End Research Group. The Internet Research Task Force, http://www.irtf.org/charters/end2end.htm. Ferguson, P., and G. Huston. *Quality of Service, Delivering QoS on the Internet and in Corporate Networks.* New York, NY: John Wiley & Sons, 1998.

ETSI GSM 03.60, "Digital Cellular Telecommunications System (Phase 2+); General Packet Radio Service (GPRS) Service Description—Stage 2," version 6.2.0, October 1998.

Fishburn, P. C. and A. M. Odlyzko. "Dynamic Behavior of Differential Pricing and Quality of Service Options for the Internet." Proc. First International Conference on Information and Computation Economies (ICE-98), 1998.

Floyd, S. and V. Jacobson. "Link-Sharing and Resource Management Models for Packet Networks." IEEE/ACM Transactions on Networking, Vol. 3 No. 4, August 1995.

———. "Random Early Detection Gateways for Congestion Avoidance." IEEE/ACM Transactions on Networking, August 1993. (Also available at `http://ftp.ee.lbl.gov/floyd/red.html`.)

Heinänen, J., F. Baker, W. Weiss, and J. Wroclawski. "Assured Forwarding PHB Group, <draft-ietf-diffserv-af-03.txt>." Internet Draft, November 1998.

Heinänen, J., and K. Kilkki. "A Fair Buffer Allocation Scheme." To appear in *Computer Communications* (written in 1995).

The Illustrated Oxford Dictionary. New York: Oxford University Press, Inc., 1998.

Integrated Services (IntServ) charter at `http://www.ietf.org/html.charters/intserv- charter.html`; mailing list archive from `ftp://ftp.isi.edu/int-serv/int-serv.mail`.

Integrated Services mailing list archive at `ftp://ftp.isi.edu/int-serv/int-serv.mail`.

ISO/IEC Final DIS 15802-3 (IEEE P802.1D/D17) "Information Technology— Telecommunications and Information Exchange Between Systems—Local and Metropolitan Area Networks—Common Specifications—Part 3: Media Access Control (MAC) Bridges (Incorporating IEEE P802.1p: Traffic Class Expediting and Dynamic Multicast Filtering), May 25, 1998.

Jacobson, V., K. Nichols, and K. Poduri. "An Expedited Forwarding PHB, a working document <draft-ietf-diffserv-phb-ef-01.txt>." November 1998.

Kalyanaraman, S., D. Harrison, S. Arora, K. Wanglee, and G. Guarriello. "A One-bit Feedback Enhanced Differentiated Services Architecture, <draft-shivkuma-ecn-diffserv-01.txt>." Internet Draft, a working document, March 1998.

Kelly, F. "Notes on Effective Bandwidths." In *Stochastic Networks: Theory and Applications.* Kelly, F. P., S. Zachary, and I.B. Ziedins (Editors). Oxford University Press, 1996. (Also at `http://www.ccsr.cam.ac.uk/Kelly.html`.)

Keshav, S. *An Engineering Approach to Computer Networking: ATM Networks, the Internet, and the Telephone Network.* Reading, MA: Addison Wesley, 1998.

Kleinrock, L. *Queueing Systems, Volume 1, Theory.* New York, NY: John Wiley & Sons, 1975.

Kleinrock, L. *Queueing Systems, Volume 2, Computer Applications.* New York, NY: John Wiley & Sons, 1975.

Kuhn, T. *Structure of Scientific Revolutions, 3rd Edition.* Chicago, IL: University of Chicago Press, 1996.

Leland, W. E., M. S. Taqqu, W. Willinger, and D. V. Wilson. "On the Self-Similar Nature of Ethernet Traffic." *Proc. ACM SIGCOMM'93.*

Loukola, M., J. Ruutu, and K. Kilkki. "Dynamic RT/NRT PHB Group, <draft-loukola-dynamic-00.txt>, a working document." November 1998.

Mankin, A. (Reported by). "Future Directions for Differential Services BOF, (fddifs) `http://www.ietf.org/proceedings/97apr/97apr-final/xrtft122.htm`." April 1998.

McKenney, P. "Stochastic Fairness Queueing," Proceedings of INFOCOM, 1990.

McKnight L. W. and J. P. Bailey (Editors). *Internet Economics.* Cambridge, MA: MIT Press, 1997.

More, Sir Thomas. *Utopia.* Wordsworth Editions Limited, 1997.

Multimedia Communications Quality of Service, Part II: Multimedia Desktop Collaboration Requirements, Multimedia Communications Forum, Inc. MMCF/95-010 (http://www.luxcom.com/library/qos.htm).

Multiprotocol Label Switching (MPLS), Description of Working Group at http://www.ietf.org/html.charters/mpls-charter.html.

Nagle, J. "Congestion Control in IP/TCP Internetworks." Request for Comments 896, September 1981.

Neil, S. "Deciphering SLAs, Service-Level Guarantees Can Differentiate a Good ISP, but Read the Fine Print." *PC Week Online*, July 13, 1998. (Also available at http://www.zdnet.com/pcweek/news/0713/13sla.html.)

Nichols, K., S. Blake, F. Baker, and D. Black. "Definition of the Differentiated Services Field (DS Field) in the IPv4 and IPv6 Headers." Request for Comments 2474, December 1998.

Nichols, K., V. Jacobson, and L. Zhang, "A Two-Bit Differentiated Services Architecture for the Internet." http://irl.cs.ucla.edu/publications.f.html, November 1997.

Odlyzko, A. "A Modest Proposal for Preventing Internet Congestion." AT&T Technical Report TR 97.35.1, September 1997.

———. "The Economics of the Internet: Utility, Utilization, Pricing, and Quality of Service." http://www.research.att.com/~amo/doc/networks.html, July 1998.

Postel, J. (Editor). "Internet Protocol, DARPA Internet Program Protocol Specification." Request for Comments 791, September 1981.

Postel, J. "Transmission Control Protocol." Request for Comments 793, September 1981.

Ramakrishnan K. K., and R. Jain, "A Binary Feedback Scheme for Congestion Avoidance in Computer Networks with Connectionless Network Layer," *Proceedings of ACM SIGCOMM '98*, August 1998.

Report Q7/13 rapporteur's meeting, Leidschendam, September 7–11 1998, Annex F, Revised text for Living List item 4: Guaranteed Frame Rate (GFR).

Roberts, J., U. Mocci, and J. Virtamo (Editors) "Broadband Network Teletraffic: Performance Evaluation and Design of Broadband Multiservice Networks: Final Report of Action Cost 242." Berlin: Springer Verlag, 1996.

Rosen, E., A. Viswanathan, and R. Callon. "Multiprotocol Label Switching Architecture, <draft-ietf-mpls-arch-04.txt>." Internet Draft (a working document), February 1999.

Ruutu, J. (Editor). "SIMA—Simple Integrated Media Access." (Available at `http://www-nrc.nokia.com/sima/`.)

Shenker, S. and J. Wroclawski. "General Characterization Parameters for Integrated Service Network Elements." Request for Comments 2215, September 1997.

Shenker, S., C. Partridge, R. Guerin. "Specification of Guaranteed Quality of Service." Request for Comments 2212, September 1997.

Stevens, W. "TCP Slow Start, Congestion Avoidance, Fast Retransmit, and Fast Recovery Algorithms." Request for Comments 2001, January 1997.

Willinger, W. and V. Paxson. "Where Mathematics Meets the Internet," *Notices of the American Mathematical Society*, 45(8), August 1998. (Also available at `ftp://ftp.ee.lbl.gov/papers/internet-math-AMS98.pdf`.)

Wittgenstein, L. *Philosophical Investigations*. Englewood Cliffs, NJ: Prentice Hall, 1973.

Wroclawski, J. (Editor). Minutes of the INTSERV meeting at the 39th IETF, `http://diffserv.lcs.mit.edu/IETF39/minutes.html`, 1997.

———. Minutes of the INTSERV Working Group Meeting, 40th IETF, `http://diffserv.lcs.mit.edu/IETF40/minutes.txt`, 1997.

Wroclawski, J. "Specification of the Controlled-Load Network Element Service." Request for Comments 2211, September 1997.

———. "The Use of RSVP with IETF Integrated Services." Request for Comments 2210, September 1997.

GLOSSARY

A

adaptive routing (also, *dynamic adaptive routing*, *alternate routing*, or *state-dependent routing*): a routing scheme in which the choice of a route depends on the load level in the network. Adaptive routing makes it possible to utilize network resources more efficiently than with static routing.

Advanced Research Projects Agency (ARPA): a U.S. federal research agency that was responsible for the funding of the network now known as the Internet. The abbreviation DARPA was also used for a while (D stands for Defense).

application: a computer program that performs a significant function directly for a user. Email and IP telephony are typical applications used in the Internet.

Assured Forwarding PHB (AF PHB): a PHB group consisting of four PHB classes. AF PHB group can be used to provide quality differentiation related to various quality aspects.

Asynchronous Transfer Mode (ATM): a connection-oriented, packet switching technology where information is carried in fixed-size cells. The objective of ATM technology has been to provide a ubiquitous network service for every imaginable purpose.

Availability of Quality: the probability that a service can meet a given quality requirement. Availability of Quality is usually measured over a long period of time.

Available Bit Rate (ABR): an ATM service category in which a network continuously informs end systems about the current available capacity in the network. An end system that can adapt its bit rate in accordance with the feedback information is expected to obtain a low cell-loss ratio.

average bit rate: a bit rate of a traffic stream measured over a relatively long period.

B

backbone: the primary connectivity mechanisms of a hierarchical system. The Internet backbone is the part of the network used to connect Internet service providers to each other.

bandwidth: formally, the difference between the highest and lowest frequencies of a transmission channel. In practice, widely used as a general term for the capacity of a transmission channel in bits per second.

best-effort service (BE): a service model in which the network transmits packets without explicit quality guarantees. This is the prevalent Internet service model.

Birds of a Feather (BoF): An informal discussion group to consider a specific issue. In an IETF meeting, BoF is a session held before the formation of a working group to decide whether the interest is sufficient.

boundary node: a network node that connects one domain to another domain. In a Differentiated Services environment, a boundary node can connect a domain to a customer, to another Differentiated Services domain, or to a domain without Differentiated Services capabilities.

buffer: a temporary storage in which data is held pending an opportunity to complete its transfer. In telecommunication networks, a buffer can be considered a technical implementation of a queue, but often buffer and queue are used as synonyms.

C

call blocking (or *call-blocking probability*): the probability that a call request is rejected because of insufficient network resources. Call-blocking standards and calculations are extensively used for planning telephone networks.

call: an association between two or more end systems connected to a network in order to use network capabilities. In multiple-service networks, a call can consist of a number of connections.

Cell Loss Priority (CLP): a bit in the ATM cell header that indicates two levels of drop priority. A CLP value of 1 in an ATM cell implies that an ATM node can discard the cell during a congestion situation.

cell: the unit of transmission in ATM networks. An ATM cell has a fixed size—a 5-octet header and 48-octet payload.

circuit switching: a communications principle in which a dedicated channel is established between end systems. The channel reserves certain network resources independent of the actual traffic sent through the channel.

Class Selector PHB (CS PHB): a PHB group that provides backward compatibility for systems using the former specification of the TOS field.

Class-based Queuing (CBQ): a queuing method that classifies packets according to certain criteria and reserves a separate queue for each traffic class. The goal of CBQ is to provide appropriated treatment for each traffic class.

classifier: an entity that selects packets according to defined rules. In a Differentiated Services network, a classifier selects the PHB class for a traffic flow.

codepoint (or *DS codepoint [DSCP]*): a specific value of the first six bits in the DS field. The codepoint of a packet informs the network about the PHB of the packet.

congestion: a situation in which there are not enough resources to appropriately handle all tasks. In packet networks, congestion occurs when the load level exceeds either the capacity of a network node or the bandwidth of a link. Congestion may last from milliseconds to weeks.

congestion control: a set of mechanisms used to avoid congestion inside the network. Congestion control includes mechanisms that enable the sender to adjust the transmission rate according to the available bit rate inside the network.

connection: a possibility to transfer information between two or more end systems. Usually, a transmission channel is explicitly established before the actual use of a connection.

Connection Admission Control (CAC): a set of actions during the call setup phase that determines whether a connection request can be accepted or should be rejected. CAC is an indispensable control mechanism in any network that gives quality guarantees.

connection oriented: a communication method in which a connection has to be established before information transfer. ATM is connection-oriented networking technology.

connectionless: a communication method in which information can be sent without first establishing a connection. IP is a connectionless protocol.

Constant Bit Rate (CBR): an ATM service category in which a constant bandwidth is allocated for a traffic stream. CBR can also be used as an attribute for any connection that sends (or is expected to send) traffic with a constant bit rate.

controlled-load service: a service model in which the network permanently offers a quality level similar to that of an unloaded network. The quality of a controlled load service is expected to be sufficient for most applications except the most demanding real-time applications.

cost efficiency (or *cost effectiveness*): economical in terms of services received for the money spent. Cost efficiency is one factor in this book used to measure whether Differentiated Services technology is providing a profitable business for the service provider and affordable services for customers.

customer service: the relationship between the customer and the service provider, including all issues that significantly affect customer satisfaction.

D

datagram: the basic information unit in the Internet that contains sufficient information to route it from source to destination. In practice, *packet* is often used rather than *datagram* as a general term for a basic information unit.

Differentiated Services (DiffServ): a service paradigm in which quality differentiation is based on the classification and marking of packets rather than explicit resource reservations for individual flows.

domain: a contiguous set of nodes operated under a common service-provisioning principle. A domain is usually managed by a single organization.

drop precedence: a value in a packet header that is used during a congestion situation to decide which packets are discarded.

DS field: the IPv4 header TOS octet or the IPv6 Traffic Class octet when used in conformance with the Differentiated Services specifications.

dynamic importance: a term used in this book to describe a system that enables customers to request a specific importance level for traffic flows or for individual packets.

Dynamic Real-Time/non–real-time PHB (DRT PHB): a PHB group that consists of two PHB classes, each with six importance levels. A DRT PHB group with appropriate traffic-condition methods can be used to build quality differentiation related to delay, loss probability, and bandwidth.

E

egress node: a collection of functions used to handle outgoing traffic streams from a network domain. Typically, a node is an egress node for some traffic streams and ingress node for some other traffic streams.

equal queuing: a term used in this book for a queuing system that attempts to divide the link capacity evenly among some entities. The entity could be an individual flow or an aggregate traffic stream.

Expedited Forwarding PHB (EF PHB): a PHB group that can be used to build a high-quality, virtual circuit service in a Differentiated Services network.

F

fair queuing: a queuing system that can provide a fair sharing of network resources even when some flows attempt to use as much resources as possible.

fairness: reasonable according to most people's ideas of justice. Fairness is used in this book to emphasize that the fundamental needs of customers are at least as important as technical requirements.

first in, first out (FIFO): a queuing system in which packets are transmitted in the order in which they are received.

flow: an association of packets transmitted between two end systems. In IP networks, packets with the same source address, source port, destination address, and destination port are often considered a flow if the packets are sent within a relatively short period of time.

flow control: a mechanism that enables the sender to adjust the transmission rate according to the available bit at a receiver.

forwarding: an operation performed by a network node in which a packet is received on an input, the right output is determined, and the packet is sent to the right output. There is a clear distinction between routing and forwarding; routing is a supporting function for the forwarding process of packets.

frame: an information unit usually related to the transmission of information over one link rather than through the whole network. *Packet* is often used rather than *frame* as a more general term.

G–H

General Packet Radio Service (GPRS): a specification for data transmission in wireless networks.

guaranteed connections: a term used for a network service used by an individual application with specific quality requirements and duration.

Guaranteed Frame Rate (GFR): an ATM service category in which a specific part of traffic flow is delivered with high probability while the excess traffic obtains best-effort service.

guaranteed service: a service model in which a network attempts to meet specific bandwidth and quality requirements with very high probability. The guaranteed-service model developed by IETF is expected to offer high enough quality for real-time applications.

header: a block of octets in the beginning of a packet that contains control information, such as source and destination addresses.

hop: a path between two network nodes that does not have any significant effect on the characteristics of traffic flows. An ATM VP between two routers is one hop, although the VP goes through several ATM nodes, if those nodes keep the traffic process virtually intact.

I

importance level: information about the relative importance of a packet to be used for traffic-management purposes. In this book, *importance level* is used (rather than *drop precedence* or similar terms) as a general term that does not refer to any specific implementation.

ingress node: a collection of functions used to handle incoming traffic streams to a network domain. Typically, a node is an egress node for some traffic streams and an ingress node for some other traffic streams.

Institute of Electrical and Electronics Engineers (IEEE): a professional society that also makes communication and network standards. IEEE has an integral role of defining standards for local area networks.

Integrated Service Digital Network (ISDN): an evolutionary step of a telephone network to integrate voice and data traffic into the same network. The main application of ISDN related to data traffic is to provide access to the Internet with a maximum bandwidth of 128kbps using ordinary telephone lines.

Integrated Services (IntServ): a service architecture in which a diverse range of services, such as voice, video, and data, are transmitted within the same network infrastructure. In IETF, Integrated Services refers to the effort made by the Integrated Services Working Group to design an advanced service model that may replace best-effort service.

interior node: a network that has links only to nodes within the same domain.

Internet (with capital "I"): a global information network that consists of a large number of smaller internets. The Internet is usually considered to cover networks with public access, whereas large networks with closed access are called intranets.

internet: a set of packet networks interconnected by routers that enable them to function as one unified network.

Internet Draft: a working document submitted by an IETF working group or by individual contributors. An Internet Draft is the first phase of the development of an RFC, but not all Internet Drafts lead to a RFC.

Internet Engineering Task Force (IETF): an organization that provides the coordination of standard and specification development for the Internet.

Internet Protocol (IP): a protocol that provides a connectionless delivery of packets in the Internet.

Internet Protocol version 4 (IPv4): the predominant version of the Internet Protocol today.

Internet Protocol version 6 (IPv6): a new version of the Internet Protocol with several enhanced features, including a larger address space. It is expected that IPv6 will replace IPv4 in the future, although the schedule is still largely uncertain.

Internet service provider (ISP): a company that sells access to the Internet.

interworking: a set of issues related to the capability of different standards, techniques, and mechanisms to work together.

J–L

jitter: a distortion of a signal, such as a flow of packets, in which the original timing relationships are altered. In the context of packet networks, *jitter* is a synonym for *delay variation*.

label: a short, fixed-length identifier in a packet header. The value of a label is usually changed in every node.

label switching: a technique based on labels that is used to alleviate the processing effort of packet forwarding.

leased-line service: a service in which a virtual circuit is leased for exclusive use of a specific customer. In this book, *leased-line service* is also used as a general term to describe a network service with permanent reservation of bandwidth and with high-quality requirements.

link: a physical connection between two network nodes.

local area network (LAN): a data network that spans small distances, up to a few kilometers. LANs are usually administrated by a single organization.

M

marking: the process of setting bits in a packet header in order to have an effect on the treatment of the packet. The term *marking* is also used in this book in a more limited sense: changing the importance level of a packet within a PHB class.

mechanism: a system of parts working together used to achieve a specific result. In Differentiated Services networks, typical parts are queuing disciplines or dropping algorithms, and the result can be a Per-Hop Behavior.

metering: a measuring process of temporal properties of a traffic stream. In this book, metering refers to cases where the result is used for packet marking, shaping, or dropping.

multicast: a technique in which a packet is delivered to more than one destination. Multicast improves the utilization of network resources by minimizing duplication of packets.

multiplexing: a technique for transmitting a number of separate signals over a single channel.

Multiprotocol Label Switching (MPLS): an IETF working group for developing label-switching standards. The development work of MPLS also includes traffic-management aspects similar to Differentiated Services.

N–O

network dimensioning (or *capacity planning*): a methodology used to manage network resources in a reasonable manner. The timescale of network dimensioning is usually at least a few weeks.

network operator: a company, organization, or person responsible for the operation and management of a network.

network service: the part of customer service that defines the technical characteristics of information transmission through a network.

node (or *network node*): a device attached to a network with capability to make connections to other devices.

Nominal Bit Rate (NBR): a parameter used in DRT PHB and in SIMA that defines the share of network resources obtained by a traffic stream.

non-real-time (NRT): a characteristic of an application or of a service without strict transmission delay and delay-variation constraints.

octet: a group of eight bits. *Byte* is often used as a synonym for *octet*, although in a strict sense byte does not define the number of bits.

operation and management (OAM): a set of functions that provides essential information about the condition of a network and that are used to make operational actions.

P

packet: a generic term used to describe an information unit that contains enough information to transmit it through a network.

packet-loss ratio (P_{loss}): the number of lost packets divided by the number of total packets. Packet-loss ratio can be defined for different levels of aggregation and for different periods of time.

packet switching: a communication principle in which information is divided into packets that are stored in network nodes before being transmitted forward.

peak rate: a bit rate of a traffic stream measured over a very short period. Peak rate is also used as a traffic parameter that defines the highest rate at which source can send data into the network.

Per-Hop Behavior (PHB): an externally observable forwarding treatment of an aggregate traffic stream in a network node. Conceptually, PHB is located between mechanisms and network services; service providers build network services based on PHBs that are implemented by using mechanisms.

PHB class: a PHB group intended to be applicable for transmitting packets of one application. A PHB class offers basically the same delay characteristics for all flows using the class.

PHB group: a set of one or more PHBs that has to be specified and implemented simultaneously. In this sense, two or more PHB groups can be used in a network domain only if the operator allocates strictly separate network resources for every PHB group.

port: (1) a physical interface to a network node. (2) an identifier used to specify a particular application running on a computer.

predictability of quality: a term used in this book to describe the capability of users to predict the actual quality of network service.

protocol: a formal description of messages and rules to be used by two or more systems to exchange information. Protocols make logical connections between applications on different computers.

Q–R

quality of service (QoS): a set of attributes that can be used to define the network's capability to meet the requirements of users and applications. Packet-loss ratio and delay variation are typical QoS attributes.

Random Early Detection (RED): a queuing principle in which packets are dropped randomly before the queue becomes full. The main goal of RED is to improve the efficiency of TCP congestion control.

real-time (RT): characteristic of an application or a service with strict transmission delay and delay-variation constraints.

Request For Comment (RFC): a document produced by IETF that contains information about the Internet. Internet standards are written in the form of an RFC, but only some RFCs are actually standards.

Resource Reservation Protocol (RSVP): a protocol used in the Internet to reserve resources for flows with specific QoS requirements.

resource sharing: a network service model in which resources are divided among all active users according to specific rules. The actual amount of bandwidth available for a user depends on the overall level of demand.

robustness: the capability to work properly under harsh conditions. Robustness is used in this book to emphasize the need to build a system that works appropriately in diverse conditions, even when some users are malicious.

router: a network node that performs routing functions and forwards packets to other nodes based on the routing information.

routing: a process in network nodes that exchanges and maintains information about paths to various destinations. The results of routing are used to forward packets through the network.

S

scheduling discipline: an algorithm that determines the order in which service requests are served.

service-level agreement (SLA): the formal part of the relationship between a service provider and a customer. The SLA contains assurances related to various issues such as service availability and transmission delays.

shaping: a mechanism that delays packets of a traffic stream to achieve better network efficiency or to ensure conformance with a traffic profile.

signaling: a process that allows end systems and network nodes to exchange information. Particularly, signaling is used for establishing and releasing connections.

Simple Integrated Media Access (SIMA): a Differentiated Services model that includes specifications for network mechanisms, traffic conditioning, and pricing.

starvation: a situation in which a traffic stream with low priority does not get any service because other traffic streams with higher priority use all the resources.

statistical multiplexing: a multiplexing principle in which there is a possibility that network resources are not sufficient for transmitting all signals. The objective of statistical multiplexing is to improve the utilization of network resources.

Stochastic Fairness Queuing (SFQ): a variant of fair queuing in which a special hash function is used to map a flow to one of a set of queues. The number of required queues is smaller than in a WFQ system.

switch: a network node that makes the forwarding decision based on a label rather than on the full destination address. Sometimes *switch* is used as a general term for all devices that transfer information from input to output.

T

throughput: the transmission capacity used by traffic streams in a channel in bits per second. *Bandwidth* is often used as a synonym for *throughput*.

token bucket: a control algorithm that regulates the bandwidth used by a traffic stream but allows some level of burstiness. *Leaky bucket* is often (but not always) used as a synonym for *token bucket*.

traffic conditioning: a set of mechanisms used to control and modify traffic flows. Traffic conditioning includes metering, marking, shaping, and dropping.

traffic handling: a set of mechanisms used by a network operator to take care of traffic in a network.

traffic management: a set of principles and mechanisms that allows the network operator to efficiently utilize network resources and to meet customer requirements.

traffic profile: a description of the temporal properties of a traffic stream. Traffic profile includes parameters (such as peak rate and maximum burst size) that are used for traffic-conditioning purposes.

traffic stream: a set of one or more flows with some common characteristics. Flows can be classified in to a stream, for instance, based on the customer group or on the quality requirements.

Transmission Control Protocol (TCP): a protocol that provides reliable connections in the Internet. The majority of traffic in the present Internet uses TCP.

Type of Service (TOS): a field in the IPv4 packet header designed to indicate the preferred treatment of the packet. The former specification of TOS bits has been replaced by Differentiated Services specifications.

U–Z

Unspecified Bit Rate (UBR): an ATM service category without QoS or bandwidth guarantees. UBR service is similar to the best-effort service used in the Internet.

User Datagram Protocol (UDP): a simple connectionless protocol used to transport packets in the Internet. As opposed to TCP, UDP does not provide any congestion-control mechanisms itself.

Variable Bit Rate (VBR): an ATM service category intended for applications with bandwidth requirements that vary with time. There are two subcategories: rt-VBR is intended for real-time applications and nrt-VBR is intended for non-real-time applications.

versatility: the capability to do many things competently. The term *versatility* is used in this book to emphasize the need of a single consistent system to realize various services and characteristics.

virtual circuit (VC): a technique that provides connection-oriented service regardless of the underlying network structure.

virtual path (VP): a set of virtual circuits established for traffic-management purposes.

virtual private network (VPN): a private network in which network nodes are at least partially connected through a public network. VPNs use secure protocols to ensure that unauthorized parties do not intercept data transfers.

Weighted Fair Queuing (WFQ): a variant of fair queuing in which each traffic flow can be given a specific proportion of the network capacity.

Weighted Random Early Detection (WRED): a variant of RED in which the packet-discarding probability depends on the characteristics of the flows or on the importance level of the packet.

World Wide Web (WWW or Web): a distributed information system used in the Internet.

X.25: a connection-oriented packet-switching protocol.

Index

The *Macmillan Technology Series* is a comprehensive and authoritative set of guides to the most important computing standards of today. Each title in this series is aimed at bringing computing professionals closer to the scientists and engineers behind the technological implementations that will change tomorrow's innovations in computing.

Currently available titles in the *Macmillan Technology Series* include

Gigabit Ethernet Networking,

by David G. Cunningham, Ph.D., and William G. Lane, Ph.D.
(ISBN: 1-57870-062-0)

Written by key contributors to the Gigabit Ethernet standard, *Gigabit Ethernet Networking* provides network engineers and architects both the necessary context of the technology and advanced knowledge of its deployment. This book offers critical information to enable readers to make cost-effective decisions about how to design and implement their particular network to meet current traffic loads and to ensure scalability with future growth.

DSL: Simulation Techniques and Standards Development for Digital Subscriber Line Systems,

by Walter Chen
(ISBN: 1-57870-017-5)

The only book on the market that deals with xDSL technologies at this level, *DSL: Simulation Techniques and Standards Development for Digital Subscriber Line Systems* is ideal for computing professionals who are looking for new high-speed communications technology, who must understand the dynamics of xDSL communications to create compliant applications, or who simply want to better understand this new wave of technology.

ADSL/VDSL Principles,

by Dr. Dennis J. Rauschmayer
(ISBN: 1-57870-015-9)

ADSL/VDSL Principles provides the communications and networking engineer with practical explanations, technical detail, and in-depth insight needed to fully implement ADSL and VDSL. Topics that are essential to the successful implementation of these technologies are covered.

LDAP: Programming Directory-Enabled Applications with Lightweight Directory Access Protocol,
by Tim Howes and Mark Smith
(ISBN: 1-57870-000-0)

This book is the essential resource for programmers, software engineers, and network administrators who need to understand and implement LDAP to keep software applications compliant. If you design or program software for network computing or are interested in directory services, LDAP is an essential resource to help you understand the LDAP API; learn how to write LDAP programs; understand how to LDAP-enable an existing application; and learn how to use a set of command-line LDAP tools to search and update directory information.

Upcoming titles in the *Macmillan Technology Series* include:

Supporting Service Level Agreements on an IP Network,
by Dinesh Verma
(ISBN: 1-57870-146-5)

Service level agreements (SLAs), which allow network service providers to contract with their customers for different levels of quality of service levels, are becoming increasingly popular. *Supporting Service Level Agreements on an IP Network* describes methods and techniques that can be used to ensure that the requirements of SLAs are met. This essential guide covers SLA support on traditional best-effort IP networks, as well as support of SLAs using the latest service differentiation techniques under discussion in the IETF and other standards organizations. *Supporting Service Level Agreements on an IP Network* provides information services managers and engineers with critical practical insight into the procedures required to fulfill their service level agreements.

Virtual Private Networks,
by David Bovee
(ISBN: 1-57870-120-1

The technologies involved in creating virtual private networks (VPNs) are still evolving and developing. A VPN can have a significant effect on reducing overall networking costs because it utilizes the free resource of the Internet instead of relying on expensive T-1 or telephone connections. *Virtual Private Networks* provides the detailed technical information that network architects need to decide how to optimally build their VPN to meet the needs of their organization and networking environment.

Directory Enabled Networking,
by John Strassner
(ISBN: 1-57870-140-6)

Directory Enabled Networking (DEN) is a rapidly developing industry and standards effort in the Desktop Management Task Force (DMTF). DEN allows network architects and engineers to manage their networks through centralized control and provisioning, which yields significant reductions in cost of ownership. DEN is also a fundamental technology for policy-based networking, which is receiving a lot of attention in the networking industry. The author, John Strassner, is the creator of the DEN specification as well as the chair of the DMTF DEN working group. *Directory Enabled Networking* is a critical resource for network architects and engineers to consider how to optimally utilize this technology in their networking environments.

Understanding the Public Key Infrastructure,
by Carlisle Adams and Steve Lloyd
(ISBN: 1-57870-166-x)

Public Key Infrastructure (PKI) is a new technology critical for securing data and communication in both enterprise and Internet environments. *Understanding the Public Key Infrastructure* provides network architects and implementers with essential information for deploying and enhancing critical business services. The authors, Carlisle Adams and Steve Lloyd, have been extensively involvement with the design, standardization, and real-world deployment of PKIs. *Understanding the Public Key Infrastructure* presents unique expertise on PKI techology not available in any other source.

SNMP Agents,
by Bob Natale
(ISBN: 1-57870-110-4)

Because SNMP is the dominant network management tool in the market, SNMP agents are included in every device that is expected to be connected to a network. Author Bob Natale, Chair of IETF Extensible SNMP Agent Working Group and the WinSNMP Industry Forum, provides critical information for network architects and engineers to manage their networks with this powerful technology. *SNMP Agents* is an essential resource for creating and implementing SNMP agents that perform optimally in a particular network environment.

Intrusion Detection,
by Rebecca Gurley Bace
(ISBN: 1-57870-185-6)

Intrusion detection is a critical new area of technology within network security. An intrusion detection system serves as a system alert for unauthorized access for networks and systems connected to the Internet. This comprehensive guide to topics in intrusion detection covers the foundations of intrusion detection and system audit. *Intrusion Detection* provides a wealth of information, ranging from commercial intrusion detection products to design considerations. Author Rebecca Bace is one of the founders of the field of intrusion detection, and is a nationally recognized expert.

The *Macmillan Network Architecture and Development Series* is a comprehensive set of guides that provides computing professionals with the unique insight of leading experts in today's networking technologies. Each volume explores a technology or set of technologies that is needed to build and maintain the optimal network environment for any particular organization or situation.

Currently available titles in the *Macmillan Network Architecture and Development Series* include

Wide Area High Speed Networks,
by Dr. Sidnie Feit
(ISBN: 1-57870-114-7)

Today, conventional telephony, ISDN networks, ATM networks, packet-switched networks, and Internet data technologies coexist in a complex tapestry of networks. This book clearly explains each technology, describes how they interoperate, and puts their various uses and advantages into perspective. *Wide Area High Speed Networks* is an authoritative resource that will enable networking designers and implementors to determine which technologies to use in their networks, and for which roles.

Switched, Fast, and Gigabit Ethernet,
by Sean Riley and Robert A. Breyer
(ISBN: 1-57870-073-6)

Switched, Fast, and Gigabit Ethernet, Third Edition is the one and only solution needed to understand and fully implement this entire range of Ethernet innovations. Acting both as an overview of current technologies and hardware requirements as well as a hands-on, comprehensive tutorial for deploying and managing Switched, Fast, and Gigabit Ethernets, this guide covers the most prominent present and future challenges network administrators face.

Understanding and Deploying LDAP Directory Services,
by Tim Howes, Mark Smith, and Gordon Goode
(ISBN: 1-57870-070-1)

This comprehensive tutorial provides the reader with a thorough treatment of LDAP directory services. Designed to meet multiple needs, the first part of the book presents a general overview of the subject matter. The next three sections cover detailed instructions for design, deployment, and integration of directory services. The text is full of practical implementation advice and real-world deployment examples to help the reader choose the path that makes the most sense for the specific organization.

Designing Addressing Architectures for Routing and Switching,
by Howard C. Berkowitz
(ISBN: 1-57870-059-0)

Designing Addressing Architectures for Routing and Switching provides a systematic methodology for planning the wide area and local area network streets on which users and servers live. It guides the network designer in developing rational systems that are flexible and that maintain a high level of service. Intended for people who are—or want to be—responsible for building large networks, this book offers a system and taxonomy for building networks that meet user requirements. It includes practical examples, configuration guides, case studies, tips, and warnings.

Wireless LANs: Implementing Interoperable Networks,
by Jim Geier
(ISBN: 1-57870-081-7)

This book provides both a context for understanding how an enterprise can benefit from the application of wireless technology and the proven tools for efficiently implementing a wireless LAN. Based on the most recent developments in the field, *Wireless LANs: Implementing Interoperable Networks* gives network engineers vital information on planning, configuring, and supporting wireless networks.

Upcoming titles in the *Macmillan Network Architecture and Development Series* include:

Local Area High Speed Networks,
by Dr. Sidnie Feit
(ISBN: 1-57870-113-9)

With Web intranets driving bandwidth needs increasingly higher, the technologies being deployed in local area networks are changing rapidly. For example, inexpensive Ethernet network interface cards and switches are now commonly available. Many networking professionals are interested in evaluating these new technologies for implementation. *Local Area High Speed Networks* provides real-world implementation expertise for these technologies, including traces, so that users can realistically compare and decide how to optimally deploy them in their network environment. This comprehensive guide covers Ethernet technologies, virtual LANs, and routing and switching technologies.

The DHCP Handbook,

by Ralph Droms and Ted Lemon

(ISBN: 1-57870-137-6)

The DHCP Handbook provides network architects and administrators with an authoritative overview of the Dynamic Host Configuration Protocol, as well as expert information on how to set up and manage a DHCP server. This book will show networking professionals already working with DHCP systems how to take full advantage of the technology to solve their management and address assignment problems. An essential resource, The *DHCP Handbook* provides the reader with critical information and expertise from author Ralph Droms, the chair of the IETF Dynamic Host Configuration (DHC) working group on automated network configuration, and author Ted Lemon, who wrote the ISC DHCP server code.

Designing Routing and Switching Architectures for Enterprise Networks,

by Howard Berkowitz

(ISBN: 1-57870-060-4)

A critical resource for network architects and engineers, Designing Routing and Switching Architectures for Enterprise Networks teaches the reader how to select the optimal switches and routers for his or her network environment, as well as guidance on effective deployment. This book provides the unique insight and experience of real-world network design from Howard Berkowitz, an experienced network designer, developer, and contributor to the standards process.